That Rob. Boll' being thus entitled under la

Our acts of assemb. have annexed to them the 2 their culture, have made that labor homogeneo efore gi-en it to him who can entitle himself to the a right to have them applied to the paiment of their debts. ...

RENTS of the tenements for the year in which the testr died, and which were not paiable till days subsequent to his death, are another part of our claim under the devise of the Buffalo lick plantation. these I understand are given up by the adv. party. they are not mentioned in the Argument. indeed the rule is settled that Rents go to him to whom the lands belong at the last moment at which they are paiable. Salk. 578. and I only mention them here that they may be made a part of the award.

A Second general claim is to the testr's Credits, burthened with his debts. the clause on which it is immediately founded is this. 'it is my will and desire that my book be given up to my brother Robert, and that he recieve all the debts due to me, and pay all that I owe'. Arch. Boll' objects that this is an appointment of Rob. Boll' his exr, and that what he recieves, he recieves as exr, and after paiment of debts, shall bring what is left of it into the residuum. on the other hand, Rob. Boll' insists that, to make this clause an appointmt of an exr is merely an artificial construction of the law; and that the testr intended by it a very different thing, to wit, to transfer to him the right to his credits, paying thereout his debts. that the intention of the testr in testamentary dispositions is not to be controuled by artificial deductions; and shall be carried into effect altho the words, in which he has happened to express himself, do in law produce an additional effect.

# Thomas Jefferson
# and
# Bolling v. Bolling

Thomas Jefferson
Physiognotrace etching by Charles Saint-Memin, 1804.
(Huntington Library)

George Wythe

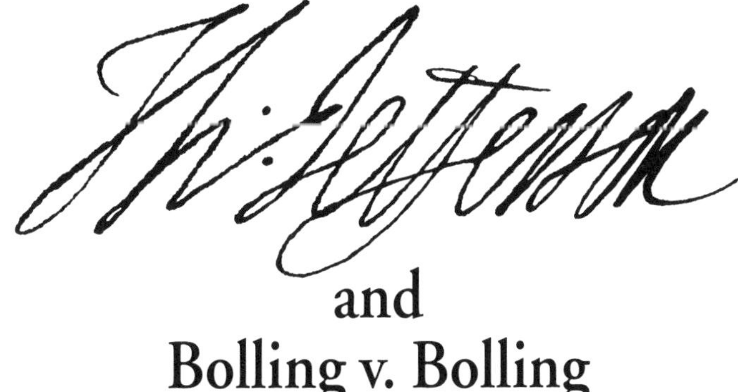


# and
# Bolling v. Bolling

## Law and The Legal Profession In Pre-Revolutionary America

Bernard Schwartz
with

Barbara Wilcie Kern
R.B. Bernstein

For Mom and Dad,
*Here* is the explanation
for my Jeffersonian handwriting.
Happy forty-third anniversary
(a *little* late).
With all my love,
Richard
9 July 1997

The Huntington Library
San Marino, California
New York University School of Law
New York City, New York

*(front endpaper)*
H 57-58, *Bolling v. Bolling* manuscript, from first argument for defendant in Jefferson's handwriting

*(back endpaper)*
H 11-12, *Bolling v. Bolling* manuscript, from first argument for defendant in Jefferson's handwriting


Printed in the United States of America

Library of Congress Cataloging-in-Publication Data
Jefferson, Thomas, 1743-1826.
Thomas Jefferson and Bolling v. Bolling : law and the legal profession in pre-revolutionary America / [edited and introduced by] Bernard Schwartz, with R.B. Bernstein, Barbara Wilcie Kern.
p. cm.
Contains edited manuscript of arguments in Bolling v. Bolling presented by Thomas Jefferson and George Wythe, largely in Jefferson's handwriting.
Includes bibliographical references and index.
ISBN 0-87328-158-6
1. Bolling, Robert, b. 1738—Trials, litigation, etc. 2. Bolling, Archibald, 1750-1827—Trials, litigation, etc. 3. Jefferson, Thomas, 1743-1826. 4. Inheritance and succession—Virginia—History—Sources. 5. Practice of law—Virginia—History—Sources. I. Schwartz, Bernard, 1923- . II. Bernstein, R. B. (Richard Bruce), 1956- . III. Kern, Barbara Wilcie, 1939- . IV. Title.
KF228.B65J44 1996 96-22569
349.73'092—dc20 CIP
[347.00922]

# Table of Contents



## Bolling v. Bolling Manuscript

# Preface

While working on a book on the development of American legal thought, I came upon the Jefferson manuscript published in this book. As soon as I received a copy from the Huntington Library, I decided that it should be made available to a wider audience. During the next few years, I spent what time I could on editing the manuscript and writing an Introduction that would both discuss the manuscript and set it in context. However, before the book could be published in its present form, my editing effort had to be supplemented by experts in the field. We were fortunate in securing Barbara Wilcie Kern and R.B. Bernstein, both outstanding historians, whose work on the manuscript has enabled it to be published in definitive form. But they have done more than merely ensure transcription of the manuscript, as their Statement of Editorial Method amply demonstrates. Without their masterful work, indeed, this publication would scarcely be the valuable contribution that we hope it will be.

I should also acknowledge the efforts of Professors John Reid and William Nelson, and Dean John Sexton, as well as the help of the Tulsa University College of Law. The result will, I trust, justify the labors of all concerned.

Tulsa, Oklahoma Bernard Schwartz

1997

# Publisher's Preface

The Huntington Library holds a significant group of autograph manuscripts written by Thomas Jefferson, the largest collection west of the Atlantic seaboard. Nearly all of the manuscript material, as well as a few books from Jefferson's personal library with his distinctive ownership inscriptions, were acquired by Henry Edwards Huntington through the dealer George D. Smith in two major purchases of 1916 and 1918. One lot came from the noted collector William K. Bixby, the second from an unidentified Jefferson descendant. The second lot is rich in personal material — retained drafts of letters written in retirement at Monticello, letters written from Paris, Philadelphia, and Washington to family members, letters on plantation operations directed to the farm managers at Monticello, and a group of receipts recording personal expenses incurred during the presidency. The collection also includes a handful of polygraph parts with Jefferson's notes on the proper maintenance of the temperamental copying device. In addition to the *Bolling vs. Bolling* manuscript, there are other pieces documenting Jefferson's law career, notably his Fee Book. Another document of some interest is Jefferson's draft of the Twelfth Amendment to the Constitution. A small group of about forty-five autograph architectural drawings includes Jefferson's plans for the first and second floor Virginia State Capitol, for a major addition to the College of William and Mary, and plans and surveys related to his homes at Monticello and Poplar Forest.

# Introduction

There is in the Huntington Library a manuscript of 239 pages — about half in the handwriting of Thomas Jefferson. It contains the arguments made by opposing counsel in *Bolling v. Bolling*, a 1770–71 Virginia case arising out of a will by the brother of the two parties in the suit. The manuscript is the most complete account in existence of the arguments made in a late eighteenth-century case. It shows the pre-revolutionary bar in action and is of special interest because the attorneys involved were Jefferson and his mentor and law teacher, George Wythe (1726–1806), then the foremost jurist in the colonies. The level of argument is strikingly high, particularly when the paucity of legal materials then available on this side of the Atlantic is considered. It shows that, had Jefferson not abandoned the law for politics, he could have had a brilliant career at the bar.

The Jefferson-Wythe arguments illustrate, better than any contemporary evidence, the conception of law that prevailed at the time and, moreover, demonstrate how the law was used in an actual case by opposing attorneys. The manuscript confirms the existence of a developed legal system and its already central place in colonial society. It shows that an instrumentalist idea of law, primarily American in its origins, was already developing. Both counsel in *Bolling* stressed the social purposes to be served by the arguments they presented.

This introduction places the *Bolling* manuscript in perspective for the reader. It contains a discussion of the law in pre-revolutionary America, the legal profession at the time, legal education (particularly that of Jefferson), Jefferson as a lawyer (with commentary on some of his cases and other legal work), and a detailed analysis of the *Bolling* arguments and what they reveal about the law and the bar just before the struggle for independence began. It is well known that the legal profession played a key role in the Revolution; the *Bolling* arguments show how both Jefferson and the bar were prepared to perform their crucial part in the conflict of ideas that paralleled the struggle on the battlefield.

## Common-Law Foundation

In the General Prologue to the *Canterbury Tales*, Chaucer says of his Serjeant of the Lawe,
In termes hadde he caas and doomes alle,
That from the tyme of kyng William were falle...
And every statut coude he pleyn by rote.

Thus, as early as the fourteenth century, a knowledge of statutes and decided cases was the mark of a learned lawyer. This indicates that even by Chaucer's day there was a developed system of English law. Of more than passing interest, this fact is of vital importance in Anglo-American history, for the development of the English constitution is intimately related to the growth of what, as early as the reign of Edward I (1272–1307), was coming to be called the *common law*.

An outstanding feature of English polity has always been that it is preeminently a legal one. If it is customary to think of English government as virtually synonymous with free government, this is only because the English are the heirs of a successful struggle to bridle governmental power by the law of the land. From the beginning, the growth of English constitutional institutions and of the rights and liberties of the English people has been influenced and controlled by legal forms and methods. By the time of Edward I, the dominant interest in Parliament was already that of the common lawyers, who, in Theodore F. T. Plucknett's phrase, "were mainly instrumental in making parliamentary supremacy a fact."[1]

It was the common lawyers who were largely responsible for developing and preserving the rule of law that was to become the central and most characteristic feature of the English system. The diffusion of the common law throughout the realm led to the realization that the law could even play a role in controlling governmental power. According to Thomas Babington Macaulay, "The principle that the King of England was bound to conduct the administration according to law, and that, if he did anything against law, his advisers and agents were answerable, was established at a very early period."[2]

Above all, it was the almost inexorable unfolding of the common law, by accretion rather than precipitation, that placed the rights of the English upon a firm case-by-case basis, enforceable in the courts of the land. There was never any need in England to write on a revolutionary tabula rasa without regard to existing tradi-

1. Theodore F. T. Plucknett, *A Concise History of the Common Law*, 2d ed. (Rochester, New York: Lawyers Co-operative Publishing Co., 1936), 235.

2. Quoted in Bernard Schwartz, *The Roots of Freedom: A Constitutional History of England* (New York: Hill & Wang, 1967), 56. See also Theodore F. T. Plucknett, *Taswell-Langmead's English Constitutional History from the Teutonic Conquest to the Present Time*, 11th ed. (Boston: Houghton Mifflin Company, 1960), 364, 522–23, 538.

tions and experience. "Even the framers of Magna Carta," Winston S. Churchill wrote: "did not attempt to lay down new law or proclaim any broad general principles. This was because both sovereign and subject were in practice bound by the Common Law, and the liberties of Englishmen rested not on any enactment of the State, but on immemorial slow-growing custom declared by juries of free men who gave their verdicts case by case in open court."[3]

From the late thirteenth century, then, English constitutional development was profoundly affected by the existence of an established system of law, upon which the rights of the English could be firmly based, and an elite professional corps ever ready to preserve the common law and the rights derived from it against any and all encroachment. Above all, the self-contained system developed by the common lawyers was, as Frederic William Maitland has commented, "tough law."[4] Its toughness enabled it not only to survive as the bulwark of English liberty but also to serve as the foundation of American law.

In an 1817 letter, Jefferson challenged the very basis of common-law authority in this respect. "I have considered," he wrote,

3. Winston S. Churchill, *History of the English-Speaking Peoples*, 4 vols. (New York: Dodd, Mead & Company, 1956), 1:225. On Magna Carta, see generally J. C. Holt, *Magna Carta*, 2d ed. (Cambridge: Cambridge University Press, 1992); A. E. Dick Howard, *The Road from Runnymede: Magna Carta and Constitutionalism in America* (Charlottesville: University Press of Virginia, 1968); and Ellis Sandoz, ed., *The Roots of Liberty: Magna Carta, the Ancient Constitution, and the Anglo-American Tradition of Rule of Law* (Columbia: University of Missouri Press, 1993).

4. Frederic William Maitland, *English Law and the Renaissance* (Cambridge: Cambridge University Press, 1901), 18.

"that respecting the obligation of the common law in this country as a very plain one, and merely a question of document. If we are under that law, the document which made us so can surely be produced; and as far as this can be produced, so far we are subject to it, and farther we are not."[5] Jefferson the lawyer knew better. In his practice, as his argument in the *Bolling* case clearly shows, he relied constantly upon common-law cases and principles. In addition, he recognized that, document or no document, the colonists had, as a matter of history, brought the common law with them as part of their English heritage. "On our arrival here," he wrote to John Tyler, "the question would at once arise, by what law will we govern ourselves. The resolution seems to have been, by that system with which we are familiar ... the English law... constituted the system adopted here."[6] In addition, he commented in his *Notes on the State of Virginia* (1785), "the rule, in our courts of judicature was, that the common law of England ... [was] in force here."[7]

Most important in this connection was Jefferson's posture on the common law when he took the lead in the effort to revise Virginia law. It was Jefferson who initiated the motion, which the

5. Thomas Jefferson to Dr. John Manners, 12 June 1817, in *The Writings of Thomas Jefferson*, ed. Paul L. Ford, 10 vols. (New York: G.P. Putnam's Sons, 1892–99), 10:86–88 (quote at 87). (Note: Putnam's republished this title in a 12-volume "Federal Edition" in 1904, a version not used by the present author.)

6. Thomas Jefferson to Judge John Tyler, 17 June 1812, quoted in Charles Warren, *A History of the American Bar*, 2d ed. (Boston: Houghton Mifflin, 1939), 225–26.

7. Thomas Jefferson, *Notes on the State of Virginia*, ed. William Peden (Chapel Hill,: University of North Carolina Press for the Institute of Early American History and Culture, 1955), 132 (Query XIV: Laws).

Virginia General Assembly passed in 1776, to set up a committee "to revise the laws."[8] The revision committee first met "to settle the plan of operation."[9] The initial point agreed upon was that the common law should remain the basis of Virginia law: "The Common Law not to be medled with, except where Alterations are necessary."[10] Edmund Pendleton and another committee member had urged that "we should propose to abolish the whole existing system of laws, and prepare a new and complete Institute." Jefferson led the vote the other way, to "preserve the general system, and only modify it to the present state of things."[11] This meant that, even after the revision, the common law would continue as the foundation of Virginia law; anything not covered by the revisors' bills would still be covered by the common law.

8. On 12 October 1776 the Virginia General Assembly named Jefferson and two other members as a committee to prepare a bill establishing a committee to revise the laws of Virginia; reported on 15 October, the measure was passed by the House of Delegates on 17 October 1776 and by the Senate on 26 October 1776. For the annotated text, see Julian Boyd, Charles Cullen, and John Catanzariti, eds., *The Papers of Thomas Jefferson*, 24 vols. to date (Princeton, N.J.: Princeton University Press, 1950), 2: 562–64 (hereafter *Jefferson Papers*). *Jefferson Papers*, 2:305–665, collects the sources used in the present study of the commission and its labors. On the motion and its significance, see the discussions in Dumas Malone, *Jefferson the Virginian* (Boston: Little, Brown, 1948), 251–57, and Edward Dumbauld, *Thomas Jefferson and the Law* (Norman: University of Oklahoma Press, 1978), 132–43. See also A. G. Roeber, *Faithful Magistrates and Republican Lawyers: Creators of Virginia Legal Culture, 1680–1810* (Chapel Hill: University of North Carolina Press, 1981), for a sensitive and intelligent analysis of the intellectual context of Virginia's evolving legal culture.

9. *Autobiography*, ca. 1821, in *Thomas Jefferson: Writings*, ed. Merrill D. Peterson (New York: Library of America, 1984), 37.

10. "Plan Agreed upon by the Committee of Revisors at Fredericksburg," 13 January 1777, in *Jefferson Papers*, 2: 325–28 (quote at 325).

11. *Autobiography*, in *Jefferson: Writings*, 37–38.

## Rights of Englishmen

In fact, at the very outset of colonization, it was recognized that the common law was to be as binding on the western side of the Atlantic as it was in England itself. Had this principle not been so established, the history of British North America might have been far different. The first colonial charter—the 1606 Virginia charter granted by James I—states the fundamental principle that the colonists were to "have and enjoy all Liberties, Franchises, and Immunities... to all Intents and Purposes, as if they had been abiding and born, within this our Realm of England."[12] Patrick Henry's 1765 resolves relied directly upon the 1606 charter provision, proclaiming that by it "the colonists aforesaid are declared entitled to all liberties, privileges, and immunities... as if they had been abiding and born within the realm of England."[13]

The Virginia Charter was only the first of a series of organic colonial documents that guaranteed the colonists all the "rights of Englishmen." The same guaranty would appear in the charters of New England (1620), Massachusetts Bay (1629), Maryland (1632), Connecticut (1662), Rhode Island (1663), Carolina (1663), and Georgia (1732).[14] And foremost among the rights of Englishmen possessed by the colonists was the common law itself. From the

12. "First Charter of Virginia, 1606," in Bernard Schwartz, ed., *The Bill of Rights: A Documentary History*, 2 vols. (New York: Chelsea House, 1971), 1:54–61 (quote at 54).

13. "Virginia Stamp Act Resolutions," 30 May 1765, in Henry Steele Commager, ed., *Documents of American History*, 9th ed., 2 vols. (New York: Appleton Century Crofts, 1973), 1:55–56 (quote at 56).

14. Richard L. Perry, *Sources of Our Liberties* (Chicago: American Bar Foundation, 1959), 35.

beginning, the colonists recognized that the common law was an essential part of their heritage. This point was first made expressly in the Maryland Act for the Liberties of the People (1639), which provided that "all the Inhabitants of this Province... Shall have and enjoy all such rights liberties communities priviledges and free customs within this Province as any natural born subject of England hath or ought to have or enjoy in the realm of England by force or vertue of the common law."[15]

The Maryland statute stated the fundamental principle that was to control the development of law in this country— that it was based upon English common law, which governed in the colonies as it did in the mother country. The situation in this respect was stated by the counsel for a defendant in a 1759 case in South Carolina, who argued that under the Carolina charter legislative power was limited to acts not contrary to the laws of England. Therefore, English law at the time of the respective charter grant was to all intents and purposes the law of Carolina.[16] As John Adams was to put it in his *Novanglus* letters, the charter provision "was intended to subject them to the Common Law... it meant to confine them to Obedience to Common Law."[17] "With us," reads the classic statement in James Kent's *Commentaries on American Law*, "the

15. "Maryland Act for the Liberties of the People, 1639," in *Bill of Rights*, 1:68.

16. Joseph H. Smith, *Appeals to the Privy Council from the American Plantations* (New York: Columbia University Press, 1950), 587.

17. "Novanglus," 1774, in *The Adams Papers, Series IV: Papers of John Adams*, ed. Robert J. Taylor et al., 8 vols. (Cambridge, Mass.: Harvard University Press, 1977–89), 2:381.

common law ... has been recognised and adopted, as one entire system, by the people of this state. It was declared to be a part of the law of the land, by an express provision in the [New York] constitution."[18]

Not only was the common law the foundation of American law, it also became an essential tool in the struggle that led to independence. As the conflict with the mother country intensified, Americans increasingly tended to rely on the common law as the embodiment of their rights. The 1774 Declaration of Rights of the First Continental Congress asserted categorically "that the respective colonies are entitled to the common law of England."[19] More and more the rallying cry was "the common law is our birthright and inheritance."[20]

## American Modifications

"The common law of England," wrote John Dickinson in his *Letters from a Farmer in Pennsylvania*, "is generally received... ; but our courts EXERCISE A SOVEREIGN AUTHORITY, in determining what parts of the common and statute law ought to be extended: For it must be admitted, that the difference of circumstances neces-

18. James Kent, *Commentaries on American Law*, 4 vols. (New York: O. Halsted, 1826–30; New York: Da Capo Press, 1971), 1:440.

19. "Declarations and Resolves of the First Continental Congress, 1774," in *Bill of Rights*, 2:215–19 (quote at 217). See generally John Phillip Reid, *Constitutional History of the American Revolution*, 4 vols. (Madison: University of Wisconsin Press, 1986–93).

20. Joseph Story, *Commentaries on the Constitution of the United States*, 3 vols. (Boston: Hilliard, Gray, 1833), sec. 157.

sarily requires us, in some cases, to REJECT the determination of both.... Some of the English rules are adopted, others rejected."[21] In other words, the colonists did not adopt the whole body of the common law, but only those portions that their different circumstances did not require them to reject.[22] "The common law of England," the U.S. Supreme Court affirmed in 1829, "is not to be taken in all respects to be that of America. Our ancestors brought with them its general principles, and claimed it as their birthright; but they brought with them and adopted only that portion which was applicable to their situation."[23] Indeed, a principal task during the formative era of American law was to adapt the common law to the situation that existed on this side of the Atlantic.

However alike two countries may be in background and tradition, a wholesale transportation of a legal system from one to another is obviously undesirable. When the England of the mid-eighteenth to mid-nineteenth centuries is compared with the America of that time, it is evident that the English law had to be remade for Americans. As an Ohio case put it in 1853, the common law had to be made "suitable to the condition and business of our people." Hence, "our courts have not hesitated to modify it to suit our circumstances."[24]

21. [John Dickinson], *Letters from a Farmer in Pennsylvania to the Inhabitants of the British Colonies*, 2d ed. (Philadelphia, David Holland William Sellers 1768), 46 (italics omitted).

22. Story, *Commentaries on the Constitution*, sec. 148.

23. *Van Ness v. Pacard*, 2 Pet. (27 U.S.) 137, 144 (1829).

24. *Bloom v. Richards*, 2 Ohio St. 387, 391 (1853).

The modifications made in the common law by American judges may be explained, first of all, by the drastically different physical setting of this country. The size of the country and the abundance of its natural resources made impossible the importation of the common law exactly as it had been developed in England. Measured by English standards, America had superabundant land, timber, and mineral wealth. American law had to serve the primary need of the new society—to master the vast land areas of the American continent. Geography, indeed, provided a new frame for U.S. law and directly affected its emphasis and direction. The classic illustration of this is the *Genesee Chief* case, decided by the Supreme Court in 1851.[25] The Court refused to follow the English rule that confined admiralty jurisdiction to the high seas and upon rivers only as far as the ebb and flow of the tide extended. This limitation might have been adequate in an island such as Britain, where practically all streams are tidal, but it could not prevail in a transcontinental America. When the first colonies were settled, the English "tidal flow" test may well have sufficed. In the original thirteen states, as in England, almost all navigable waters were tidewaters. The westward movement, and the growth of commerce on the Mississippi and other inland waterways, revealed the law's inadequacy. "It is evident," declared the *Genesee Chief* opinion, "that a definition that would at this day limit public rivers in this country to tide waters is utterly inadmissible. We have thousands of miles of public navigable waters, including lakes and rivers in which there is no tide. And certainly there can be no reason for admiralty power

25. *The Propeller Genesee Chief,* 12 How. (53 U.S.) 443 (1851).

over a public tide water, which does not apply with equal force to any other public water used for commercial purposes."[26]

The physical setting also worked to free America from restrictive English legal traditions.[27] The land law in England was not only feudal in origin, it also still retained much of its feudal character, with its labyrinth of primogeniture, fee tail, seisin, attornment, seigniories, reversions, remainders, and the like. Of course, there were attempts to introduce the feudal land law into the colonies. Perhaps the most curious one was contained in the 1669 Fundamental Constitutions of Carolina, drafted by John Locke.[28] Here is the rare example of the Platonic ideal in operation—a frame of government drawn up by one of the greatest political philosophers.

Unfortunately, as all too often happens, Plato-become-Solon produced a fundamental law that, however attractive to the speculative theorist, proved wholly unworkable. It is suprising that a mind as acute as Locke's could have produced so clumsy a document, with its reliance on feudal concepts and Graustarkian layers of nobility, and with its palatines, seigniories, baronies, manors, court-leets, landgraves, and caziques. Certainly the elaborate structure was bizarre in the Carolina colony, which could scarcely be settled as a miniature feudal kingdom based on institutions that had become anachronisms even in the Old World.

26. Id., 457.

27. Compare James Willard Hurst, *The Growth of American Law: The Law Makers* (Boston: Little, Brown, 1950), 8.

28. "Fundamental Constitutions of Carolina, 1669," in *Bill of Rights*, 1:108–24.

Such efforts to transfer feudal institutions from England (where they may still have had some meaning) were doomed to fail, although they lingered on in scattered places, notably the Hudson River Valley in New York, until after the Revolution. Primogeniture, entailed estates, and other common-law fundamentals were the worst possible foundations for American property law, for they destroyed the incentive that would induce people to settle and develop the constantly expanding frontier. Alexis de Tocqueville contrasted the European expectation of passing on to sons land held in a long family line with his observation of American practice, where the farmer "brings land into tillage in order to sell it again, ... on the speculation that, as the state of the country will soon be changed by the increase of population, a good price may be obtained for it."[29]

Feudal land law, like the royal prerogative in government and the navigation acts in commerce, was an obstacle to Americans' ability to utilize their own resources as they saw fit. As vestiges of colonialism, the feudal rules had to go. The old common-law abuses gradually were overcome, although not without a few sharp clashes. Primogeniture and entails were not saved by their antiquity, nor the rules of descent by their incongruity, nor fines, recoveries, and real actions by their absurdity and costliness.[30] As a New York court noted in 1835, decent oblivion was provided for most of

29. Alexis de Tocqueville, *Democracy in America*, trans. Francis D. Reeve, ed. Phillips Bradley, 2 vols. (New York: Alfred A. Knopf, 1954), 2:16.

30. Compare "The Law of Real Property," 1879, in *The Collected Papers of Frederic William Maitland*, ed. H. A. L. Fisher, 3 vols. (Cambridge: Cambridge University Press, 1911), 1:162–201 (esp. 198–99).

the "monarchial machinery of landed tenures...This ancient, complicated and barbarous system...is entirely abrogated in relation to the tenure, the acquisition, the enjoyment and the transmission of property."[31] The result was to make all tenure allodial, with the freehold established as the normal type of land title.[32] In America, the governing policy ultimately became that proposed during the 1846 New York constitutional debate on the abolition of feudal tenures: "There should be no more restrictions placed upon the alienation of real estate than upon personal property. Property was improved by passing from hand to hand."[33] As will be shown, perhaps the most important contribution by Jefferson to private law was his work in reforming the land law.

## An American System of Law

As early as 1704, an *Abridgement of the Laws in Force and Use in Her Majesty's Plantations* was printed in London, devoted to the laws of Virginia, Maryland, and Massachusetts, together with a smattering of items from New York and the Carolinas.[34] This was a clear recognition that a body of American law already existed, distinct from the English law from which it was derived. Those having dealings with the colonies could no longer rely solely on English legal authorities.

31. *Coster v. Lorillard*, 14 Wend. 265, 374–375 (N.Y. 1835).

32. See Kent, *Commentaries on American Law*, 4:3.

33. Quoted in James Willard Hurst, *Law and the Conditions of Freedom in the Nineteenth-Century United States* (Madison: University of Wisconsin Press, 1946), 13.

34. Richard B. Morris, *Studies in the History of American Law* (New York: Columbia University Press, 1930), 11.

Even more important was the fact that an American conception of law was coming into being. The underlying notion of English law was stated in Sir William Blackstone's conception of law as command: "Law... is that rule of action, which is prescribed by some superior, and which the inferior is bound to obey."[35] American jurists rejected this idea of superiority. That concept, declared Justice James Wilson of the U.S. Supreme Court in his 1790–91 law lectures in Philadelphia, "contained the germ of the divine right of princes to rule," and was hence inappropriate for a nation founded upon repudiation of that doctrine. "In its place," Wilson stated, "I introduce—the consent of those whose obedience the law requires. This I conceive to be the true origin of the obligation of human laws."[36]

Here was a distinctly American conception of law—that laws derive their force from consent. This concept was the one generally accepted in American jurisprudence in the latter part of the eighteenth century. Thus, George Wythe, Jefferson's law teacher and the opposing counsel in the *Bolling* case, stated in a judicial opin-

35. Sir William Blackstone, *Commentaries on the Laws of England*, 4 vols. (1765–69; photographic reprint, Chicago: University of Chicago Press, 1979), 1:38. On Blackstone's influence, see Daniel J. Boorstin, *The Mysterious Science of the Law* (Cambridge, Mass.: Harvard University Press, 1941); and Julius S. Waterman, "Thomas Jefferson and Blackstone's Commentaries," *Illinois Law Review* 27 (1933): 629–59, reprinted in David H. Flaherty, ed., *Essays in the History of Early American Law* (Chapel Hill: University of North Carolina Press for the Institute of Early American History and Culture, 1969), 451–88.

36. "Lectures on Law, Part One, Lecture II: Of the general principles of law and obligation," ca. 1790–91, in *The Works of James Wilson*, ed. Robert G. McCloskey, 2 vols. (Cambridge, Mass.: Belknap Press of Harvard University Press/John Harvard Library, 1967), 1:121.

ion, "rational civil liberty... is to be free from all civil obligations, except such as laws, enacted by consent of the society, or representatives of their election, had created; and to be free from those obligations, when the same society, of representatives, shall signify their will to abrogate the laws, which did create the obligations."[37] Such an approach to law was natural to a Virginian whose state adopted a bill of rights that expressly declared, "all men... cannot be... bound by any law to which they have not... assented [by] their own consent or that of their Representatives so elected."[38] This was particularly true of so close an associate of the man who asserted in the Declaration of Independence that governments (and presumably the laws enacted by them) derive "their just powers from the consent of the governed."[39]

It is true that British law was by then also based on the notion that statutes derived their force from the fact that the people had consented to them because they were approved by elected parlimentary representatives. Before the great electoral reforms of the nineteenth century, however, the concept of consent through parliamentary representation was largely a fiction. Not until the doctrine of "virtual" representation gave way to one in which the House of Commons became directly representative of a democratic electorate could it truly be said that British laws were based upon

37. *Page v. Pendleton*, in George Wythe, reporter, *Decisions of Cases in Virginia by the High Court of Virginia, with Remarks upon Decrees of the Court of Appeals, Reversing Some of Those Decisions* (1793), 129–31 n. e.

38. "Virginia Declaration of Rights, 1776," art. 6, in *Bill of Rights*, 1:234–236 (quote at 235).

39. "Declaration of Independence, 1776," in id., 251–55 (quote at 252).

the consent of the governed.[40]

The Wilson and Wythe conception that laws derive their force from consent was better suited to the needs of the new nation than Blackstone's imperative conception of law. If consent was the basis of law, then the law could be changed to meet the "felt necessities of the times."[41] Americans were coming to look upon the law as an instrument of social change rather than one for preserving the social status quo—the idea that prevailed on the other side of the Atlantic. The law's goal was to further ambition and energy;[42] its job was to furnish the legal tools needed for effective mobilization of the society's resources. This was the conception of law held not only by Jefferson but also by his arch-rival, Alexander Hamilton.

Few would dispute this so far as the latter is concerned. Elsewhere I have called Hamilton "The First Instrumentalist" in American jurisprudence.[43] In its two centuries of existence, American public law has been essentially Hamiltonian in its

40. Schwartz, *Roots of Freedom*, 227. Compare John Phillip Reid, *The Concept of Representation in the Age of the American Revolution* (Chicago: University of Chicago Press, 1989), passim (arguing that American understanding of representation had roots in English constitutional history and law at least as firm as those anchoring English conceptions of "virtual" representation).

41. Oliver Wendell Holmes, Jr., *The Common Law* (Boston: Little, Brown, 1881), 1.

42. Compare Hurst, *Growth of American Law*, 195; Hurst, *Law and the Conditions of Freedom*, passim; William E. Nelson, *Americanization of the Common Law: The Impact of Legal Change on Massachusetts Society, 1760–1830* (Cambridge, Mass.: Harvard University Press, 1975; reprint, with new introduction, Athens: University of Georgia Press, 1994); Morton J. Horwitz, *The Transformation of American Law, 1780–1860* (Cambridge, Mass.: Harvard University Press, 1977).

43. Bernard Schwartz, *Main Currents in American Legal Thought* (Durham, N.C.: Carolina Academic Press, 1993), 23.

approach. The two fundamental principles for which Hamilton stood—the doctrine of judicial review and that of implied powers[44]—have become the very cornerstones of the constitutional system. Hamilton did not advocate the doctrines he urged as mere academic exercises. On the contrary, he intended the principles that he promoted to ensure attainment of the social and economic ends that he favored. He interpreted the Constitution to provide for an energetic national government, because its powers could be used to foster the strong productive economy that he foresaw and desired. Hamilton was ready to make affirmative use of the law to advance the economy, by doctrines such as that of implied powers or by reliance on the General Welfare Clause to justify the power to enact protective tariffs.[45]

Jefferson's constitutional principles were the virtual opposites of those urged by his rival. Yet Jefferson, too, advocated his opposed concept of public law to further the type of polity and society that he favored. His goal of national development emphasized an idealistic agrarianism to counter (or complement) the centralizing capitalism that was emerging. Jefferson warned of the danger of a consolidated government, which invariably tended toward self-aggrandizement—the inevitable result being a political Leviathan.[46] The danger could be avoided by circumscribing cen-

44. Id., 26–31.

45. Compare James Willard Hurst, *Law and Social Order in the United States* (Ithaca, N.Y.: Cornell University Press, 1977), 23, 45; James Willard Hurst, "Alexander Hamilton: Law Maker," *Columbia Law Review* 78 (1978): 483–547.

tral power and emphasizing states' rights.

For both Jefferson and Hamilton, legal doctrine had become a tool to attain political, social, and economic ends. Their constitutional disagreements were a prime example of the evolving American instrumentalist conception of law in action, with each protagonist using legal doctrines to further the goals that he favored.

## The Legal Profession

By the time of the *Bolling* case, the role of the law in America had already become evident. According to Edmund Burke, on the extent of legal influence in the American colonies: "in no country, perhaps, in the world, is the law so general a study."[47] In a broad sense, the struggle for American independence was a legal struggle; or, at the least, it was framed in terms of legal issues. The conflict that led to the Revolution was in large part over differing interpretations of the colonies' status under the British constitution. "In

46. Compare Vernon L. Parrington, *Main Currents in American Thought*, 3 vols. (New York: Harcourt, Brace, 1924–1930, 2:10–12, 356; David N. Mayer, *The Constitutional Thought of Thomas Jefferson* (Charlottesville: University Press of Virginia, 1994); Joyce Oldham Appleby, *Capitalism and a New Social Order: The Republican Vision of the 1790s* (New York: New York University Press, 1984); Joyce Oldham Appleby, *Liberalism and Republicanism in the Historical Imagination* (Cambridge, Mass.: Harvard University Press, 1992); James R. Stoner, Jr., *Common Law and Liberal Theory: Coke, Hobbes, and the Origins of American Constitutionalism* (Lawrence: University Press of Kansas, 1992).

47. "On Conciliation with the Colonies," 22 March 1775, in *The Works of the Right Honorable Edmund Burke*, 12 vols. (Boston: Little, Brown and Company, 1865–67), 2:101–82 (quote at 124). On the place of the American Revolution in Burke's thought, see Conor Cruise O'Brien, *The Great Melody: A Thematic Biography and Commented Anthology of Edmund Burke* (Chicago: University of Chicago Press, 1992), 87–182, 202–34.

Britain," wrote Governor Sir Francis Bernard of Massachusetts in 1765, "the American Governments are considered as Corporations empowered to make by-Laws, existing only during the Pleasure of Parliament.... In America they claim... to be perfect States, no otherwise dependent upon Great Britain than by having the same King."[48]

The legal nub of this constitutional controversy could scarcely be resolved by compromise between the diametrically opposed English and American viewpoints. While London was willing to appease the colonists by revoking exactions such as the Stamp Act, it could not give way on its constitutional right to legislate for the colonies. The Americans, for their part, could hardly assent to the parliamentary interpretation. The colonists may have faced no greater risk of actual impoverishment from the British tax on tea than John Hampden did when he refused Charles I's demand for payment of ship money,[49] but both Hampden and the Americans were convinced that their constitutional rights were being violated and that acquiescence on their part would have disastrous consequences.

Framing the controversy between the colonies and the mother country in legal terms was possible only because of the widespread influence that the law and lawyers already had in the American system. "I have been told by an eminent bookseller," said Burke, "that

48. Quoted in Claude H. Van Tyne, *The Causes of the War of Independence* (Boston: Houghton Mifflin, 1922), 217.

49. Compare Charles H. McIlwain, *The American Revolution: A Constitutional Interpretation* (1923; reprint, Ithaca, N.Y.: Cornell University Press, 1958), 189.

in no branch of his business... were so many books as those on the law exported to the plantations." He also noted that "The greater number of the deputies sent to Congress were lawyers,"[50] and General Thomas Gage complained "that all the people in his government [i.e., Massachusetts] are lawyers, or smatterers in law,"[51] and a similar comment could have been made about the other colonies. By the outbreak of the Revolution, an established legal profession existed throughout the country. This was true despite the fact that the early colonists attempted to get on without lawyers. Legislation hostile to the practice of law was continuous from the middle of the seventeenth century to the middle of the eighteenth century.[52] Typical was a 1658 Virginia statute providing that no attorney should "pleade in any courte of judicature within this collony, or give council in any cause, or controvercie whatsoever, for any kind of reward or profit."[53] The attempt to administer justice without lawyers is characteristic of both utopias and revolutions. The cry of Shakespeare's Dick the Butcher, "The first thing we do, let's kill all the lawyers," soon gives way, however, to the realization that the legal profession is an essential element of any functioning society. When the *Bolling* case was argued, there was a trained bar in all of the colonies.

50. "Conciliation," in *Works of Burke*, 2: 124.

51. Id., 125.

52. Roscoe Pound, *The Lawyer from Antiquity to Modern Times* (St. Paul, Minn.: West Publishing Co., 1953), 136.

53. John B. Minor, *Institutes of Common and Statute Law*, 2d ed. (1883), 4:177. A similar prohibition was contained in article 26 of the Massachusetts Body of Liberties (1641); for its text, see *Bill of Rights*, 1:74.

The rise of a legal profession accelerated rapidly in the generation before the Revolution. When he was admitted to practice in the middle of the eighteenth century, John Adams could state: "Looking about me in the Country, I found the practice of Law was grasped into the hands of Deputy Sheriffs, Pettifoggers, and even Constables, who filled all the Writts upon Bonds, promissory notes, and Accounts, received the Fees established for Lawyers, and stirred up many unnecessary Suits."[54] Typical of the pettifoggers he encountered was a tavern keeper. "In Kibby's Barr Room, in a little Shelf within the Barr, I spied 2 Books. I asked what they were. He said every Man his own Lawyer, and Gilberts Law of Evidence. Upon this I asked some Questions of the People there, and they told me that Kibby was a sort of Lawyer among them—that he pleaded some of their home Cases before Justices and Arbitrators &c."[55] Adams ends by saying that he told Kibby to purchase a copy of Blackstone.

Adams also noted the existence of a flourishing bar in the province: "Boston was full of Lawyers and many of them of established Characters for long Experience, great Abilities and extensive Fame."[56] Massachusetts had had a strong bar since the beginning of the eighteenth century, when a statute required an oath of office for admission to practice. (By the end of the colonial period, this

54. *Autobiography*, in *The Adams Papers, Series I: Diary and Autobiography of John Adams*, ed. Lyman H. Butterfield et al., 4 vols. (Cambridge, Mass.: Belknap Press of Harvard University Press, 1961), 3:274.

55. Diary entry, 5 June 1771, in id., 2:27.

56. *Autobiography*, in id., 3: 270.

was also true in the other colonies.) Particularly in the generation before the Revolution, lawyers came to the fore. They were the most influential members of the colonial legislatures and the Continental Congress. Not only did they lead the revolutionary movement, they also, perhaps more importantly, translated the Revolution into institutions that gave its peculiarly legal cast to the American polity.

Thus, as Chief Justice Harlan Fiske Stone wrote, "Burke's portrayal of the position and influence of the legal profession in Revolutionary America was not overdrawn.... Such names as James Otis, John Adams, Josiah Quincy, Robert Payne of Massachusetts, Peyton Randolph, Patrick Henry, Edmund Pendleton of Virginia, Charles Carroll and Samuel Chase of Maryland, and Alexander Hamilton and James Kent of New York recall vividly to mind... the ascendance of the legal profession in legislation and in the political and social life of the growing nation."[57] During the earlier colonial period, the leadership may have been furnished by others—for example, the clergy in New England; toward its end the lawyers assumed increasing prominence. Their position is graphically shown by statistics: of the fifty-six signers of the Declaration of Independence, twenty-five were lawyers; of the fifty-five members of the Constitutional Convention, thirty-one were lawyers; in the first Congress, ten of the twenty-nine senators and seventeen of the

57. Harlan Fiske Stone, "The Lawyer and His Neighbors," *Cornell Law Quarterly* 4 (1919): 175–89 (quote at 177).

fifty-six representatives were lawyers.[58] If, as the New York legal reformer David Dudley Field asserted over a century ago, "the condition of the legal profession is an index of the civilisation of a people,"[59] the new nation had already attained an unusually high level of development.

## Education of a Lawyer

In an oft-quoted comment, President John F. Kennedy told a White House dinner for Nobel laureates, "I think this is the most extraordinary collection of talent, of human knowledge, that has ever been gathered together at the White House, with the possible exception of when Thomas Jefferson dined alone."[60] Jefferson's protean activities and interests are so dazzling that the fact that he began his professional life as a practicing lawyer is easily overlooked. After having received what was probably the best legal education in the colonies under the tutelage of George Wythe, Jefferson devoted seven years to the practice of law. He built up a successful practice and, as John W. Davis once put it, "if he had not been called away to public life…, he would still have won his place in the history of

58. Warren, *History of the American Bar*, 211.

59. David Dudley Field, "The Study and Practice of the Law," *Democratic Review* 14 (1844): 345.

60. Kennedy added: "Someone once said that Thomas Jefferson was a gentleman of 32 who could calculate an eclipse, survey an estate, tie an artery, plan an edifice, try a cause, break a horse, and dance the minuet. Whatever he may have lacked, if he could have had his former colleague, Mr. Franklin, here we all would have been impressed." "Remarks at a Dinner Honoring Nobel Prize Winners of the Western Hemisphere," 29 April 1962, in *Public Papers of the Presidents—John F. Kennedy: 1962* (Washington, D.C.: Government Printing Office, 1963), 347–48 (quote at 347).

Virginia as one of the brightest ornaments of an illustrious bar."[61] In 1790, John Marshall could list Jefferson among the "ablest men and soundest lawyers" of the day.[62] As the most recent Jefferson biography sums it up, "By the time he decided to abandon his legal practice..., he represented many of the colony's wealthiest and most prominent citizens, including many of the leading lawyers."[63] Jefferson's legal knowledge was summarized after his death by James Madison: "The Law itself he studied to the bottom, and in its greatest breadth, of which proofs were given at the Bar which he attended for a number of years, and occasionally throughout his career."[64] Wythe's great rival Edmund Pendleton thought him qualified to be a judge;[65] according to Justice Lewis F. Powell, "Jefferson almost certainly could have had a judgeship had he

61. John W. Davis, "Thomas Jefferson, Attorney at Law," *Proceedings of the Virginia State Bar Association* 38 (1926): 361–77 (quote at 364); Davis's article also appeared in *American Bar Association Journal* 13 (1927): 63–68.

62. John Marshall to Patrick Henry, 31 August 1790, in *The Papers of John Marshall*, ed. Charles T. Cullen and Herbert A. Johnson, 6 vols. to date (Chapel Hill: University of North Carolina Press for the Institute of Early American History and Culture, 1977), 2:60–61 (quote at 61).

63. Willard Sterne Randall, *Thomas Jefferson: A Life* (New York: Henry Holt, 1993), 95.

64. James Madison to Samuel H. Smith, 4 November 1826, in *The Writings of James Madison*, ed. Gaillard Hunt, 10 vols. (New York: G.P. Putnam's Sons, 1900–1910), 9:256–61 (quote at 260).

65. "I am not able to answer your reasons for not engaging in the Judiciary... However, I can but lament that it is not agreeable and convenient to you, for I do not Assent to your being unqualified, tho' I readily do to your usefulness in the Representative body, where... I hope you'll get cured of your wish to retire so early in life from the memory of man, and exercise Your talents for the nurture of Our new Constitution, which will require all the Attention of it's friends to prune exuberances and Cherish the Plant." Edmund Pendleton to Thomas Jefferson, 10 August 1776, in *Jefferson Papers*, 1:489.

wanted it."[66] Long after Jefferson had given up his practice, Aaron Burr (certainly no admirer) was heard to say of him, "Our president is a lawyer and a great one too."[67]

When Jefferson decided to study law, there was no formal legal education in this country. That was to start only after independence, when, on Jefferson's urging, George Wythe was appointed by the College of William and Mary in 1779 as the first American law professor and when Judge Tapping Reeve set up the nation's first law school in Litchfield, Connecticut, in 1784. At the time Jefferson studied law, John W. Davis tells us, "he had but [three] avenues of approach to the gateway of the bar,"[68] and those were study at the Inns of Court in London, independent reading, and apprenticeship.

The first was, by its very nature, available only to a small minority of the profession. In the century before the Revolution, only twenty members of the Virginia bar had studied in London.[69] Among them, however, were some of its leaders, notably Jefferson's cousins Edmund and Peyton Randolph, as well as prominent lawyers in other colonies, such as Charles Carroll of Carrollton in

66. Lewis F. Powell, Jr., "Thomas Jefferson and American Justice," *Los Angeles Daily Journal*, 28 April 1981, p. 4, cols. 3–6 (quote at col. 3) (reprint of Powell's commencement address at the University of West Virginia).

67. Quoted in Dumbauld, *Jefferson and the Law*, xi, from Isaac Jenkinson, *Aaron Burr: His Personal and Political Relations with Thomas Jefferson and Alexander Hamilton* (Richmond, Indiana: M. Cullaton, 1902), 261.

68. Davis, "Thomas Jefferson, Attorney at Law", *American Bar Association Journal*, quote at p. 64.

69. Randall, *Thomas Jefferson: A Life*, 46.

Maryland and John Rutledge of South Carolina, later a member of the U.S. Supreme Court.

The best-known revolutionary leader who had been trained in the Inns of Court was John Dickinson of Pennsylvania—one of the few lawyers outside the southern colonies able to complete his legal education in England. His direct exposure to English law at the Middle Temple had an indelible effect upon the young Dickinson. Like most of the other colonial lawyers trained at the Inns of Court, he acquired a conservative approach to law that colored his whole attitude on the great political and legal issues with which Americans were soon presented. At the Inns of Court, Dickinson steeped himself in the common law to an extent impossible for John Adams, who worked in a law office, or Alexander Hamilton, who read the law on his own. The lawyer taught in the Temple acquired a profound respect for the English system and its orderly processes. During the dispute with the mother country, he based his theories of resistance upon the English law and traditions that he had been taught. Maitland's aphorism that taught law is tough law[70] is supported by no better example than the revolutionary approach of the Inn-taught lawyers such as Dickinson.

According to Justice Robert H. Jackson, colonial lawyers such as Dickinson were "considered the elite of the Bar, who had imbibed the law of England, along with its best port, at London Inns of Court."[71] That was true even though the Inns themselves

70. See supra, note 4.

71. Robert H. Jackson, "The Genesis of an American Legal Profession: A Review of 150 Years of Change," *American Bar Association Journal* 38 (1952): 547–50, 615–18 (quote at 548).

were then at their nadir, so far as their teaching of law was concerned. In fact, the pre-revolutionary period was "concurrent with the decadence of Inns of... Court into mere social institutions rather than disseminators of professional education."[72] Charles Carroll, who was enrolled at the Inner Temple, wrote to his father in 1762 that, though "being entered at the Temple is a necessary... opening to all preferments in the law; 't is attended with no other advantages, but many and great inconveniences; the chiefest is the frequenting loose and dissolute companions."[73] In a letter the next year, Carroll asserted, "Nothing can be more absurd than the usual manner of young gentlemen's studying the law" at the Temple.[74] Jefferson apparently agreed; in 1781 he wrote to James Monroe, "An entrance in the Temple, or gown from thence, would scarcely add to your character here."[75]

The second method of studying law in Jefferson's day was followed by Abraham Lincoln over half a century later, when he prepared for the profession by self-directed reading. There were two outstanding examples of the self-trained attorney in the latter part of the eighteenth century. The first was Patrick Henry. He was admitted to the bar after six weeks solitary study of *Coke on Littleton* and the Virginia statutes. According to one commentator,

72. Tommy R. Ledbetter, "Comment: The Early History of the Legal Profession," *Baylor Law Review* 18 (1966): 380–93 (quote at 389).

73. Warren, *History of the American Bar,* 193.

74. Id.

75. Thomas Jefferson to James Monroe, 5 October 1781, in *Jefferson Papers,* 6:126–28 (quote at 127).

"this self-directed reading was not altogether successful [as] may be gathered from the fact that George Wythe, one of his 'bar examiners' (in Virginia all candidates for admission to the bar were examined by a committee of lawyers appointed by the [General] Court), refused to sign Patrick Henry's license. John Randolph, who passed him rather reluctantly, 'perceived him to be a young man of genius... [but] very ignorant of the law.'"[76] The second example of the self-directed law student was Alexander Hamilton, a student of an entirely different caliber. Hamilton had started to read legal works while enrolled at Columbia (then called King's College). His early tract, *The Farmer Refuted*,[77] written in February 1775 while he was still at King's College, cites both the standard law books of the day and works on natural law by Locke and Continental writers, indicating the breadth of his legal reading even at that early date.[78]

When Hamilton left Washington's army toward the end of 1781, he decided to become a lawyer. A three-year clerkship was

76. Warren, *History of the American Bar*, 165; Anton-Hermann Chroust, *The Rise of the Legal Profession in America*, 2 vols. (Norman: University of Oklahoma Press, 1965), 1:30. See also the discussion in Henry Mayer, *A Son of Thunder: Patrick Henry and the American Republic* (New York: Franklin Watts, 1986), 51–56.

77. [Alexander Hamilton], *The Farmer Refuted: or A more impartial and comprehensive View of the Dispute between Great-Britain and the Colonies, Intended as a Further Vindication of the Congress: In Answer to a Letter from A. W. Farmer, Intitled A View of the Controversy Between Great-Britain and Her Colonies: Including a Mode of determining the present Disputes Finally and Effectually, &c...*, in *The Papers of Alexander Hamilton*, ed. Harold C. Syrett, Jacob E. Cooke, and Barbara Chernow, 27 vols. (New York: Columbia University Press, 1961–87), 1:81–165.

78. See Julius Goebel, Jr., and Joseph H. Smith, Jr., eds., *The Law Practice of Alexander Hamilton*, 5 vols. (New York: Columbia University Press, 1964–81), 1:5–6. See also the fullest and most reliable intellectual biography: Gerald Stourzh, *Alexander Hamilton and the Idea of Republican Government* (Stanford: Stanford University Press, 1970).

then required of candidates for the New York bar. This requirement, however, was suspended for Hamilton by the state supreme court in April 1782 because he "has in Court declared that he had previous to the war directed his Studies to the profession of the Law and... entered into the Army in defence of his Country."[79] All Hamilton had to do was to pass an examination in open court, which he did some months later, and he was admitted as an attorney qualified to practice before the New York Supreme Court in July 1782.[80] Hamilton read on his own for about six months to prepare for his bar examination. It is not known what his preparation consisted of, but he doubtless read the traditional texts used at the time, particularly Coke, as well as Blackstone, whose masterly analysis of English law was by then widely available in this country. Some idea of the effort he made can be obtained by examining the practice manual he wrote while studying for the bar. This manual, consisting of 177 manuscript pages, was entitled *Practical Proceedings in the Supreme Court of the State of New York.*[81] It was later copied[82] and, according to Robert Troup, Hamilton's college friend who helped him prepare for the bar, "served as an instructive grammar to future students and became the groundwork of subse-

79. Paul M. Hamlin, "Legal Education in Colonial New York" *New York University Law Quarterly Review*, (1939): 128.

80. Goebel and Smith, *Law Practice of Alexander Hamilton,* 1:46–47.

81. *Practical Proceedings in the Supreme Court of the State of New York*, ms. copy of lost original ms. ca. 1782, in Goebel and Smith, *Law Practice of Alexander Hamilton*, 1:55–166. See discussion in id., 1:37–54.

82. Id., 1:38–39.

quent enlarged practical treatises."[83] The first printed book on New York practice made extensive use of the Hamilton work.[84]

Not only is Hamilton's manual "the first work in the field of private law by one of the great lawyers of the early Republic,"[85] his practice manual also shows that, even as a student, he understood the law well enough to recognize the need for procedural reforms. Writing of suing out a *scire facias* in certain cases, he wrote, "this proceeding seems to be without use, nor do the Books explain its Intention." Similarly, referring to the use of an English writ in the process of summoning a jury, he asserted, "there seems to be no reason for this." He declared of another practice, "this is among the Absurdities with which the Law abounds." He summarized his theme in a sardonic passage: "the Court... lately acquired... some faint Idea that the end of Suits at Law is to Investigate the Merits of the Cause, and not to entangle in the Nets of technical Terms."[86] Although Hamilton's manual shows deep dependence upon existing procedure, the work is full of defections in favor of "the Merits of the Cause."[87]

To be sure, only a Hamilton could obtain any systematic

83. Nathan Schachner, "Alexander Hamilton Viewed by His Friends: The Narratives of Robert Troup and Hercules Mulligan," *William and Mary Quarterly*, 3d ser., 4 (1947): 215.

84. William Wyche, *A Treatise on the Practice of the Supreme Court of Judicature of the State of New York in Civil Actions* (New York, 1792).

85. Goebel and Smith, *Law Practice of Alexander Hamilton,* 1:41.

86. Id., 51–52 (quoting and discussing "Practical Proceedings").

87. Id., 52. Compare Lawrence M. Friedman, *A History of American Law*, 2d ed. (New York: Simon and Schuster, 1985), 146.

knowledge of the law by reading on his own the texts and reports then available on this side of the Atlantic. Instead most would-be lawyers at the time, including Jefferson, followed the third method of studying law, apprenticeship. "It is," Jefferson himself noted, "a general practice to study the law in the office of some lawyer."[88] At that time, training for the bar was almost entirely through journeyman training; indeed, well past 1850 the chief method of American legal education was service as an apprentice with an established lawyer. The outstanding example before Jefferson was John Adams. For two years, he served as an apprentice to James Putnam, a Massachusetts lawyer considered so expert that "he could get a man hanged for stroking his neighbor's cat."[89] The young apprentice spent his time following court sessions, doing rudimentary jobs for his mentor, studying the law books in Putnam's library, and generally learning the practical requirements of the profession. Charles Carroll, who (as already apparent) had a low opinion of legal education at the Middle Temple, was an advocate of apprenticeship. He wrote to his father in 1763, "The best way to become a good lawyer is to be under an attorney.... Most of our great lawyers have been brought up under attorneys." If he had followed that method, Carroll averred, "I should then have known the practical part of the

88. Thomas Jefferson to John Garland Jefferson, 11 June 1790, in *Jefferson Papers,* 16:480–82 (quote at 480).

89. The quotation is from the fictionalized biography by Catherine Drinker Bowen, *John Adams and the American Revolution* (Boston: Little, Brown, 1950), 137. For a more reliable analysis of John Adams's training as a lawyer, see *The Adams Papers, Series III: The Legal Papers of John Adams,* ed. L. Kinvin Wroth and Hiller Zobel, 3 vols. (Cambridge, Mass.: Belknap Press of Harvard University Press, 1965), 1:lii–lvii, 1–25.

law, by which knowledge many difficulties would be removed, which, for want of it, are so insurmountable."[90]

In practice, however, the apprentice system was usually far from satisfactory. George Wythe, under whom Jefferson was to study, had himself read law in the law office of his uncle, Stephen Dewey. Wythe later complained bitterly about his own apprenticeship. He wrote that he had been less an apprentice at law than a mere clerk, spending most of his time in the drudgery of copying mostly routine papers.[91] The only benefit of this experience, says one Wythe biographer, is that it "may have shown him 'how not' to train lawyers, for the guidance he gave to his own charges was vastly different from that which he received."[92] James Wilson, next to Wythe perhaps the leading jurist of the day, was described as of little help to the students in his office: "As an instructor he was almost useless to those who were under his direction. He would never engage with them in professional discussions; to a direct question he gave the shortest possible answer and a general request for information was always evaded."[93] William Livingston, who had been in the law office of James Alexander, then the leader of the New

90. Quoted in Warren, *History of the American Bar,* 193.

91. Robert Bevier Kirtland, *George Wythe: Lawyer, Revolutionary, Judge* (New York: Garland, 1986), 32; Imogene E. Brown, *American Aristides: A Biography of George Wythe* (Rutherford, N.J.: Fairleigh Dickinson University Press, 1981), 22; Alonzo Thomas Dill, *George Wythe: Teacher of Liberty* (Williamsburg: Virginia Independence Bicentennial Commission, 1979), 9.

92. Brown, *American Aristides,* 22.

93. Warren, *History of the American Bar,* 167.

York bar, was even blunter in a 1745 newspaper invective against the drudgery to which law clerks were subjected. The apprentice system, Livingston declared, "is an outrage upon common honesty, a conduct scandalous, horrid, base, and infamous to the last degree! These gentlemen must either have no manner of concern for their clerk's future welfare and prosperity, or must imagine, that he will attain to a competent knowledge in the Law, by gazing on a number of books, which he has neither time nor opportunity to read; or that he is to be metamorphos'd into an attorney by virtue of Hocus Pocus."[94]

The problem with the apprenticeship system, Jefferson later wrote, was "that the services expected in return have been more than the instructions have been worth."[95] According to Richard B. Morris, "Much of the law clerk's time was consumed in tedious copying in longhand of writs, pleading, wills and deeds—all tasks that a photocopying machine does today."[96] In most cases, law clerks in Jefferson's time spent their office day in the kind of routine that Herman Melville was to immortalize in his "Bartleby the Scrivener" — the "dull, wearisome, and lethargic" task of copying legal documents. "I averr," Livingston wrote, "that 'tis a monstrous absurdity to suppose, that the law is to be learnt by a perpetual

94. Quoted in id., 168.

95. Thomas Jefferson to John Garland Jefferson, 11 June 1790, in *Jefferson Papers,* 16:480–82 (quote at 480).

96. Richard B. Morris, "The Legal Profession in America on the Eve of the Revolution," in Harry W. Jones, ed., *Political Separation and Legal Continuity* (Chicago: American Bar Association, 1976), 3–34 (quote at 15).

copying of precedents."[97] Yet, despite Livingston's "ridicule of this monstrous practice,"[98] it did succeed in turning out attorneys who have remained legends in the profession. It is as difficult to explain such success as it is to account for the level of statesmanship of the revolutionary generation.

## Diffusion of Legal Knowledge

One of the striking facts about pre-revolutionary America, at least to the present-day observer, was the diffusion of legal knowledge outside the profession itself. Charles Carroll's father wrote to him in 1759:

> it is a shame for a gentleman to be ignorant of ye laws of his country and to be dependent on every dirty pettifogger whose interest it may be to lead him by such a dependence into endless difficulties. On the other hand, how commendable is it for a gentleman of an independent fortune... to be able to advise and assist his friends, relatives and neighbors. What weight must such a one have on ye circle of his acquaintance![99]

In his March 22, 1775, speech on conciliation with the American colonies, Edmund Burke noted, "In no country perhaps in the world is the law so general a study. The profession itself is numerous and powerful; and in most provinces it takes the lead.... But all

97. Quoted in Warren, *History of the American Bar*, 168.

98. Id.

99. Quoted in id., at 191–92.

who read, and most do read, endeavour to obtain some smattering in that science."[100]

The most outstanding example of the layman as Founding Father was James Madison. Deemed the "father of the Constitution,"[101] Madison also drafted the Bill of Rights and was the leader in its adoption. He may thus be considered the father of American public law, even though he had little legal training (other than some desultory study of Coke and Blackstone) and no legal experience.

Madison had once considered a legal career. In 1773 he told a friend, "Intend myself to read law occasionally and have procured books for that purpose."[102] In 1785, long after he had struggled for some months over what he once called "the coarse and dry study of the law,"[103] Madison wrote to Edmund Randolph that, although "I keep up my attention to the course of reading... I am however far from determined ever to make a professional use of it."[104]

To the young Madison, the law may have been a "barren Desert," but he qualified the characterization by writing, "perhaps I

100. "Conciliation," in *Works of Burke,* 2:124.

101. Irving N. Brant, *James Madison: Father of the Constitution, 1787–1800* (Indianapolis and New York: Bobbs Merrill, 1950).

102. James Madison to William Bradford, 1 December 1773, in *The Papers of James Madison,* ed. William T. Hutchinson, et al., 17 vols. to date (vols. 1–10, Chicago: University of Chicago Press, 1962–1975; vols. 11–17, Charlottesville, University Press of Virginia, 1977), 1:100–102 (quote at 100–101) (hereafter *Madison Papers*).

103. James Madison to William Bradford, 24 January 1774, in *Madison Papers,* 1:104–6 (quote at 105).

104. James Madison to Edmund Randolph, 26 July 1785, in *Madison Papers,* 8:327–29 (quote at 328).

should not say barren either, because the law does bear fruit, but it is sour fruit, that must be gathered and pressed and distilled before it can bring pleasure or profit."[105] With Madison the "fruit" ultimately borne came from both his reading (particularly in public law — his wish, he once wrote to Jefferson, was to read "whatever may throw light on the general constitution & droit public")[106] and political experience— although he never did become a lawyer.

To a member of today's lawyer-dominated polity, it must remain a source of wonder that a gentleman-planter with a relative smattering of legal reading and without experience in the law could play the seminal role in drawing up the documents that are the foundation of the American system. Yet Madison was not the only nonlawyer who played a crucial part in the constitution drafting of the time. George Mason — the principal architect of both the Virginia Constitution of 1776 and its Bill of Rights — was, as Hugh Grigsby wrote in 1855, only "a planter,... whose life had been spent in a thinly settled colony."[107] Yet Mason, Madison, and their

105. James Madison to William Bradford, 24 January 1774, in *Madison Papers,* 1:104–6 (quote at 105).

106. James Madison to Thomas Jefferson, 16 March 1784, in *Madison Papers,* 8:6–15 (quote at 11). For the most thorough documentation of Jefferson's and Madison's fifty-year friendship, see James Morton Smith, ed., *The Republic of Letters: The Complete Correspondence between Thomas Jefferson and James Madison, 1776–1826,* 3 vols. (New York: W. W. Norton, 1995); see also Adrienne Koch, *Jefferson and Madison: The Great Collaboration* (New York: Alfred A. Knopf, 1950).

107. Quoted in Bernard Schwartz, *The Great Rights of Mankind: A History of the American Bill of Rights,* rev. ed. (Madison, Wis.: Madison House, 1992), 69. On Mason, see *The Papers of George Mason,* ed. Robert Allen Rutland, 3 vols. (Chapel Hill: University of North Carolina Press for the Institute of Early American History and Culture, 1970); Helen Hill

fellow statesmen knew Locke, Montesquieu, and Algernon Sydney — the trio that gave the American Revolution its theoretical underpinnings — and were widely read in the classics and in English and Continental public law.

## Thomas Jefferson: Law Student

Unlike Madison, his principal disciple, Jefferson was not just a layman who had studied some law. Despite Woodrow Wilson's famous assertion that "he was no lawyer,"[108] Jefferson had what may have been the best legal education of any pre-revolutionary American lawyer not trained at the British Inns of Court. He became a leader of the Virginia bar and had a flourishing practice before the law became only a peripheral part of his life.

In 1762, when he was nineteen and had finished college at William and Mary, Jefferson decided to study law under George Wythe, who had his law office in Williamsburg. Wythe, then thirty-five, was already the foremost legal scholar in the colonies, although he had little formal schooling. With his mother's help and by continuous reading and self-education, he mastered Latin, Greek, mathematics, the classics, moral philosophy, and the natural sciences, as well as the law. He became a leading classicist and, in 1778, a judge of the Virginia Court of Chancery. In 1788 he was named chancellor of the state.

Miller, *George Mason: Gentleman Revolutionary* (Chapel Hill: University of North Carolina Press, 1975); Robert Allen Rutland, *George Mason: Reluctant Statesman* (Williamsburg, Va.: Colonial Williamsburg, 1961).

108. Woodrow Wilson, *A History of the American People*, 2d ed. (New York: Harper, 1918), 3:183–84; 6:69.

In 1779 Wythe assumed the first American law professorship, established by the College of William and Mary at Jefferson's behest, as mentioned earlier. Modeled on Blackstone's chair at Oxford — the first common-law professorship in England, set up only twenty-one years before — the chair at William and Mary was occupied by Wythe for ten years. In addition to Jefferson, he numbered John Marshall and James Monroe among his students.

Historians have generally assumed that Jefferson studied under Wythe's tutelage from 1762 to 1767, and then began the practice of law. This version was accepted by Dumas Malone in his definitive biography,[109] as well as by Julian Boyd, the founding editor of the modern landmark edition of Jefferson's papers.[110] Five years of law study was unheard of at the time; two years was thought more than enough and most spent only a year or even less.[111] The most recent study of Jefferson's legal career concludes that the traditional account is erroneous and that Jefferson actually spent only two years studying under Wythe — from 1763 to 1765. Since a list of fees paid "by Gentleman examin'd to practice the Law for the use of the Examiners" in Virginia indicates that Jefferson was examined for the bar toward the end of 1765, it may well be that his time as a law student was shorter than the accepted version.[112] That does not,

109. Malone, *Jefferson the Virginian*, 113.

110. Frank Dewey, *Thomas Jefferson, Lawyer* (Charlottesville: University Press of Virginia, 1986), 9.

111. Id.

112. Id., 9–12.

however, change the fact that Jefferson did receive what, for the day, was an eminently superior legal education.

In later life, Jefferson constantly gave advice to young men on the study of law. When asked to recommend a course of reading for a law student, Jefferson listed the leading texts on common law and Chancery, from Coke to Blackstone, but he also advised that only the hours from 8 a.m. to noon should be devoted to reading law. "Till VIII o'clock in the morning employ yourself in Physical studies, Ethics, Religion..., and Natural law." At the noon hour, the student should "Read Politics" and "In the AFTERNOON. Read History." Then, "From Dark to Bed-time, Belles lettres, criticism, Rhetoric, Oratory." Jefferson recommended books in all the fields listed — from Lavoisier to Buffon, Locke to Cicero, Montesquieu to Gibbon, and Shakespeare to Demosthenes.[113] Jefferson, the Renaissance man, maintained that the student should devote himself to becoming the Renaissance lawyer.

Jefferson's study under Wythe probably did not attack learning on so wide a front. Wythe "did not expect his protégé, along with the law, to study physics, ethics, religion, natural philosophy, belles-lettres, criticism, rhetoric, politics and history."[114] Jefferson himself may have done as much reading in these subjects as he could; his so-

113. Thomas Jefferson to General John Minor, 30 August 1814, in Ford, *Writings of Jefferson,* 9:480–85. This letter is also reproduced in facsimile, transcribed, and set in context in Morris L. Cohen, "Commentary: Thomas Jefferson Recommends a Course of Law Study," *University of Pennsylvania Law Review* 119 (1971): 823–44.

114. Malone, *Jefferson the Virginian,* 69. But compare Randall, *Thomas Jefferson: A Life,* 56: "the scientific regimen Jefferson outlined... was not the half of his own daily labors over the books."

called Literary Bible indicates the broad range of the authors he managed to read. But he undoubtedly spent most of his time on the "dreary ramble" (John Adams's phrase) of technical law study. In 1826, just after Jefferson's death, Madison wrote, "The law itself he studied to the bottom, and in its greatest breadth."[115]

There is no doubt that Wythe had Jefferson begin his law studies with *Coke on Littleton.* According to a striking passage in a lecture by Frederic W. Maitland:

> Perhaps we should hardly believe if we were told for the first time that in the reign of James I a man who was the contemporary of Shakespeare and Bacon, a very able man too and a learned, who left his mark deep in English history, said, not by way of paradox but in sober earnest, said repeatedly and advisedly, that a certain thoroughly medieval book written in decadent colonial French was 'the most perfect and absolute work that ever was written in any human science.' Yet this was what Sir Edward Coke said of a small treatise written by Sir Thomas Littleton.[116]

The technical minutiae of the medieval land law, as developed in Littleton's intricate and turgid prose, strikes the present-day reader as an egregious example of the dryness of legal immortality and well justifies John Adams's caustic comment, "It contains a vast mass of

115. Adams quoted in Malone, *Jefferson the Virginian,* 69; Madison to Samuel H. Smith, 4 November 1826, in Hunt, ed., *Writings of Madison,* 9:260.

116. Rede Lecture, in *Selected Historical Essays of F. W. Maitland,* ed. Helen M. Cam (Cambridge: Cambridge University Press, 1957), 136.

law learning, but heaped up in such an incoherent mass that I have derived very little benefit from it."[117]

It is true that in later life both Adams and Jefferson realized how much their training owed to the masterful Elizabethan—"our juvenile oracle," as Adams was to term him in 1816. Coke's *Commentary upon Littleton,* Jefferson was to concede, "was the universal elementary book of law students and a sounder Whig never wrote nor of profounder learning in the orthodox doctrines of... British liberties."[118] All the same, when a law student, Jefferson could complain of the drudgery of having to labor through Coke's crabbed medieval style. "I do wish the Devil had old Cooke [Coke]," plaintively wrote Jefferson soon after he began his law studies, "for I am sure I never was so tired of an old dull scoundrel in my life."[119]

From *Coke on Littleton* Jefferson went on to the other three parts of Coke's *Institutes.* From them, he learned the legal foundation of the "doctrines of... British liberties." Jefferson later wrote, "Ld. Coke has given us the first view of the whole body of law worthy now of being studied... Coke's Institutes are a perfect digest of the law."[120] In an 1814 letter, Jefferson "lament[ed] the general defection of lawyers and judges, from the free principles of govern-

117. Quoted in Schwartz, *Roots of Freedom,* 113.

118. Quoted in Catherine Drinker Bowen, *The Lion and the Throne* (Boston: Atlantic-Little, Brown, 1957), 514.

119. Thomas Jefferson to John Page, 25 December 1762, in *Jefferson Papers,* 1:3–6 (quote at 5).

120. Quoted in Dumbauld, *Jefferson and the Law,* 7–8.

ment. I am sure they did not derive this degenerate spirit from the father of our science, Lord Coke. But it may be the reason why they cease to read him, and the source of what are now called 'Blackstone lawyers.'"[121] Two years earlier, Jefferson had compared "those who have drawn their stores from the rich and deep mines of Coke Littleton" and "Blackstone lawyers ... these ephemeral insects of the law."[122] It could not, however, be denied that, for the legal neophyte Coke was sheer drudgery. Still, as John Adams wrote when he was studying law, "You must conquer the *Institutes*.... I must get [Coke] and read over and over again. And I will get [it] and break through, as Mr. Gridley expresses it, all obstructions."[123]

We are not certain what other treatises Jefferson read after he suffered through Coke. In an 1821 letter, Jefferson outlined a course of reading for a prospective law student:

> 1st. Begin with Coke's four Institutes. These give a complete body of the law.... 2. Then passing over (for occasional reading as hereafter proposed) all the reports and treatises to the time of Matthew Bacon, read his abridgment.... Here, too, the student should take up the chancery branch of the law, by reading the first and sec-

121. Thomas Jefferson to Dr. Thomas Cooper, 16 January 1814, in *The Writings of Thomas Jefferson*, ed. H[enry] A[ugustine] Washington, 7 vols. (New York: Riker, Thorne & Co., 1854), 6:292–96 (quote at 296).

122. Thomas Jefferson to Judge John Tyler, 17 June 1812, quoted in Waterman, "Thomas Jefferson and Blackstone's Commentaries," in Flaherty, *Essays in the History of Early American Law*, 458.

123. Quoted in Warren, *History of the American Bar*, 172–73.

> ond abridgments of the cases in Equity.... by the same Matthew Bacon.[124]

Despite his deprecating statement about Blackstone, Jefferson also strongly recommended his *Commentaries*, which he praised in other letters as "the inimitable Commentaries"[125] — "the most lucid in arrangement which had yet been written, correct in its matter, classical in style, and rightfully taking its place by the side of the Justinian Institutes."[126]

Presumably the books listed were the primary texts that Jefferson read when he studied law. These books as well as others he recommended, Jefferson wrote, would involve "reading four or five hours a day [and] would employ about two years."[127] Yet Jefferson, as already indicated, scarcely intended the legal neophyte to spend the rest of the day giving in to idle temptations — to be, as he wrote of his college days, "as merry as agreeable company and dancing with Belinda in the Apollo could make me."[128] In 1821, "He recommended at least four hours reading of the law, and here six hours

124. Thomas Jefferson to Dabney Terrell, Esq., 26 February 1821, in Washington, *Writings of Jefferson*, 7:206–9 (quote at 207–8).

125. Thomas Jefferson to General John Minor, 30 August 1814, in Ford, *Writings of Jefferson*, 9:482 n. 1.

126. Thomas Jefferson to Dr. Thomas Cooper, 16 January 1814, in Washington, *Writings of Jefferson*, 6:293.

127. Thomas Jefferson to Dabney Terrell, Esq., 26 February 1821, in Washington, *Writings of Jefferson*, 7:208.

128. Thomas Jefferson to John Page, 7 October 1763, in *Jefferson Papers*, 1:11–12 (quote at 11).

of law reading, light and heavy, and [besides] those necessary for the repasts of the day, for exercise and sleep, which suppose to be ten or twelve, there will still be six or eight hours for reading history, politics, ethics, physics, oratory, poetry, criticism, &c., as necessary as law to form an accomplished lawyer."[129]

However much such a regimen might contribute to intellectual development, it was bound to make the student's days dull at best. Jefferson himself recognized this in a 1763 letter to his friend, John Page, when he was in the midst of his law studies:

> All things here appear to me to trudge on in one and the same round: we rise in the morning that we may eat breakfast, dinner and supper and go to bed again that we may get up the next morning and do the same: so that you never saw two peas more alike than our yesterday and today.[130]

But Jefferson did not spend all his time as a law student reading tedious law treatises. As the editors of *The Law Practice of Alexander Hamilton* have pointed out, "Books alone could not supply the sort of technical command of [law] practice of which a postulant for admission would stand in need. This was, of course, the point where a preceptor experienced in the 'practick part' of the law was close to being indispensable."[131]

129. Thomas Jefferson to Dabney Terrell, Esq., 26 February 1821, in Washington, *Writings of Jefferson*, 7:209.

130. Thomas Jefferson to John Page, 20 January 1763, in *Jefferson Papers*, 1:7–9 (quote at 7).

131. Goebel and Smith, *Law Practice of Alexander Hamilton*, 1:49.

In his letter to Monroe, as noted, Jefferson deprecated the value of training in the Inns of Court. However, he also observed, "could you attend Westminster hall a term or two, no doubt you would catch something in the manner of doing business which, formed as our habits are on that model, might be of advantage to you."[132] Jefferson spent much of his time as a law student observing the courts. In an October 1763 letter to John Page, he noted, "The court is now at hand, which I must attend constantly."[133] Jefferson was referring to the General Court (then the highest Virginia court), which began its semiannual session on October 10 and sat for twenty-four days. Presumably Jefferson also attended sessions of the lower, county courts, which met monthly in Williamsburg. These contacts with the law in action helped relieve the tedium of trudging through Coke and his confreres.

Unfortunately, much of the time Jefferson spent in Wythe's office must have been comparable in dullness to the study of Coke. Not long after he finished his apprenticeship, Jefferson wrote, "I always was of the opinion that the placing a youth to study with an attorney was rather a prejudice than a help. We are all too apt by shifting on them our business, to incroach on that time which should be devoted to their studies."[134]

132. Thomas Jefferson to James Monroe, 5 October 1781, in *Jefferson Papers,* 6:126–28 (quote at 127).

133. Thomas Jefferson to John Page, 7 October 1763, in *Jefferson Papers,* 1:11–12 (quote at 12).

134. Thomas Jefferson to Thomas Turpin, 5 February 1769, in *Jefferson Papers,* 1:23–24 (quote at 24).

As noted above, too much of the work of the apprentice student consisted of copying of documents. Yet, however much students may have wished to say, with Melville's Bartleby, "I prefer not to," however boring that work may have been—"drudgery [was] the beginning (if not the end) of the profession," as one clerk wrote[135]—it did train the student in the drafting of pleadings and other legal documents. Much of Jefferson's subsequent practice involved caveats, petitions for lapsed lands, and other proceedings involving land titles.[136] He scarcely would have had the expertise needed to draw up the necessary legal documents if his pre-practice experience had consisted of mere reading, however learned. Mechanical and dull though it was, the work in Wythe's office did enable Jefferson to master the basics of law practice sufficiently to practice in the General Court without having any other experience in court.

The meagerness of the law student's education in Jefferson's day was, of course, compounded by what Justice Robert H. Jackson called "the barren state of the American legal bookshelf"[137] at the time. Despite Burke's comment about the number of books "on the law exported to the plantations," the present-day observer is struck by how scanty were the legal materials available to the colonial lawyer. Jefferson himself, in outlining a course of law study for a

135. Quoted in Charles McKirdy, "The Lawyer as Apprentice: Legal Education in Eighteenth Century Massachusetts," *Journal of Legal Education* 28 (1976): 124–36 (quote at 128).

136. Dewey, *Thomas Jefferson, Lawyer,* 13.

137. Jackson, "Genesis of an American Legal Profession," 548.

friend's son, pointed out, "One difficulty only occurs, that is, the want of books.... for a lawyer without books would be like a workman without tools."[138]

With all its theoretical and practical flaws, however, the apprentice system gave rise to a bar whose competence set a standard rarely attained by any profession. So high was that standard that, according to an 1813 letter describing the pre-revolutionary Virginia bar by St. George Tucker (Wythe's successor at William and Mary), "The truth is, that Socrates himself, would pass unnoticed... in Virginia."[139]

Charles Warren asserted in his pioneering *History of the American Bar* that the very "meagreness of a [colonial] lawyer's education ... was a source of strength." Warren further contended:

> *Multum in parvo* was particularly applicable to the training for the Bar of that era. There was truth in the reply of a great lawyer, when asked how the lawyers who formed the United States Constitution had such a mastery of legal principles,—"Why they had so few books."... Chancellor Kent's remark "that he owed his reputation to the fact that, when studying law during the war, he had but one book, Blackstone's *Commentaries*, but that one book he mastered," sums up very concisely the cause of the greatness of many an early American jurist.[140]

138. Thomas Jefferson to Thomas Turpin, 5 February 1769, in *Jefferson Papers*, 1:23–24 (quote at 24).

139. Quoted in John P. Kennedy, *Memoirs of the Life of William Wirt*, 2 vols. (Philadelphia: Lea & Blanchard, 1849), 1:354.

140. Warren, *History of the American Bar*, 187.

The rationale that Warren offered does not explain the high level of the pre-revolutionary American bar. Yet it remains true that the competence of the colonial lawyer was in almost inverse ratio to the quality of legal education and quantity of legal materials in the colonies at that time. It makes one who has devoted his life to the teaching of law wonder whether the development of formal legal education marked the advance that most people believe it did.

## The Student versus the Oracle

One of the things Jefferson did while he studied law was to prepare reports of the earliest Virginia cases. These were published in 1829 as *Jefferson's Reports of Cases Determined in the General Court of Virginia. From 1730 to 1740; and from 1768 to 1772.* The first set of these cases was based on manuscript reports by earlier lawyers, which were given to Jefferson by John Randolph, then attorney general. The later cases were reported by Jefferson himself, who noted that, in 1768, "I began to commit to writing some leading cases of the day"— a practice "I continued… until… the Revolution… called those attatched to [the courts] to far other occupations."[141]

An appendix to *Jefferson's Reports* contains a trenchant and precocious opinion entitled, *Whether Christianity is a part of the Common Law?*[142] It was, Jefferson explained, added to the *Reports*

141. *Reports of Cases Determined in the General Court of Virginia. From 1730, to 1740; and from 1768, to 1772.* By Thomas Jefferson (Charlottesville, Virginia: F. Carr and Co., 1829), 5 (hereafter *Jefferson's Reports*).

142. Id., 137. See also Thomas Jefferson to Dr. Thomas Cooper, 10 February 1814, in *Jefferson: Writings*, 1321–29, in which Jefferson sets forth his memorandum on Christianity

as "a Disquisition of my own on the most remarkable instance of Judicial legislation, that has ever occurred in English jurisprudence, or perhaps in any other. It is that of the adoption in mass of the whole code of another nation, and its incorporation into the legitimate system, by usurpation of the Judges alone, without the particle of legislative will having ever been called on, or exercised towards its introduction or confirmation."[143]

The accepted principle— "christianity is part of the laws of England"[144]— was stated by Blackstone, then the very oracle of the law, who, Jefferson wrote in 1810, "is to us what the Alcoran is to the Mahometans."[145] This was precisely the principle that Jefferson sought to refute. His opinion notes that Blackstone had merely repeated the view stated by leading English authorities, from Lord Hale to Lord Mansfield. Jefferson traced their statements to a Year Book case (the earliest English reports) during the reign of Henry VI, where the "question was, How far the ecclesiastical law was to be respected in this matter by the Common law court?" During his discussion, Chief Justice Prisot said (in the monstrous law French of the day), "a tiels leis que ils de seint eglise ont en ancien scripture, covient a nous a donner credence; car ceo common ley sur quel touts manners leis sont fondes. Et auxy, Sir, nous sumus obliges de

and the common law and explains its origins. The memorandum is also reprinted in Saul K. Padover, ed., *The Complete Jefferson* (New York: Duell Sloan Pearce, 1943), 931–37.

143. *Jefferson's Reports*, 137.

144. Blackstone, *Commentaries on the Laws of England*, 4:59, quoted in *Jefferson's Reports*, 138.

145. Thomas Jefferson to John Tyler, 26 May 1810, in *Jefferson: Writings*, 1225–27 (quote at 1226).

conustre lour ley de saint eglise. Et semblablement ils sont obliges de conustre nostre ley."[146] Jefferson translated this passage as follows: "It is proper for us to give credence to such laws as they of holy church have in ancient writing; for it is common law on which all kinds of laws are founded, and also sir, we are obliged to recognize their law of holy church, and likewise they are obliged to recognize our law."[147] He pointed out that this passage was mistranslated by Sir Henry Finch, whose treatise on the common law was a pre-Blackstone elementary law book: "Finch misstates this in the following manner: 'to such laws of the church as have warrent in *holy scripture*, our law giveth credence.'" In this passage, "we find 'ancien scripture,' converted into 'holy scripture;' whereas it can only mean the antient written laws of the church. It cannot mean the scriptures."[148] It was Prisot as mistranslated by Finch that was the source of the later statements, culminating in Blackstone, that Christianity was part of English law.

Both Justice Joseph Story and John Quincy Adams strongly supported Finch and criticized Jefferson's translation. "My own opinion," wrote Adams, "has been... that it was Mr. Jefferson him-

146. Quoted in *Jefferson's Reports*, 137.

147. Quoted in Dumbauld, *Jefferson and the Law*, 211 n41. For another Jefferson translation, see Thomas Jefferson to John Adams, 24 January 1814, in Lester J. Cappon, ed., *The Adams-Jefferson Letters*, 2 vols. (Chapel Hill: University of North Carolina Press for the Institute of Early American History and Culture, 1959), 2: 421–25 (quote at 422). Compare an authoritative modern translation: "To such laws as they of Holy Church have in ancient writing (*en ancient scriptur*) it is right for us to give credence. For that is common law, on which all manner of laws are founded." Courtney Kenny, "The Evolution of the Law of Blasphemy," *Cambridge Law Journal*, 1 (1922): 127–42 (quote at 131).

148. See supra, n142.

self, and not the succession of English lawyers for three hundred years, who had mistaken the meaning of this dictum of Prisot. Judge Story said that he had looked into the case in the year-book, and found the exposition of it by Mr. Jefferson so manifestly erroneous that he cannot even consider it an involuntary mistake."[149] This time, however, it was "the most learned scholar ever to sit on any American Court"[150] who was mistaken. Jefferson's version is supported by the leading modern inquiry into the matter: "Finch does give, in his margin, Prisot's actual words, but he misunderstands and mistranslates them. The misunderstanding was first detected, so far as I am aware, not by an English lawyer, but by an American one, less known to us indeed, as a lawyer, than as a statesman — the acute and brilliant President Jefferson."[151]

His opinion on Christianity and the law shows Jefferson the practicing lawyer at his best, but the essentials of the opinion were

149. *Memoirs of John Quincy Adams*, ed. Charles Francis Adams, 12 vols. (1876; reprint, New York: AMS Press, 1971), 8:291. See also William W. Story, *Life and Letters of Joseph Story*, 2 vols. (Boston: Little, Brown & Co., 1851), 1:430–33, 2:8–9; James McClellan, *Joseph Story and the American Constitution* (Norman: University of Oklahoma Press, 1971), 118–59; and R. Kent Newmyer, *Supreme Court Justice Joseph Story: Statesman of the Old Republic* (Chapel Hill: University of North Carolina Press, 1985), 183–84. See also *State v. Chandler*, 2 Harrington 443, 562 (Del. 1837), where the court also rejected Jefferson's translation and asserted, "we... are well satisfied that if Finch construed '*auncient scripture*' to mean *holy scripture*, such a translation of the Norman french would be the true translation." For discussions of Jefferson's part in the argument, see Mayer, *Constitutional Thought of Jefferson*, 185; Merrill D. Peterson, *The Jefferson Image in the American Mind* (New York: Oxford University Press, 1960), 96–98.

150. So characterized in Bernard Schwartz, *The American Heritage History of the Law in America* (New York: American Heritage Publishing Co./McGraw Hill, 1974), 110.

151. Kenny, "Evolution of Law of Blasphemy," 130.

written when Jefferson was only a law student or, at most, a young lawyer. "When I was a student of law, now half a century ago," Jefferson wrote in an 1814 letter to Thomas Cooper, "I was in the habit of abridging and common-placing what I read meriting it, and of sometimes mixing my own reflections on the subject."[152] In this respect, Jefferson followed the practice common to law students in his day. "On their own time," Richard B. Morris tells us, "law clerks customarily attempted to systematize their legal studies by preparing what they would call a Commonplace Book.... A law clerk's Commonplace Book was essentially a topical summary of the law."[153] Thus, in his Commonplace Book, "Jefferson made extensive briefs of the English printed reports, chiefly of Salkeld and Raymond, and abstracts of Coke's *Institutes*, Lord Kames's *Historical Law Tracts*, Hale's *History of the Common Law*, and of Spelman and Somers."[154] In another letter, Jefferson explained how to "commonplace" legal matters:

> In reading the Reporters, enter in a Common-place book every case of value, condensed into the narrowest compass possible which will admit of presenting distinctly the principles of the case. this operation is doubly useful, inas-

152. Thomas Jefferson to Dr. Thomas Cooper, 10 February 1814, in *Jefferson: Writings*, 1321–29 (quote at 1321).

153. Morris, *Studies in the History of American Law*, 67.

154. Major portions of the Commonplace Book are published in *The Commonplace Book of Thomas Jefferson*, ed. Gilbert Chinard (Baltimore: Johns Hopkins University Press, 1928), and in Douglas L. Wilson, *Jefferson's Literary Commonplace Book* (Princeton: Princeton University Press, 1989). Jefferson also kept an Equity Commonplace Book. See Edward Dumbauld, "Thomas Jefferson's Equity Commonplace Book," *Washington and Lee Law Review* 48 (1991): 1257–83.

> much as it obliges the student to seek out the pith of the case, and habituates him to a condensation of thought, and to an acquisition of the most valuable of all talents, that of never using two words where one will do. it fixes the case too more indelibly in the mind.[155]

Apparently Cooper had asked for a sample from his Commonplace Book and Jefferson enclosed "the extract from these entries which I promised."[156] The extract enclosed was an early version of the opinion on Christianity and the law, later published in *Jefferson's Reports.* The version in the *Reports* is similar to that in the Commonplace Book; at most there are only minor modifications, as well as some toning down of language in the published version. The latter was necessary because, as the letter to Cooper conceded, the commonplace extract was "written at a time of life when I was bold in the pursuit of knowledge, never fearing to follow truth and reason to whatever results they led, and bearding every authority which stood in their way."[157]

There are good passages in the commonplace extract that are absent from the published version. The commonplace essay reads, "We might as well say that the Newtonian system of philosophy is a part of the Common law, as that the Christian religion is. The truth is that Christianity and Newtonianism... are protected under

155. Thomas Jefferson to General John Minor, 30 August 1814, in Ford, *Writings of Jefferson* 9:483 n1.

156. Thomas Jefferson to Dr. Thomas Cooper, 10 February 1814, in *Jefferson: Writings,* 1321.

157. Id., 1321–22.

the wings of the Common law from the dominion of other sects, but not erected into dominion over them.... The Common law protects both... but enacts neither into law."[158] One wonders why Jefferson deleted from the *Reports* what in the Age of Enlightenment would have been considered a most apt comparison.

If, as stated, his published opinion on Christianity and the law shows Jefferson the lawyer at his best, think of what the essentially similar commonplace version tells us about Jefferson's ability when he may have been only a law student. It should, however, be pointed out that Frank L. Dewey questions whether Jefferson did write the commonplace essay when he was a law student. He relies on the numbering of the essay as item 873 in Jefferson's Legal Commonplace Book, pointing out that items with lower numbers were probably entered after his law student days were finished. At the same time, he recognizes, "Clearly one cannot say how much, if any, of Jefferson's commonplace books represent reading he did as a student."[159]

Possibly, as Dewey says, "Jefferson's memory of distant events was fallible."[160] When he wrote to Cooper, Jefferson was seventy years old; anyone who reads his correspondence can only hope to retain comparable acuity at that age. Still, is it likely that Jefferson

158. Chinard, *Commonplace Book*, 356.

159. Dewey, *Thomas Jefferson, Lawyer*, 16.

160. Id., 12. In 1824 Jefferson wrote about his essay, "I do not remember the occasion which led me to take up this subject while a practitioner of the law." Thomas Jefferson to Edward Everett, 15 October 1824, in Washington, *Writings of Jefferson* 7:380–83 (quote at 383).

forgot when he first wrote an essay so close to his heart and important enough to be published in his *Reports*?[161] Even if Dewey is right, the conclusion can be drawn, according to Gilbert Chinard, "that the Commonplace Book [essay] was written when Jefferson was still a young man ... during his formative years."[162] If he wrote the essay not as a law student but as a fledgling lawyer in his twenties, it scarcely detracts from his reputation. The important thing, after all, is the quality of the legal analysis by the young Jefferson. Not only did he have the better in his legal argument with the contemporary oracle of the law, as well as later leading legal authorities in the new nation, notably Justice Joseph Story, but Jefferson also stated the view on the matter that is accepted today.

A century and a half later it is apparent that the Blackstone-Story approach might well have meant "the transplanting of the seeds of establishment... from English to American shores."[163] In 1989, Justice Sandra Day O'Connor wrote a letter "to the effect that this is a Christian nation."[164] To Jefferson, of course, such a notion was political, if not religious, heresy. He knew that English deci-

161. See W. Jennings Price, "'The Characteristic Bent of a Lawyer' in Jefferson," *Georgetown Law Journal* 16 (1927): 41–54 (quote at 47) (review of Chinard, *Commonplace Book*), which concludes that the date of the Jefferson essay is earlier than that argued by Chinard or Dewey; and Lynton K. Caldwell, "The Jurisprudence of Thomas Jefferson," *Indiana Law Journal* 18 (1943): 193–213 (quote at 201), which argues that the essay was "apparently written about 1764."

162. Chinard, *Commonplace Book*, 11–13.

163. Mark DeWolfe Howe, *The Garden and the Wilderness: Religion and Government in American Constitutional History* (Chicago: University of Chicago Press, 1965), 28.

164. Quoted in *Washington Post*, 16 March 1989, A3.

sions holding that Christianity was a part of the law had led to establishment of religion by law and denied religious freedom to dissenters from the Anglican church. The outcry provoked by Justice O'Connor's statement shows that Americans today agree with Jefferson. Jefferson, whether as law student or young lawyer, has plainly triumphed in his difference with Blackstone and Story over Christianity and its place in the law.

## Thomas Jefferson: Lawyer

"In 1767," Jefferson recalled in his *Autobiography*, "[Mr. Wythe] led me into the practice of the law at the bar of the General court, at which I continued until the revolution shut up the courts of justice."[165] Jefferson practiced as a lawyer for seven years — until 1774, when, in the words of an August 27 printed circular letter by Edmund Randolph, "Mr. Jefferson having declined his Practice in the General Court,... consigned the Business, which he left there unfinished, into my Hands."[166] Jefferson kept a Case Book, a Fee Book, and account books in which he meticulously recorded all the cases in which he took part as counsel. These provide some idea of his practice, although they do not record the details of the cases that he took or reveal the manner in which he presented them. In the Case Book, two hundred and fifty-three cases are marked with an asterisk and a notation such as, "1774, Aug. 11. E.R. to finish."[167]

165. *Autobiography*, in *Jefferson: Writings*, 5.

166. Quoted in Dewey, *Thomas Jefferson, Lawyer*, 107.

167. Quoted in id., 108.

Presumably these were the cases turned over to young Randolph; their number indicates the success of the practice built up by Jefferson.

Summarizing Jefferson's own case documentation, John W. Davis concluded that Jefferson's "success [in practice] was striking and immediate.... He makes record of 68 cases in the General Court in 1767; 115 in 1768; 198 in 1769; 121 in 1770; 137 in 1771; 154 in 1772; 127 in 1773; and 29 in 1774, up to the time when he gave up his business to his cousin, Edmund Randolph."[168] The extent of Jefferson's success is shown by the fact that, as recorded in his Case Book, when Robert Carter Nicholas, "the acknowledged leader of the bar," sought to retire in 1771, he "put his business into my hands to be finished." Jefferson, however, as he expressed it, was "under a necessity of declining it"—another indication of his success, since he could not take on additional cases—and Nicholas had to turn over his practice to Patrick Henry.[169]

Most commentators on Jefferson's practice have assumed that it was prosperous as well as successful. The traditional account has it that Jefferson's professional income averaged three thousand dollars a year. This, said Davis, "may not seem a dazzling figure in this auriferous age, but it bulked large in that day and time."[170] In fact,

168. Davis, "Thomas Jefferson: Attorney at Law," a bar association address of over fifty years ago, 364. The figures Davis gave apparently derive from the first important Jefferson biography: Henry S. Randall, *The Life of Thomas Jefferson,* 3 vols. (New York: Derby & Jackson, 1858; New York: Da Capo Press, 1972), 1:47.

169. Dumbauld, *Jefferson and the Law,* 93.

170. Davis, "Thomas Jefferson, Attorney at Law," 364.

according to one writer, Jefferson doubled his substantial inherited estate by his law practice "and the young Virginia lawyer might be called a very prosperous young gentleman."[171] Here, too, Dewey disagrees with the accepted version. He asserts that Jefferson's collected fees during all his years at the Bar only totaled about twelve hundred pounds.[172] It is true that legal fees in Virginia were then fixed by law—with a five-pound limit in the General Court. A 1903 estimate was that "it was as though a lawyer of the present day received fifty dollars for arguing a case before the Supreme Court of the United States."[173] It is also true that Jefferson joined every member of the General Court bar (with the exception of George Wythe) in a 1773 notice in the *Virginia Gazette* complaining about unpaid fees, which asserted, "The fees allowed by law, if regularly paid, would barely compensate our incessant labors, reimburse our expenses, and the losses incurred by neglect of our private affairs."[174] This, however, is the normal complaint of even the well-paid lawyer. It may be doubted that Dewey has really disproved the traditional account. After all, it was Jefferson's executor who first stated that his average profit was about three thousand dollars a

171. Eugene L. Didier, "Thomas Jefferson as a Lawyer," *Green Bag* 15 (1903): 153–59 (quote at 156).

172. Dewey, *Thomas Jefferson, Lawyer*, 7. Justice Powell also asserts that Jefferson's "practice was disappointing from a financial standpoint. Many of his clients did not pay their bills." Powell, "Jefferson and American Justice," p. 4, col. 3.

173. Didier, "Jefferson as a Lawyer," 156.

174. "Notice Concerning Legal Fees," 20 May 1773, in *Jefferson Papers*, 1:98–99 (quote at 98).

year — a handsome sum for the day, even if some of it remained uncollected.[175] In addition, the number of General Court cases handled by Jefferson indicates that his practice was a flourishing one.

Jefferson's Case Book contains 939 cases "and there a lawyer's life marches, eight notations to a page."[176] In Jefferson's day, law practice meant working as a general practitioner. Like his confreres, Jefferson's practice ran the gamut—with most of his cases concerned with land or slaves. Other cases were likely to concern estates and, ultimately, the wealth of estates then was in land and slaves.

Although the number of clients does indicate that Jefferson's reputation at the bar stood high, his own records, as noted, are insufficiently detailed to make possible a judgment of his legal work. It is Jefferson's arguments, where we have records of them, that indicate he was a first-rate lawyer. In addition to *Bolling, v. Bolling*, two other cases provide some idea of the arguments made by Jefferson as counsel. The two cases, contained in Jefferson's own *Reports*, are devoted almost entirely to the arguments he presented to the court.

The first case is of particular interest, for Jefferson's argument was an early version of the theme he was to immortalize in the Declaration of Independence. The case, *Howell v. Netherland*, was

175. "With the very low rate of fees then paid in Virginia, this was a decidedly successful practice for a young lawyer, or indeed for a lawyer of any age, unless possibly with the exception of three or four of the greatest old luminaries of the bar, like Wythe, Pendleton, Peyton and John Randolph, and Nicholas." Randall, *Life of Thomas Jefferson* 1:48.

176. John P. Frank, review of Dumbauld, *Jefferson and the Law*, *American Bar Association Journal* 66 (1980): 336.

argued before the General Court in April 1770 [177]. It was brought by a mulatto seeking a release from servitude. Plaintiff's grandmother, also a mulatto, had been bound to service until the age of thirty-one. During her servitude, "she was delivered of plaintiff's mother, who, during her servitude… was delivered of the plaintiff, and he was again sold… to the defendant."

Jefferson framed his argument for plaintiff in broad terms that anticipated his assertion of liberty and equality six years later. "Under the law of nature," Jefferson declared to the court, "all men are born free, every one comes into the world with a right to his own person, which includes the liberty of moving and using it at his own will. This is what is called personal liberty, and is given him by the author of nature, because necessary for his own sustenance." To Jefferson, "reducing the mother to servitude was a violation of the law of nature: surely then the same law cannot prescribe a continuance of the violation to her issue, and that too without end."[178] Jefferson's report summed up his *Howell* argument as follows:

> I have endeavored to shew;
> That the [statute] subjected to servitude, the first mulatto only.
> That this did not, under the law of nature, affect the liberty of the children,
> Because, under that law we are all born free.[179]

177. *Jefferson's Reports*, 90 (Va. 1770).

178. Id., 92.

179. Id., 95.

The reliance upon the natural law concept of freedom could, without a doubt, be used as the basis for an attack upon slavery itself. It was to be used in that way by George Wythe in 1806, when he sat as chancellor. Plaintiffs in the case before Wythe were the descendants of an Indian woman, who were about to be sent out of the state by defendant, who claimed to be their master. They sought a writ of *ne exeat* on the ground that they were entitled to freedom because they were descended from a free Indian woman.

Wythe determined that plaintiffs were entitled to their freedom. According to the sketchy account we have of his decision, he laid down two principles. The first was "that whenever one person claims to hold another in slavery, the *onus probandi* lies on the claimant." The second was more far-reaching, since it was based "on the ground that freedom is the birth-right of every human being, which sentiment is strongly inculcated by the first article of our 'political catechism,' the bill of rights."[180] Wythe was referring to Article I of the Virginia Declaration of Rights, adopted in 1776, under which "all men are by nature equally free and independent."[181]

Wythe's decision was appealed to the Virginia Supreme Court of Appeals, which affirmed the chancellor on the ground that plaintiffs were descended from an Indian woman, who was not a slave under Virginia law. But the appellate judges went out of their way to state that they disagreed with Wythe's broad reasoning on slavery. This disagreement was best expressed by Judge St. George Tucker,

180. 1 Hening and Munford 133, 134 (Va. 1806).

181. "Virginia Declaration of Rights, 1776," art. 6, in *Bill of Rights*, 1:234–36 (quote at 234).

who had been Wythe's student and holder of the William and Mary chair after Wythe. Tucker declared:

> I do not concur with the chancellor in his reasoning on the operation of the first clause of the Bill of Rights, which was notoriously framed with a cautious eye to this subject, and was meant to embrace the case of free citizens, or aliens only; and not by a side wind to overturn the rights of property, and give freedom to those very people whom we have been compelled from imperious circumstances to retain, generally, in the same state of bondage that they were in at the revolution.[182]

The other appellate judges specifically stated their concurrence with Tucker's view. Their decree stated that they were "entirely disapproving ... of the Chancellor's principles and reasoning in his decree."[183] Thus, instead of the legal landmark which it might have been, Wythe's decision became not even a minor footnote in early American jurisprudence.

In *Howell v. Netherland*, however, Wythe appeared as counsel for defendant and was doubtless prepared to do what the Virginia Court of Appeals was to do to his own decision that slavery violated the state's bill of rights—to argue that positive law, not natural law, governed in an actual case. That was even more true, Wythe was ready to argue, because a 1723 statute expressly provided that any mulatto or Indian child born to a mother in servitude "shall serve" the mother's master or mistress on the same terms as the mother.[184]

182. 1 Hening and Munford 141.

183. Id., 144.

184. *Jefferson's Reports*, 96.

Wythe did not have the opportunity to make his argument, however. Jefferson's report of the case tells us, "Wythe, for the defendant, was about to answer, but the court interrupted him and gave judgment in favor of his client."[185] The irony, of course, is that Wythe himself was to make a broader version of Jefferson's natural law argument the basis of his 1806 decision as chancellor—only to be rebuffed as sharply as Jefferson had been in *Howell v. Netherland.*

Jefferson's Case Book also contains a brief summary of the case: "Samuel Howell, a pauper v. Wade Netherland (Cumbd.) the pl's great-grandmother was a white woman and had a daur. by a negro man, whose grandson the pl. is; and sues for freedom. charge no fee."[186] The tradition of *pro bono* service by the bar is thus an old one. As a typical note in Jefferson's Case Book explained, "The pl. being poor charge no fee."[187]

The second case reported by Jefferson in which he gave his argument as counsel was *Godwin v. Lunan*, an October 1771 case.[188] Jefferson represented the churchwardens and vestrymen of a parish, who filed a libel in the General Court for the removal of a clergyman, charging

> that he was of evil fame and profligate manners; that he was much addicted to drunkenness...; that he officiated in ridiculous apparel unbecoming to a priest; that he was a common disturber of the peace, and often quarrelling and

185. Id.

186. Quoted in Dumbauld, *Jefferson and the Law*, 90.

187. Id.

188. *Jefferson's Reports*, 96 (Va. 1771).

> fighting; that he was a common and profane swearer; that on the 10th of July 1767, and at other times, he exposed his private parts to view in public companies, and solicited negro and other women to fornication and adultery with him;... that he had declared that he did not believe in the revealed religion of Christ, and cared not of what religion he was so he got the tobacco, nor what became of the flock so that he could get the fleece.

Defendant claimed that the court had no ecclesiastical jurisdiction and therefore could not censure or remove him.

The case was apparently an important one, for Wythe was also counsel for the libellants and John Randolph, the attorney general, appeared for the defendant. However, Jefferson's report of the case gave only his own argument in detail. Jefferson explained that "I was of counsel for the libellant[s] also." He then wrote in a footnote: "This circumstance is the apology for the little justice done to the arguments of the other counsel in this case; being prevented taking them down minutely by the necessity of considering in the instance, how they might be answered."[189]

Jefferson started his *Godwin* argument by stating, "I thought the ecclesiastical jurisdiction of the court established beyond a doubt." He then had to show how "visitation and deprivation are... parts of the office of an ecclesiastical judge." He recorded how he intended to demonstrate this:

> To prove this it was proposed,
>
> To enquire into the first establishment of Christian churches in Great Britain;

189. Id., 97.

> To develope their several kinds and constitutions;
>
> To see who is entrusted with their care and visitation; and to apply the principles which this enquiry would revolve to the parochial churches of our own country.[190]

There followed an elaborate technical analysis of both history and law on the matters listed. Jefferson not only cited the obvious authorities, such as Coke and Blackstone, but also relied on a mass of statutes, cases, and texts, starting with a Saxon law of Ethelwulf. The modern observer is overwhelmed by the legal learning of the young attorney, and more generally the ability of the pre-revolutionary bar to deal with a highly technical legal subject. One wonders whether the attorney today, armed with all the tools available in the computer age, could do as well as the practitioner in an age characterized by a paucity of legal references.

Jefferson won his case, for his report states, "The court adjudged that they possessed ecclesiastical jurisdiction in general, and that as an ecclesiastical court they might proceed to censure or deprive the defendant, if there should be sufficient cause."[191] For his work in the case, Jefferson received a fee of five pounds.

## Thomas Jefferson: Lawyer-Politician

After Jefferson turned over his unfinished cases to Edmund Randolph in 1774, he never again appeared in court as a lawyer. It

190. Id.

191. *Jefferson's Reports*, 108. However, the court granted the attorney general's petition for rehearing. The case was still awaiting the rehearing three years later when Jefferson retired from practice. Malone, *Jefferson the Virginian*, 122. The decision on rehearing is not known.

is not, however, entirely accurate to say that he never again practiced law. In 1782, after his term as governor of Virginia had expired, Jefferson temporarily "abandoned public life and resumed a more genteel practice of formulating legal opinions for a fee."[192] Several legal opinions written by Jefferson during the resumption of his practice have been published,[193] and three others are known to have been written, though their texts have not been found.[194] The texts that have been published confirm Jefferson's great legal ability.

Jefferson's second stint of legal practice lasted only six months. Largely owing to Madison's influence, he returned permanently to public life, giving up his law practice for good in the process. Apparently, however, he continued to write legal opinions for those seeking his advice, at least after he returned to Virginia upon completion of his Presidential terms. An example is his 1824 opinion for an attorney seeking advice on certain questions arising out of a conveyance of land that was originally part of the tract on which Jefferson built Monticello.[195] All of Jefferson's later work, however,

192. John Cooke Wyllie, "The Second Mrs. Wayland: An Unpublished Jefferson Opinion on a Case in Equity," *Journal of Legal Education* 9 (1965): 64–68 (quote at 64).

193. "From John Lyne, with Jefferson's Memoranda for a Legal Opinion," ca. 13–16 January 1782, in *Jefferson Papers,* 6: 145–46 (contains only memoranda for Jefferson's opinion); "The Case of Mace Freeland," 12 February 1782, in *Jefferson Papers,* 6:151–58 (editorial note, 151–52; "Jefferson's State of the Case and Opinion thereon," 15 February 1782, 152–54; "Petition of Mace Freeland to the Governor and Council," 155–56; and "Petition of Mace Freeland to the House of Delegates," 156–58); and "From Thomas Watkins, with Jefferson's Opinion concerning a Will," 9 May 1782, in *Jefferson Papers,* 6:179–82.

194. Dumbauld, *Jefferson and the Law*, 90.

195. "Note: A Legal Problem of Mr. Jefferson's," *Virginia Law Review* 22 (1936): 362–65 (reprints and comments on 1824 letter from Jefferson to unidentified correspondent analyzing legal issues pertaining to land in Albemarle County, Va., conveyed by Jefferson's son-in-law John W. Eppes to Jefferson's grandson Thomas Jefferson Randolph).

had a legal cast— far-removed though it may have seemed from the practice of law— and he had always acknowledged the role of law in public life and in politics. In a 1787 letter to the son of a friend who had "fixed on... Politics as your principal pursuit," Jefferson advised the study of law, as well as politics and history. "Every political measure," Jefferson wrote, "will for ever have an intimate connection with the laws of the land; and he who knows nothing of these will always be perplexed and often foiled by adversaries having the advantage of that knolege over him."[196] Even after he had retired from law practice, Jefferson, in Justice Powell's phrase, "continued his interest in the law in a larger sense."[197] During his entire career, he took an interest in legal matters and approached problems and issues with a law-trained mind.

After Jefferson gave up his practice to young Randolph, the lawyer-in-operation can best be seen in his leadership of the effort to revise the Virginia laws and in his pursuit of instrumentalist objectives within the framework of the common law. As seen above, Jefferson, the theorist, could question common-law authority, but when it came to legal work, he realized that the common law had to carry the day. He knew that it was, practically speaking, the only system that was or could be workable with the available materials.[198] In the *Bolling* case, indeed, Jefferson delivered what Judge

196. Thomas Jefferson to Thomas Mann Randolph, Jr., 6 July 1787, in *Jefferson Papers,* 11:556–59 (quote at 557–58).

197. Powell, "Jefferson and American Justice," p. 4, col. 3.

198. Compare Roscoe Pound, "The Place of Judge Story in the Making of American Law," *American Law Review* 48 (1914): 676–97 (quote at 685).

Edward Dumbauld, in his authoritative study of Jefferson and the law, has termed "an eloquent encomium in favor of *stare decisis*"[199]—the essential doctrine upon which the common law itself is grounded. Jefferson declared in his argument:

> I cannot suppress the anxiety I ever feel when an attempt is made to unhinge those principles, on which alone we depend for security in all the property we hold, and to set us again adrift to search for new.... they should therefore be sacred, and not wantonly set aside when ingenuity can persuade us to believe they are unfit, or inconsonant with other decisions. we should not, under a momentary impression, demolish what has been the growth of ages. this deference to adjudged cases is enjoined by our laws.[200]

Having shown that the decided cases were in his favor, he stressed that stare decisis "is enjoined by our laws." His well-known 1785 letter to Philip Mazzei shows that his advocacy of adherence to precedent was more than a tactic designed to win his case. Without stare decisis, the common law would be as much governed by the "Chancellor's foot" as the equity of which John Selden spoke. "This," according to Jefferson's letter, "will be worse than running on Scylla to avoid Charybdis." The common law and its reliance on precedent avoids this, for "The object of [its] judges has been to render the law more and more certain."[201]

199. Dumbauld, *Jefferson and the Law*, 102.

200. *Bolling v. Bolling*, Huntington Library ms., original page H38, reprinted infra.

201. Thomas Jefferson to Philip Mazzei, [28] November 1785, in *Jefferson Papers*, 9:67–72 (quote at 70–71).

Despite his sense of the general value of the common law, Jefferson's role in the revision of the Virginia laws also shows that he had an essentially instrumentalist conception of law. He later wrote in his *Autobiography* that he had led the law revision movement "in the persuasion that our whole code must be reviewed, adapted to our republican form of government, and, now that we had no negatives of Councils, Governors & Kings to restrain us from doing right, that it should be corrected, in all it's parts, with a single eye to reason, & the good of those for whose government it was framed."[202] In line with this goal, the revisors produced a far-reaching revision of the Virginia laws in 126 draft bills. The last of them provided for the repeal of the existing statute-law (both English and Virginian), with a few exceptions (notably the state constitution and bill of rights), and its replacement by the preceding bills reported by the revisors.[203] Almost all of the revisors' bills were drafted by Jefferson and Wythe, with by far the major share of the work being done by Jefferson. Of the 126 bills, 51 have been identified as being Jefferson's handiwork, and 7 as written by Wythe.[204] That leaves 68 bills unaccounted for. Jefferson probably did the major work on them also. At any rate, the bills known to have been drafted by Jefferson include all the major substantive ones recommended by the revisors.

To Jefferson, the revision presented the opportunity to recast

202. *Autobiography*, in *Jefferson: Writings*, 37.

203. "[Bill No.] 126. A Bill for repealing Certain Acts of Parliament and of General Assembly," in *Jefferson Papers*, 2:656–57.

204. "Editorial Note," *Jefferson Papers*, 2:320; Brown, *American Aristides*, 179.

the land law in republican terms. This could be done by a simple "repeal of the law" authorizing entailed estates and primogeniture.[205] As Jefferson saw it, "The repeal of the laws of entail would prevent the accumulation and perpetuation of wealth in select families, and preserve the soil of the country from being daily more and more absorbed in Mortmain. The abolition of primogeniture, and equal partition of inheritances removed the feudal and unnatural distinctions which made one member of every family rich, and all the rest poor, substituting equal partition, the best of all Agrarian laws." This, he said, was essential for "forming a system by which every fibre would be eradicated of antient or future aristocracy; and a foundation laid for a government truly republican."[206]

In 1776, as a member of the legislature, Jefferson had submitted a bill abolishing entails; despite opposition, it speedily passed. His attack on primogeniture came as part of the work of the revision committee. Among the revisors' bills drafted by Jefferson was "A Bill Directing the Course of Descents."[207] It did away with primogeniture by "chang[ing] the laws of descent, so as that the lands of any person dying intestate shall be divisible equally among all his children."[208] In his *Notes on the State of Virginia*, Jefferson listed this change first in his list of "the most remarkable alterations pro-

205. In practice, however, both primogeniture and entail had begun to disappear in Virginia by the end of the colonial period. See C. Ray Keim, "Primogeniture and Entail in Colonial Virginia," *William and Mary Quarterly*, 3d ser., 25 (1968): 545–68.

206. *Autobiography*, in *Jefferson: Writings*, 32, 44.

207. "[Bill No.] 20. A Bill Directing the Course of Descents," in *Jefferson Papers*, 2:391–93.

208. Jefferson, *Notes on the State of Virginia*, 137.

posed" by the revisors.[209] His reforms were the catalyst for a movement that swept through all the states and soon resulted in the abolition of primogeniture and entails in practically all of them.[210]

The English preoccupation, until well into the nineteenth century, was the danger of meddling with as old a structure as the land law, almost untouched for centuries. If, in England, improving the land law was beyond the power of mortal man, that plainly was not the case for Jefferson. Under his lead, the English law gave way to a system in which land became readily transferable. Feudal land tenure was abolished and the freehold established as the basic type of land title. Freedom of contract and the autonomy of private decision-making could capture the land, as it was soon to capture other areas of American law.[211]

Writing to a Dutch friend, Jefferson noted, "our Revised code of laws... contains not more than three or four laws which could strike the attention of the foreigner."[212] As Dumas Malone pointed out, European scholars would scarcely be interested in the bulk of the revision, which dealt with purely local matters, such as the militia, prevention of infection in cattle, improvement of the breed of horses, and horse thieves.[213] However, the few bills that Jefferson

209. Id.

210. Malone, *Jefferson the Virginian*, 256.

211. Compare Hurst, *Growth of American Law*, 71, and Hurst, *Law and the Conditions of Freedom*, 12.

212. Thomas Jefferson to G. K. van Hogendorp, 13 October 1785, in *Jefferson Papers*, 8:631–34 (quote at 632).

213. Malone, *Jefferson the Virginian*, 263.

deemed of broader interest bear directly upon his conception of law as a tool "by which every fibre would be eradicated of antient or future aristocracy; and a foundation laid for a government truly republican."[214]

"I have sometimes asked myself," Jefferson once wrote, "whether my country is better for my having lived at all?" He then listed the things which "I have been the instrument of doing."[215] Among them were his bills ending entails and primogeniture, as well as his bill on citizenship.[216] It provided for citizenship for all white persons born or resident two years in Virginia, as well as those who later migrated into the state and gave an oath or affirmation of intent to reside there. It also included a strong statement of "that natural right, which all men have of relinquishing the country, in which birth, or other accident may have thrown them."[217]

Jefferson's position on citizenship was a logical corollary of his conception that law was based upon the notion of consent, not command. "It is the will of the nation," he wrote to Edmund Randolph, "which makes the law obligatory." Indeed, "The law [is] law because it is the will of the nation."[218]

214. *Autobiography*, in *Jefferson: Writings*, 9.

215. Thomas Jefferson, "A Memorandum (Services to My Country)," ca. 1800, in *Jefferson: Writings*, 702–04 (quote at 702).

216. "[Bill No.] 55. A Bill Declaring Who Shall Be Deemed Citizens of This Commonwealth," in *Jefferson Papers*, 2: 476–79.

217. Id., 477.

218. Thomas Jefferson to Edmund Randolph, 18 August 1779, in *Jefferson: Writings*, 1066–68 (quote at 1067). It should, however, be noted that the "doctrine that the legitimacy of governmental authority came from the consent of the governed was not an

Jefferson's citizenship bill also recognized a right of expatriation by simple declaration or assumption of citizenship in another country. This made for a significant modification in existing law.[219] The common-law rule originally followed by the courts in this country barred an individual from divesting himself of citizenship without the consent of the government.[220] To Jefferson, on the contrary, the right of expatriation was one that "We do not claim ... under the charters of kings or legislators, but under the King of Kings.... we may safely call on the whole body of English jurists to produce the map on which Nature has traced, for each individual, the geographical line which she forbids him to cross in pursuit of happiness."[221]

Jefferson also listed his bill on religious freedom as one of the things "I have been the instrument of doing" and later wrote to George Wythe from Paris, "Our act for freedom of religion is extremely applauded."[222] The applause has continued down to the present, for religious freedom and toleration became the foundation

American invention.... legitimization by consent was ancient English legal theory." John Phillip Reid, *Constitutional History of the American Revolution: The Authority to Legislate* (Madison: University of Wisconsin Press, 1991), 97.

219. Jefferson himself denied this, asserting "that there is not another nation, civilized or savage, which has ever denied this natural right." Thomas Jefferson to Dr. John Manners, 12 June 1817, in Ford, *Writings of Jefferson,* 10:87.

220. See, e.g., *Shanks v. Dupont,* 3 Pet. (28 U.S.) 242, 246 (1830). The common-law rule was abrogated by 15 Stat. 223 (1868). See *Perez v. Brownell,* 356 U.S. 44, 48 (1958).

221. Thomas Jefferson to Dr. John Manners, 12 June 1817, in Ford, *Writings of Jefferson,* 10:87.

222. Thomas Jefferson, "Memorandum," in *Jefferson: Writings,* 702; Thomas Jefferson to George Wythe, 13 August 1786, in *Jefferson Papers* 10:243–45 (quote at 244).

of both the First Amendment guaranty and the subsequent jurisprudence.

Jefferson's Bill for Establishing Religious Freedom[223] was also a natural product of the lawyer's conception of government and law. Julian Boyd observed in his classic edition of Jefferson's papers that the bill was a necessary consequence of the approach followed in the Declaration of Independence: "as the Declaration of Independence asserted the natural right of a people to choose any form of government conducive to their safety and happiness, so the Bill for Establishing Religious Freedom asserted the natural right of a person to choose his beliefs and opinions free of compulsion."[224] If government and law rest ultimately upon consent, the bill declared, the same must be true of religious belief: "to suffer the civil magistrate to intrude his powers into the field of" belief violates the principle of consent upon which public power is based: "the opinions of men are not the object of civil government, nor under its jurisdiction."[225] The substantive portion of the religious freedom bill drafted by Jefferson is short and simple—albeit with a lawyerlike elegance of its own:

> *We the General Assembly of Virginia do enact* that no man shall be compelled to frequent or support any religious

223. "[Bill No.] 82. A Bill for Establishing Religious Freedom," in *Jefferson Papers,* 2:545–53. See generally Merrill D. Peterson and Robert D. Vaughan, eds., *The Virginia Statute for Religious Freedom: Its Evolution and Consequences in American History* (Cambridge: Cambridge University Press, 1986), and Thomas J. Buckley, *Church and State in Revolutionary Virginia, 1776–1787* (Charlottesville: University Press of Virginia, 1977).

224. *Jefferson Papers,* 2:547.

225. Id., 546.

> worship, place, or ministry whatsoever, nor shall be enforced, restrained, molested, or burdened in his body or goods, nor shall otherwise suffer, on account of his religious opinions or beliefs; but that all men shall be free to profess, and by argument to maintain, their opinions in matters of religion, and that the same shall in no wise diminish, enlarge, or affect their civil capacities.[226]

By now, freedom of belief has become so deeply ingrained in American public law that it is easy to forget how far-reaching Jefferson's bill was in its day. When he sought "to establish religious freedom on the broadest bottom,"[227] heresy was still a capital crime at common law, and a statute imposed imprisonment as a penalty "for not comprehending the mysteries of the trinity."[228] Jefferson's bill swept away both state support and state coercion from the field of religion. Instead, it affirmed the right to have religious beliefs reign in the private kingdom of the individual mind.

Jefferson's revision of the laws also proposed important changes in the criminal law. As Jefferson himself explained it, his principal bill on the subject "proposes to proportion crimes and punishments."[229] Not long before Jefferson did his revisory work, the Marquis Cesare di Beccaria had begun his landmark advocacy of

226. Id.

227. Jefferson, *Notes on the State of Virginia,* 137.

228. Id., 161.

229. Id., 143. For the bill's text, see "[Bill No.] 64. A Bill for Proportioning Crimes and Punishments in Cases Heretofore Capital," in *Jefferson Papers,* 2:492–507.

criminal-law reform.[230] Very few, if any, other colonial lawyers had even heard of the great Italian penal reformer.[231] Jefferson, however, had not only read Beccaria,[232] he also relied upon the approach of the "Philosophical Legislator"[233] in drafting his criminal punishment bill. Jefferson observed that "Beccaria... had satisfied the reasonable world of the unrightfulness and inefficacy of the punishment of crimes by death."[234] Following Beccaria, Jefferson sought in his bill to mitigate the harshness of the common law, which made all felonies punishable by death. He got the revisors to agree "that the punishment of death should be abolished except for treason and murder."[235] In his commentary on Beccaria, Voltaire wrote, "It is an old saying that a man after he is hanged is good for

230. Beccaria first published his landmark *Essay on Crimes and Punishments* in Italian in 1764; the English translation published in London in 1770 quickly made its way to British North America. On Beccaria, see Marcello T. Maestro, *Cesare Beccaria and the Origins of Penal Reform* (Philadelphia: Temple University Press, 1973), and Janet Funston and Richard Funston, "Cesare Beccaria and the American Founding Fathers," *Italian Americana* 3 (1976): 73–92. See also the new edition of Beccaria's principal writings: *On Crimes and Punishments and Other Writings*, trans. Richard Davies, with Virginia Cox and Richard Bellamy, ed.Richard Bellamy (Cambridge: Cambridge University Press, 1995).

231. One who had was John Adams. See "Argument for the Defense in [No. 64], Rex v. Weems (Suffolk Superior Court, Boston)," 3–4 December 1770, in *Legal Papers of John Adams*, 3:242–70 (quote at 242).

232. See the lengthy extracts from Beccaria (in the original Italian) in Chinard, *Commonplace Book*, 298–316.

233. The phrase is James Madison's. See James Madison to Thomas S. Grimké, 15 January 1828, in *Writings of Madison*, 9:298–301 (quote at 300). The full letter suggests that Madison had a less enthusiastic opinion of Beccaria, and of the reforms his writings inspired, than did Jefferson.

234. *Autobiography*, in *Jefferson: Writings*, 40.

235. Id., 39.

nothing, and that the punishments invented for the welfare of society should be useful to that society."[236] Jefferson agreed and wrote that, for felonies other than treason and murder, "should be substituted hard labor in the public works."[237] His bill did just that, though it also reverted to the *lex talionis* in certain cases, even if he conceded that it "will be revolting to the humanised feelings of modern times."[238] Still, his use of "an eye for an eye, a tooth for a tooth"[239] in cases of rape, polygamy, sodomy, or maiming does not change the overall intent of his bill to relax the severity of punishments and make them more humane in the spirit of the enlightened liberalism that he so well embodied.[240]

Jefferson's effort here can be best appreciated by comparing it with the criminal law it sought to replace. Blackstone listed 160 capital offenses and the number rose to 225 before the reforming legislation early in the nineteenth century.[241] When Jefferson drafted his bill, authorities often executed thieves, robbers, counterfeit-

236. Voltaire, *Candide and Other Writings* (New York: Modern Library, 1956), 375.

237. *Autobiography*, in *Jefferson: Writings*, 39.

238. Thomas Jefferson to George Wythe, 1 November 1778, in *Jefferson Papers*, 2:229–30 (quote at 230).

239. *Autobiography*, in *Jefferson: Writings*, 39.

240. Malone, *Jefferson the Virginian*, 270.

241. John Laurence, *A History of Capital Punishment* (New York: Citadel Press, 1960), 13. Leading modern discussions of capital punishment in English legal history include Frank McLynn, *Crime and Punishment in Eighteenth-Century England* (London: Routledge, 1989), 257–76 (165 in 1775 and 225 by 1815); Peter Linebaugh, *The London Hanged: Crime and Civil Society in the Eighteenth Century* (Cambridge: Cambridge University Press, 1992); and V. A. C. Gattrell, *The Hanging Tree: Execution and the English People, 1770–1868* (Oxford: Oxford University Press, 1994).

ers, and other felons.[242] Well could Jefferson state that his bill was aimed at "the sanguinary hue of our penal laws."[243]

Jefferson's criminal punishment bill was another expression of his conception of law and the society he intended it to serve. "Capital punishments," wrote Benjamin Rush in 1792, "are the natural offspring of monarchical governments.... Kings consider their subjects as their property;... they shed their blood with as little emotion as men shed the blood of their sheep or cattle."[244] To Jefferson, too, "the principles of republican governments speak a very different language."[245] He described capital punishment "as the last melancholy resource against those whose existence is become inconsistent with the safety of their fellow citizens." Except for those who fall within that category, the law should seek reform so that the lapsed citizen should still be able to play his part in the republican society. But "capital punishments... exterminate instead of reforming," and "weaken the state by cutting off so many who, if reformed, might be restored sound members to society."[246]

Jefferson's humanitarian (at least for his time) approach to criminal law also extended to the law of his day's greatest violation of human dignity—the law of slavery, which reduced human beings

242. Louis Masur, *Rites of Execution: Capital Punishment and the Transformation of American Culture, 1776–1865* (New York: Oxford University Press, 1989), 71.

243. Thomas Jefferson to Edmund Pendleton, 26 August 1776, in *Jefferson Papers,* 1:503–07 (quote at 505).

244. Quoted in Masur, *Rites of Execution,* 65.

245. Quoted in id.

246. "A Bill for Proportioning Crimes and Punishments," in *Jefferson Papers,* 2: 493.

to the status of property in a large part of the country. As part of his revision, Jefferson prepared a bill "to emancipate all slaves born after passing the act."[247] It was not, however, included among the bills presented by the revisors because, as Jefferson put it, "it was found that the public mind would not yet bear the proposition, nor will it bear it even in this day"—1821, when Jefferson wrote his *Autobiography.* In writing about his aborted slavery bill, Jefferson did, however, declare, "Nothing is more certainly written in the book of fate than that these people are to be free."[248]

Like the *Bolling* argument, Jefferson's revisory work shows him at his best as a lawyer. He intended his revision of the laws to produce an American statute book that, in Madison's words, was "adapted to the Independent & Republican form of Government."[249] It was to be a law that would enable "this American, this new man" celebrated by Crèvecoeur to be the kind of republican citizen who would make the nation's new institutions succeed. Jefferson's bills on criminal punishment and slavery were intended to help achieve this goal. Even more adapted to that end were the bills on land descent, religious freedom, and citizenship. Plainly, to Jefferson, the law was to be a primary instrument to enable Americans to construct the type of society that he favored.

247. "[Bill No.] 55. A Bill Concerning Slaves," in *Jefferson Papers,* 2:470–73. See also Jefferson's discussion of this bill and its fate (with its unsettling display of Jefferson's racist rationalization of slavery) in Jefferson, *Notes on the State of Virginia,* 137–43.

248. *Autobiography,* in *Jefferson: Writings,* 44.

249. James Madison to Samuel Harrison Smith, 4 November 1826, in *Writings of Madison,* 9:257.

## *Bolling v. Bolling*: The Manuscript

The bar in action can, of course, best be seen in the courtroom. That was particularly true before the founding of law schools and the age of the first treatise writers, before formal legal education was available. The law then was taught primarily through practice—first in the office of a preceptor and then in the courtroom. Hence, there is no better way to observe early American jurisprudence than through its application in actual cases.

There is, nevertheless, a critical problem in attempting to see the early American Bar in action: the lack of materials, such as transcripts, recording what went on in the eighteenth-century courtroom. Because of this, the lawyer of Jefferson's day has largely remained hidden from the sight of history.[250] The difficulty was stated over a century ago by the biographer of William Wirt, a leading early American lawyer. Wirt, "who, with a full measure of contemporary fame, has left but little on record by which the justice of that fame might be estimated."[251] As Justice Story once said of the early Supreme Court bar, "no reports in print exhibit correctly the vast compass and variety of their powers."[252]

By happenstance, however, there has been preserved the text of the arguments delivered by Thomas Jefferson and George Wythe as opposing counsel in an important case. On December 2, 1770, Jefferson made the following entry in his Case Book: "Archbld.

250. Hurst, *Growth of American Law*, 18.

251. Kennedy, *Memoirs of Life of William Wirt*, 1:14.

252. Story, *Life and Letters of Joseph Story*, 2:326.

Bolling v. Robt. Bolling (Buckingham). Case in Canc. Referred to arbitration. Desired by R. Bolling to state it with arguments at length in writing. Charge £5.—1771 Sep. 13. Recd. £9-17."[253]

Jefferson himself apparently thought highly of the *Bolling* arguments. In 1780 he sent his copy to William Short, his young protégé,[254] to whom Jefferson frequently referred as his adopted son.[255] At that time, Short had (in the words of his 1781 petition for admission to the bar) "been for a considerable time engaged in the Study of the Law."[256] Jefferson thought that the manuscript would help the legal neophyte. "I send you," Jefferson wrote, "by Col. Digges (the first opportunity which has occurred) Mr. Wythe's and my arguments in *Bolling vs Bolling* bound up together. The former are valuable in themselves, the latter to none but myself; but being so to myself, I am induced to recommend the book to your particular care. It will enable you better to foresee your adversary's objections, than to answer them."[257]

The *Bolling* manuscript itself consists of 239 pages (including a

253. Fee book, case no. 489 (*Bolling v. Bolling*), 2 December 1770, in *Jefferson Papers,* 15:587 note. also quoted in Dumbauld, *Jefferson and the Law*, 94.

254. So characterized in Samuel Flagg Bemis, *Pinckney's Treaty: America's Advantage from European Distress* (New Haven: Yale University Press, 1926), 186. See also the historical novel by Max Byrd, *Jefferson* (New York: Bantam, 1994).

255. George C. Shackelford, "William Short, Jefferson's Adopted Son, 1758-1849" (Ph.D. diss., University of Virginia, 1955).

256. Petition by William Short to the Governor and Council, undated but ca. 1781, quoted in *Jefferson Papers,* 6:122 n. (accompanying "Jefferson's Certification of William Short as an Attorney," 30 September 1781, in id.).

257. Thomas Jefferson to William Short, 1 June 1780, in *Jefferson Papers,* 15:586-87 (quote at 586).

title page for George Wythe's first argument for plaintiff); 124 of these are in Jefferson's handwriting and 112 in what Jefferson termed the "elegant hand writing" of his friend Anderson Bryant. According to a note in Jefferson's *Papers*, Anderson Bryan (as his name is there given) was another Jefferson protégé whom Jefferson "took... into my family, and gave him his board for some years. In return he now and then aided me in writing."[258] The reader today is struck not only by the lucidity of the arguments presented but also by the clarity (and even beauty) of the handwriting itself.

The present edition strikes a balance between a reading text of the manuscript and a literal transcription of Jefferson's and Bryant's script. Editorial insertions are denoted by brackets; footnotes identify any material that Jefferson or Bryant enclosed in brackets in the original manuscript. As noted in the Statement of Editorial Method, spelling and punctuation are those in the original manuscript, even where they differ substantially from modern practice. The reader should consult the Statement of Editorial Method for a detailed explanation of these and related matters.

## *Bolling v. Bolling*: The Case

The Bollings were a prominent Virginia family. John, a brother of the two parties in the case, had married Jefferson's sister Martha; he came to be known as Colonel John Bolling.[259] The case

258. "Thomas Jefferson's state of the case between himself and Harvie," ca. July 1795, quoted in *Jefferson Papers,* 16:84 n. (Thomas Jefferson to Anderson Bryan [i.e., Bryant], 6 January 1790, in id., 83–84).

259. Malone, *Jefferson the Virginian,* 39. See also Suzanne Lebsock, *The Free Women of Petersburg: Status and Culture in a Southern Town, 1784–1860* (New York: W. W. Norton & Co., 1984), 112–16.

arose out of the will of Edward Bolling. The two parties were brothers of the testator; the plaintiff was Archibald Bolling and the defendant Robert Bolling. Edward's will left his Buffalo Lick plantation to Robert and, after several other legacies, "declared it was his will and desire that his book be given up to his bro[the]r Robert, and that he recieve all the debts due to him (the test[ato]r) and pay 'all that he owed.'"

To Archibald, Edward devised other lands, including "his warehouse at Pocahontas." In addition, "the rest of his estate, negroes, harvest, clothes, and every other part of his estate not already given he gave and bequeathed to his bro[the]r Archibald Bolling for him and his heirs for ever" — a clause that made Archibald residuary devisee and legatee.

The will also left a slave to the testator's sister Mary Bland, a legacy of £100 to his sister Sarah Tazewell, a slave to his sister Anne Bolling, a slave to his friend, Richard Meade and one to his cousin Bolling Eldridge.

After he made his will, Edward Bolling sold his Pocahontas warehouse to Neill Buchanan for £500. In contemplation of the money from the Pocahontas sale, Edward purchased other property for more than £500. These purchases (except one of £120) passed to plaintiff as residuary legatee.

The testator died in August 1770. Robert Bolling then probated the will and acted as executor. His action was not contested by Archibald Bolling.

The *Bolling* case, as the quoted extract from Jefferson's Case Book indicates, was brought as a Chancery case in the Virginia

General Court and was referred to arbitration. Presumably the arguments preserved in the Jefferson manuscript were those presented to the arbitrator. It should be noted that the issues in the case involve highly technical questions of property and inheritance law. The General Court, which had both common-law and equity jurisdiction, was composed of the same men who made up the Governor's Council. As Jefferson himself put it, they were "chosen from among the gentlemen of the country, for their wealth and standing, without any regard to legal knowledge."[260]

The General Court was scarcely competent to try a case presenting knotty legal issues of the sort at the heart of *Bolling*. Instead, "Arbitration was particularly well suited to complex issues that might baffle lay judges."[261] A qualified lawyer could be chosen who could deal with the technical matters involved. Thus, Jefferson's Case Book tells of a case in which the arbitrator was Benjamin Waller, the clerk of the General Court and later a judge.[262] His ability is shown by a 1779 comment by Edmund Pendleton: "We have had sad blundering among the Clerks, and shall have worse, now that they will not have a Mr. Waller at their head to apply to in cases of difficulty."[263] The use of arbitration in *Bolling* would enable the case to be tried before a comparable lawyer, rather than the lay judges of the General Court, who could

260. *Jefferson's Reports*, 5.

261. Dewey, *Thomas Jefferson, Lawyer*, 24.

262. Jefferson Case Book, no. 233, cited in Dewey, *Thomas Jefferson, Lawyer*, 24.

263. Edmund Pendleton to Thomas Jefferson, 11 May 1779, in *Jefferson Papers*, 2:266–67 (quote at 266).

hardly be expected to understand, much less resolve, the complicated issues involved.

## Wythe's First Argument

The *Bolling* manuscript begins with a two-page statement summarizing the complaint and answer, which was probably prepared by Jefferson. Then comes George Wythe's first argument for the plaintiff. It has been assumed that the *Bolling* arguments were written arguments presented to the arbitrator. According to Judge Dumbauld, Jefferson "evidently copied [Wythe's] argument, perhaps from an original in Wythe's large handwriting."[264] However, the heading of Wythe's first argument (in Jefferson's handwriting) reads, "G. Wythe's argum': verbal." Samuel Johnson's *Dictionary* defines "verbal" as "1. Spoken, not written. 2. Oral; uttered by mouth." The implication is that the manuscript argument was delivered orally by Wythe and recorded by Jefferson.[265]

Jefferson's transcript of Wythe's *Bolling* argument is remarkably detailed if, in fact, he took it down while it was delivered verbally, or even if he followed the practice of Madison during the Constitutional Convention in 1787—that is, taking shorthand notes during the proceedings and writing them up during the evening. At any rate, if the manuscript argument was only the written argument in the case, it is difficult to explain why Jefferson used the word "verbal" at the beginning of the Wythe argument.

264. Dumbauld, *Jefferson and the Law*, 220 n84.

265. Note, however, Judge Dumbauld's suggestion that Wythe's argument "is evidently copied from another paper, and not notes taken during argument." Id, 221 n97.

As far as the *Bolling* case itself was concerned, two main issues were presented: (1) whether defendant was entitled to the crops growing on the Buffalo Lick plantation at the time of the testator's death, or whether they should instead pass to plaintiff, the residuary legatee, as part of Edward's personal estate; and (2) whether the gift to defendant of the testator's "Book" was a legacy to him of the surplus of amounts collected over the debts to be paid, or whether that surplus also was an undisposed part of decedent's personal property that should pass under the residuary clause of the will to plaintiff.

The most interesting part of the argument dealt with the first issue, for it was to it that both Jefferson and Wythe devoted their major attention. This portion is also of greatest interest because resolution of the first issue turned on the type of common-law legal reasoning that best shows the early American bar in action.

In law, the growing crops such as those in dispute are termed "emblements." Are emblements to be treated as real or personal property? Wythe, opening the case for plaintiffs, began, "Emblements are not part of the inheritance nor considered as fixed to the freehold, but are chattels personal... yea they are in law, before they be severed, mobilia." As such they "are no part of the inheritance, but mere personal chattels following the sower, the consequence is, that they will not pass with land by a devise." Hence, "emblements, do not descend to the heir with the inheritance which the law casts upon him." Wythe stressed the social purpose behind the rule advocated by him: "[T]he law gives the emblements to the representative of a sower when he dies before they be reaped to encourage agriculture and they are as much his separate property and subject to the regulations which concern personal chattels as his cattle, household furniture, and the like." That being the case, "they must go as all other personal chattels go, without distinguishing such plants &c. as are cut from what are standing."

Wythe devoted much of his argument to criticism of the authorities he expected Jefferson to cite. Thus, referring to a case reported in Godbolt, he said, "I cannot allow such a book as this to deserve much credit." Wythe dismissed another legal commentator, who had mentioned a case under which emblements passed with the land, with the comment, "Wentworth was a compiler only, and what he sais of the sale or conveiance, since he quotes no authority is but his opinion." In particular, Wythe objected to the authority of a case reported by Sir Humphrey Winch. According to Wythe, "this is another unauthoritative publication, translated, as it is said, from a fair copy of Sir Humphrey Winch's in French. but all the cases were not collected by him, for in one of them (pa. 125) there is an eulogy of himself upon occasion of his death." Wythe concluded his criticism of the authorities to be relied on by his opponent by asserting "that emblements will pass with land by a simple devise or conveiance of the latter does not appear to have been a point judicially determined in any reporter of authority; but the sayings of judges to that purpose... were obiter opinions, and such are of no great weight at any time."

Wythe also relied upon a statute which provided that, if a person died after March 1 while his crop was in the ground, all slaves then employed on the crop would continue to work on it until

December 25, and then the crop would be deemed assets in the hands of the executor and the slaves would be delivered to the legatees. Wythe interpreted this law as, in effect, treating the growing crops and the slaves' labor similarly:[266] "by this confusion of the emblements of land with the profits of slaves the legislature has declared them to be homogeneous, and the former consequently to be personal chattels, and then they must go as all other personal chattels go, without distinguishing such plants &c as are cut from what are standing." Here, too, Wythe stressed the social purpose behind the statute. He noted that, "our lands being cultivated mostly if not altogether by slaves, if they should be removed immediately after the owner's death the crop on his ground must perish. to prevent this public as well as private loss, the act directs the crop... to be finished by the slaves, who should for that purpose be continued on the plant[atio]n till Christmas."

Wythe then turned to the words in the will, "it is my will and desire that my book be given up to my bro[the]r Robert, and that he recieve all the debts due to me, and pay all that I owe." Wythe argued that this "does not import a gift of the debts, and is no more than the appointment of an ex[ecuto]r. the surplus in this case being expressly bequeathed to Archibald Bolling that must prevail against the gift to Rob[ert] Bolling, implied in the appointment of him to the ex[ecuto]rship."

Wythe concluded his first argument: "It is therefore hoped the def[endant] will be deemed to pay to the pl[aintiff] the surplus of

266. Compare id., 97.

the debts, with the emblements. and for that purpose that an account be taken. in this account the def[endant] must be debited with the money he owed."

## Jefferson's First Argument

Jefferson's first argument, which follows in the manuscript, is much longer and more detailed than the Wythe argument just summarized. Arguing for defendant, Jefferson dealt with both the legal status of emblements and "the objections made to my authorities." Jefferson's reply to Wythe's objections shows him at his best as both an advocate and legal scholar. So successful was he in answering the objections to his authorities that Wythe was later to concede that the cases at common law supported Jefferson's position on emblements.

Jefferson answered Wythe's "objections... to my authorities" after he had shown by these authorities that his client was "entitled to the Emblements unsevered at the death of the test[ato]r." He began, "What first presents itself to us as a guide thro' this enquiry is the maxim 'quicquid plantatur solo, solo cedit,' [whatever is planted in the soil belongs to the soil] a maxim derived from our earliest ideas of property." It follows, Jefferson continued, that "whatever of an inferior value, is annexed to a subject of much greater, seems naturally to be a part of, and to belong to, that subject, and ought therefore as a dependant, or accessory, to pass with it's principal." This, Jefferson urged, meant that the crops growing on the land should pass with the land itself to his client to whom the land had been devised.

Jefferson rejected Wythe's contention that emblements were to be treated in all respects as personal chattels. Instead, emblements "seem in truth to be chattels of a <u>mixt nature</u>, partly personal, partly real"; in a case such as this, they pass with the land on which they are sown. Jefferson's conclusion, "unimpeached by any of [plaintiff's] objections," was as follows:

> 'Emblements go to the ex[ecuto]r of the sower if his estate was rightful, not joint, of incertain continuance, and determined by the act of god or of the law: but if it was wrongful, or joint, or of certain continuance, or determined by his own act, as by desertion, forfeiture, alienation without reserve &c. they go with the lands.'

Jefferson cited a mass of common-law authorities to support his position. Indeed, as far as the authorities themselves were concerned, Jefferson was certain that they supported his view on emblements. He therefore spoke strongly in favor of *stare decisis*, as noted in the economium already quoted,[267] which he supported with a quotation from a Mansfield opinion[268] and with Blackstone's statement that adherence to precedent served "to keep the scale of justice even and steady, and not liable to waver with every new judge's opinion."[269]

But Jefferson, with his instrumentalist conception of law, also

267. Supra, text at notes 199, 200.

268. *Windham, Esq., versus Chetwynd, Esq.*, 1 Burrow 414–431 (K.B., 25 Nov. 1757), 97 E.R. 377–87. Additional reports of this case appear in 1 W. Blackstone 96–103, 96 E.R. 53–57; 1 Kenyon 253–56, 96 E.R. 984–85; and 2 Kenyon 121–62, 96 E.R. 1128–42.

269. Blackstone, *Commentaries on the Laws of England*, 1:69.

stressed the social purpose behind the rule that he advocated. Although he began with the maxim that whatever is planted in the soil belongs to the soil, he showed that this principle had to give way in certain cases to the maxim, "he who sows shall reap"—as in the case giving the legatee or executor of a tenant "the corn which he had sowed but had not lived to reap." This was done "on a political principle, to encorage agriculture for the benefit of the state." This was true for the sower "unless his estate determine by his own act" — that is, he voluntarily terminated his interest in the land. Jefferson gave an "account of the progress of alienation" in English law, starting with feudal law, "to shew that a devise is but another mode of alienation or conveiance; and that when the testamentary alienation becomes perfect, by the death of the devisor, the alienee is on the same footing as he would have been if the conveiance had been by deed."

Consequently, he continued, "I think I may add, on the adjudications I have produced,... the devisee or alienee takes all the unreserved accessories, among which are the emblements." Jefferson shrewdly noted that, in this respect, his position was similar to Wythe's, with one crucial difference: "It will be perceived that this is the same with the conclusion drawn in the argument for the pl[aintiff] 'that emblements follow the person of the sower... unless his estate determine by his own act.' Only the pl[aintiff]'s counsel does not consider a conveiance by... will as a determination 'by the act of the party.'"

Jefferson showed that, both "in a legal point of view," through the cases on the matter, and "before the eye of reason," the position of a devisee in this respect was different from that of an heir: "therefore to say the emblements will not pass by a devise... 'because no more passes to the devisee... than would descend to the heir' is a plain non-sequitur; the rights of these persons being not analogous." Hence, Jefferson concluded, since the testator's estate "was determined by his own act, i.e. by devise without reserving the emblements when he had opportunity to reserve them if he had meant to do so. they therefore return to their natural channel and pass with the land to Robert Bolling."

The skill with which Jefferson argued the emblements issue is best shown by Wythe's concession, in his second argument in reply to Jefferson, that "the common law supposed the owner of the soil to have a right to emblements." Thus, when Jefferson started his second argument with the proposition "that at the Common law by the devise of these lands the emblements would have passed to Rob[ert] Bolling," he could say, "the first of these propositions the adverse counsel now admits, to wit, that, putting our acts of assembly out of the question, Rob[ert] Bolling would be entitled to the emblements growing on the land at the testator's death."

Jefferson then dealt with Wythe's argument that the common-law rule in this respect had been changed by statute—namely, the act which provided for the use of the slaves employed on a crop to continue working on it until Christmas, with the crop then to be deemed assets in the hands of the executor and the slaves to be delivered to the legatees. According to Jefferson, the purpose of the act was to provide labor to harvest emblements, not to affect their ownership. In his first argument for the defendant, Jefferson stressed the social purpose of the law: "our legislature at that time took up into consideration, that tho' for the encoragement of agriculture, the law in certain instances had given the emblements to the sower, and in others to the owner of the lands, yet it had in neither case given them reapers[.]" In England, this presented no problem, "because any number of reapers may be there hired on short warning." But "this could not be done in our country, where the lands are cultivated by slaves alone, and he who has them not of his own cannot hire them." The legislature "therefore, to save the emblements to the community as well as to the individual, determine to give him reapers also." Thus, Jefferson argued, the statute did not affect the title to emblements: "'this act has annexed the labor of slaves to the Emblements... and given it to him (whether sower or owner of the soil) who can entitle himself to the Emblements.'"

## Emblements and "Assets"

Jefferson dealt with the statutory provision that the crop was to be deemed "assets" in the hands of the executor (which, Wythe had claimed, made them personal chattels which go to the residuary legatee) by an argument that demonstrates his forensic skill. Pointing out that the word "assets" comes "from the French *Assez*" (enough), he asserted, "*Assets,* then signifies in English *Enough,* and this calls for two other questions, to wit, *Of what*? answer. of *goods* and *chattels. For what*? answer. to satisfy *debts* and *legacies....* by use we have made the adverb *assez,* or *assets* or *assetz,* as it was spelt in old French, to carry in it the whole idea of 'goods and chattels *enough* to pay debts and legacies.'"

Jefferson's position here was that the term "assets" meant only the "goods and chattels [that] will be applied to the paiment of debts and legacies; but when they are all paid, what remains is not called *assets*..." The term did not denote

> the personal estate in general, abstracted from the idea of paying debts and legacies, or in other words, it is never used to denote the *distributable* or *residuary surplus.* what I infer from all this is, that the word assets denotes that part of the personal estate which will actually be applied to the paiment of debts and legacies, and that as soon as these are paid there are no such things as *assets* in existence. so that where an act of assembly directs that any thing 'shall be *assets* in the hands of ex[ecuto]rs and adm[inistrato]rs,' it means only that 'it shall be considered as a *chattel* for the purpose of paying *debts* and *legacies*, if there be a deficiency without it' but if not, it remains in the hands in which it would have remained had such act never been made.

To us, Jefferson's argument seems farfetched, for the word "assets" now has a broader meaning that would bring the relevant statutory provision into line with Wythe's interpretation. But "assets" in Jefferson's day had a more restricted connotation, as he asserted. In support, Jefferson quoted Cowell's *Interpreter*, which noted that "assets" is derived from the French "assez" and defined it as "*goods enough* to discharge that burthen, which is cast upon the ex[ecuto]r or heir, in satisfying the test[ato]rs debts and legacies."[270]

270. John Cowell (Cowel), *The Interpreter of Words and Terms, Used either in the Common or Statute Laws of this Realm, and in Tenures and Jocular Customs...* (London: J. Place, A. & J. Churchill, and R. Sare, 1701). This definition is borne out by the many legal dictionaries and word books used by both Jefferson and Wythe in their arguments in *Bolling v. Bolling.*

## Gift of the Book

Jefferson also rebutted Wythe's interpretation of the provision in the will that the testator's "book be given up to his bro[the]r Robert," who was to "recieve all the debts due to him (the testator) and 'pay all that he owed.'" Wythe, as noted, had urged that the provision was only an appointment of defendant as executor and that, after the debts were paid, the surplus should go to plaintiff as residuary legatee.

Jefferson, relying on the term "give up," argued that it was a devise of the testator's credits, with the surplus remaining to Robert after the debts were paid. As summed up by Jefferson near the beginning of his first argument, "Under the bequest of the test[ato]r's Book he claims His test[ato]r's Credits burthened with his Debts." Jefferson argued that Wythe's contention that the will provision only made Robert executor "is merely an artificial construction of the law." The testator's intention was "to transfer to him the right to his credits, paying thereout his debts." The "gift" of the Book "carried [more than] the paper and leather of which it was made." Yet, Jefferson asked, "how idle and nugatory would the gift of the paper and leather be, if their appendages, the Credits, were not to follow them? nobody can suppose the test[ato]r intended to give his brother merely a parcel of waste paper." Instead, "the word *give*, imports a transfer of the *use*, as well as *legal property*, of the thing given."

Jefferson gave various other reasons why the "Book" provision should be interpreted as he contended. In discussing them in detail, he proved himself a master of what he called, in this portion of his argument, "the subtle reasonings of the law." Jefferson's argument here was intended to show that his interpretation was supported by the words of the will.

In addition, Jefferson asked rhetorically "Whether [the testator's] intention may not be ascertained by *Parol proof* dehors of the will"—clearly assuming that it could, both in fact and in law. His conclusion, based upon cited English authorities, was "that it may be safely laid down that *Parol proof* is admissible and proper here to explain what the test[ato]r is supposed to have expressed doubtfully, vid' the capacity in which Rob[ert] Boll[ing] was to recieve his debts." Jefferson then used the depositions of the testator's overseer and his wife to support his interpretation. Indeed, Jefferson asserted, "this part of the testimony I take to be conclusive. for who can best judge of the test[ato]r's intention: we who see nothing but the written letter? or those who saw him write it; to whom he repeated and explained the substance of what he wrote; and with whom he often conversed on the subject?"

In the conclusion of his first argument, Jefferson summarized his argument on the "Book" issue:

> That the test[ato]r did intend this a beneficial bequest appears
> On the *Face* of the *will* itself, and principally
> from the import or efficacy of the word *give.*
> from that of the word *recieve.*
> from the *location* of the clause, to wit, in the midst of *donations.*
> from its *circumlocution,* which shews the test[ato]r did not mean it as an appointment of an

ex[ecuto]r; and therefore that he had
another meaning.
from his not *enumerating* it in the *residuary* clause.
From *Parol proof* dehors of the will, which is *admissible*; and is
that the test[ato]r spoke of having 'left' and 'given'
his lands, slaves and debts in the same sense.
that he never mentioned that Rob[ert] Boll[ing] was
to be his *executor*. but
that he meant his debts as a *legacy*.
Among the *Credits* we are entitled to is to be reckoned *Buchanan's*
£500.
because the sale of the warehouses *revoked* the
devise[.]
because Arch[ibald] Boll[ing] has the *fruits* of the
sale, in his residuum.

## Jefferson's Defense of His Authorities

In many ways, the most interesting part of Jefferson's first argument came at an earlier stage, when he defended the authorities upon which he relied to support his position on emblements at common law. Recall that Wythe in his opening argument had strongly criticized the authorities upon which Jefferson relied. After discussing the common law on the matter and the authorities supporting his position, Jefferson stated, "Having now settled what I think the rule with respect to Emblements, I shall answer the objections made to my authorities, which I was unwilling to do as I cited them, lest it should interrupt the course of our ideas, and divert our attention from what was then to be proven."

In particular, Wythe had objected to a case reported by Sir Humphrey Winch. Because Jefferson relied strongly upon that case and another reported in Winch, he first answered Wythe's objections to Winch's reports. Jefferson started by plaintively noting, "I have so few of the old reporters, in my possession." However, his detailed discussion of the different old reporters plainly belies his self-deprecation. To Wythe's assertion that Winch "is an unauthoritative publication," Jefferson referred to other reporters whose "books are cited universally, without objection for want of the license." Even more important, he stressed, "the character of Sir Humph[rey] Winch however, as a judge, should seem to give as much authority to his book, as it would have given to that of any other, to have had an imprimatur prefixed, signed by him. and yet such signature would have made such book authoritative." In addition, Winch "is as often cited by both bar and bench... as any reporter.... I never before met with an objection to his authority. indeed I have ever considered 'all Reporters to be authoritative, whether licensed or not, if they have been usually cited by, and before, the judges in Westminster hall, and were never, by them, denied.'" To Wythe's objection that the Winch reports were only a translation of the original in French, Jefferson noted, "Coke's, Plowden's, Noy's, Levintz's, Lutwyche's cases were collected and published in French. they are since translated." But that does not affect their authority. In fact, their "English editions are held equally authoritative with the French, and are most sought after."

Wythe had noted that Winch's cases "were not collected by him, for in one of them (pa. 125) there is an eulogy of himself upon occasion of his death." Jefferson countered with a sarcastic analogy: "we might as well endeavor to destroy the authority of the

Pentateuch, by observing, that all the chapters thereof were not written by Moses, because in one of them, Deut. XXXIV. 5–12 'is an eulogy on himself, on occasion of his death.' in both cases the passage, which could not be by the author himself, is easily and equally distinguishable." Wythe had objected to a case reported in Godbolt on the ground that his work was a compilation of cases collected by others, not those reported by him personally. Jefferson answered, "That the cases in any reporter were all taken in court by the reporter himself, is I believe in no instance true." Instead, the reporter "is furnished, by his friends of the long robe, with manuscript cases in their possession. these, if important and well taken, would hardly be rejected, merely because not taken by himself." In fact, said Jefferson, "we know, in many instances, it was impossible the reporter should have taken every case himself." To prove this point, Jefferson's argument at this point contains a table with the names of seven English reporters, with the dates covered by their reports. Their reports ranged in coverage from 58 to 408 years. "[N]ow," Jefferson then said, "we know it impossible men should have lived at all, much less enjoyed that vigor of mind requisite for such works, thro so long spaces of time. and tho' we know they could not have taken all the cases themselves, yet as they declare they collected them, we are satisfied with their judgment and fidelity, and admit the authority." Thus, the reporters named in the table "are acknoleged authorities." Wythe's objections to the reporters cited by Jefferson completely missed the mark: "the questions which determine [a reporter] authoritative or not, are these, Is he cited in Westminster hall? ans. he is… Was he ever there denied to be authority? ans. Never."

Jefferson next refuted Wythe's objections to a case on which defendant had placed great reliance. The opinion that "'*by the devise of the lands* they' i.e., the emblements 'pass with it'" was, Jefferson noted, "my Lord Coke's opinion, in which too 'he said he was clear' and his opinion, when clear, I consider as no mean authority." Moreover, "all three judges, with Coke and Popham, unanimously agreed the question, so far as it concerns us, that 'by the devise of the lands the emblements passed.'" To the argument that the case "was not an *adjudged* case, but an extra judicial opinion," Jefferson conceded that there was no judgment entered of record: "but I conceive the *opinion* of the judges is the essence of every authority; and if that opinion be given on a full state of the case, on mature deliberation, and on the point, in support of which it is adduced; then their opinion so given must influence ours, i.e., it becomes an authority, whether, when they pronounced it, their clerk took a minute of it or not."

Wythe had also objected to the report of the case on the ground that the reporter, Sir George Croke, "was then but twenty-seven years of age." Jefferson was only a year older himself and he began his reply with a bow in the direction of age, perhaps in deference to Wythe (to the young lawyer his forty-six year old mentor must have seemed already aged): "far be it from me to detract from that superiority of wisdom to which years give title, because they bring it. the longer a man has lived, the more facts have come under his observation, and the more time he has had for reflection." At the same time, Jefferson urged, his age did not militate against Croke's authority: "if this part of his book be not authority because of his youth, say whereabouts he begins to be old enough, that at that place we may draw a line in the book. our law books do not inform us; they cite equally every part of his work."

Wythe, it will be recalled, had criticized Wentworth, another reporter relied on by defendant, as "a compiler only." Jefferson retorted by asking, "what are the authorities produced in support of the pl[aintiff]'s right? Swinburne a compiler; Blackstone a compiler, Broke a compiler, Perkins a compiler; and Viner a compiler."

Jefferson also objected strongly to what he alleged were the distortions in the authorities cited by the other side. He complained that, "if such a liberty as this may be taken with the cases in the books, I will say they do not furnish a case, which may not be disarmed, or even pointed in it's opposite direction by the insertion of a single word."

Jefferson concluded this portion of his argument with his eulogy on *stare decisis.* Having demonstrated the authenticity of the authorities upon which he relied and believing correctly that they were firmly in his favor, he naturally urged, quoting Lord Mansfield, that "'they must be adhered to'" as binding precedents. (Jefferson's defense of *stare decisis* is doubly ironic—both because, nearly two decades later, he urged in letters to Madison that "[t]he earth belongs always to the living generation" and because in the years following the American Revolution, Jefferson bitterly reprobated the Tory Mansfield for his conservatism.)[271]

271. For Jefferson's and Madison's 1789–90 correspondence on Jefferson's proposition that "[t]he earth belongs always to the living generation," see Smith, *The Republic of Letters,*

Jefferson also strongly appealed for the adoption of a simple, uniform rule to govern the case.[272] After discussing the statutory provision for the continuance of slave labor on a crop after its planter died, Jefferson concluded:

> I think it is to be wished that now, when questions on this subject are first arising, an end should be put to them, by carrying the Labor of the slaves with the Emblements, and subjecting them at once to the same rules. if that were done, we have a set of rules, already formed, which will apply to every case that can arise; and judges will determine, counsel advise, and even the people themselves proceed, at once with certainty and precision. but on the other hand, if a set of rules is to be now built up express for this particle of property, I fear we shall find that (like the jumble of real and personal rules which our legislature made it necessary to compound when they altered the legal nature of the slaves themselves) it will introduce infinite contest, and time, and expence, before they can be framed consistent with themselves, and with the other parts of the law.

## Second Arguments and Reply

The next fifty-one pages of the *Bolling* manuscript are in the copperplate hand of Anderson Bryant. They start with a transcript of the report of *Wankford v. Wankford*, a 1703 English case on which Jefferson had relied for an alternative argument on the "Book" pro-

1:631–36 (Jefferson to Madison, 6 September 1789), 650–53 (Madison to Jefferson, 4 February 1790). See also id., 1:603–04 (editor's comments), and the discussion in Adrienne Koch, *Jefferson and Madison: The Great Collaboration* (New York: Alfred A. Knopf, 1950), 62–96. For Jefferson's critical comments on Mansfield, see John P. Foley, ed., *The Jefferson Cyclopaedia...* (New York: Funk & Wagnalls, 1900), 528, col. 1.

272. Dumbauld, *Jefferson and the Law*, 104.

vision — that, if it did not give his client the surplus of the testator's credits over his debts, the appointment of defendant as executor by operation of the provision at least extinguished his debt to the testator. In his argument, Jefferson had referred to the case and, in a bracketed note in the manuscript, he noted, "this case is too long to be transcribed, but if there be any doubt on this question I beg it may be turned to and read, because I rely on it as decisive." Presumably Jefferson included the transcript at the end of his argument to enable the reader to follow his advice that the case be read.

Next in the manuscript comes Wythe's second argument (also transcribed by Anderson Bryant), followed by Jefferson's second argument (in his hand), and, concluding the manuscript, Wythe's reply (again in Bryant's writing). These will be discussed more briefly than the first arguments, since they only repeat, elaborate, and refine the points already made. Furthermore, the analysis given of the first arguments should give the reader an adequate idea of Jefferson's and Wythe's forensic techniques.

Wythe began his second argument with a justification of the title of the landowner "to the corn that he hath sown on the land, tho' the property of the land is altered." Wythe's reasons were based upon an instrumental conception of law emphasizing that "it is a public benefit that the lands should be sown and cultivated, and all things that tend to plenty and increase ought to have the uttermost security that the law can give it; for hence it is fit that they should suppose a property in the corn distinct from that of the soil, and that this property should be at the intire disposal of the owner distinct and separate from the land." Wythe cited the purpose for such a rule, "that all incouragement possible might be given to tillage, and that no man might decline cultivation under this fear, lest the profits should be swallowed by any person that he disliked."

Wythe also urged that, if his rule that the crop belongs to the one who has sown it were not followed, "men would break in upon other peoples grounds and sow them, and keep men out of the disposal of their own estates, and thereby they would raise a property to themselves from another's estate, and put the owner to the trouble of controverting it." Despite his argument in this respect, Wythe then conceded that Jefferson had stated the correct common-law rule and that, under it, the emblements would go to the devisee in a case such as *Bolling.* But, Wythe urged, "this distinction is abolished, and the common law altered by" the Virginia statute already discussed. Under it, the crop was annexed to the labor of slaves and no longer belonged to the freehold. Instead, "it is annexed to another kind of interest, [and] is expressly directed to go to a different person from him who takes the land; this going to the devisee, that to the executor" for distribution to plaintiff as residuary legatee. The statute, in effect, suspended the devisee's right to the land until the slaves had finished work on the crop. "[H]ow then can the crop, as emblements, belong to him, who has no right to take possession of the land till after the crop is finished, and actually severed?"

Wythe also argued that Jefferson's definition of "assets" as "goods and chattels... to pay debts" was contrary to the statute, which makes the crop "assets, not when it is paid away... but when, i.e. so soon as it is made and finished." Indeed, Wythe asserted, "If no part of the estate be assets but what will actually be applied in payment of debts and legacies; and if consequently, it is not assets before it is so applied; it seems there is no such thing as assets." That was true because, "the moment it is paid away it is not the testator's or intestates assets, but the creditors or legatees property." Wythe contended that all the testator's "personal estate be assets" (much closer, of course, to the present-day meaning) and hence the surplus over debts and legacies went to the residuary legatee.

Wythe then argued that the "Book" provision did "not import a gift of the debts thereby appearing to be due to the testator"; instead they made "his brother Robert not only his receiver, but his Bursar." In the latter function, he was to pay the debt surplus to the legatees, and in particular to plaintiff as residuary legatee. The "Book" provision did not give the debts to Robert Bolling; on the contrary, "we claim the debts, as a part of the residuum, undeniably, as we think, comprehended by" the clause making plaintiff residuary legatee.

Wythe had conceded that his adversary was correct on the common-law rule and that, as Jefferson put it at the beginning of his second argument, "to wit, that, putting our acts of assembly out of the question, Rob[ert] Bolling would be entitled to the emblements growing on the land at the testator's death." Jefferson therefore began his second argument by disputing Wythe's contention "that our acts of assembly have taken these emblements from the devisee." "Turn to the words of the act... ," Jefferson urged, "and you will not find a syllable expressing that the emblements are to be taken from the devisee; nor yet that they are to be given to any other person." Based on his reading of the statute, Jefferson maintained, "if property in the soil then will draw to it property in the plant, where both the plant & the labor are accessions, much rather shall a property in the soil and plants (as Rob[ert] Bolling had) draw to them the accession of labor alone"—here the "accession of labor" of the slaves as provided by the statute. "Justice and Analogy with the fabric of the law in similar cases," Jefferson declared, "carry it to the proprietor of the soil, and authorize my position that the labor of the slaves is annexed, or is an accession to the Emblements, is become homogeneous with them, and consequently is the property of him who can entitle himself to them: i.e. of the devisee of the lands in the present case." This line of reasoning "contradict[s] the position of the pl[aintiff]'s counsel 'that the emblements are annexed to, & incorporated with the labor of the slaves.'" To argue the other way, Wythe "has been oblige[d] to go out of the circle of nature and reason: for I think I may say his case is framed so extravagantly, that... it never can have happened."

Jefferson repeated his argument on the meaning of "assets." When the statute said that the crop was to "be assets in the hands of ex[ecuto]rs," he urged, it singled out only one of its properties—"liableness to debts." This meant that "it clearly remains as it was as to the other two, to wit, not liable to pecuniary legacies, nor to be thrown into the residuum." Jefferson urged "that these plants were a specific legacy to Rob[ert] Boll[ing]." If the testator had expressly given "'to Rob[ert] Boll[ing] my Buffalo-lick lands with the emblements now growing thereon', the emblements would have been admitted to be as much a specific legacy as the lands themselves." Yet, "when he sais 'I give to Rob[ert] Boll[ing] my Buffalo lick lands' this in law includes a bequest of the emblements then growing as perfectly as if he had expressed himself in the first form. The words therefore used in the first form 'with the emblements now growing thereon' would have been surplusage." Jefferson referred to the "maxim in law that 'the omission of that which would have been surplusage shall not vitiate.' the latter form therefore carries them clearly as a specific legacy." Hence, "let the act 'untortured, unperverted, uninterpolated' speak for itself," and what it said plainly supported Jefferson's interpretation.

Jefferson then used the analogy of an estate *pur autre vie*, where the leading case, *Oldham v. Pickering*, supported his view. The only difference was that *Bolling* involved a freehold estate. Jefferson sarcastically stated that "the pl[aintiff]'s counsel seems to think there is some magick quality in a freehold estate which will exempt that from being made distributable by words which would at the same time make any other estate, not possessing that particular magic quality, liable to distribution." There was no "mystical quality supposed to be in a freehold estate" to support such a distinction between freehold and other estates.

According to Jefferson, what the cases showed as to the effect of the Virginia statute was "'that an act introducing new alterations in the nature of any estate, shall not be intended to reverse the whole nature of that estate in every point, but only to alter those qualities particularly expressed to be altered.' and consequently that in the present case the act of ass[embly] by making emblements liable to *debts* has not taken away their deviseable quality, nor yet given them a distributable one where they had it not before."

Jefferson devoted the remainder of his second argument to rebutting Wythe on the "Book" provision in the will. Here, Jefferson asserted, "I shall still rest on what was said in the argument for the def[endant]. which does not appear to be shaken by any thing advanced on the other part." Two portions of Jefferson's argument on the "Book" question are of particular interest, though they do not concern the merits of that question. Wythe had accused Jefferson "of 'interpolating' a clause in the will." Jefferson pointed out that he "had said 'a gift of his book' is synonimous with a 'gift of his debts paying thereout what he owed.' and again... 'it is as if he had said "I give him my outstanding debts except so much as is requisite to pay what I owe."'" Jefferson explained that "these expressions were in both instances intended to be paraphrastical on the testator's words: for I take that to be paraphrase where you professedly use words of your own to explain more at large what you conceive the writer to have expressed shortly. whereas an interpolation is a wilful substitution of words in the writer's text with design that they shall pass as the words of the writer." No one who understood the distinction, said Jefferson, could accuse him of misquoting the will. Instead, "let him only for a moment then attend to the expressions objected to and say whether they are offered to the reader as the identical words of the test[ato]r, or as my own paraphrase on his words."[273]

Jefferson also got back at his opponent by mocking Wythe's earlier effort to question the authorities cited by Jefferson.[274]

273. Compare the issue of fabricated quotations. *Masson v. New Yorker Magazine*, 501 U.S. 496 (1991).

274. Compare Dumbauld, *Jefferson and the Law*, 113.

Wythe had relied upon *Brown v. Selwin*, in which Lord Chancellor Talbot had said that "it is not necessary to be determined" whether "a debt be assets to pay legacies in general," but had then stated, "I am at present inclined to think it may; but shall not bind myself by giving my opinion 'til the case happens." Referring by implication to Wythe's punctilio in attacking his authorities, Jefferson retorted, "All delicacy about authorities seems now to have subsided." He then declared,

> here is the inclination of a Chancellor on a point which had not been argued, which was not in question, which could never come but incidentally before the court of which he was judge but belonged properly to the department of the Common law, and on which he does not pronounce even an obiter dictum, but expressly reserves his opinion till the case should happen; this I say is produced to contradict a judge within whose proper province the question lay, who declared it to be his opinion, not merely his inclination, who supported this opinion by authorities, & whose judgment in a question of Common law (tho' perhaps it might give way to that of a Holt, as would the opinion of any judge who had lived since the days of Lord Coke, yet) surely is not to be controlled by that of a Lord Chancellor Talbot.

Respect for his mentor did not lead Jefferson to tone down his attacks upon opposing counsel in the case. Yet it was Wythe who had the last word, for it is his lengthy reply (it takes up sixty-two pages, this portion also recorded in Anderson Bryant's hand) that ends the *Bolling* manuscript. Judge Dumbauld has characterized Wythe's reply as "largely a repetition of previous points, punctuated with cunning jabs at any maladroit expressions which Jefferson had chanced to use in the course of his discussion of the case."[275] Wythe's ripostes tend to belie his reputation as only an "engaging pedant."[276]

Two examples illustrate a skill in forensic fencing that one does not usually associate with the legal scholar. Referring to Jefferson's attempts to define "assets," Wythe noted:

> lawyers and judges frequently speak of a sufficiency of assets[,] and a deficiency of assets. the defendants counsel uses that language several times in the last page of his argument of which this explanation makes as good english as a sufficiency of a sufficiency and a deficiency of a sufficiency, or enough of enough and not enough of enough. but enough of this logomachy; especially as the defendant's counsel emancipating the word we have so much reason to be tired with, objects not to the adoption of another, to wit, liableness...

Wythe's "word play"[277] is as adroit as any of the Jefferson sallies which have been mentioned. In his argument on the "Book" provision, Jefferson had relied on the term "give up," contending that it was a devise of the testator's credits versus his debts, with the surplus remaining to Robert Bolling after the debts were paid. Wythe argued that, under Jefferson's interpretation of the term, "'given up' must be understood in a sense the plaintiff's counsel cannot find it

275. Id., 114.

276. David J. Mays, *Edmund Pendleton: A Biography*, 2 vols. (Cambridge, Mass.: Harvard University Press, 1952), 2:292.

277. Dumbauld, *Jefferson and the Law*, 115.

to have been ever understood in before." Contrary to Jefferson's interpretation, Wythe asserted, "there is not any [instance] wherein, the word signifies to part with, and transfer the property of a thing one hath an undisputed right to dispose of to another; which is conceived to be included in the idea of a legacy." Indeed, Wythe testily noted,

> To give up the ghost is to die. an apostate is said to give up his religion; a woman to give up her virtue, when she becomes a prostitute. to give up a friend is to betray him, to desert him, to have no further connection with him.... to give up an argument is no longer to continue the dispute; which was the meaning of the defendant's counsel when he said 'I might venture to give up the question.'

Mention should also be made of Wythe's reply to Jefferson's defense of his paraphrases of the will—what Wythe called "the mutilation and metamorphosis it suffers by such a paraphrase." Jefferson's argument, Wythe maintained,

> is founded... not in the will but, in a paraphrase, as it is called, supposed to be more expressive of the testator's meaning than his own language[,] a dangerous kind of reasoning. two or three paraphrases have been made of this clause, and then the author singling out one of them makes it his thesis for an argument, leaving the will as if we had nothing more to do with it.

## *Bolling* and the Bar

It is not known who won the *Bolling* case, but since Jefferson's

Case Book records that he charged his client £5, but received £9.17 from the latter, it is probable that he prevailed. The case was still on the General Court's chancery docket in October 1772, doubtless awaiting confirmation of the arbitrator's decision. The records do not reveal when that occurred.

If we are not entirely certain about the ultimate outcome in *Bolling*, we can nevertheless be clear on what the case tells us about the state of legal advocacy on the eve of the American Revolution. Judge Dumbauld, who discusses the *Bolling* arguments in his *Thomas Jefferson and the Law*, concludes his discussion:

> The arguments of counsel in *Bolling v. Bolling* constitute a splendid specimen of the professional powers and proficiency of the Virginia bar in the years immediately preceding the American Revolution. Both Thomas Jefferson and his former preceptor George Wythe displayed enormous erudition and handled with skill and resourcefulness the pertinent legal materials relating to the novel, intricate, and difficult questions under consideration. Statutory provisions were scrutinized with thoroughness; the language of judicial decisions and authoritative treatises was analyzed with acute perceptivity. Considerations of logic, history, and public policy were attentively weighed. But likewise both adversaries exhibited astute alertness in the rough and tumble combat of forensic conflict, in quoting an opponent's own words against himself, in sprightly sallies of wit, in resort to *argumentum ad hominem* and *reductio ad absurdum*, in clearness and cogency of expression. In every respect their performance was worthy of renown,

> and added lustre to the high esteem in which both men were held by fellow lawyers and their countrymen.[278]

One who reads the *Bolling* argument is bound to agree with Dumbauld. The *Bolling* argument is of great interest two centuries later, not only because it presents two outstanding legal minds in action, but, also and even more so, for what it reveals about the early American bar. *Bolling* shows that at the least the leaders of the American bar were as learned in the law as their counterparts on the other side of the Atlantic. More than that, it strikingly demonstrates that American law was still essentially the common law. The Jefferson and Wythe arguments are outstanding examples of the common law in action; with regard to both substance and technique, Westminster Hall and the Virginia General Court were not as far apart as they might have seemed.

Considering the relative paucity of legal materials available in the colonies at the time, Jefferson and Wythe cite an impressive number of English authorities, including both cases and treatises going back to the origins of English law. The American conception of law was thus already based on a system of case law. To practitioners such as Jefferson and Wythe, the famous Holmes conception of law, which seemed so "audacious and even revolutionary for the time,"[279] would not have appeared strange at all. As explained by Jerome Frank, Holmes's concept was that "Law is made up… of the

278. Id., 119–20.

279. Benjamin Kaplan, "Encounters with O.W. Holmes, Jr.," *Harvard Law Review* 96 (1983): 1828–52 (quote at 1829).

decisions [of the courts] themselves."[280] This was, of course, the conception of law upon which Jefferson, Wythe, and their contemporaries at the bar relied in their legal arguments. The law to which they appealed was primarily that contained in the law reports available to them.

The big gap in this respect was, of course, the lack of American law reports. "When I came to the bench [1798]," writes James Kent, "there were no reports or State precedents."[281] The situation in Virginia was similar. At the time of *Bolling*, decisions there were reported only in manuscript and were not generally available.[282] Jefferson himself, as noted, collected these whenever he could and also "began to commit to writing some leading cases of the day."[283] They formed the basis for Jefferson's *Reports*, among the earliest cases in any Virginia law reports.

In the eyes of Jefferson and Wythe as well as their contemporaries at the bar, the law consisted of both cases and the legal principles and maxims inductively derived from court decisions. Thus, Jefferson's *Bolling* argument contains a strong plea in favor of *stare decisis*—the principle requiring adherence to precedent. It also relies on the maxim *ejusdem generis*, under which, in Jefferson's way of putting it, "words of doubtful meaning may receive illustration

280. Jerome Frank, *Law and the Modern Mind* (New York: Tudor Publishing Co., 1930), 125.

281. *Memoirs and Letters of James Kent*, ed. William Kent (Boston: Little, Brown & Co., 1898), 117.

282. Dumbauld, *Jefferson and the Law*, 75.

283. *Jefferson's Reports*, 5.

from others in their neighborhood." Thus, referring to Wythe's claim that the gift of the testator's "Book" for "receipt of the debts" only gave defendant the fiduciary duties of executor. Jefferson replied, "For a moment suppose it doubtful whether the 'receipt of his debts' was intended to be beneficial, or fiduciary. The context, to wit, the 'gift of the book' explains the doubt and proves a beneficial devise intention."

Jefferson also used *ejusdem generis* to support his argument by reference to the will's provision making plaintiff residuary legatee. "We cannot believe that in enumerating the principal articles of the residuum he was giving he would mention such trifles as his horses and clothes, and omit the capital article of outstanding debts." Jefferson illustrated this point by the following analogy: "so a man who had just made the tour of America, would hardly say 'he had visited the towns of Contocook, Kenderhook, Concord, and all the other towns of America.' Boston, New York, Philadelphia, as being the great and principal objects, would first strike his mind in recollecting and enumerating the places he had visited, and would most certainly be mentioned."

The *Bolling* arguments, of course, recognized the principle, by then accepted in the law on both sides of the Atlantic, that statutes might modify and even override the common law. Much of the Jefferson-Wythe efforts were devoted to the statutes that, Wythe contended, had changed the common-law rules governing emblements, as well as to relevant English statutes. The statutory arguments are comparable in quality to those on the common law, showing the facility of the bar in working with statutory materials.

A suggestive passage in Wythe's argument indicates that there may be limits to the legislative power to override the common law. Wythe gave the example of a legislative act that set plants in the soil of Robert Bolling. In such a case, "they are not the plants of Rob[ert] Bolling; unless the act of assembly set them there by *wrong*." But, Wythe asserted, "an act of assembly cannot work injustice or wrong, whereas in such a case as this, it violates no divine or moral precept."

Wythe as a judge is remembered today largely because of his opinion in the 1782 case of *Commonwealth v. Caton*.[284] There, as summarized in the notes of Edmund Pendleton, who presided over the *Caton* court, Wythe "urged several strong and sensible reasons… to prove that an Anti-constitutional Act of the Legislature would be void; and if so, that this Court must in Judgment declare it so, or not decide according to the Law of the land."[285] According to Call's *Virginia Reports*, Wythe was even more eloquent, declaring that, if a statute conflicted with the Constitution, "I shall not hesitate, sitting in this place, to say, to the general court, Fiat Justitia, ruat coleum; and, to the usurping branch of the legislature, you attempt worse than a vain thing."[286] In *Caton*, an early American judge declared the power of judicial review. Is it too fanciful to find the germ

284. 4 Call 5 (Va. 1782).

285. Notes of "The Case of the Prisoners" in the Court of Appeals, 29 October 1782, in *The Letters and Papers of Edmund Pendleton*, ed. David J. Mays, 2 vols. (Charlottesville: University Press of Virginia for Virginia Historical Society, 1967), 2:416–27 (quote at 426).

286. 4 Call 8.

of Wythe's opinion in *Caton* in his suggestion in *Bolling* that there were limits on legislative power?

The sophistication in the use of statutes at the time is shown by Jefferson's animadversion in *Bolling* on the use of statutory preambles in statutory interpretation: "nothing is less to be depended on than the allegations in the preambles of modern statutes. the facts set forth in them, are most commonly mere creatures of the brain of the penman, & which never existed but in his brain. that this is true with respect to our own acts of ass[embly] we all know too well.... it is also true with respect to the English acts."

Jefferson also adopted a most unlawyerlike attitude toward the language in which statutes are usually drafted. "I dislike the verbose and intricate style of the English statutes," Jefferson wrote in an 1817 letter. He enclosed a bill he had drafted in "the simple [style] of the ancient statutes." He sarcastically suggested, "You, however, can easily correct this bill to the taste of my brother lawyers, by making every other word a 'said' or 'aforesaid,' and saying everything over two or three times, so that nobody but we of the craft can untwist the diction, and find out what it means; and that, too, not so plainly but that we may conscientiously divide one half on each side."[287]

It is of particular interest that both counsel in *Bolling* stressed the social purpose to be served by the rules that they stated. Wythe urged that it would encourage agriculture to have emblements go to

287. Thomas Jefferson to Joseph C. Cabell, 9 September 1817, in *The Writings of Thomas Jefferson*, ed. Andrew A. Lipscomb and Albert Ellery Bergh, 20 vols. (Washington, D.C.: Thomas Jefferson Memorial Foundation, 1903), 17:417-18 (quote at 417).

the sower's representative, for the same reasons that induce the law to have personal chattels go to the representative carrying out a testator's will. Jefferson countered with the claim that the social interest would be furthered by recognizing a devise as comparable to a conveyance. Jefferson traced the development of the right to alienate property, starting with Glanville in the twelfth century. The basic theme was the removal of restrictions on alienation in order to encourage agriculture and other productive enterprises. Jefferson based much of his argument on this development: "the purpose of this short account of the progress of alienation is to shew that a devise is but another mode of alienation or conveiance." Hence, "when the testamentary alienation becomes perfect, by the death of the devisor, the devisee is on the same footing as he would have been if the conveiance had been by deed."

Jefferson also relied on social purpose in his interpretation of the Virginia statute that provided for continued labor by slaves on crops in the ground when the landowner died. Wythe had argued that "it is unjust that the devisee of the land should have the profit of slaves devised to another person." Jefferson replied that the principle "is in some degree unjust. but yet this private injury is made to give way to public good, which is promoted by the encoragement of agriculture.... in fact there is no way wherein so little injustice will be done to individuals, and so much good effected for the state as by annexing the labor of slaves to the Emblements, and making it follow them into whatever hands they go."

Both Jefferson and Wythe were relying upon the instrumentalist conception that was to be the foundation of American law. The law was stated as a means, not an end. The legal rules advocated were put forth as instruments to bring about desired practical results. In this respect the *Bolling* argument indicates that the instrumentalist conception was characteristic of American jurisprudence at an earlier date than had been thought. In *The Transformation of American Law, 1780–1860*, the leading work on the subject, Morton J. Horwitz writes that it was only after the Revolution that American lawyers and judges "for the first time" began "to reason about the social consequences of particular legal rules." Referring to the "increasing preoccupation with using law as an instrument of policy in the early years of the nineteenth century," Horwitz asserts that "[t]wo decades earlier it would have been impossible to find an American judge" using such an approach.[288] The *Bolling* argument shows that such a view is mistaken.

As men of the eighteenth century, both *Bolling* counsel also appealed to what Jefferson called "the laws of nature… the great original from which our Saxon ancestors as well as the Roman lawyers copied their several institutions." Yet, if they relied on "the circle of nature and reason" (as Jefferson termed it in another portion of his argument), they did so more as a matter of form than substance. Their presentation was made almost entirely in terms of the common law and statutes. In this respect, their argument was one that could have been made not only by their confreres at Westminster but also by attorneys at the present time.

The *Bolling* argument thus indicates that the basic legal techniques used by lawyers today were well known during our law's for-

288. Horwitz, *Transformation of American Law*, 2–3.

mative era. It is even more significant that both Jefferson and Wythe relied not only on cases and statutes but also on the social purposes to be served by the legal principles they were advocating. The early jurist could, with Jefferson in *Bolling*, deliver encomia on *stare decisis* and stress the need for fixed legal rules so that, as Jefferson put it in his argument, "judges will determine, counsel advise, and even the people themselves proceed, at once with certainty and precision." But emphasis on the social purposes served by law necessarily meant that legal rules that no longer served those purposes should be replaced by those that would.

Jefferson the lawyer thus soon gave way to Jefferson the law revisor. American jurists had to construct a legal system that would answer the needs of what would become a continental community and economy, rather than those of the confined island kingdom in which the common law had developed. But it was not only the physical setting that differed so drastically from that on the other side of the Atlantic. American law had to be adapted to the new nation's political and social institutions. As early as the *Bolling* argument, the law had received the instrumentalist cast that was ultimately to predominate in American jurisprudence.

## On the Eve

A revolution made by lawyers? The very phrase is an oxymoron, "since as a class, lawyers are among the most conservative elements in the community."[289] By training and temperament, the

289. Edwin C. Surrency, "The Lawyer and the Revolution," *American Journal of Legal History* 8 (1964): 125–35.

legal profession emphasizes continuity rather than revolutionary transformation. "Then why should the majority of leaders in this revolutionary movement have been lawyers?"[290]

The *Bolling* argument can help answer this question. It graphically demonstrates the caliber of the American bar on the eve of the struggle for independence. By the latter part of the century, the leaders of the bar had become the leaders of the society. By the time of *Bolling* the lawyers had come to the fore and were already the most influential members of the colonial legislatures. The *Bolling* argument shows that the lawyers were well qualified to assume the leadership role. And assume it they plainly did. As General Gage wrote from Boston, "The Lawyers are the Source from whence the clamors have flowed in every Province."[291]

The legal profession ensured that the struggle for American independence never went to the later extremes of the French and Russian revolutions. In 1775, John Adams met a horse jockey who had been his client, who expressed his joy that the courts were closed and said, "I hope there will never be another!" After this meeting, Adams asked himself, "Is this the Object for which I have been contending?"[292] Adams and his colleagues at the bar saw to it that the Revolution did not degenerate into the extremes, so common to revolutions. Instead, "the colonial bar managed the Revolution, kept it one for liberty under law."[293]

290. Id.

291. Quoted in id.

292. *Diary and Autobiography of John Adams*, 3:326.

293. Robert F. Boden, "The Colonial Bar and the American Revolution," *Marquette Law Review* 60 (1976): 1–28 (quote at 22; italics omitted).

Lawyers such as those who had argued the *Bolling* case found it natural to frame the revolutionary conflict in legal terms. Steeped in the common law, they would use it as the source of their political liberties. George Mason spoke for the majority of his compatriots when he declared in 1766 that the colonists claimed "nothing but the liberties and privileges of Englishmen, in the same degree as if we had still continued among our brethren in Great Britain."[294] In one of his early published papers, John Adams referred to his

> settled opinion that the liberty, the unalienable, indefeasable rights of men, the honor and dignity of human nature, the grandeur and glory of the public, and the universal happiness of individuals, was never so skillfully and successfully consulted, as in that most excellent monument of human art, the *common law* of England. A law that maintains a great superiority, not only to every other system of laws, martial, or cannon, or civil, but to all officers, and magistrates civil and military, even to majesty itself.[295]

Daniel Boorstin has written, "The American Revolution itself, led... by men who called themselves lawyers, was a vindication of legal rights."[296] For lawyers such as Adams, the conflict with Britain was basically a legal one. The dispute could be settled as other legal questions were, by appeal to the legal principles recog-

294. Quoted in id., 7.

295. [John Adams], "'U' to the *Boston Gazette*," 5 September 1763, in *Papers of John Adams*, 1:84–90 (quote at 86).

296. Daniel J. Boorstin, *The Americans: The National Experience* (New York: Random House, 1965), 35.

nized in common on both sides of the Atlantic. The colonial resistance to the ministerial measures was to be based on the ground that they were violations of English law, not of natural law. It was, at least before independence, a constitutional resistance within the lines of English law. To the lawyers, the notion of the Rights of Man made sense only when based upon the rights recognized by the common law.

Thus, the colonial lawyers, led by Adams, strongly opposed the courts of Vice Admiralty, which had been established to enforce the trade and navigation laws that controlled colonial commerce. Customs officers could bring enforcement suits in the Admiralty courts, which provided them with a more friendly forum, notably because recoveries by them could not be thwarted by hostile juries.[297] But the very factors that made the royal officials prefer the Admiralty courts made them anathema to lawyers like Adams. To Adams, the Admiralty courts represented the denial to Americans of basic rights guaranteed to Englishmen by the common law. In particular, the Admiralty courts did not follow common-law rules of procedure and evidence. "We are here to be tryed by a Court of civil not of common Law, we are therefore to be tryed by the Rules of Evidence that we find in the civil Law, not by those We find in the common Law. We are to be tryed, both Fact and Law is to be tryed by a single Judge, not by a Jury."[298]

297. Editorial Note, "Admiralty — Revenue Jurisdiction," in Wroth and Zobel, *Legal Papers of John Adams,* 2:99.

298. John Adams, copy of information and draft of argument in No. 46, *Sewall v. Hancock* (Court of Vice Admiralty, Boston), October 1768–March 1769, in id., 2:203.

What made the situation worse for the American lawyer like Adams defending his client in the Boston Court of Vice Admiralty was the fact that his English counterpart was not subject to the same handicaps. Thus, the American Act of 1764 provided expressly that comparable cases in Britain were to be tried only in the common-law courts.[299] "Here is the Contrast that stares us in the Face! The Parliament in one Clause guarding the People of the Realm, and securing to them the Benefit of a Tryal by the Law of the Land, and by the next Clause, depriving all Americans of that Privilege. What shall we say to this Distinction? Is there not in this Clause, a Brand of Infamy, of Degradation, and Disgrace, fixed upon every American? Is he not degraded below the Rank of an Englishman?" Indeed, urged Adams, the subjection to Admiralty jurisdiction amounted to "a Repeal of Magna Charta, as far as America is concerned."[300]

The spokesmen for the revolutionary cause, notably Adams and John Dickinson, wrote as traditional lawyers. The revolutionary documents drafted by them were legal papers that treated the dispute with the mother country as one involving essentially a conflict over different interpretations of English law. They argued that the actions of the British Government were gross violations of English law. In effect, their writings were the legal briefs that supported the American position during the nation's formative period. Their arguments were legal arguments that relied upon the common law as the basis upon which American grievances rested.

299. 4 Geo. III, c. 15, § 40 (1764): *American Act*, quoted and discussed in id., 200.

300. Id.

One who reads the *Bolling* argument is anything but surprised at the skill of the colonial bar in drafting the documents that supported the revolutionary cause. In addition, the argument shows Jefferson as fully able to make the transition from law to politics. The *Bolling* manuscript contains a convincing display of the ability that would enable both Jefferson and his colleagues at the bar to play their crucial roles in the national arena.

# Statement of Editorial Method

This edition of the Jefferson-Bryant manuscript of *Bolling v. Bolling* follows guidelines derived from the editorial methods of modern documentary editions, such as *The Papers of Thomas Jefferson, The Papers of John Jay*, and *The Mansfield Manuscripts.*

## I. Relationship between the Manuscript and this Edition

***Spelling*** follows the manuscript, reproducing Jefferson's and Bryant's spelling. For example, Jefferson habitually reversed "i" and "e" — as in "recieve" and "Mansfeild" — and often used "i" instead of "y" — as in "conveiance." (Because "habitually" does not mean "consistently," this edition also reflects the manuscript's inconsistencies of spelling.) Where the original spelling might confuse the reader, the modern equivalent appears in brackets following the word in question or in a footnote otherwise required. This edition does not use [*sic*].

***Abbreviated words and contractions*** omitting one or two letters have been expanded to full length silently. For abbreviated words and contractions omitting three or more letters, the supplied letters appear within square brackets. Letters given in superscript in the manuscript appear in normal size. This edition silently drops (1) words inadvertently repeated by the original copyists, as when the last word of a page is repeated as the first word of the next page, and (2) "page-turning" words that appear in the bottom-right corner of each page of the manuscript.

***Capitalization*** follows the manuscript. Jefferson did not capitalize the first words in sentences; Bryant's transcriptions of Wythe's pleadings and arguments display similar patterns of capitalization, suggesting that Jefferson might have learned this practice from Wythe or that it was a common practice in the 1770s.

***Punctuation*** follows the manuscript. This transcript reproduces Jefferson's and Bryant's eclectic mix of periods, colons, semicolons, and dashes to indicate the ends of sentences. Jefferson and Bryant also used single quotation marks to indicate quoted material and double quotation marks to indicate quotations within quotations. This edition follows their practice, while silently standardizing inconsistencies — for example, it supplies opening or closing quotation marks (in brackets) omitted in the manuscript. This edition also drops the marginal quotation marks used in the manuscript to indicate quotations running longer than one line. For cancelled material given in footnotes, and for quoted material not indicated as such in the original manuscript, see paragraphs (d) and (e) under *Typography*.

***Typography*** follows the manuscript:

(a) The relationship between ***typefaces used in this edition*** and the orthography of the manuscript is complex. Jefferson and Wythe used a variety of means to emphasize words and to present citations. Thus, most of the manuscript — written in ordinary script — appears in normal type; words printed in the manuscript appear in *italics*; words underscored in the manuscript appear underlined.

(b) ***Paragraphing and indenting*** reproduce those of the manuscript as closely as possible.

(c) This edition omits the ***ornamentation*** that Jefferson and Bryant used to fill out lines or provide the manuscript equivalent of justified margins. Jefferson and Bryant sometimes used ***spacing within paragraphs*** to indicate pauses or to break up trains of thought; this edition silently standardizes spacing between sentences within paragraphs.

(d) ***Crossed-out words and symbols***, where diverging in substance from the finished manuscript, appear in footnotes, enclosed in angled brackets: for example, <&>. Crossed-out words and symbols merely duplicating material in the manuscript are dropped silently.

(e) ***Quoted material not indicated as such***: Jefferson and Wythe sometimes transcribed extracts from cases, statutes, and legal commentaries without labeling such extracts as quotations. Their practice is consistent with that of other writers in the eighteenth century.[1] Quoted material not so indicated in the manuscript appears within double angle brackets; for example: <<it was so ordered.>>

(f) The ***manuscript's pagination***, established in 1975 by the Henry E. Huntington Library, is indicated by boldface numbers preceded by the letter H and enclosed in ornamental brackets — **{H16}** — placed to indicate the beginning of the relevant manuscript page. Marginal page numbers, which Jefferson and Bryant

1. See the discussion of John Adams's *A Defence of the Constitutions of Government of the United States* (1787–1788), *Discourses of Davila* (1790–1791), and other writings in Zoltan Haraszti, *John Adams and the Prophets of Progress* (Cambridge, Mass.: Harvard University Press, 1952), 46–48, 155–65, 169–71.

used intermittently to indicate the pagination of the original pleadings and arguments, have been dropped; where the manuscript refers to the original pagination, footnotes give references to the Huntington pagination.

## II. Annotation

***Legal terms and phrases in Latin and Law French*** are translated and defined in footnotes the first time they appear, and in the glossary. Passages in Latin longer than ten words — for example, extracts from Justinian and Bracton — are translated in notes but not in the glossary, with annotation indicating (where possible) the source of such quotations. The index indicates the first appearance in the text of each defined legal term. Definitions appearing in the footnotes and the glossary are based on *Black's Law Dictionary* (6th ed.); the *Oxford English Dictionary* (1st and 2nd editions); the *Oxford Latin Dictionary*; Henry Broom, *A Selection of Legal Maxims,* 8th American edition from 5th London edition (Philadelphia: T. & W. Johnson & Co., 1882); and other law dictionaries and reference works.

***Identifications*** of judges, lawyers, legal commentators, and other persons mentioned in the manuscript appear in footnotes. Each note giving identifying information appears at the first mention of the person identified, and is listed in the index. Reference works these footnotes draw on include:

- the *Dictionary of National Biography*;
- the *Dictionary of American Biography*;

☐ J. H. Baker, *The Legal Profession and the Common Law: Historical Essays* (London: Hambledon Press, 1986);

☐ J. H. Baker, *The Order of Serjeants at Law: A chronicle of creations with related texts and a historical introduction* (London: Selden Society, 1984) (supplemental series, volume 5);

☐ John D. Cowley, *A Bibliography of Abridgments, Digests, Dictionaries and Indexes of English Law to the Year 1800* (London: Quaritch [for the Selden Society, 1932]; reprint, Holmes Beach, Fla.: Wm. W. Gaunt & Sons, Inc., 1979);

☐ Edward Foss, *Biographia Juridica: A Biographical Dictionary of the Judges of England from the Conquest to the Present Time, 1066–1870* (London: John Murray, 1870; reprint, Glashütten im Taunus: Detlev Auvermann KG, and London: Wiley & Sons Ltd., 1971);

☐ N. G. L. Hammond and H. H. Scullard, eds., *The Oxford Classical Dictionary*, 2nd edition (Oxford: Clarendon Press of Oxford University Press, 1970);

☐ Sir William S. Holdsworth, *A History of English Law*, 16 vols. (London: Methuen, 1922–1966);

☐ Sir John Sainty, *The Judges of England, 1272–1990* (London: Selden Society, 1993) (supplemental series, volume 10);

☐ Sir John Sainty, *A List of English Law Officers, King's Counsel, and Holders of Patents of Precedence* (London: Selden Society, 1987) (supplemental series, volume 7);

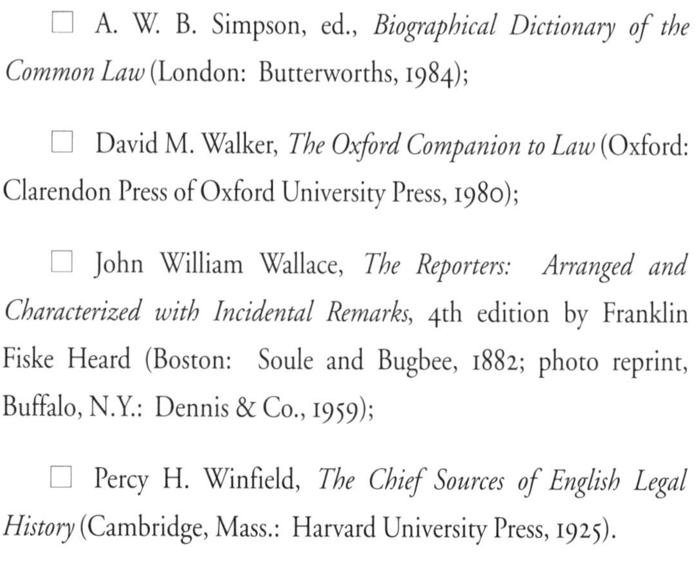

- A. W. B. Simpson, ed., *Biographical Dictionary of the Common Law* (London: Butterworths, 1984);

- David M. Walker, *The Oxford Companion to Law* (Oxford: Clarendon Press of Oxford University Press, 1980);

- John William Wallace, *The Reporters: Arranged and Characterized with Incidental Remarks*, 4th edition by Franklin Fiske Heard (Boston: Soule and Bugbee, 1882; photo reprint, Buffalo, N.Y.: Dennis & Co., 1959);

- Percy H. Winfield, *The Chief Sources of English Legal History* (Cambridge, Mass.: Harvard University Press, 1925).

## III. Citations

***Citations of statutes, cases, and legal authorities*** follow the manuscript. Jefferson and Wythe placed quotations either before or after the relevant citations; no clear pattern explains why citations sometimes precede and at other times follow quotations. To avoid confusion, footnotes indicate the connections between citations and quotations.

The forms of citation in the manuscript demonstrate the many differences between practices of legal citation and quotation in the era of *Bolling v. Bolling* and modern standards. Footnotes give equivalent modern citations; the reader seeking explanations for specific abbreviations should consult the table of abbreviations following this statement of editorial method. Reliable guides to the law books available to Jefferson and Wythe include:

- W. Hamilton Bryson, ed., *Census of Law Books in Colonial Virginia* (Charlottesville, Va.: University Press of Virginia, 1978);

- E. Millicent Sowerby, ed., *Catalogue of the Library of Thomas Jefferson*, 5 vols. (Washington, D.C.: Government Printing Office, 1952–1959).[2]

As shown by the *Bolling v. Bolling* manuscript, Jefferson and Wythe were well-versed in the bewildering variety of English legal reports, treatises, and commentaries; the modern reader will find an authoritative exposition in J. H. Baker, *An Introduction to English Legal History*, 3rd edition (London: Butterworths, 1990), chap. 11.

### Statutes

Footnotes give modern citations to statutes cited in the manuscript. Jefferson and Wythe cited statutes only by regnal year, chapter, and sometimes section, or by general descriptive phrases, such as "the statute of frauds," "the statute of distribution," or "the slave act." They often failed to distinguish between English and Virginia statutes; when they did make such distinctions, they referred to an "act of Parliament" to signify an English or British statute and an "act

2. Sowerby's catalogue details the holdings of Jefferson's library as of 1814, when he sold it to the United States to replace the original Library of Congress, burned in the fires set by British forces during the occupation of Washington, D.C. See Dumas Malone, *Jefferson and His Time: The Sage of Monticello* (Boston: Little, Brown, 1981), 169–184; Sowerby, *Catalogue*, 1: *passim*; and Thomas Jefferson (James C. Gilreath and Douglas L. Wilson, eds.,), *Thomas Jefferson's Library: A Catalog with the Entries in His Own Order* (Washington, D.C.: Library of Congress, 1989), *passim*. Jefferson's library was similarly destroyed by fire in 1770; thus, there is no record of the law books he owned at the time of *Bolling v. Bolling*. See Dumas Malone, *Jefferson the Virginian* (Boston: Little, Brown, 1948), 125–126.

of assembly" to signify a Virginia statute. Occasionally, they referred only to "the statute" or "the act of assembly;" in such instances, footnotes identify the statute under discussion. Sometimes, they provided the wrong citation for the statute they were discussing. When the statutory citation given in the manuscript is incorrect, the correct chapter or section number appears bracketed in text.

The first note to each statute gives its full title and citation, as explained below. Subsequent notes provide only the regnal year, chapter, jurisdiction (if a Virginia statute), and date. If the manuscript quotes a statute, the note cites that provision, with a page reference to the appropriate statutory compilation.

For **English statutes**, footnotes cite the most widely-available contemporary edition: Danby Pickering and G. K. Richards, eds., *The Statutes at Large, From Magna Charta to the End of the Eleventh Parliament of Great Britain, Anno 1761–1869*, 109 vols. (Cambridge: J. Bentham for C. Bathurst, 1762–1869).[3]

For **Virginia statutes**, footnotes cite to William Waller Hening, ed., *The Statutes at Large*, 13 vols. (Richmond, Va.: Franklin Press, 1820–1823; reprint, Charlottesville, Virginia: University Press of Virginia for the Jamestown Foundation of the Commonwealth of Virginia, 1979).[4]

3. This edition appears in notes and the index of authorities as *Statutes at Large* (Pickering). Readers are also referred to *Statutes of the Realm*, 12 vols. (London: G. Eyre and A. Strahan, 1810–1822; reprint, London: Dawson of Pall Mall, 1963), and to Owen Ruffhead, ed., *The Statutes at Large: From Magna Charta to the... 39th Year of the Reign of King George the Third, Inclusive*, 8 vols. (London: M. Baskett et al., 1763–1799).

4. Footnotes cite to Hening, ed., *Statutes at Large*. The 1979 edition reprints the second editions of vols. I–IV: Volumes I–II (New York: Printed for the editor by R. and W. and G. Bartow, 1823); Vol. III (Philadelphia: Printed for the editor by Thomas DeSilver, 1823); Volume IV (Richmond: Printed for the editor by Franklin Press, 1820).

## *Cases*

For **English reported cases**, footnotes cite to the authoritative and accessible compilation *The English Reports*,[5] by volume and page numbers, court (where noted), and date and calendar term (where given),[6] with parallel citations to the original reporter, and to any other reports of the same case in *English Reports*. The first note to each case gives its full citation. Subsequent notes give the case name and its citation in *English Reports* only; subsequent citations to cases with more than one reported version give the name of the original reporter in parentheses following the case name. Where the manuscript refers to a case having multiple reported versions already cited, but does not provide a specific cite or quote, such references are not annotated. Cases often vary widely, even wildly, in their spelling of parties' names and the designations of plaintiff and defendant;[7] the notes to this edition reprint case names exactly as given in *English Reports*, with no attempt to standardize case names. Readers should remember the warning of James Burrow (or Burrough), compiler of one of the most highly regarded series of English law reports: "No sort of inaccuracy is

5. *The English Reports*, 176 vols. (Edinburgh: W. Green, and London: Stevens, 1900–1932; reprint, Abingdon, Oxon.: Professional Books Ltd., 1980).

6. The English high courts (King's Bench, Chancery, Common Pleas, and Exchequer) sat during four terms: Hilary (beginning in January); Paschal (beginning after Easter Sunday); Trinity (beginning after Whitsunday, 50 days after Easter Sunday); and Michaelmas (beginning in November).

7. See the valuable discussion of this problem in James Oldham, *The Mansfield Manuscripts and the Growth of English Law in the Eighteenth Century*, 2 vols. (Chapel Hill, N.C.: University of North Carolina Press, 1992), 1: xxix ¶ 11.

more frequent amongst note-takers, than an inattention to the precise names of the cases and the transposing of the names of the plaintiffs and defendants."[8] Annotations to the manuscript's transcriptions of cases indicate substantive divergences or omissions — but not mere mechanical differences — from the texts as given in *English Reports.*

**English cases from the Year Books**[9] appear in the manuscript designated only by regnal year and either *placitum* (pl. — the paragraph or case number within the term) or page number (to the compilation described below). Year Book entries do not bear case names with the familiar form of named plaintiff *versus* named defendant. Each term of each regnal year has its own case numbering, and in printed compilations each regnal year has its own pagination. Footnotes cite a compilation of Year Book reports generally used by eighteenth-century lawyers:

☐ *Les Reports del Cases en Ley, Que furent argues en le temps de tres Haut & Puissant Princes Les Roys Henry le IV. & Henry le V. Ore Novelment Imprimes, Corriges, & Amendes, avec le Notations & References al Brook, Fitzherbert & Statham.* (London: Printed by George Sawbridge, William Rawlins, and Samuel Roycroft, Assigns of Richard and Edward Atkins Esquires, 1679);

8. Quoted in id., from 5 Burr. 2659–2660.

9. See William Craddock Bolland, *The Year Books* (Cambridge: Cambridge University Press, 1921); William Craddock Bolland, *A Manual of Year Book Studies* (Cambridge: Cambridge University Press, 1925), esp. 61–82, on the published editions; and Baker, *Introduction to English Legal History*, 204–207, 225–27.

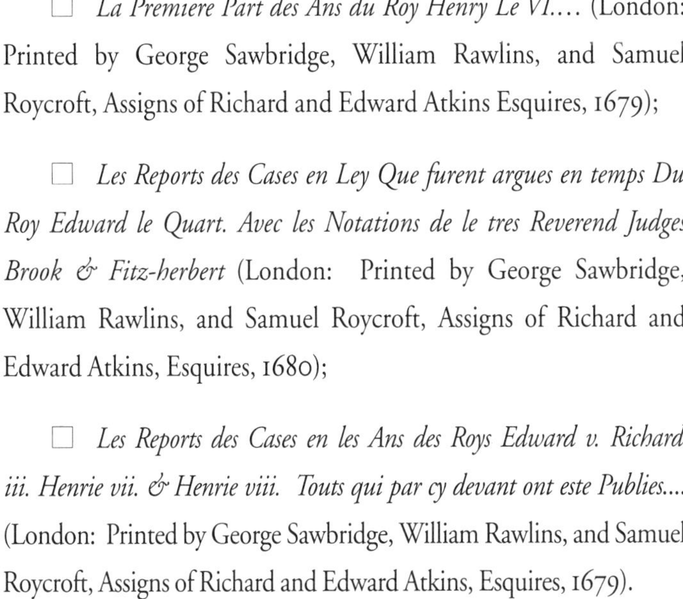

☐ *La Premiere Part des Ans du Roy Henry Le VI....* (London: Printed by George Sawbridge, William Rawlins, and Samuel Roycroft, Assigns of Richard and Edward Atkins Esquires, 1679);

☐ *Les Reports des Cases en Ley Que furent argues en temps Du Roy Edward le Quart. Avec les Notations de le tres Reverend Judges Brook & Fitz-herbert* (London: Printed by George Sawbridge, William Rawlins, and Samuel Roycroft, Assigns of Richard and Edward Atkins, Esquires, 1680);

☐ *Les Reports des Cases en les Ans des Roys Edward v. Richard iii. Henrie vii. & Henrie viii. Touts qui par cy devant ont este Publies....* (London: Printed by George Sawbridge, William Rawlins, and Samuel Roycroft, Assigns of Richard and Edward Atkins, Esquires, 1679).

Although historians of English law have subjected this seventeenth-century compendium to rigorous and justifiable criticism,[10] it was the only compilation of Year Book entries available to eighteenth-century American lawyers such as Wythe and Jefferson.

**Virginia cases** were not regularly reported until after the American Revolution. Thus, colonial lawyers had access only to colleagues' manuscript notes. The manuscript cites only one Virginia case, from a report then available only in manuscript but since published.[11]

10. See Baker, *Introduction to English Legal History*, 207–208.

11. *Tucker &c. vs. Tucker's Exors* (April Court, 1740), in R. T. Barton, ed., *Virginia Colonial Decisions, II: The Reports by Sir John Randolph and by Edward Barradall of Decisions in the General Court of Virginia 1728–1748* (Boston: Boston Book Co., 1909), B100–B105. The case was reported by Barradall.

### *Legal authorities*

Jefferson and Wythe used terse, often cryptic citation forms for legal authorities; footnotes give citations in modern form. Footnotes cite (1) the edition most likely to have been used by Jefferson or Wythe, (2) accessible reprints of contemporary editions, or (3) modern editions. The index of authorities gives a ready reference to the legal commentaries, treatises, dictionaries, and form-books that Jefferson and Wythe cited in *Bolling v. Bolling.*

Grateful acknowledgments to the following for scholarly and research assistance:

Professor J. H. Baker, Cambridge University and New York University Law School; Professor William P. LaPiana, New York Law School; Professor James Oldham, Georgetown University Law Center; Professor David Thomas Konig, Washington University, St. Louis, Missouri;

Ene Sirvet, Editor, *The Papers of John Jay*, Columbia University; Dr. Gaspare J. Saladino, Co-Editor, *The Documentary History of the Ratification of the Constitution and the Bill of Rights*, University of Wisconsin — Madison; Dr. Kenneth Russell Bowling, Co-Editor, *The Documentary History of the First Federal Congress*, George Washington University; Dr. John Catanzariti, Editor, *The Papers of Thomas Jefferson*, Princeton University;

Laura Bedard, Special Collections Librarian, Georgetown University Law Library; Elizabeth Evans, Gretchen Feltes, Carol Alpert, and Ron Brown, New York University Law Library; Chris

Knott and Whitney Bagnall, Special Collections Librarians, Columbia University Law Library; and Deborah Paulus, Marta Kiszely, Kate McLeod, Camille Broussard, and Roy Basit, New York Law School Library;

Joanne B. Freeman, Department of History, University of Virginia; Phillip A. Haultcoeur; Steven Geoffrey Kern; L. D. Kern; and Homer Higgins.

Special thanks to Professor John Phillip Reid of New York University Law School, who shared with us his unpublished monograph demonstrating that, when President Franklin Pierce installed the first Christmas tree in the White House, he chose a tree that was an emblement from those once at issue in *Bolling v. Bolling.*

R. B. Bernstein Barbara Wilcie Kern

## Table of Abbreviations

| | |
|---|---|
| **A.G.** | Attorney General |
| **B.R.** | *Banco Regius* — King's Bench |
| **C.B.** | *Common Banco* — Common Pleas |
| **C.J.** | Chief Justice |
| **C.P.** | Court of Common Pleas |
| **Ch.** | Court of Chancery |

| | |
|---|---|
| **Exch.** | Court of Exchequer |
| **J.** | Justice |
| **K.B.** | Court of King's Bench |
| **L.C.J.** | Lord Chief Justice |
| **n.c.** | no court given |
| **n.d.** | no date given |
| **pl.** | *placitum* — the paragraph or case number, a component of the citation form for both Year Books and legal treatises arranged by numbered paragraphs. |
| **Q.B.** | Court of Queen's Bench |
| **S.C.** | same case |
| **S.G.** | Solicitor General |

# {H1} A[rchibald] Bolling v. Rob[ert] Bolling[1]

Archib[ald] Bolling sets forth that Edward Bolling[2] was siesed[3] of the lands &c hereafter ment[ione]d in fee,[4] and poss[esse]d of slaves, & personal estate viz, household furniture, money, plate, stocks &c. & outstand[ing] debts: July 13, 1769 made his will, wherein, inter alia,[5]

he divised[6] his Buffalo lick plant[atio]n and 5 negroes with the increase of 2. of them to def[endant] & his heir. the Old town plantation, his warehouse at Pocahontas, and lots at Bermuda hundred to Archibald in fee

£100 to his sister Sara [Sarah] Tazewell

declared it was 'his will and desire that his book be given up to his bro[the]r Robert, that he recieve all the debts due to him

1. The statement of facts is in Thomas Jefferson's handwriting. It summarizes the plaintiff's bill in equity, the defendant's answer, and two depositions. Archibald Bolling (1750–1827), the plaintiff, was the youngest of the three sons of John Bolling of Cobbs (1700–1757). Robert Bolling (1738–1775), the defendant, was John Bolling's oldest son. See generally J. A. Leo Lemay, ed., *Robert Bolling Woos Anne Miller: Love and Courtship in Colonial Virginia*, 1760 (Charlottesville: University Press of Virginia, 1990).

2. Edward Bolling (1746–1770), the testator, was the second son of John Bolling of Cobbs.

3. possessed of real property under claim of freehold estate.

4. a type of possessory interest in an estate in land; usually short for "fee simple absolute," the broadest form of possessory interest in land, with no limits on duration of possession or the holder's ability to transfer the interest.

5. among other things.

6. devised; disposed of real property by will.

(the test[ato]r)[7] and pay 'all that he owed.'

gave several other legacies, and

'the rest of his estate, negroes, horses, clothes, and every other part of his estate not already given he gave and bequeathed[8] to his bro[the]r Archibald Bolling for him and his heirs for ever.'

after making the said will he sold the warehouse at Pocahuntas to Neill Buchanan for £500

Aug. 10. 1770. departed this life.[9]

Rob[ert] Boll[ing] proved the will[10] and undertook [e]x[ecutio]n thereof, as virtually appointed [e]x[ecuto]r.[11]

complains that said Rob[ert] Boll[ing] retains the crop of Indian corn, wheat, tob[acc]o and other things growing and made at Buffalo lick — the outstanding debts, — the £500 due from Buchanan — 8 h[ogs]heads tob[acc]o shipped by the test[ato]r to Gr. Britain and not acc[ounte]d for when he died, as specifically devised to him, and not chargeable with the test[ato]r's proportion of a debt due from the estate of his father John Bolling to mess'rs Hyndman

7. one who devises or transfers real and personal property by a will.

8. given (of personal property) to another person by a provision of a will.

9. The date of Edward Bolling's death is given as 18 August 1770 in Edward Dumbauld, *Thomas Jefferson and the Law* (Norman, Okla.: University of Oklahoma Press, 1978), 99 and 220–21n91.

10. to offer a will for confirmation by the authorities according to law. The will was probated on 1 October 1770, and Robert Bolling qualified as executor on 5 November 1770. Dumbauld, *Jefferson and the Law*, 221n93, citing Amherst County (Va.) Will Book (1761–1780), 184–86, Virginia State Library, reel 17.

11. a person appointed by a testator to carry out directions and requests in the testator's will, including offering the will for probate after the testator's death and disposing of the property in the testator's estate according to the will's provisions.

& Lancaster, nor to the paiment of Sara [Sarah] Tazewell's legacy.
insists that whatever was growing on the lands of annual produce the year the test[ato]r died, is, by law, his personal estate and included in the residuum[12] and
that the clause desiring the said Rob[ert] to receive and pay debts does not purport a legacy to him of the outstanding debts, but they passed to pl[aintiff] as part of Residuum.
prayer is that def[endant] may make inventory of all test[ato]r's estate

an acc[oun]t of the crops made on test[ato]r's lands the year he died

and of all the debts due to him

and pay and deliver the residue with interest after discharging test[ato]r's debts and legacies

**{H2}** Answer. admits the facts stated in the bill and adds

that after selling the Pocahuntas warehouses the test[ato]r in contempl[atio]n of the money due to him for them made purchases to a greater amount, which purchases (except one [of] about £20. value) go to the complainant under the residuary devise;[13] so that the def[endant] has these purchases to pay for, ought to have the money which was intended to pay them; but be this as it will, the sale was a revoc[atio]n of the devise and the price cannot be claimed

12. residuary estate — the part of a testator's estate not otherwise specifically bequeathed by the testator's will.

13. the clause of a will by which the testator grants the residuary estate (or residuum); also a grant by provision of a will.

by the pl[aintiff] under that devise.

he claims also an extinguishment[14] of a debt of £235. due from the def[endant] to the test[ato]r.

he gives up the proceeds of the 8 h[ogs]heads of tobacco,[15] and only considers them as equalling the other parts of the residuum subject to the paiment of the test[ato]r's prop[ortio]n of John Boll[ing]'s debt to Hyndman and Lancaster, and of Sara [Sarah] Tazew[ell]'s legacy, which are not by the test[ato]r charged on the fund given this def[endant].

he has deliv[ere]d all the residuum except the price of the 8 h[ogs]heads tob[acc]o — the crop severed before the test[ato]r's death — a few hogs, cattle &c purchased by this def[endant] of the pl[aintiff] for £162.2 — all which he proposes to apply to Hyndman's debt, and Sara [Sarah] Tazew[ell]'s legacy.

he asserts his claims in opposition to the pl[aintiff]'s claims in the bill stated, except what is before given [up] refers to a stated acc[oun]t as part of his answer.

## Dep[ositio]ns[16] taken by consent. Archelaus Mitchell.

he was present when E[dward] Boll[ing] made his will; after making it test[ato]r told him he had left his

14. the destruction or cancellation of a right, power, contract, or estate.

15. <except>

16. a written record of a witness's sworn answers to questions posed to the witness by an attorney.

bro[the]r Rob[ert] his lands on this side the river, such and such slaves, and 'that he was to pay all his debts and recieve what was due to him.'

heard him often after say the same, but never heard him say any thing of his being the ex[ecuto]r or accountable for [what] he sh[oul]d recieve of his outstanding debts.

from his convers[atio]n always understood and verily believes he intended the outstanding debts a legacy to Rob[ert].

Hanna Mitchell

was present when test[ato]r made his will and deliv[ere]d to her husband to keep. her husband said he s[houl]d be sorry to see his will take place.

test[ato]r answ[ere]d it w[oul]d make no odds, for he had given his land on this side the river (on which her husband was then living as overseer) to his bro[the]r Rob[ert] and several slaves which he named 'and that his bro[the]r Rob[ert] was to pay what he owed and to recieve what was due to him' and that he [was] as good an emploier as any in the country.

She understood and believes E[dward] B[olling] intended his outstanding debts as a legacy to his bro[the]r Rob[ert] and that he sh[oul]d pay all the debts due from him.

{H3}

# Archib[ald] Bolling v. Rob[ert] Bolling

## G[eorge] Wythe's Argum[ent] for pl[aintiff][17]

17. This section of the manuscript, in Thomas Jefferson's handwriting, gives George Wythe's first argument for the plaintiff, Archibald Bolling.

{H4} Archibald Bolling v. Robert Bolling, G. Wythe's argum[ent]: verbal

[I.] Emblements[18] are not part of the inheritance nor considered as fixed to the freehold,[19] but are chattels personal,[20] to be put in the inventory Swinb. VI. 7.(3)[21] may be taken in exec[utio]n Vent. 222.[22] Swinb. III. 6 (10)[23] 2. Black. 222. 145. 246. 403.[24] yea they are in law, before they be severed, mobilia.[25] Swinb. VII. 10.[26]

the property of Emblements is distinct from the ownership of the soil. Bro. Emblem'ts. ¶ 9. 15. 26.[27] Park. 512.[28] they therefore fol-

18. crops annually produced by the labor of a tenant.

19. an estate in land for life or in fee of uncertain duration.

20. articles of personal property (as opposed to real property). Also known as "movables."

21. Henry Swinburne, *A Treatise of Testaments and Last Wills*, 6th ed. (London: Printed by Henry Linton, 1743), Part VI, "Of divers Questions about the Making of an Inventory: And, first, Whether it be of Necessity that an Inventory be made," chap. 7, ¶ 3, at 420. On Swinburne, see infra note 272.

22. *Perrot versus Bridges*, 1 Ventris 222, 86 E.R. 149 (K.B., Trinity 1673).

23. Swinburne, *Treatise of Testaments and Last Wills*, Part III, "What Things may be devised by will," chap. 6, ¶ 10, at 219.

24. Sir William Blackstone, *Commentaries on the Laws of England*, 4 vols. (1765–1769; reprint, Chicago: University of Chicago Press, 1979), 2: 222 (fee simple); 2: 145 (emblements); 2: 246 (escheats); 2: 403 (emblements). See infra note 273.

25. movable things; personal property or chattels personal.

26. Swinburne, *Treatise of Testaments and Last Wills*, Part VII, "What Things are to be put into the Inventory," at 421.

27. Sir Robert Brooke, *La Graunde Abridgement, Collecte & escrie par le Judge tres reverend Syr Robert Brooke Chivalier...* ([London]: Richard Tottell, 1576), s.v. "Emblements," ¶¶ 9, 15, 26, at fol. 260a–260b. Sir Robert Broke (or Brooke) (d. 1558), serjeant-at-law (1552), C.J., C.P. (1554–1558), author of *La Graunde Abridgement* (1568).

28. John Perkins (or Parkins), *A Profitable Booke... Treating of the Lawes of England...* (London: Printed by R.B..., 1641), chap. 8, "Devises," ¶ 512, at 224–25. See infra note 274.

low the person of the sower, if he have interest in the land, the continuance whereof is incertain, at the time of sowing unless his estate determine by his own act. If it be true that emblements are no part of the inheritance, but mere personal chattels following the sower, the consequence is, that they will not pass with land by a devise, or by a conveiance[29] of the latter, unless there be some other word used to include them: for 1. a devise or conveiance of land passes only such things as are fixed to the freehold, among which emblements are confessedly not reckoned. 2. a devise or conveiance of land simply, passes no more than would descend without it; but emblements, do not descend to the heir with the inheritance which the law casts upon him.

Obj. Cro El. 61. fol. 3.[30]

Ans 1. Coke[31] taking it for granted that the ex[ecuto]r of the devisor[32] had no right to the Emblements, propounded to the justices this question only; whether the ex[ecuto]r of ten[ant] for life,[33] or he in rem[ainde]r[34] should have them? their opinion therefore was

29. conveyance — a disposition of property by written agreement executed by a living person.

30. *Case 3. Anonymous*, Croke, Elizabeth 61–62, 78 E.R. 321–22 (Q.B., 1587–1588).

31. Sir Edward Coke (1552–1634), barrister, Inner Temple (1578), S.G. (1592), A.G. (1594), C.J. C.P. (1606–1613), C.J. K.B. (1613–1616; author of Reports (parts 1–11, 1600–1615; unfinished parts 12–13, 1656–1659), *First Part of Institutes (Coke on Littleton)* (1628); *Second Part of Institutes* (1642); *Third and Fourth Parts of Institutes* (1644; *Fourth Part* unfinished at Coke's death).

32. one who disposes of real property by will.

33. a tenant who holds possession of premises by permission of a landlord or owner for the duration of the tenant's life.

34. that possessory interest in an estate in land left over after those interests specifically limited by time or identity have expired—for example, O gives a life estate to A, remainder to B.

hypothetical, not a determination of the point in dispute between us, which is, whether or not the emblements passed by the devise of the land?

2. Wray[35] and Shute[36] contradict themselves. they supposing the emblements to have passed with the land. by the devise of the latter, infer from thence that the first ten[ant] for life dying before severance had no right to them. yet they admit expressly that the same ten[ant] for life might have granted them to another. nor is it necessary for the establishment of this opinion as authority and to clear it from inconsistency to explain how one can grant to another what he has no right to himself.

**{H5}** 3. there was a diversity of sentiments among the judges upon the question in that case.

4. it was not an adjudged case, but an extrajudicial opinion.[37] Vau. 382.[38]

Note. Sir G[eorge] Croke[39] was then but 27 years old. see his life by Sir Harbottle Grimstone[40]

35. Sir Christopher Wray (1524–1592), barrister, Lincoln's Inn (1550); serjeant-at-law (1567); J. Q.B. (1572–1574); C.J. Q.B. (1574–1592).

36. Robert Shute (d. 1590), barrister, Gray's Inn (1576); Baron, Exch. (1577–1585); J. Q.B. (1585–1590).

37. an opinion given by a judge or judges that did not grow out of an actual case or controversy legitimately before the court.

38. *Bole v. Horton*, Vaughan 359–92, 124 E.R. 1113–1129 (n.c., n.d.).

39. Sir George Croke (1560–1642), barrister, Inner Temple; J. C.P. (1625–1628); J. K.B. (1628–1641); reporter (in Norman French) of cases from 1580 to 1640.

40. Sir Harbottle Grimstone (or Grimston) (1603–1685), barrister, Lincoln's Inn; Master of the Rolls (1660–1685).

Obj. Cro El. 263 [463] fol. 11.[41]

Ans: Nothing can be concluded from the judgment in this case against the principle I rely on. A lessee for years of a ten[ant] for life is disseised;[42] the disseisor[43] lets the land to a ten[ant] for years[44] who sows it and before the crop is gathered, the ten[ant] for life dies. if lessee of ten[ant] for life had sown the land himself, he would have had a right to the corn, altho' it had not been severed before the ten[ant] for life had died. if he had entered and regained the possession before ten[ant] for life died, he would have had the same right to the corn as if he had sown it himself. for a man has a right to whatever is planted in or put upon his ground by another, without lawful authority. there the rule holds 'quicquid plantatur solo, solo cedit'.[45] Bro. Emblem 1. 3. 8. 11.[46] the sowing therefore by the lessee of the disseisor, who was a wrong doer was for the benefit of the lessee of ten[ant] for life. consequently the judgment of the court that the corn appurtained to Hawkins the lessee of the ten[ant] for life affirms the principle that emblements follow the person of the sower, if he have interest in the land the continuance whereof is incertain at the time of sowing.

41. *Sir Henry Knevett against Pool and Hawkins and Two Others,* Croke, Elizabeth 463–64, 78 E.R. 701–702 (Q.B., Trinity 1594).

42. dispossessed or deprived of a possessory interest in land.

43. one who dispossesses or deprives another of a possessory interest in land.

44. one who holds possession of premises by permission of a landlord or owner for a specified period of time.

45. Whatever is affixed to the soil, belongs to the soil.

46. Brooke, *La Graunde Abridgement,* s.v. "Emblements," ¶¶ 1, 3, 8, 11, at fol. 260a.

In the argument of this case Tanfeild[47] said 'if a man sows land and lets it for life and the lessee for life dies before the corn be severed, his ex[ecuto]r shall not have them, but he in reversion,'[48] i.e. he who sowed. 'but if he himself i.e. the ten[ant] for life, sowed the land and died, it were otherwise, i.e. the ex[ecuto]r of ten[ant] for life who sowed, not he in rev[ersio]n, who had a right to the soil, should have[49] the corn.'[50] so far the case is an authority for the pl[aintiff].

But it will perhaps be quoted by the other side for this part of it.[51] 'So adds Tanfeild Mich. 29. 30. Eliz.[52] there was a case in this court, where a man sowed his land, and devised his land for life, rem[ainde]r in fee, ten[ant] for life dies, the corn not severed; the quest[ion] was whether the ex[ecuto]r or he **{H6}** in rem[ainde]r should have it? and held that he in rem[ainde]r.' which case sais the reporter they 'all agreed.' the case alluded to by Tanfeild is that of

47. Sir Lawrence Tanfield (or Tanfeild) (d. 1625), barrister, Inner Temple (1569); Chief Baron, Exch. (1607–1625); J. K.B. (1606–1607). The quotations following this note are from Tanfield's argument for the plaintiff in *Sir Henry Knevett against Pool and Hawkins and Two Others*, Croke in 78 E.R. at 701–702.

48. the residue possessory interest in an estate — belonging to the grantor or his heirs (or the heirs of a testator) — which takes effect by operation of law at the termination of a particular possessory interest granted or devised. For example, when O gives Blackacre to A for life, O and his heirs retain a reversion by which Blackacre returns to their hands on A's death.

49. <a right to>

50. This quotation from Tanfield's argument breaks off after the word "otherwise."

51. *Sir Henry Knevett against Pool and Hawkins and Two Others*, Croke in 78 E.R. 701–702: quote at 702.

52. 1577–1578.

Cro El. 61.[53] which I have before attempted, and shall further endeavor to shew is of no authority, and against which the case I am animadverting upon, militates. for in that it was agreed by Gawdy[54] and Popham[55] 'if ten[ant] for life sows the land, and grants over his estate, and the grantee dies before the corn severed, his ex[ecuto]r shall not have the corn, but he who sowed the land.'[56] now if in that case the person who sowed the land had a right to the crop, why should not the ex[ecuto]r of him who sowed the land in the case of Cro. El. 61.[57] and devised it, have the corn likewise? if the grant of the estate did not convey the emblements in one instance, why should the devise of the land convey them in the other instance? has not a purchaser who pays an equivalent, as much right, as a devisee[58] whose title is founded in the testator's benevolence? this case of Sir Henry Knevett is also reported in Goldsbor. 145. 60.[59] note in this reporter it is said to have been

53. *Case 3. Anonymous*, 78 E.R. 321–22.

54. Sir Thomas Gawdy (d. 1589), barrister, Inner Temple (1551); serjeant-at-law (1567); J. Q.B. (1574–1588).

55. Sir John Popham (1531?–1607), barrister, Middle Temple; S.G. (1579); A.G. (1581); C.J. Q.B. (after 1603, K.B.) (1592–1607).

56. *Sir Henry Knevett against Pool and Hawkins and Two Others* (Croke), 78 E.R. 701–702: quote at 702.

57. *Case 3. Anonymous*, 78 E.R. 321–22.

58. one who receives real property by will.

59. *Sir Henry Knevett against Pool and Hawkins and Two Others*, Gouldsborough 143–45, 75 E.R. 1053–1054 (Q.B., Trinity 1594). John Gouldsborough (1568–1618), law reporter; Middle Temple. On his *Reports* (1653), see J. H. Baker, *The Legal Profession and the Common Law: Historical Essays* (London: Hambledon Press, 1986), 250.

adjudged that Pool should have the corn; in Croke[60] that Hawkins should have it.

Obj. Hob. rep. 132. case 174.[61]

Ans. Altho' the judges in this case indeed agree [with] the case in Cro. El. 61.[62] yet they admit the sower to have a kind of property, ipso facto,[63] in the emblements distinct from the land; which is irreconcileable, unless we suppose the conveiance or will, in the case reported by Croke, to have expressly transferred or bequeathed the corn, by the word 'profits' or some other; and if so the case in Croke is nothing to the purpose. be that as it may, the case in Hob. admits expressly the principle I contend for. and what the case may be relied upon by the def[endant]'s counsel for was not the point in quest[ion]. therefor the lease was for a certain number of years, and as in that case, the emblements not severed at the expiration of the term, would not belong to the ten[ant]. it was covenanted that the ten[ant] might carry away the corn which should be growing at the end of the last year, and the only question was, whether, by such a covenant the lessee, or his ex[ecuto]r, had aright [a right] to the corn, there being no doubt that he would not have been entitled without such a cove**{H7}**nant, because the time of continuance of his interest was certain.

60. *Sir Henry Knevett against Pool and Hawkins and Two Others* (Croke), 78 E.R. 701–702.

61. *Grantham against Hawley*, Hobart 132–33, 80 E.R. 281–82 (K.B., Trinity 1616).

62. *Case 3. Anonymous*, 78 E.R. 321–22.

63. by the fact itself, by the very fact.

Obj. Godbolt. case 219.[64] <<it was adjudged in this court that if land, which was sowed, be leased to one for life, the rem[ainde]r to another for life, that if the ten[ant] for life dieth before the severance of the corn, that he in rem[ainde]r shall have the corn.>>
Ans. the case said to have been adjudged I suppose to be that reported by Croke. but if it were not, I cannot allow such a book as this to deserve much credit, the title of which is 'Reports of certain cases collected by very good hands, and lately reviewed, examined, and approved of by the late learned Justice Godbolt and now published by W. Hughes'.[65]

Obj. Winch 51. Mr Spencer's case.[66]

What was said in answer to Cro. Eliz. 61.[67] is partly applicable to this case. to which may be added that this is another unauthoritative publication, translated, as it is said, from a fair copy of Sir Humphrey Winch's in French. but all the cases were not collected by him, for in one of them (pa. 125) there is an eulogy of himself upon occasion of his death. whether this case was collected by Sir H[umphrey] Winch himself, or by some other hand the editor does not inform us.

64. *Case 219*, Godbolt 159, 78 E.R. 97 (C.P., 1609): quotation in 78 E.R. at 97. The quotation follows this citation. John Godbolt (d. 1648), barrister, Gray's Inn, 1611; serjeant-at-law, 1636; J. C.P., 1647–1648; reports revised by Godbolt were published in 1653.

65. William Hughes (1587?–?), barrister, law writer, and publisher; Gray's Inn (1606).

66. *Mr. Spencers Case*, Winch 51–52, 124 E.R. 44 (C.P., Michaelmas 1623). Sir Humphrey Winch (1555?–1625), barrister, Lincoln's Inn (1581); J. C.P. (1611–1625); legal compilations published posthumously.

67. *Case 3. Anonymous*, 78 E.R. 321–22.

Obj. Wentworth's office of executor pa. 59.[68] 'put the case that a man dies in July &c. —[69] all these shall pass to one to whom the land is sold or conveied, if not excepted, though never so near reaping, felling or gathering.'

Ans. Wentworth was a compiler only, and what he sais of the sale or conveiance, since he quotes no authority is but his opinion, which was probably founded upon that leading case in Cro. El. 61.[70]

Having made these particular remarks upon the books that probably will be cited by the def[endant]'s counsel, I shall now

68. Thomas Wentworth, *The Office and Duty of Executors: or, A Treatise directing Testators to Form, and Executors to Perform their Wills and Testaments according to Law... And now enlarged with a Supplement,... by H[enry] Curson, of the Inner-Temple* (orig. ed., 1641; London: Printed by Eliz. Nutt and R. Gosling, 1728), chap. V, "What Things shall come unto Executors, and be Assets in their Hands, and what not," 59. Wentworth (1568?–1628) was a member of Lincoln's Inn. Some authorities attribute the book to Sir John Doddridge (or Dodderidge) (d. 1628), king's-serjeant; J. K.B. (1612–1628).

69. The dash replaces the following from Wentworth, *Office and Duty of Executors*, 59:

> (before Harvest I mean) seized for Life, or in Fee or Tail, in his own Right or his Wife's, or estated for Years of Land in the Right of his Wife, being sown with Corn or any manner of Grain, the common Saying is, *Quicquid plantatur solo, solo cedit*: Yet this shall go to the Executor of the Husband, and not to the Wife or Heir, who shall have the Land; but Hay, growing, viz. Grass ready to be cut down, Apples, Pears, and other Fruit upon the Trees, shall go to the Wife; as also if they had been upon a Man's own Land of Inheritance, they should go to the Heir, though the Corn should go to the Executor. The Reason of the Difference is, because this latter comes not merely from the Soil without the Industry and Manurance of Man, as the other do: And I take Hops, though not sown, if planted, and Saffron and Hemp because sown, to pertain as Corn to the Executor.

70. *Case 3. Anonymous*, 78 E.R. 321–22.

shortly review them, and subjoin an observation, or two upon the same subject.

1. that emblements will pass with land by a simple devise or conveiance of the latter does not appear to have been a point judicially determined in any reporter of authority; but the sayings of judges to that purpose in Croke and Hob. were obiter opinions,[71] and such are of no great weight at any time. Vau 382.[72]

**{H8}** 2. some of the books relied on for the def[endant] contradict one another, and almost every one contradicts itself and besides they are ill reported.

3. authors of the best credit establish the principles from whence it undeniably follows that emblements do not pass by a conveiance or devise of the land to a purchaser or devisee any more than they descend to an heir, with the land, as it is admitted they do not. and

4. in conformity with these principles the point hath been expressly so determined. In Leon. Launton's ca. Hil. 20 Eliz.[73] Vin. abr. Emblements pa. 373. pl. 82.[74]

It is admitted that the emblements which were severed the 18th day of August when Edward Bolling died, were part of his personal

71. *obiter dictum* — an observation or remark made by a judge in pronouncing an opinion in a case, concerning some rule, principle, or application of law, or a solution of a question suggested by a case at bar, but not necessarily involved in that case or essential to its determination. Any statement of the law enunciated by the court merely by way of illustration, argument, analogy, or suggestion.

72. *Bole v. Horton*, 124 E.R. 1113–1129.

73. *Launton's Case*, 4 Leonard 1, 74 E.R. 685 (Q.B., Hilary 1578).

74. Charles Viner, *A General Abridgment of Law and Equity...*, 23 vols. (Aldershot: Printed for the Author, 1741–1753), s.v. "Emblements," 9: 373 ¶ 82. See infra note 275.

estate and bequeathed with the residue. harvest was then over, so that Arch[ibald] Bolling is entitled to the wheat. part of the tobacco was cut, and to that he is equally intitled. how then can we distinguish the plants which were severed from those which were standing when he died? in truth the crop after severance is not properly emblements, which are sown &c growing. the law gives the emblements to the representatives of a sower when he dies before they be reaped to encorage agriculture and they are as much his separate property and as subject to the regulations which concern personal chattels as his cattle, household furniture, and the like. the distinction therefore between crops growing and crops gathered, is unsound and not warranted.

but if Rob[ert] Bolling had a right to the plants which were standing when the test[ato]r died, he has lost it. if Titius intermixes his own corn &c and that of Gaius,[75] without consent of the latter, so that the one cannot be known from the other so the quantities be ascertained, the whole mass becomes the property of Gaius.

If the principles upon which the pl[aintiff]'s claim to the crop is founded be true, as they certainly are, the conclusion from them in support of his title cannot be avoided and then the cases in Croke &c. are not law. for they directly dispute the conclusion unless a good reason can be shewn why a deviser of **{H9}** land should have more right to the emblements than an heir. but the contrary is true for an heir is ever more favored than a devisee. indeed the matter does not appear to have been so well discussed, or so maturely con-

75. Writers on civil law use the fictitious names Titius and Gaius in examples, as writers on common law use the fictitious names John Doe and Richard Roe.

sidered in those cases as that they ought to have any weight.

By 22. G2 c.5. s.30.[76] when any person shall die between the 1st. of March and the 25th. of Dec[ember] his servants and slaves shall be continued and emploied upon his plantation until the 25th of Dec[ember] for making and finishing the crop, which crop shall be assets in the hands of ex[ecuto]rs and adm[inistrato]rs[77] after deducting charges and sect. 31.[78] after the 25th. of Dec[ember] the servants and slaves shall be delivered to the persons having legal right to demand them. this act meddles not with the profits of land, leaving them as they were at the common law, but our lands being cultivated mostly if not altogether by slaves, if they should be removed immediately after the owner's death the crop on his ground must perish. to prevent this public as well as private loss, the act directs the crop, which might be in some forwardness by the 1st of March, to be finished by the slaves, who should for that purpose be continued on the plant[atio]n till Christmas. but how are their profits to be disposed of? the next produce of the whole crop is to go together: all shall be assets in the hands of ex[ecuto]rs and adm[inistrato]rs, i.e. shall be part of the decedent's chattels, subject

76. 22 Geo. II, c. 5, § 30 (Virginia 1748): *An Act directing the manner of granting probate of Wills, and Administration of Intestates Estates*, in Hening, ed., *Statutes at Large*, 5: 454–67: quote at 464.

77. a person appointed by the court or other legal authority to administer the assets and liabilities of a decedent who either has died without making a will, or whose will does not satisfy the legal requirements for a will.

78. 22 George II, c. 5, § 31 (1748), in Hening, ed., *Statutes at Large*, 5: 464–65.

to debts funerals and legacies. so that if it had been a question, whether emblements by the common law would pass by a devise of the land they grew upon, this act has resolved the question in the negative. by this confusion of the emblements of land with the profits of slaves the legislature has declared them to be homogenous, and the former consequently to be personal chattels, and then they must go as all other personal chattels go, without distinguishing such plants &c. as are cut from what are standing, indeed the law having directed the slaves to be worked upon the plant[atio]n until the crop be finished, it would be unreasonable that a devisee of the land should have the emblements. for if so, when a man devised his lands to one and bequeathed his slaves to another the former would have the benefits of both for the first year. in that instance land and the crop growing upon the land devised to R[obert] Bolling **{H10}** was finished by the very slaves bequeathed to A[rchibald] B[olling] or some of them. as to the intention of the test[ato]r in this case, since we can only conjecture what it was no conclusive argument is deducible from it either way. one thing is certain, if he had died in the month of November, when the crop would probably have been gathered and housed, instead of August, every grain and ounce of it would have belonged to the pl[aintiff] by the bequest[79] to him of the rest of the estate not already given. and it is apprehended he has in this case the same title to it, the emblements unsevered being part of the test[ato]r's personal estate disposed of by that clause, and not by the devise of the land to the def[endant].

79. a gift of personal property by will.

II. By these words 'it is my will and desire that my book be given up to my bro[the]r Robert, and that he recieve all the debts due to me, and pay all that I owe,' the def[endant] insists that he is entitled to all the test[ato]r's outstanding debts and amongst them to £500. the price of a warehouse at Pocahuntas, devised to his bro[the]r Archibald, but afterwards sold by the test[ato]r, that sale being an ademption[80] of the legacy. 'it is my will and desire that my book be given up to my brother Robert' can import no more than that his book, I suppose he meant his book of acc[oun]ts, should be deliv[ere]d to his bro[the]r, or that he should take charge of the book. the book did not contain all the debts, so that giving up that, be the meaning what it can, did not extend to other debts. this book was to be given up or delivered to him, that he might 'recieve all the debts due to the test[ato]r and pay all that he owed.' the debts due to him exceeding what he owed, the question is what shall become of the surplus? a reciever does indeed represent the person by whom he is appointed, as to the power of calling the debtors to account, and acquitting them, but does not succeed him in the right to use or dispose of the money, without some other act to transfer it. he is by the very nature of his substitution an agent for the benefit of, and accountable to, others. thus bailiffs, attornies, factors, must pay what they collect to their landlords, constituents, principals, or their successors. and so ex[ecuto]rs and adm[inistrato]rs are answerable to legataries[81] and next of kin. in truth the whole clause we are

80. extinction or withdrawal of a legacy by testator's act that, by indicating testator's intention to revoke, is equivalent to a revocation.

81. legatees; those to whom a testator devises or bequeaths personal property.

considering is but the appointment of an ex[ecuto]r enumerating and empowering him to perform the most **{H11}** eminent parts of that office, which are recieving and paying debts. and that will not entitle him to the surplus of the outstanding debts; for 1. he hath particular legacies by the will. 2. the whole surplus is in express terms bequeathed to the def[endant]. 'the rest of my estate not already given' includes the surplus of the debts.

Evidence parol[82] of a contrary intention not admissible; and if it were the evidence in this case proves nothing.

The appointment of a man ex[ecuto]r formerly, was a gift in law to him of all the test[ato]r's personal chattels, not disposed of in legacies to others, so that if one appointed an utter stranger ex[ecuto]r, and did not dispose of the residue of his estate, he retained it in exclusion of the test[ato]r's relations. but later determinations on this point have changed the law, which is now settled and agreed universally to be thus. 1. if particular legacies be given to the ex[ecuto]r, altho' the residue be not disposed of, the ex[ecuto]r shall be no more than a trustee for the next of kin, as to the surplus, unless it be proved by some kind of evidence, that the test[ato]r designed the surplus for the ex[ecuto]r. but 2. if the surplus be given away from the ex[ecuto]r, he is excluded, whether he have a particular legacy or not; neither can he be permitted to prove, by any extraneous evidence, that the test[ato]r designed the surplus, or any part of it, for him: for an express gift of the surplus to another is inconsistent with and so must prevail against, the gift which is

82. parol evidence — oral (spoken) evidence as opposed to documentary or physical evidence.

only implied in the appointment of an ex[ecuto]r, and shews that appointment to be fiduciary.[83] and evidence that the test[ato]r did design for one person part of that surplus, which he himself says another shall have, would not explain, but contradict the words of a will, which never was and never ought to be admitted. if then the clause 'it is my will and desire that my book be given up to my brother Robert, and that he recieve all the debts due to me and pay all that I owe' does not import a gift of the debts, and is no more than the appointment of an ex[ecuto]r; the surplus in this case being expressly bequeathed to Archibald Bolling that must prevail against the gift to Rob[ert] Bolling, implied in the appointment of him to the ex[ecuto]rship. it is agreed on all hands that the words 'recieve all the debts **{H12}** due to me and pay all that I owe' is a proper appointment of an ex[ecuto]r. the appointment of an ex[ecuto]r where the surplus is given away, and a legacy, are different things. The words therefore, which appoint the ex[ecuto]r, are not a legacy in this case. If the test[ato]r had said 'I appoint my bro[the]r Robert ex[ecuto]r' the book must have been given up to him; he must have received debts and paid what the test[ato]r owed. on the other hand, if R[obert] B[olling] had renounced the ex[ecuto]rship, he could not have claimed by this clause, which therefore must be fidei commissary,[84] not legatory.[85] the power 'to recieve debts' no more authorized the ex[ecuto]r to apply the

83. person bound by an obligation, as a trustee.

84. one who has the real or beneficial interest in an estate, the title or administration of which is temporarily confided to another.

85. of or pertaining to a legacy.

money to his own use, than the direction to 'pay all that the test[ato]r owed' obliged him to discharge out of his own estate the test[ato]rs debts if his estate had not been sufficient. This supplies matter for another objection against the def[endant]'s claim to the outstanding debts. if the debts due to the test[ato]r had been less than what he owed, the residuum, bequeathed to the pl[aintiff], must have made good the deficiency: for out of the residuary estate debts must be first paid. if then in case of a deficiency, the residuum must have been diminished, that, in the contrary event, it should be increased, is as true as that, quod sentit onus sentire debit et commodum,[86] is a maxim of pure equity. indeed if this clause is a legacy of the outstanding debts to the defendant, he is not obliged to apply any part of them to the paiment of what the test[ato]r owed, except in aid of the residuary estate, if that fund should be exhausted. This clause 'it is my will that my book be given up to my brother Robert, and that he recieve all the debts due to me, and pay all that I owe', is no more than the appointment of an ex[ecuto]r. it is not ex vi terminorum[87] a bequest of the surplus of debts. it is not a gift in law of the surplus, because the ex[ecuto]r hath particular legacies; and because the whole surplus is disposed of to the pl[aintiff] to construe this clause a legacy would be unequitable, because the residuum might be burthened, in one event, and yet not be relieved in another. Nay the residuum must be wholly burthened with the debts due from the test[ato]r; whereas all that are due to him will belong to the def[endant]: which

86. What has sustained the burden ought to derive the advantage.

87. from or by force of the term.

must appear the harder because the warehouse was certainly designed for the pl[aintiff] by the test[ato]r, who probably did not alter his will[88] **{H13}** after the sale, supposing the consideration money to be included in the residuum, as it would unquestionably have been if the test[ato]r had recieved the money.

It is therefore hoped the def[endant] will be decreed to pay to the pl[aintiff] the surplus of the debts, with the emblements. and for that purpose that an account[89] be taken. in this account the def[endant] must be debited with the money he owed. Brown v. Selwin Ca. temp. Talb. 240.[90]

88. <by the>

89. <may>

90. *Brown v. Selwin et contra,* Cases Temp. Talbot 240–44, 25 E.R. 756–58 (Ch., Michaelmas 1734).

{H14}

# Archibald Bolling v. Rob[ert] Bolling

## Argum[ent] for def[endant][91]

{H15 — blank}

91. This section of the manuscript, in Thomas Jefferson's handwriting, gives Jefferson's first argument for the defendant, Robert Bolling.

**{H16}** Edward Bolling was seised and poss[esse]d of certain lands, slaves, and chattels and on the 13th. day of July 1769 made his will in these words.

'In the name of god amen. I Edward Bolling of the county of Chesterfield being in perfect health of body and mind, but knowing it is appointed for all men born to die, am willing, and do dispose of my estate in the manner and form following; to wit: I give and bequeath to my brother Thomas Bolling and my brother John Bolling my plantation called and known by the name of Falling river, to be equally divided between them, the line to be run by my brother John Bolling and my brother Thomas to have his choice, for them, the said John and Thomas their heirs, ex[ecuto]rs, adm[inistrato]rs, and assigns for ever. I give and bequeath to my brother Robert Bolling my plantation called and known by the name of the Buffalo lick on the North side of James's river for him and his heirs for ever, as also my negroes Will, Joe, Bristol, Ball, Sarah, and Cis, with the children belonging to Sarah and Cis, for the said Robert Bolling and his heirs for ever. I give and bequeath to my brother Archibald Bolling my plantation called and known by the name of the Old town, as also my warehouses at the place called Pocahuntas, and my lots at Bermuda hundred, for him and his heirs for ever. I give and bequeath to my sister Mary Bland my negro woman Jane and all her children, except Louisa, for her and her heirs for ever[.] I give and bequeath to my sister Sarah Tazewell one hundred pounds for her and her heirs for ever. I give and bequeath to my sister Anne Bolling my negro girl Louisa and her increase for her and her heirs forever. I give and bequeath to my friend Richard Kid[der] Meade[92] my trusty servant Jack for him and his heirs for ever. it is my will and desire that my Book be given up to my brother Robert and that he recieve all the debts due to me, and pay all that I owe. I give and bequeath to my cousin Bolling Eldridge my negro fellow Bob that is now at work with him for him and his heirs for ever. the rest of my estate, negroes, houses, clothes and the other parts of my estate, not already given, I give and bequeath to my brother Archibald Bolling, for him and his heirs for ever[.] **{H17}** this is my last will and testament wrote this thirteenth day of July in the year of our lord one thousand seven hundred and sixty nine in my writing and as a proof whereof I have set my sig[nature] and affixed my seal. Edward Bolling. l.S.[93] before these witnesses Archilaeus Mitchell. Hannah Mitchell.'

sometime in the month of November 1769 he sold the warehouses at Pocahuntas to one Neill Buchanan. for £500. and in contemplation of the moneys due to him on this account made purchase to a greater amount, which (except one of about £20 value) now go to the pl[aintiff] as part of the residuum. he died on the 10th of August 1770 indebted to a considerable amount, but had also large sums of money owing to him: of which the £500 aforesaid due from Buchanan, and about £235 due from the def[endant] made a part. he kept a Book of accounts in which were stated the greater

92. Richard Kidder Meade (1749–1805), Virginia plantation owner and politician, later a soldier in the Continental Army and aide-de-camp to General George Washington in the Revolutionary War.

93. abbreviation for "locus sigilli," the place of the seal, indicating where the seal was affixed in the original document.

part, tho' not the whole of his Debts and Credits. an inconsiderable part of the tobacco at his Buffalo lick planta[tio]n of the growth of that year was severed at the time of his death: but far the greater part thereof. and all the Indian corn was then unsevered. this crop was finished by the slaves then working on the lands, seven of whom were among those bequeathed to the pl[aintiff]: six, being the residue, were those given to the def[endant]; There were two tenants on the land, one of whom was to pay a certain sum of money rent; the other was to pay a certain proportion of the clear profits of his tenemant; and the days of paiment were subsequent to the death of the test[ato]r. two years after his death, to wit, when Archibald Bolling attained his age, Then test[ato]rs estate became chargeable, in common with those of his other brothers, with the debts of John Bolling his deceased father. it happened thus. the said John Bolling had in his will directed that his debts and legacies should be paid out of the profits which should arise from the estates of his sons during their minority: each as he came of age being to take his part of the estate and have the unpaid debts a charge on the estates of his minor brethren till they should attain age. however when Archibald (the youngest of them) came of age, it was found that a consid[era]ble prop[ortio]n of the debts were still unpaid. then therefore it became necessary to divide equally among the several brothers, each of whom it is estimated, will have about £400 sterl[ing] and £50 currency to pay.

**{H18}** These are the facts which give rise to the opposite pretensions of Archibald Bolling the pl[aintiff] and Robert the def[endant]. those of the latter are to be now discussed in the following order.

I. under the devise of the Buffalo lick plant[atio]n he claims

1. the Emblements unsevered at the death of the test[ato]r
2. the Rents growing and not paiable till after his death

II. under the bequest of the test[ato]r's Book he claims

His test[ato]rs Credits burthened with his Debts. but

1. in the Credits he means to include the £500. due from Buchanan and
2. among the Debts charged on this fund, he does not reckon
   (a) Edward Bolling's proportion of his father's debts, nor
   (b) the legacy of £100. to Sarah Tazewell.

but if it should be thought the bequest of the book was merely fiduciary he then insists

III. That the debt of £235. due from him to the test[ato]r is extinguished.

I. That the def[endant] is entitled to the Emblements unsevered at the death of the test[ato]r

What first presents itself to us as a guide thro' this enquiry is the maxim 'quicquid plantatur solo, solo cedit.' a maxim derived from our earliest ideas of property. for whatever of an inferior value, is annexed to a subject of much greater, seems naturally to be a part of, and to belong to, that subject, and ought therefore as a dependant, or accessary to pass with it's principal. so sais Puffendorf[94] B. 4. c.7. §. 2.[95] 'it is a general rule in this case that

94. Samuel Pufendorf (or Puffendorf), Freiherr [Baron] von Pufendorf (1632–1694), German jurist and historian, early theorist of natural law and international law.

95. Samuel, Baron Pufendorf (Basil Kennet, trans.), *The Law of Nature and Nations: or,*

whoever is owner of a thing, to him likewise belong the accessions of it: which evidently flows from the very nature of property, and from the end for which it was first introduced, inasmuch as the possession of many things would be vain and useless should the fruits of them accrue to others.' and again sect. 5[96] 'it is likewise a common rule that things planted or sown shall go with the soil; because they are not only nourished by it, but, growing into a most strict union, and made as it were parts of the same body.' such too was the Roman law. Inst. L. 2. Tit. 1. §. 31.[97] 'Si Titius alienam plantum in[98] solo possuerit, **{H19}** ipsius erit, et ex diverso, si Titius suam plantam in Maevii solo possuerit, Maevii planta erit; si modo utroque casu radices egerit.'[99] et sect. 32. 'qua ratione autem plantae, quae terrae coalescunt, solo cedunt, eadem ratione frumenta

*A General System of the most Important Principles of Morality, Jurisprudence, and Politics. In Eight Books... To which is prefix'd M. Barbeyrac's Prefatory Discourse..., The Fifth Edition, carefully Corrected* (London: Printed for J. and J. Bonwicke, R. Ware, J. and P. Knapton, S. Birt, T. Longman, R. Hett, C. Hitch, T. Osborne, J. Hodges, S. Austen, E. Wicksteed, E. Comyns, T. Waller, J. and J. Rivington, J. Ward, and M. Cooper, 1749), Book IV, chap. 7, "Of Additional Acquirements," sec. 2, at 398. The quotation follows this citation.

96. Id., Book IV, chap. 7, "Of Additional Acquirements," sec. 5, at 399. The quotation follows this citation.

97. *The Institutes of Justinian with English Introduction, Translation, and Notes* (Thomas Collett Sandars, ed.; London: Longman, Green & Co., 1922), Lib. II, Tit. I, § 31, at 107. Justinian I, Emperor of the East (483?–565). The quotation follows this citation.

98. omitted: "suo"

99. "If Titius places another man's plant in ground belonging to himself, the plant will belong to Titius; conversely, if Titius places his own plant in the ground of Maevius, the plant will belong to Maevius— that is, if, in either case, the plant has taken root; for, before it has taken root, it remains the property of its former owner."

quoque, quae sata sunt, solo cedere intelligentibur.'[100] accordingly trees, grains, fruits, corn, roots, and whatever else nature had affixed to the earth, would doubtless originally pass with the earth to the same proprietor. yet at a period of our law, so early that our books tell us not when it was otherwise, our ancestors did so far dissolve this natural connection as to give to the legatee or ex[ecuto]r of the ten[ant] in fee simple[101] the corn which he had sowed but had not lived to reap. and this as the books all testify, on a political principle, to encorage agriculture for the benefit of the state. however the same reasons should have extended the constitution to other tenants also, yet we are informed by Brooke, tit. Emblements 10.[102] that it was not so extended till the stat[utes] of Merton 20 H.3.[103] his words are 'by Fortescue[104] and Danby[105] tinant [tenant] at will, and for term of life, for the life of another, and ten[ant] in tail,[106] shall have the emblements by the stat[ute] of Merton cap. 2. and

100. *Institutes of Justinian*, Lib. II, Tit. I, § 32, at 108: "As plants rooted in the earth accede to the soil, so, in the same way, grains of wheat which have been sown are considered to accede to the soil."

101. a possessory interest in land clear of any condition or restriction to a particular period of time or to particular heirs; the broadest interest that one can have in land.

102. Brooke, *La Graunde Abridgement*, s.v. "Emblements," ¶ 10, at fol. 260a.

103. 20 Hen. III, c. 1–11 (1235): *Statutes of Merton*, in *Statutes at Large* (Pickering), 1: 24–31.

104. Sir John Fortescue (1394?–1476?), C.J. K.B. (1442–1461); author, *De Laudibus Legum Angliae* (first published in 1537).

105. Sir Robert Danby (d. 1471?), serjeant-at-law (1443); J. C.P. (1453–1461); C.J. C.P. (1461–1471).

106. limited to a certain order of succession or to certain heirs.

ten[ant] in fee-simple shall have them by the common law.' these tenants seem to have been included within the equity of the stat[ute] of Merton (a mode of construction much used, and indeed necessary, at that time; when their laws were but short texts to be extended by the reason of their judges) for that stat[ute] only gives the unsevered Emblements to a <u>Dower</u>. Coke indeed 2. inst. 81.[107] seems to think she was entitled to them so early as the 4 H.3.[108] but Bracton[109] and Fleta[110] there cited, expressly say she was not till the 'nova provisio apud Merton facta,'[111] and they lived nearest the time spoken of, and thus was introduced a second maxim 'he who sows shall reap' which was made in many instances to controul the former 'quicquid plantatur solo, solo cedit.' yet are there occasions wherein the antient rule prevails to this day, and the Emblements following their natural connection, pass with the lands to which they adhere. thus, Brooke. Emblements 15.[112] 'baron and feme[113]

107. Sir Edward Coke, *The Second Part of the Institutes of the Lawes of England. Containing The Exposition of many ancient, and other Statutes*... (London: Printed by M. Flesher, and R. Young, 1642), 81.

108. 1220.

109. Henry de Bracton (d. 1268), judge; reputed author of *De Legibus et Consuetudenibus Angliae*, earliest known attempt at a systematic and practical treatment of English law.

110. *Fleta*: a Latin text of English law, written circa 1290, which took its name from the Fleet Prison. The unknown author of *Fleta* was probably a judge imprisoned by Edward I. See infra note 634.

111. new provision made at Merton.

112. Brooke, *La Graunde Abridgement*, s.v. "Emblements," ¶ 15, at fol. 260b. The manuscript translates from Brooke's Law French. The quotation follows this citation.

113. husband and wife.

tenants in tail sow the land. the baron dies before severance, the wife shall have the emblements and not the son of the baron.' and Co. Lit. 55. b[114] 'if husband and wife be jointenants[115] of the land and the husband soweth the ground, and the land serviveth [surviveth] to the wife, it is **{H20}** said that she shall have the corn.' and tho' in Rowney's case 2. Ver. 322.[116] the court in a similar instance being doubtful recommended a compromise, yet was it agreed that if the parties had been strangers jointenants, instead of husband and wife jointenants, no doubt could have been entertained but that the emblements would have gone with the land. this case then of jointenancy, where the emblements do not follow the person of the sower, but go with the soil to which they belong — seems to be a remain of our antient law. another remain of this law shews itself in these instances. a man having no right to the land enters and sows. the disseisee re-enters, or recovers by action.

114. Sir Edward Coke, *The First Part of the Institutes of the Lawes of England. or, a Commentarie upon Littleton, not the name of a Lawyer Onley, but of the Law it selfe*, 2 vols. (London: Printed for the Societie of Stationers, 1628), chap. 8, "Of Tenant at Will": quote at 1: 55. b. 7. (Hereafter *Coke on Littleton.*) Sir Thomas Littleton (1422–1481), serjeant-at-law (1453), J. C.P. (1466); author of *Tenures*, first published without title or date in London. The quotation follows this citation.

115. joint tenants; in common law, a form of ownership of real property in which two or more persons (usually a husband and a wife) hold real property. Joint tenants have one and the same interest and a right of survivorship; if either joint tenant dies, the other succeeds to the full interest in the property.

116. *Rowney's Case*, 2 Vernon's Cases in Chancery 322–23, 23 E.R. 808–809 (Ch., 1694). Thomas Vernon (1654–1721), barrister, Middle Temple (1679); compiler of chancery decisions (1681–1718; published 1726–1728).

he shall have the emblements. Bro. Emblem. 5. 8. 11.[117] a villein[118] leases. the lessee sows and dies. the lord of the villein enters. he shall have the emblements. ib. 25.[119] here the 'nova provesis [provisio]'[120] as Bracton calls it — and the adjudications founded on that, having failed to extend themselves to this sower because he was a wrong-doer, the emblements return into their natural channel, and become the property of him to whom the soil belongs. so where the sower has by his own act determined his estate in the land, the emblements follow their principal. thus if lessee at will determines his estate by desertion of it, Co. Lit. 55. b.[121] if a tenant during widowhood determines it by marriage, Moore. 512.[122] if a ten[ant] for life forfeits by aliening[123] in fee; or a copy holder[124] by non-performance of services Bro. Emblem 3. 4.[125] in all these cases the emblements go with the soil; the judges having not extended the new maxim 'he who sows shall reap' to reserve emblements to those who

117. Brooke, *La Graunde Abridgement,* s.v. "Emblements," ¶¶ 5, 8, 11, at fol. 260a–260b.

118. in feudal law, a person attached to the manor; a subject of property of the lord of the manor.

119. Brooke, *La Graunde Abridgement,* s.v. "Emblements," ¶ 25, at fol. 260b.

120. new provision.

121. *Coke on Littleton,* 1: 55. b. 1.

122. *Le Seignior Buckhursts Case,* Moore 512, 72 E.R. 726–27 (K.B., n.d.). The case is in Law French.

123. conveying or transferring an item of real or personal property.

124. a tenant by copyhold tenure — a type of estate at will, or customary estate, the only visible title to which consisted of the copies of the court rolls; the general or common-law tenure of the country.

125. Brooke, *La Graunde Abridgement,* s.v. "Emblements," ¶¶ 3, 4, at fol. 260a.

have wilfully or tortiously[126] relinquished their right to them. so in cases where he has determined his interest by any other act of his own which he might have qualified so as to reserve his emblements, if he meant to reserve them, he is left to make that reservation in explicit terms. as when a man by deed or will conveys his lands, without reservation of any of it's accessaries. there the law gives up the labor which the laborer himself has given up, and permits the emblements, like the houses and trees, to return to their wonted channel of passage with the soil on which they grow. this has been determined in many instances. 18 Eliz.[127] Allen's case.[128] a man sows land and devises it to one for life, rem[ainde]r in fee. the devisor dies; the devisee for life dies; both before severance; and to **{H21}** whom the emblements should go, was the question. the exe[cuto]r of the devisor could not take them, because his test[ato]r had departed with the principal to which they were annexed without reserving them: the devisee for life could not make title to them under the maxim 'he who sows shall reap'; they were adjudged therefore to go to the devisee in rem[ainde]r as belonging to the soil to which they were annexed. cited in Spencer's case. Winch. 51.[129]

Godbolt's rep. ca. 219.[130] <<adjudged that if lands which are sowed be leased to one for life, rem[ainde]r to another for life, if

126. wrongfully.

127. 1574.

128. *Allen's Case* (n.c., 1574?), cited in *Mr. Spencers Case*, Winch 51–52, 124 E.R. 44 (C.P., Michaelmas 1623).

129. *Mr. Spencers Case*, Winch 51–52, 124 E.R. 44 (C.P., Michaelmas 1623).

130. *Case 219*, 78 E.R. 97: quotation at 97. The quotation follows this citation.

ten[ant] for life dies before severance, he in rem[ainde]r shall have the corn.>> this case is similar to the former, only that this is of a deed, and that of a will.

29. Eliz.[131] Ten[ant] in fee sowed the land and devised to A. for life, rem[ainde]r to B. for life, test[ato]r and A. die before severance. every body agreed the exe[cuto]r of the devisor had no color to have the emblements, and the only question was whether the ex[ecuto]r of A. or B. was entitled. and adjudged by Wray and Shute that B. should take them: Clench[132] doubting in favor of A's ex[ecuto]r, but all agreeing against the ex[ecuto]r of the devisor as did also Sir Edward Coke who was to arbitrate the case, and Popham attorney who was consulted by the court. Cro. El. anon. 61.[133]

38 Eliz.[134] Sir Henry Knevet v. Poole et al. Cro. El. (463). Gouldsbor. 145.[135] the last case is cited in these words 'Mich. 29 & 30. Eliz[136] there was a case in this court where "a man sowed his land and devised his lands for life, rem[ainde]r in fee. ten[ant] for life dies, the corn not severed. the quest[ion] was whether the

131. 1587.

132. John Clench (d. 1607), barrister, Lincoln's Inn (1568); Baron, Exch. (1581–1584); J. Q.B. (1584–1602).

133. *Case 3. Anonymous*, 78 E.R. 321–22.

134. 1594; should be 36 Eliz.

135. *Sir Henry Knevett against Pool and Hawkins and Two Others* (Croke), 78 E.R. 701–702; (Gouldsborough), 75 E.R. 1053–1054 (summary). The quotation in text paraphrases Gouldsborough's report, in 75 E.R. at 1054.

136. 1587–1588.

ex[ecuto]r or he in rem[ainde]r should have it? and held that he in rem[ainde]r." which case they all agreed.'

13. Jac. [1.][137] it was agreed by the court in the case of Grantham and Hawley[138] 'that if A siesed of land sow it with corn and then convey it away to B. for life, rem[ainde]r to C. for life, and then B. die before the corn reaped; now C. shall have it and not the ex[ecuto]rs of B. tho' his estate was incertain. note the reason of industry and charge in B. fails.' Hob. 132.[139] and the Chief Baron Gilbert[140] citing this case, Law of Evdce. 250[141] explains it's reason in these words 'for B. had not the property of this corn, from his own charge and industry, but merely from the donation of A. the corn appurtaining to the land that was given['] and for **{H22}** the only principle on which the law separates the emblements from their principal. they were then, according to the course of their nature, to go with the land on which they were growing.

20. Jac. 1.[142] Ten[ant] in fee sows the land, devises to I.S., and

137. 1616.

138. *Grantham against Hawley*, 80 E.R. 281–82.

139. Id.

140. Sir Geoffrey Gilbert (1674–1726), Baron, Exch. (1722–1725); Chief Baron, Exch. (1725–1726); author, *Law of Uses and Trusts* (1734), *Law of Evidence* (1754, 2d ed. 1760), *History and Practice of Civil Actions in the Court of Common Pleas* (1737), and *Treatise of Tenures* (1754).

141. [Sir Geoffrey Gilbert], *The Law of Evidence. By a late Learned Judge. The Second Edition, corrected; and many new References added* ([London] In the Savoy: Printed by Catherine Lintot, 1760), 250. The quotation follows this citation, with emphasis added.

142. 1623.

dies before severance. Hobart,[143] Winch, and Hutton[144] all agreed the devisee should have the emblements, and not the ex[ecuto]r of the devisor. Winch. 51. Spencer's case.[145] for sais Baron Gilb[ert] 'the devisee in relation to the chattels belonging to the land is put in the place of the exe[cuto]rs by the words of the will.['] Law of Evidence 251.[146]

2 Ro: abr' 727.[147] [']if a man siesed in fee sows copy hold lands and surrenders them to the use of his wife and dies before the severance, it seems that the wife shall have the corn and not the ex[ecuto]rs of the husband; for this is a disposition of the corn that being appurtenant to the land, and since the husband hath disposed of it during his life, it cannot go to his ex[ecuto]rs.' Gilb. L. of Evd'ce. 249.[148]

Wentworth's office of an ex[ecuto]r 59.[149] apples pears and

143. Sir Henry Hobart (1610–1681), serjeant-at-law; barrister, Gray's Inn (1669); author, *Reports of Cases in the Exchequer 1655–1670* (published in 1693).

144. Sir Richard Hutton (1561?–1639), barrister, Gray's Inn (1586); serjeant-at-law (1603); J. C.P. (1617–1639).

145. *Mr. Spencers Case*, 124 E.R. 44.

146. Gilbert, *Law of Evidence*, 251.

147. Henry Rolle, *Un Abridgment des Plusieurs Cases et Resolutions del Common Ley, Alphabeticalment digest desouth severall Titles* (London: Printed for A. Crooke, W. Leake, A. Roper, F. Tyton, G. Sawbridge, T. Dring, T. Collins, J. Place, W. Place, J. Starkey, T. Basset, R. Pawlet, and S. Heyrick, 1668), s.v. "Emblements," 1: 727 ¶ 17 (not volume 2, as given in the manuscript). Henry Rolle (1589–1656), serjeant-at-law (1640); J., K.B. (1645); C.J., K.B. (1648–1655). Rolle's *Abridgment* was published posthumously in 1668, edited by Sir Matthew Hale.

148. Gilbert, *Law of Evidence*, 249 (emphasis added).

149. Wentworth, *Office and Duty of Executors*, 59. The quotation follows this citation.

other fruits, corn and other grain, hops, saffron, and hemp 'shall pass to one, to whom the land is sold or conveied: if not excepted, tho' never so near reaping, felling, or gathering.'

Gilbert's law of Evidence. 250.[150] after stating that emblements shall pass by a conveiance of the lands 'because they appurtain thereto' adds a 2d reason in these words.

'Objection. But why doth the corn pass to the donee as appertaining to the soil, when the property of the soil alters; and yet shall not descend to the heir, as appertaining to the soil, when the property of the soil remains in the first owner?

'Answer. Every man's donation being taken most strongly against himself shall pass not only the land itself, but the chattels that belong to the land; but no chattels can descend to the heirs[,] they go to the ex[ecuto]r.'

These are the cases and authorities, wherein, as I before said, it has been settled that whenever a man's interest in land is determined, by the act of god, or of the law, so that he has no opportunity of reserving himself the emblements he has sown, the law takes care, and reserves them, for him. but, where he determines his interest by his own act, no matter whether it be an act in pais[151] (as relinquishment by ten[ant] at will, forfeiture by ten[ant] for life, conveiance by deed or will) and might and yet **{H23}** has not made reservation of the emblements, the law does not, in his favor, separate them from the soil, of which they are an adjunct, but suffers them to go therewith as their natural union directs.

150. Gilbert, *Law of Evidence*, 250 (the source of the two paragraphs following this one).

151. an act done out of court, and not a matter of record.

But lest it should be thought that the decisions abovementioned in the cases of deeds, are not authorities in our case, which is of a will, I shall shew, in a few words, that they are so strictly as to the quantity of interest they convey.

While the feudal law prevailed in England, the lands of nearly the whole kingdom, being divided among the lords, were let out to their vassals as usufructuaries,[152] at first during will, afterwards for life, and advancing step by step were granted at length to the vassal and his heirs, and so became inheritable in perpetuum. yet was it very long before the feuditary could alienate the inheritance, a fixed right being vested in his heir by the terms of the grant. the right of alienation began in those lands which a man had acquired himself. 'acquisitiones suas det cui mages velit; si bocland autem habeat quam si parentis sui dedorint, non mittat eam, extra cognationem suam.' Leg. H. 1. No. 70.[153] afterwards it was allowed to alien a part of the family inheritance, for particular purposes, as to a vassal for services, to a daughter in frank-marriage,[154] to the church in

152. in civil law, those who have the *usufruct* or right of enjoying anything in which they have no property interest.

153. [A]cquisitions of his to whomever he prefers (21); if a person has bocland which his Kinsmen have left him, he shall not dispose of it outside his kindred....(21a)

L. J. Downer, ed. and trans., *Leges Henricus I [Laws of Henry I]* (Oxford: Clarendon Press of Oxford University Press, 1972), 70, c. 21 and 21a. "Bocland" (boc land or bookland), a term from Saxon law, is allodial lands held by deed or other written evidence of title. Allodial lands are free lands, not subject to any feudal tenure. On this anonymous legal commentary, see T. F. T. Plucknett, *Edward I and Criminal Law* (Cambridge: Cambridge University Press, 1960), 45–49.

154. a species of entailed estates.

frank-almoigne.[155] the license was then extended to one fourth, and in process of time, to one half the patrimony. At length the stat[ute] Quia emptores terrarum 18. E. 1. c. 1.[156] allowed the feuditory free alienation of the whole: but that was to be by deed in the life time of the alienor. alienation by Will crept in more lately. Thus Glanvil lib. 7. c. 1. 'possit donatis, in ultima voluntate alieni facta, ita tenere, vi cum convenvis haeredis confirmaretur.'[157] without tracing these steps particularly, which is unnecessary for my purpose; I shall observe only that testimentary alienation of lands, not held in knight's service[158] was by the statute 32 & 34 H. 8.[159] permitted in all the latitude of alienations inter vivos.[160] and when the tenure of knight's service was at length abolished, this last

155. free alms; a spiritual tenure whereby religious corporations, aggregate or sole, held lands of the donee to them and their successors forever.

156. 18 Edw. I, c.1 (1290): Statute *Quia emptores terrarum,* in *Statutes at Large* (Pickering) 1: 255–57. The Latin phrase used as the statute's common title comes from its preamble; it means: "Because purchasers of land...."

157. "However, a gift of this kind made to another in a last will can hold good if made and confirmed with the heir's consent." Ranulf de Glanville (G. D. G. Hall, trans., ed., and intro.), *The Treatise on the Laws and Customs of England commonly called Glanvill* (London: Thomas Nelson and Sons, Ltd., 1965), Book VII, "Marriage Portions," chap. 1: quote at 70. Ranulf de Glanville (also Glanvil or Glanvill) (d. 1190), chief justiciar of England (1180–1189), presumed author of *Treatise on the Laws and Customs of England.*

158. personal feudal obligation to render military service to one's lord; later taking the form of pecuniary commutation of the obligation to give service.

159. 32 Hen. VIII, c. 1, § 1 (1540): The Act of Wills, Wards and Primer Seisins, whereby a Man may devise two Parts of his Land, in Statutes at Large (Pickering), 5: 1–6; and 34 & 35 Hen. VIII, c. 5 (1542–1543): *The Bill concerning the explanation of wills,* in *Statutes at Large* (Pickering), 5: 136–43.

160. alienation between the living; a transfer of property from one living person to another, as distinguished from a testamentary gift or case of succession or devise.

restriction on alienation fell of course. the purpose of this short account of the progress of alienation is to shew that a devise is but another mode of alienation or conveiance; and that when the **{H24}** testamentary alienation becomes perfect, by the death of the devisor, the alienee is in on the same footing as he would have been if the conveiance had been by deed. so sais 2. Blackst. 378.[161] 'a will of lands[162] is considered by the courts of law, not so much in the nature of a testament, as of a conveiance, declaring the uses to which the lands shall be subject.' 'and upon this notion, that a devise affecting lands is merely a species of conveiance, is founded this distinction between such devises and testaments of personal chattels, that the latter will operate upon whatever the testator dies possessed of, the former only on such real estates as were his at the time of executing and publishing his will.' if then a conveiance by will transfers the same interests to the alienee, which would have been transferred had the alienation been by deed; a determination of what accessories shall pass by a conveiance of their principal in the one way, is determination of what shall pass in the other. and the interests, thus conveied by the act of the party, are very different from those, which would have been transferred by the law, to an heir, had the lands been left unconveied. the contrary of which seems however to be implied in the argument for the pl[aintiff] where it is said that 'a devise, or conveiance, of land simply, passes no more than would descend without it.' if by this is meant, that a

161. Blackstone, *Commentaries*, 2: 378. The quotation follows this citation.

162. omitted: "made by the permission and under the controll of these statutes"

devisee, or other alienee, is an instituted heir, quoad hoc,[163] and so that his rights are commensurate with those of an heir; this must be denied. the differences between the rights, of an heir and devisee, are as follows.

1. an heir takes by Descent, a devisee by Purchase: the consequences of which difference are That the estate shall descend to the purchaser's blood in general, and not to the blood on that part only, from which the land descended, as would be the case if it came by descent: in this instance, I concieve, the devisee takes <u>more</u> than the heir would have taken: That a purchaser is not subject to the acts of his ancestor, as he is, who takes by descent; as a ten[ant] in tail, for instance, who, taking by purchase, is not bound **{H25}** by the act of any ancestor, intermediate between the donor and himself. here also the devisee takes <u>more</u> than an heir would, because he takes clear of all defalcation.[164]

2. where an infant, or insane person, conveys; his heir may avoid it, but not a subsequent alienee, who claims by alienation, made after he became of full age, or of sound mind. Whittingham's case 8. Co. 42.b. 43.a.[165] and so, in all other cases which depend on privity[166] of blood, the heir has the same privilege. here the alienee takes <u>less</u> than the heir.

163. as to this; with respect to this.

164. The act of embezzling; failure to meet an obligation; misappropriation of trust funds or money held in any fiduciary capacity; failure to account properly for such funds.

165. *Whittingham's Case,* 8 Coke Reports 42b–45a, 77 E.R. 537–41 (K.B., Hilary 1603).

166. mutual or successive relationship to the same rights of property; *privity of blood* indicates that the relationship is one of family or blood.

3. in cases of Exchange, or Partition, there is a special warranty annexed to each parcel of lands. under this warranty, the heirs of either party, if evicted, may vouch the other, and recover the lands given on the exchange or partition: but an alienee cannot. Bustard's case. 4. Co. 121.[167] here also the alienee takes <u>less</u> than the heir.

4. the heir of a disseisor, dying seised, is privileged against the entry of the disseisee, but his alienee is not. Co. L. 237. b.[168]

5. it is said by Lord Mansfeild[169] in the case of Windham v. Chetwynd[170] that 'devises of land differ extremely from wills' [he means 'wills at the civil law' which he was then contrasting with English devises][171] 'they are no appointment of an heir; they create no representation; the devisee does not stand in the place of the devisor, as to simple contract debts, and, till the stat[ute] of K[ing] W[illia]m,[172] the devisee was not liable to specialty debts,[173] (because he was considered as an alienee, and not as the heir)[.]

167. *Bustard's Case,* 4 Coke Reports 121a–123a, 76 E.R. 1114–1118 (K.B., Paschal 1603).

168. *Coke on Littleton,* chap. 6, "Descents which Toll Entries," 2: 237. b.

169. William Murray, Lord Mansfield (1705–1793), barrister, Lincoln's Inn; S.G. (1742–1754); A.G. (1754–1756); C.J. K.B. (1756–1788).

170. *Windham, Esq., versus Chetwynd, Esq.*, 1 Burrow 414–31, 97 E.R. 377–87 (K.B., 25 Nov. 1757). Additional reports appear in 1 W. Blackstone 96–103, 96 E.R. 53–57; 1 Kenyon 253–56, 96 E.R. 984–85; and 2 Kenyon 121–62, 96 E.R. 1128–1142.

171. Brackets in original.

172. 3 & 4 Wm. and Mary, c. 14 (1691), *An Act for relief of creditors against fraudulent devises,* in *Statutes at Large* (Pickering), 9: 154–56.

173. a debt due by deed or instrument under seal.

they are conveiances, or dispositions mortis causâ:[174] and that is the reason why a man cannot devise land which he shall afterward acquire.' 1. Burr. 429.[175] other instances of difference between the rights of an heir and devisee might be adduced, but these suffice to prove them not commensurate.

And I think it will be found that the terms 'haeres factus,'[176] and 'haeres natus'[177] are taken altogether from the civil law. that law gives to the person who is called to the succession, by the will of the test[ato]r, and whom it calls the 'haeres factus', all the privileges which the heir ab intestata,[178] **{H26}** who is the 'haeres natus' would have had; and subjects him to the same charges. Lord Coke 1. inst. 237. b.[179] pointing out the difference between the Civil, and Common law, sais 'the Civilians call him haeredem, qui ex testamento succedit in universum jus testatoris.[180] but, by the Common law, he is only heir, who succeedeth by right of blood.' or as the maxim expresses it 'solus deus facit haeredem, non homo.'[181] the term of 'haeres factus' is never used, in the common law, but in the sense of Co. Lit. 15.b.[182] where a sister, coming in under the

174. by reason of, or in contemplation of, death.

175. *Windham, Esq., versus Chetwynd, Esq.*, 97 E.R. 377–87: quotation at 386.

176. in civil law, an heir made by a will (a testamentary heir).

177. in civil law, an heir born; the next of kin by blood, in cases of intestacy.

178. from an intestate, in case of intestacy.

179. *Coke on Littleton*, 1: 237. b. The quotation follows this citation.

180. heir, because by the testament he succeeds to all the testator's right.

181. God alone makes the heir, not man.

182. *Coke on Littleton*, "Of fee simple," 1: 15. b.

maxim 'possessio fratris facit sororem esse haeredem',[183] is called 'haeres facta', and the younger brother 'haeres natus.' but, even in this instance, she is the true common law heir, because she is heir of the blood of the elder brother, who was last seised of the fee simple.

So that the position, laid down in the argum[ent] for the pl[aintiff] that 'a devise, or conveiance, of land simply, passes no more than would descend without it'; is not true, if taken in it's most restricted sense: because there passes to the devisee or other alienee a right of transmitting his estate to both his paternal and maternal heirs, which is doubling the duration of the estate in his family: because the devisee, or other alienee, also takes it clear of any defalcation on account of his ancestors: and, I think I may add, on the adjudications I have produced, because the devisee or other alienee takes all the unreserved accessories, among which are the emblements. and, if the position be laid down in a sense still larger, to mean, that a devisee, or other alienee is an 'haeres factus' and his rights perfectly commensurate with those of the 'haeres natus', this is still less true; because, it is before shewn, that the common law knows no heir 'natus' or 'factus' who is not heir of the blood of him who was last seised: and because it was also shewn that the rights of the devisee are broader in some instances, and narrower in others, than those of the heir; insomuch that the rights of the one can, in no instance, be inferred from those of the other. and therefore to say the emblements will not pass by a devise or conveiance of the lands, 'because no more passes to the devisee or **{H27}** other

183. The brother's possession makes the sister to be heir.

alienee, than would descend to the heir,' is a plain non-sequitur;[184] the rights of these persons being not analogous.

Obj. pa. 14. 'that an heir is ever more favored than a devisee'[185]

Ans. Lord Hardwicke[186] does not say so. his words are 'another reason was given that it is in favor of the heir; but that can be no reason at all; because, in a court of justice, there ought to be no favor shewn to one man more than to another.' 1. Atk. 380.[187] whenever any court declares it has a favorite, it ceases to be a court of justice.

From the whole premisses then I draw this conclusion. 'formerly, Emblements went with the land. — at a later time, our laws have given them to the ex[ecuto]r of the sower, if his estate was rightful, not joint of incertain continuance, and determined by the act of god or of the law: but if it was wrongful, joint, of certain continuance, or determined by his own act, as by disertion, forfeiture, alienation <u>without reserve</u> &c. they still go with the lands.' it will be percieved that this is the same with the conclusion drawn in the argument for the pl[aintiff] 'that emblements follow the person of the sower, if he have interest in the land, the continuance whereof is incertain at the time of sowing, unless his estate determine by

184. something that does not follow logically.

185. Supra, at H9.

186. Philip Yorke, Earl of Hardwicke (1690–1764), barrister, Middle Temple; S.G. (1720–1724); C.J. K.B. (1733–1737); Lord Chancellor (1737–1756).

187. *Harvey v. Aston*, 1 Atkyns 361–81, 26 E.R. 230–43 (Ch., 30 April & 2 May 1737): quotation in 26 E.R. at 243.

his own act.' only the pl[aintiff]'s counsel does not consider a conveiance by deed, or will, as a determination 'by the act of the party.'

Having now settled what I think the rule with respect to Emblements, I shall answer the objections made to my authorities, which I was unwilling to do as I cited them, lest it should interrupt the course of our ideas, and divert our attention from what was then to be proven.

Allen's case. 18. Eliz. Winch's rep. 51.[188] is the first in point of time. this was not the principal case there adjudged, but was cited by Harris,[189] as having been adjudged, and was not denied. so far therefore as the credit of the reporter is requisite to support this case, we will now examine it, more especially as it will save the trouble of doing it when we come to Spencer's case,[190] which was the principal.

**{H28}** Obj. 1. this is an unauthoritative publication; 2. it is translated from Sir Humphrey Winch's French; 3. all the cases were not collected by him, because in one of them there is an eulogy on himself on occasion of his death.

Ans. 1. I have so few of the old reporters, in my possession, that I cannot fully state which have, or have not, the license of the judges. Noy[191] has it not. T. Jones[192] has it signed faintly by one

188. *Allen's Case*, cited in *Mr. Spencers Case*, 124 E.R. 44.

189. Probably Thomas Harris II (d. 1627), Serjeant's Inn (1603).

190. *Mr. Spencers Case*, 124 E.R. 44.

191. William Noy (or Noye) (1577–1634), barrister, Lincoln's Inn (1602); A.G. (1631); wrote on tenure of property and prepared reports of cases.

192. Sir Thomas Jones (d. 1692), barrister, Lincoln's Inn (1634), serjeant-at-law (1669),

judge only. Shower's[193] parliamentary cases, and I believe his [Shower's] reports [*marginal note: They have no license.] which are not in my possession, have it not. to my edition of Plowden[194] and Coke. no license is prefixed; but they are English ed[itio]ns, the former a very late one, and perhaps it may be omitted, as the license has been lately thought of little consequence. yet these books are cited universally, without objection for want of the license. these are the only Reporters, prior to Winch, of whom I can speak with certainty. among the moderns, the license is utterly laid aside. Foster,[195] Andrews,[196] Burrow,[197] Prec. in Chanc. Cases temp. Talbot,[198] Barnardeston,[199] Atkyns,[200]

J.K.B. (1676), C.J. C.P. (1683). Author of *Reports of Special Cases in the Courts of King's Bench and Common Pleas from 19th to 36th year of Charles II* (Latin edition, 1695, French and English edition, 1729).

193. Sir Bartholomew Shower (1658–1701), barrister, Middle Temple (1680).

194. Edmund Plowden (1515–1585), barrister, Middle Temple; jurist and publisher of legal compilations.

195. Sir Michael Foster (1689–1763), barrister, Middle Temple (1707); J. K.B. (1745–1763); *Reports* (London, 1764).

196. George Andrews, (fl. 1776), of the Middle Temple, barrister-at-law, published reports of cases argued in King's Bench for the years 1737–1740.

197. James Burrough (or Burrow) (1701–1782), barrister, Inner Temple; editor of law reports 1756–1780.

198. Charles Talbot, Baron Talbot (1685–1737), barrister, Inner Temple (1711), member of Lincoln's Inn (1719), S.G. (1726), Lord Chancellor (1733–1737). Cases collected in Peere Williams's *Reports and in Cases in Equity during the Time of Lord Chancellor Talbot* (1741).

199. Thomas Barnardiston (d. 1752), legal reporter for cases in Chancery and King's Bench.

200. Sir Robert Atkyns (or Atkins) (1621–1700), J. C.P. (1672–1680), publisher of legal treatises.

prove this. The character of Sir Humph[rey] Winch however, as a judge, should seem to give as much authority to his book, as it would have given to that of any other, to have had an imprimatur prefixed, signed by him. and yet such signature would have made such book authoritative. he was a judge of the Com[mon] Pleas from 9. Jac. 1. to 22. Jac. 1.[201] and reports only the cases determined before him the last four years of that time. he is as often cited by both bar and bench in all our books subsequent to him, as any reporter of so contracted a period. See 1. Ld. Ray. 582.[202] he is cited by Counsel. ib. 296 [297].[203] by Turton[204] justice. ib. 343[205] by the court, I suppose by Holt[206] who was Chief justice, and yet no objection to him, either from bench or bar. and my Lord Holt, who, according to the reporter, was present in the cases page 296. 343.[207] and probably in the other, tho' not mentioned, was remarkable for never citing himself, nor suffering others in his presence to cite, books which deserved little credit, without declaring his disallowance of the authority. this same Reporter is cited 1 Sho. 130.

201. 1612–1625.

202. *Rex vers. Chandler*, 1 Ld. Raymond 581–83, 91 E.R. 1288–1290 (K.B., Trinity 1701): cite to Winch 541, 547, in 1 Ld. Raymond at 582, 91 E.R. at 1289.

203. 1 Ld. Raymond 297, 91 E.R. 1094.

204. Sir John Turton (d. 1708), barrister, Gray's Inn (1673), Baron, Exch. (1689), J. K.B. (1696–1702).

205. 1 Ld. Raymond 343, 91 E.R. 1126.

206. Sir John Holt (1642–1710), barrister, Gray's Inn (1663); L.C.J. K.B. (1689–1710); chief authority on law of bailments; edited reports of cases in pleas of the crown under Charles II (published in 1708).

207. See notes 203 and 205 supra.

138. 433.[208] 4. Bac. 63.[209] 3. Bl. 142.[210] and equally[211] in all other Reporters and compilers: and yet I never before met with an objection to his authority. indeed I have ever considered 'all Reporters to be authoritative, whether licensed or not, if they have been usually cited by, **{H29}** and before, the judges in Westminster hall,[212] and were never, by them, denied.'

2. but these are a translation from Winch's cases which were collected in French.

Ans. Coke's, Plowden's, Noy's, Levintz's,[213] Lutwyche's[214] cases were collected and published in French. they are since translated; Plowden, Noy and Levintz I know by different hands, and perhaps Coke and Lutwyche. the English editions are held equally authoritative with the French, and are most sought after.

3. all the cases in Winch are supposed not to have been collected by him; because, in one of them, is an eulogy on himself, on occasion of his death.

208. No cite to Winch appears in either the Chancery reports or the Parliamentary (House of Lords) reports of Sir Bartholomew Shower.

209. Matthew Bacon, *A New Abridgment of the Law. The Third Edition, Corrected; with many Additional Notes and References*, 5 vols. (London: Printed by his Majesty's Law-Printers, 1768–1770), 4: 63 (citation to Winch 19).

210. Blackstone, *Commentaries*, 3: 142 and note m (citing to Winch 51 on actions on contract).

211. <by>

212. The building in London where the English law and chancery courts met.

213. Sir Cresswell Levinz (1627–1701), barrister, Gray's Inn (1661); A.G. (1679); author, *The Reports of Sir Cresswell Levinz, Knight* (1722).

214. Sir Edward Lutwyche (d. 1709), barrister, Gray's Inn (1661); J. C.P. (1686–1689); author, *Reports of Cases in the Common Pleas*, 1704 (published in 1718).

Ans. we might as well endeavor to destroy the authority of the Pentateuch, by observing that all the chapters thereof were not written by Moses, because in one of them, Deut. XXXIV. 5–12. 'is an eulogy on himself, on occasion of his death.' in both cases the passage, which could not be by the author himself, is easily and equally distinguishable.

Godbolt. ca. 219.[215]

Obj. the title of the book 'Cases collected by very good hands' reviewed examined and approved by the late learned justice Godbolt,' 'and published by William Hughes.' and again this is supposed to be the same case with Cro. El. 61.[216]

Ans. That the cases in any reporter were all taken in court by the reporter himself, is I believe in no instance true. a person, who intends to publish, is furnished, by his friends of the long robe, with manuscript cases in their possession. these, if important and well taken, would hardly be rejected, merely because <u>not taken by himself</u>. Lord Raymond[217] points out, in his book, the cases taken by others. 'ex relatione magistri[218] Jacob,'[219] 'magistri Place,'[220] 'mag-

215. *Case 219*, 78 E.R. 97.

216. *Case 3. Anonymous*, 78 E.R. 321–22.

217. Robert, Lord Raymond (1673–1733), barrister, Gray's Inn (1697); S.G. (1710–1714); A.G. (1720–1724); J. K.B. (1724–1725); C.J. K.B. (1725–1733).

218. upon relation or information of the authority named.

219. This is possibly a reference to Giles Jacob (1686–1744), compiler of the *New Law Dictionary* (1729).

220. Place has not been identified. A "Mr. Place" is noted as having appeared with the Attorney General for the King in *Rex et Regina v. Episcopum Cestr. Piers & Scroope*, 1 Ld. Raymond, 292–305, 91 E.R. 1091–1099 (K.B., 1698): mentioned in 91 E.R. at 1094.

istri Nott,'[221] is subjoined to a great number of his cases.[222] The title-page of his book sais, with the rest, 'Reports of Cases &c. taken and collected by Robt. Ld. Raymond.' and sais it with truth. for some he took himself in court, and others he collected from his friends, and that, I concieve to be the purpose of inserting the word 'collected' in the title-page of this, and every other, book of reports.[223] The cases, we know, are collected and revised by the reporter; we rely on his fidelity and judgment in doing this, and **{H30}** that he admits among them, none, which are not genuine. this is the light in which Godbolt's reports are to be considered. they were taken, some by himself, no doubt, others, collected from his friends; but all 'reviewed examined, and approved' by him. it is possible they might be determined before himself while a judge, tho' I cannot certainly say they were, as I am unable to find the precise time of his service in that office. we know, in many instances, it was impossible the reporter should have taken every case himself.

221. Probably a reference to Fetiplace Nott (d. 1726), Inner Temple, serjeant-at-law (1724).

222. For example: 1 Ld. Raymond 3–4 and 22, 91 E.R. 899–900 and 911 ("ex relatione m'ri place"); 1 Ld. Raymond 35–39, 91 E.R. 920–23 ("Ex relatione m'ri Nott."); 1 Ld. Raymond 95 and 99, 91 E.R. 959–60 and 962 ("ex relatione m'ri Jacob").

223. The reports published under [Lord Raymond's] name mark the transition from the generally poor seventeenth-century reports to the modern methods of reporting which were perfected in the eighteenth century.... It is not generally realised that even such an authoritative series as this is of dubious authorship. The first volume is full of reports communicated by others: *ex relatione* Place, Nott, Mather, Daly, Salkeld, Jacob, Shelley, Northey, Lutwyche, Cheshyre, Thornhill, Peere Williams, Bury and Pengelly.

J. H. Baker, "The Dark Age of English Legal History, 1500–1700," in Baker, *Legal Profession*, 435–60: quotation at 457.

| | | |
|---|---|---|
| Leonard[224] | reports from | |
| | 1558. to 1615. that is thro' a space of | 58. years. |
| Anderson[225] | 1532. – 1603. | 71. years |
| Dyer[226] | 1510. – 1584. | 72. years |
| Noy | 1558. – 1648. | 91. years |
| Benloe[227] | 1485. – 1578. | 94. years |
| Moore[228] | 1485. – 1616. | 132. years |
| Jenkins[229] | 1218. – 1625. | 408. years |

now we know it impossible men should have lived at all, much less enjoyed that vigor of mind requisite for such works, thro so long spaces of time. and tho' we know they could not have taken all the cases themselves, yet as they declare they collected them, we are satisfied with their judgment and fidelity, and admit the authority. and

224. William Leonard (fl. 1558–1625), member of Gray's Inn; *Reports* translated by William Hughes from the Law French (London, 1658–1675; second improved edition, 1687).

225. Sir Edmund Anderson (1530–1605), C.J. C.P. (1582–1605).

226. Sir James Dyer (ca. 1510–1582), barrister, Middle Temple (ca. 1537); serjeant-at-law (1553); J. C.P. (1557), J. Q.B. 1558), C.J. C.P. (1559–1582). See generally J. H. Baker, ed., *Reports from the Lost Notebooks of Sir James Dyer*, 2 vols. (London: Selden Society, 1994: *Selden Society Publications*, vols. 109 and 110).

227. William Bendlowes (also Benloe or Benlows) (1515–1584), Serjeant's Inn, serjeant-at-law (1555).

228. Sir Francis Moore (1558–1621), barrister, Middle Temple (1580); serjeant-at-law (1614); author of law reports (1512–1621; published in 1665).

229. David Jenkins (1582–1663), Welsh jurist and legal reporter; Gray's Inn (1602), judge of Great Sessions (1642). Author of *Rerum Judicatarum Centuriae Octo* (London, 1661; new edition as *Eight Centuries of Reports*, London, 1734).

accordingly the books last mentioned are acknoleged authorities.

that 'they were published by Hughes' is another part of the objection.

Ans[.] they were so. Moore, was published by Sir Geoffrey Palmer;[230] Yelverton[231] by Wylde;[232] Croke by Sir Harbottle Grimstone; Freeman[233] by Dixon, Vaughn[234] by his son; Peere-Williams[235] by his son; Bunbury[236] by Wilson;[237] and Leonard from whom Launton's case[238] is cited on the other side, by the very same W[illia]m Hughes who published Godbolt. The questions which determine him authoritative or not, are these. Is he cited in Westminster hall? ans. he is. see 1. Ray. 140. 159. 228. 236. 453.

230. Sir Geoffrey Palmer (1598–1670), barrister, Middle Temple; A.G.

231. Sir Henry Yelverton (d. 1629/30), Serjeants Inn, serjeant-at-law (1625), J. C.P. (1625–1630) and reporter of cases in King's Bench.

232. Sir William Wilde (or Wylde) (d. 1679), Serjeant's Inn, king's-serjeant (1660–1668), J. C.P. (1668–1673), J. K.B. (1673–1679).

233. Richard Freeman (d. 1710), Lord Chancellor of Ireland (1707–1710); *Reports* (London, 1742).

234. Sir John Vaughan (1603–1674), barrister, Inner Temple (1630); C.J. C.P. (1668–1674). Editor of *Reports* (1677).

235. William Peere Williams (1664–1736), barrister, Gray's Inn (1687), co-editor of Vernon's *Reports* (London, 1726–1728), and editor of *Reports of Cases Argued and Determined in the High Court of Chancery, and of Some Special Cases adjudged in the Court of King's Bench* (1740).

236. William Bunbury (fl. 1710s–1740s), Postman of Courts of Exchequer and law reporter; *Reports* of Court of Exchequer, 1713–1742 (published posthumously, London, 1755).

237. George Wilson (d. 1777), serjeant-at-law (1753).

238. *Launton's Case*, 74 E.R. 685.

&c.[239] 1. 3. Ba. 179.[240] see also[241] the compilers, as 4. Bac. 2. 14. 37. 44. 56. 72. &c.[242] 2. Bl. 449.[243] 3 Bl. 4. 92.[244] and others. Was he ever there denied to be authority? ans. Never.'

**{H31}** The last part of the objection is 'that this is supposed to be the same case reported in Cro. El. 61.'[245]

Ans. it cannot be the same; because the case in Croke was of a *devise*; that in Godbolt of a *lease*. and besides, the case in Godbolt is mentioned as a present, not as a past adjudication.

Cro. Eliz. 61. 27 Eliz.[246]

1. Obj. Coke took it for granted the ex[ecuto]r of the devisor was not to have them; and so propounded the question as only lying between an ex[ecuto]r of ten[ant] for life, and him in remainder.

Ans. this then, by the bye, gives us my Lord Coke's opinion, in which too 'he said he was clear.' and his opinion, when clear, I con-

239. Godbolt is cited in 1 Ld. Raymond 140 and 453, 91 E.R. 990 and 1202. Godbolt is not cited in 1 Ld. Raymond 159, 228, and 236, 91 E.R. 1003, 1049, and 1054–1055.

240. Barnardiston's Chancery reports and his King's Bench reports do not cite Godbolt at the pages indicated, though 1 Barn. K.B. 179, 94 E.R. 123, cites to Croke.

241. <of>

242. Bacon, *A New Abridgment of the Law*, 4: 2, 14, 37, 44, 56, 72 (citations to Godbolt).

243. Blackstone, *Commentaries*, 2: 449 (citing Godbolt on the custom of the market place).

244. Godbolt is not cited on the pages of Blackstone mentioned in the manuscript; but see Blackstone, *Commentaries*, 3: 84 (citing Godbolt on privileges in chancellor's courts for universities of England), 109 (citing Godbolt on procedure in courts of admiralty).

245. *Case 3. Anonymous*, 78 E.R. 321–22.

246. Id.

sider as no mean authority. but I insist it must also have been the opinion of the judges. Lord Coke proposed these circumstances. 'a man sows, devises to A. for life, rem[ainder]r to B. for life. A dies before severance,' and asks 'has his ex[ecuto]r, or has B. a right to the emblements, for I think the ex[ecuto]r of the devisor has no color'? if they thought otherwise, their answer was naturally 'we differ from you in opinion; neither A's ex[ecuto]r nor B. have a right, but the ex[ecuto]r of the devisor.' but, agreeing with Coke, their answer was consistent, 'that B. was entitled.' when it was stated to them, that the devisor sowed; how could they say the right was in a devisee, if they thought it in the ex[ecuto]r of the devisor? suppose a case thus stated to a judge or att[orne]y. 'a ten[ant] in fee simple is dead intestate, leaving a son and several daughters. whether does his eldest daughter alone, or all his daughters, take the lands, for I hold it clear the son has no color to have them.' the answer would be 'Sir you are mistaken; neither the eldest daughter nor all the daughters will take them, but the son.'

but their words are express that '<u>by the devise of the lands</u> they' i.e. the emblements 'pass with it; and when they pass <u>by reason of the land</u>' &c. on view of these words, how could it be said 'their opinion did not determine whether the emblements passed by the devise of the land'?

**{H32}** 2. Obj. Wray and Shute contradict themselves in admitting A. might have granted them, tho' they had determined he had no right to them; and how can one grant, to another what he has no right to himself?

Ans. let the terms of the objection be accurate. they did not say that A. had no right to them while living; but that his ex[ecuto]r after his death, has none. I answer then, the ten[ant] for life took the emblements in this case, as he did his *Estovers*,[247] i.e., wood for building, burning, utensils of agriculture, and inclosing. he had right to use them, if he thought proper; but if he used none, was his ex[ecuto]r entitled to them? no: to the wood which might reasonably have been used for these purposes, but was not, the right is now passed on with the land. here then is an instance where a man's ex[ecuto]r has no right, tho'[248] himself had. exactly similar is the case now objected to: by the devise to A. for life, a right to use the emblements in any way he thought proper, passed. their several uses, or ways of being used, were to depasture, to cut, to sell &c. any of these uses he had power to make, if he chose, and it would have been confirmed, as Wray and Chute said. he exercised none of his powers. the subject therefore, say they is gone over with the land. where now is the inconsistency? Another instance similar to this is, where a man marries a woman possessed of a term for years, or other chattel real.[249] the law sais, he has a modified right to this, he may alone alien it if he will: but if he fails to do it, and dies, his ex[ecuto]r has no right, but it goes over to the wife. here then is another instance, where a man may grant, not what 'he had no right to' as the objection states it, but that to which his ex[ecuto]r would have no right. nor is there any greater inconsistence in this, than in

247. a tenant's right or privilege to furnish himself with wood from the demesned premises as may be sufficient or necessary for fuel, fences, or agricultural operations.

248. <he>

249. article or item of real property; an interest in real estate less than a freehold or fee.

every other case of a modified or restricted right, where the restriction must work it's effect, if the event happens on which it was to take effect.

3. Obj. there was a diversity of sentiment among the judges upon the question in that case.

Ans. one judge indeed doubted, in favor of the ten[ant] for life, but two others and Popham attorney, whom they consulted, were of opinion for the rem[ainde]r-man. **{H33}** yet all three judges, with Coke and Popham, unanimously agreed the question, so far as it concerns us, that 'by the devise of the lands the emblements passed.'

4. Obj. it was not an adjudged case, but an extrajudicial opinion.

Ans. if to an adjudged case it be essential that there be a judgment entered of record, this is not entitled to be so called. for as there had been no curial proceedings[250] in it before, there was no need to record the judgment. it was a friendly reference to Sir Edward Coke, who took the advice of the court, and the parties were ready to perform their dictum of what was the law. but I conceive the opinion of the judges is the essence of every authority; and if that opinion be given on a full state of the case, on mature deliberation, and on the point, in support of which it is adduced; then their opinion so given must influence ours, i.e. it becomes an authority, whether, when they pronounced it, their clerk took a minute of it or not.

250. civil, as distinguished from ecclesiastical, proceedings.

5. Obj. Sir Geo[rge] Croke was then but 27. years of age.

Ans. far be it from me to detract from that superiority of wisdom to which years give title, because they bring it. the longer a man has lived, the more facts have come under his observation, and the more time he has had for reflection. but the understanding of Sir Geo[rge] Croke must have been of slow growth indeed, if at the age of 27. he was yet unable to apprehend a case so simplified as this, when canvassed among the judges and counsel in court, and again explained to him in conversation with Coke: besides if this part of his book be not authority because of his youth, say whereabouts he begins to be old enough, that at that place we may draw a line in the book. our law books do not inform us; they cite equally every part of his work. — but let us see what confirmation there is of Croke's report of this case. 1. in the case of Knevet v. Poole, reported by Croke,[251] when he was 36. years of age, and also by Gouldsborough.[252] Tanfeild cites this case, now under consideration, as having been adjudged. he states the time, circumstances, and judgment. Popham, who, as an amicus curiae,[253] had been consulted in that case, was now on the bench. and he, and the rest of the court, confirm that there **{H34}** was such a case, and agree the doctrine. 2. in Grantham v. Hawley. Hob. 132[254] this case is

251. *Sir Henry Knevett against Pool and Hawkins and Two Others* (Croke), 78 E.R. 701–702.

252. *Sir Henry Knevett against Pool and Hawkins and Two Others* (Gouldsborough), 75 E.R. 1053–1054.

253. friend of the court; one who is invited to submit briefs or arguments to the court to aid in the decision of a case, though not a party in interest before the court.

254. *Grantham against Hawley*, 80 E.R. 281–82.

again cited and agreed by the court.

6. Obj. again it is said this case is of no authority, because a passage in the case Cro. Eliz. (463)[255] militates against it, which passage is thus cited. 'if ten[ant] for life sows the land, and grants over his estate, and the grantee dies before the corn severed, his ex[ecuto]r shall not have the corn, but he who sowed the land.'

Ans. the latter words 'but he who sowed the land' are not in the book, tho', from a mistake in prefixing a comma to them, we might understand they were. they are only an inference by the pl[aintiff]'s counsel of the principle on which he supposes the court went. but I will shew they could not go on that principle. the case then, as stated in the book, is in these words 'if ten[ant] for life sows the land, and grants over his estate, the grantee dies before the corn severed, his ex[ecuto]r shall not have the corn.' who then shall have it? the ten[ant] for life who sowed? no. for where the case sais, if the grantee die 'before severance' his ex[ecuto]r shall not have the corn, it supposes undeniably that if he died after severance, he should have it, and not the ten[ant] for life. why else is the circumstance of his death mentioned at all? if the ten[ant] for life did not pass away his right to the emblements by the grant, he keeps that right whether the grantee be living or dead at the time of severance; if he did pass it away, the grantee would have it if he lived till severance; but[256] otherwise not. on this supposition alone then, to wit,

255. *Sir Henry Knevett against Pool and Hawkins and Two Others* (Croke), 78 E.R. 701–702: quotation at 701. The quotation follows this citation, but, as Jefferson pointed out, the last six words do not appear in the opinion.

256. <if>

that the grant of the lands did pass the emblements, the death of the grantee before or after severance becomes worthy [of] mention. but if neither the ex[ecuto]r of the grantee, nor the ten[ant] for life grantor, has the emblements, who shall have them? whoever becomes Occupant of the land. for Co. Lit. 41.b.[257] sais 'if ten[ant] for his own life grant over his estate to another, if the grantee dieth, there shall be an occupant.' and upon what principle does the Occupant of the land take also the emblements? upon this 'he who sows shall reap'? no. upon the other 'quicquid plantatur solo, solo cedit.' a principle which the law does indeed infringe to encorage the sower; but where the claimant cannot say 'he sowed' or 'that

Williamsburg courthouse reprinted from *Williamsburg, The Old Colonial Capital* by Lyon Gardiner Tyler (Whittet & Shepperson, Richmond, VA, 1907)

257. *Coke on Littleton,* "Tenant for Term of Life," 1: 41. b.

some person sowed while the possesion was in him,' as was Hawley's Case, Cro. El. (463)[258] there the emblements **{H35}** follow nature, i.e., cedunt solo.[259] now this the grantee of ten[ant] for life, or his exec[uto]r, could not say. for neither 'they sowed' nor 'any person while the possession was in them.' — where therefore the adverse counsel asks 'if in that case the person who sowed the land had a right to the crop, why should not the ex[ecuto]r of him who sowed the land in Cro. El. 61.[260] and devised it, have the corn likewise'? I answer. if indeed it were shewn that in this case 'the person who sowed the land' had a right to the crop as sower, and not as occupant, the inference would be undeniable, and all my authorities contradicted. but I have already observed these words 'he who sowed the land', are not in the book, that on the contrary the book plainly infers the right is not in the sower, who was the grantor, but would have been in the grantee if he had lived to sever; which is sufficient to shew the sower had, by his grant of the lands, parted with his right to the emblements. — Again where it is asked 'if the grant of the estate did not convey the emblements in one instance' to wit, the instance of ten[ant] for life granting over his estate; 'why should the devise of the land convey them in the other instance' to wit, of Cro. El. 61?[261] I answered this under the 2d

258. This citation is to *Sir Henry Knevett against Pool and Hawkins and Two Others,* 78 E.R. 700–701; the quoted language preceding the citation paraphrases id., 78 E.R. at 701, and not *Grantham against Hawley.*

259. in the same way.

260. *Case 3. Anonymous,* 78 E.R. 321–22.

261. Id.

obj[ectio]n, thus. a grant of the estate did convey the emblements, as it did his *Estovers*, to be used, if the grantee chose it: but, if he chose it not, they passed on with the land. so that in the instances cited both of the grant and devise it did convey the emblements from the conveior; and in both cases the first alienee, having praetermitted[262] his right, it goes over to the next who makes title to the land. this in the case of the devise was the rem[ainde]rman; in that of the grant, it was the occupant. which shews the two cases to proceed on the same principle, and not to militate, as is objected.

Sir Henry Knevet v. Poole. Cro. Eliz. (463.) Gouldsb.[263]

Obj. this case is put by Tanfeild. 'if a man sows land, and lets it for life, and the lessee for life dies before the corn be severed, his ex[ecuto]r shall not have them, but he in reversion. but if he himself,' i.e. the tenant for life, 'sowed the land and died, it were otherwise.'[264] and 'so far, sais the argument, the case is an authority for the pl[aintiff].'

**{H36}** Ans. it is most clearly an authority for the def[endant]. i.e. an affirmation of the maxim 'quicquid plantatur solo, solo cedit.' 'if a man sows and leases the land for life, and the lessee dies before severance, his ex[ecuto]r shall not have the corn:' but if he die after severance, he shall have it, is an implication irresistible: and consequently, that he had acquired the title to the corn, and the

262. let pass or neglected.

263. *Sir Henry Knevett against Pool and Hawkins and Two Others* (Gouldsborough), 75 E.R. 1053–1054, and (Croke), 78 E.R. 701–702.

264. *Sir Henry Knevett against Pool and Hawkins and Two Others*, 78 E.R. at 701–702 (Croke); paraphrased in 75 E.R. at 1053 (Gouldsborough).

lessor parted with it, by leasing the land. Again let me state what precedes the case here put. sais Tanfeild 'quicquid plantatur solo, solo cedit; and therefore if a man sows land, and lets it for life, and the lessee for life dies before the corn severed, his ex[ecuto]r shall not have them, but he in revers[io]n.'[265] here then he plainly puts this case to illustrate the rule quicquid plantatur &c. and sais that under this rule in the case he here puts the corn shall go with the land, to the reversioner. this is so far then from being an authority for the pl[aintiff] as his counsel supposes, that it is produced by Tanfeild as an instance wherein the maxim on which he relies, to wit, 'he who sows shall reap' has no authority. the word he uses too is remarkeable 'it shall go to him in reversion' i.e. it belongs to the reversion, or in other words to the land. if the grantor who sowed happened to be living when the lands reverted, the emblements would go to him indeed, not as sower, but as reversioner, i.e. owner of the soil: but if he was dead, to whom would it go, by this authority? to his ex[ecuto]r? no. because he is not reversioner, but to his heir, who is. he is the person described by Tanfeild. it is clear to me that Tanfeild is here shewing where the two principles take place. in the first part of the sentence 'if a man sows, and leases, and the lessee dies before severance, the reversioner shall have the corn' he shews where the rule quicquid plantatur &c. takes place, and carries the emblements with the land: in the next words 'but if the lessee sowed and died, it were otherwise,' he shews where the rule 'he who sows &c.['] takes place and carries them to the sower. This is

265. Id.

enough, I hope to shew that the case put by Tanfeild proves the right to the emblements did pass from the lessor to the lessee, by the grant, if the lessee had chosen to sever them: but as he did not, that they became, like the **{H37}** trees, parcel of the land to which they were annexed, and would go with that to the reversioner, who would be the lessor, if living, or his heir, if dead, and not his ex[ecuto]r: and so instead of being an authority for the pl[aintiff] is such for the def[endant].

Grantham v. Hawley. Hob. 132.[266]

Obj. 'the judges here admit the sower to have a <u>kind of property</u> and yet agree the case Cro. El. 61.[267] which is irreconcileable'. that is, I suppose, they <u>admit</u> the sower has a kind of property here, but <u>denied</u> he had any in the case of Cro. El. 61. which is irreconcileable.

Ans. Nothing is more consistent. they denied the sower in Cro. El. 61. had any right, because <u>he had parted with it</u> by devise: they admit he has a kind of right here because <u>he has not parted with it</u>. is there any thing so irreconcileable in this as to render it necessary for us to frame a new case by inserting the word 'profits' into the case Cro. El. 61. and making it a devise of the land and profits, in order to accomodate it to the reasoning on the other side. so far from our being at liberty to insert such a word, the judges expressly guard against it and say that 'by a devise of the <u>land</u> the emblements passed.' but if such a liberty as this may be taken with the cases in the books, I will say they do not furnish a case, which may not be disarmed, or even pointed in it's opposite direction by

266. *Grantham against Hawley*, 80 E.R. 281–82.

267. *Case 3. Anonymous*, 78 E.R. 321–22.

the insertion of a single word.

20. Jac. 1. Spencer's case. Winch 51.[268]

The objections to this are the same as to Allen's case,[269] and so have been answered.

1. Rolle's abridgement. 727.[270]

This case is not noticed by the counsel on the other side.

Wentworth's Office of an ex[ecuto]r. 59.[271]

Obj. Wentworth was a compiler.

Ans. what are the authorities produced in support of the pl[aintiff]'s right? Swinburne[272] a compiler; Blackstone[273] a compiler, Broke a compiler, Per**{H38}**kins[274] a compiler; and Viner[275] a

268. *Mr. Spencers Case,* 124 E.R. 44.

269. *Allen's Case,* cited in *Mr. Spencers Case,* 124 E.R. 44.

270. Rolle, *Abridgment,* 1: 727 ¶ 17.

271. Wentworth, *Office and Duty of Executors,* 59.

272. Henry Swinburne (1560?–1623), ecclesiastical lawyer; author of *A Briefe Treatise of Testaments and Last Willes* (1591 and later editions). See J. H. Baker, "Famous English Canon Lawyers: Henry Swinburne," *Ecclesiastical Law Journal* 3 (1993): 5–9.

273. Sir William Blackstone (1723–1780); barrister, Middle Temple (1741); J. K.B. (1770); J. C.P. (1770–1780); author, *Commentaries on English Law,* 4 vols. (1765–1769).

274. John Perkins (or Parkins) (d. 1545), barrister, Inner Temple; author of *Perutilis Tractatus* (1530; English translation, *A Profitable Booke... Treating of the Lawes of England...,* 1642).

275. Charles Viner (1678–1756), member of Middle Temple (1700, 1727); published *General Abridgment of Law and Equity,* 23 vols. (1741–1753). Viner bequeathed his unsold copies of his *General Abridgement of Law and Equity* to Oxford University; he directed that Oxford sell the books and apply the revenue thus generated to the creation of the Vinerian Professorship of Law at Oxford, first held by Sir William Blackstone, whose *Commentaries* were based on his lectures.

compiler. Ventris[276] a reporter is cited to prove these words 'emblements may be taken in execution' and Leonard for the short case called Launton's case.[277] then, as to the merit of Wentworth's book, I shall only observe the credit given him by two of our best modern compilers. Blackstone quotes him in almost every page, while treating on Wentworth's subject; and Bacon[278] has transcribed I believe every word in the book.

Gilb's Law of Ev'dce

I know not whether any objection will be made to this. he is, like Wentworth, a compiler, but I have ever supposed him unquestionable authority.

And here I cannot suppress the anxiety I ever feel when an attempt is made to unhinge those principles, on which alone we depend for security in all the property we hold, and to set us again adrift to search for new. and by the time these are found, they will again be sent off after the old. when rules of property have been settled, on their faith we buy things, and call them our own. they should therefore be sacred, and not wantonly set aside when ingenuity can persuade us to believe they are unfit, or inconsonant with other decisions. we should not, under a momentary impression, demolish what has been the growth of ages. this deference to adjudged cases is enjoined by our laws. Lord Mansfeild sais 'when

276. Sir John Ventris (d. 1691), barrister, Middle Temple (1661); J. C.P. (1689–1691); *Reports* (1645–1691; published in 1696).

277. *Launton's Case,* 74 E.R. 685.

278. Matthew Bacon, (fl. 1730), author of *The Compleat Arbitrator* and *A New Abridgement of Law and Equity* (1736), based largely on materials by Sir Geoffrey Gilbert.

solemn determinations, acquiesced under, have settled precise cases, and become a rule of property; they ought, for the sake of certainty, to be observed, as if they had originally made a part of the text of the statute.' and again 'if judicial determinations, acquiesced under, and become a rule of property, since the statute have extended' the incapacity 'further, they must be adhered to.' 1. Burr. 419. 423.[279] and 1 Bl. 69.[280] 'even so early as the conquest, we find the praeteritorum memoria eventorum,[281] reckoned up as one of the chief qualifications of those, who were held to be legibus patriae optime instituti.[282] for it is an established rule to abide by former precedents, **{H39}** where the same points come again in litigation: as well to keep the scale of justice even and steady, and not liable to waver with every new judge's opinion; as also because the law in that case being solemnly declared and determined, what before was uncertain, and perhaps indifferent, is now become a permanent rule, which it is not in the breast of any subsequent judge to alter or vary from, according to his private sentiments: he being sworn to determine, not according to his own private judgment, but according to the known laws and customs of the land; not delegated to pronounce a new law, but to maintain and expound the old one.'

I shall now therefore subjoin some observations, supported by this review of the cases, and in answer to those of the pl[aintiff]'s counsel.

279. *Windham, Esq., versus Chetwynd, Esq.* (Burrow), 97 E.R. 377–87: quotes at 380 and 382.

280. Blackstone, *Commentaries,* 1: 69. The quotation follows this citation.

281. memory of past events.

282. those best instructed in the laws of their country.

1. That emblements will pass with the land by a simple devise or conveiance of the land, has been judicially determined in these several instances. 1. In Allen's case 18. Eliz.[283] 2. in Godbolt 219.[284] 3. in 29. 30. El. Cro. El. 61.[285] 4. in Spencer's case 20. Jac.[286] 5. in the case Ro.'s abr.' 727.[287] add to this that one of these cases has been cited and approved in Cro. El. (463.)[288] and in Hob. 132.[289] and the spirit of them all in Wentworth and Baron Gilbert.

2. none of the books contradict themselves, or one another, if you go on this rule 'that the emblements go to the sower, where his estate was rightful, not joint, of certain duration, and determined by the act of god or of the law: but that they go with the lands in all other cases, and particularly where the sower determines the estate by desertion, forfieture, alienation without reserve, or any other his own act.'

Objection. Launton's ca. 4 Leon.[290]

'A. is bound in an obligation that B. shall enjoy a lease of

283. *Allen's Case*, cited in *Mr. Spencers Case*, 124 E.R. 44.

284. *Case 219*, 78 E.R. 97.

285. *Case 3. Anonymous*, 78 E.R. 321–22.

286. *Mr. Spencers Case*, 124 E.R. 44.

287. Rolle, *Abridgement*, 1: 727 ¶ 17.

288. *Sir Henry Knevett against Pool and Hawkins and Two Others* (Croke), 78 E.R. 701–702.

289. *Grantham against Hawley*, 80 E.R. 281–82.

290. *Launton's Case*, 74 E.R. 685. The quotation follows this citation.

Blackacre immediately after his death: the land being sown, the ex[ecuto]r of A. take the corn, it was holden the obligation was not forfieted, for that by the laws, the corn did belong to the ex[ecuto]r.'

**{H40}** Ans. the reporter has here given us only the outlines of the case, with the judgment of the court that the corn belonged to the ex[ecuto]r. but the process of reasoning by which that conclusion is deduced, is left for our investigation. — There is great difference between a lease actually executed, to commence in possession immediately after a death; and an agreement or obligation to lease immediately after a death. the actual lease would vest the property of the lands and emblements in the lessee at the instant of his lessor's death, and to take them would be a trespass[291] in the ex[ecuto]r. the agreement or obligation to lease which was Launton's case transfers no property to the obligee, nor has he any till the lease be actually executed. and tho' the obligation sais he shall enjoy it immediately, yet some time will be requisite before he can enjoy it. for instance, the obligee must make his demand of the heir, who has no other way of being notified that he is bound to make a lease; the heir must have time to write and execute, and even to consult with counsel, if he takes only a reasonable time to do it. now all this must have been understood between the obligor and obligee, who when they say the lease shall be made immediately, mean it shall be done with as little delay as the several necessary

291. unlawful interference with one's person, property, or rights; in civil as opposed to criminal law, a form of action to recover damages for any injury to one's person, property, or relationship with another.

steps will admit; or in other words, it shall be done in convenient time. they could not mean 'in articulo temporis'[292] for the writing and sealing alone are not the works of an instant. thus Bro. Condicions. 164.[293] 'Debt on an obligation that the def[endant] will make an obligation to the pl[aintiff] by the advice of W. N. of £40. immediately. and by Brian,[294] Choke[295] and others he may say that the first bond was made such a day and hour, and that he, such a day and hour after, made an obligation of £40 by advice of W.N. and shall not speak of this word immediately, and good. for it cannot be made immediately, for he ought to have time to have the advice of W. N. and afterwards to write and seal it. 18. E. 4. 21.'[296] here then this same word 'immediately' in a bond, is construed, not 'in articulo temporis,' but, in 'convenient time after.' which the judges in this particular case extended to days, it appearing, I suppose, to them, that the condition could not with any convenience be performed **{H41}** sooner. this convenient time in Launton's case,[297] would be more, or less, according to the delay of

292. at that point in time.

293. Brooke, *La Graunde Abridgement*, s.v. "Condicions," ¶ 164, at fol. 154b. The following quoted passage translates Brooke's Law French.

294. Sir Thomas Bryan (d. 1500), Gray's Inn, serjeant (1463), C.J. C.P. (1471–1500).

295. Sir Richard Choke (d. 1483?), J. C.P. (1452–1461, 1461–1470).

296. *Les Reports des Cases en Ley Que furent argues en temps Du Roy Edward le Quart. Avec les Notations de le tres Reverend Judges Brook & Fitz-herbert* (London: Printed by George Sawbridge, William Rawlins, and Samuel Roycroft, Assigns of Richard and Edward Atkins, Esquires, 1680), "De Termino Michaelis Anno xviii Edwardi. IIII.," ¶ 21, at 17. Each regnal year has its own pagination, and each term has its own case numbering.

297. *Launton's Case*, 74 E.R. 685.

the pl[aintiff] in making his demand, and the distance the heir might be obliged to go, to advise with counsel and have his lease written. in the mean time the emblements are clearly vested in the ex[ecuto]rs, who may sever them without doing wrong; for, sais the book, and I agree [with] it, 'by the laws the corn did belong to the ex[ecuto]rs.'[298] thus we see that between the death of the obligor and actual execution of the lease to the obligee, some time must necessarily intervene. during that time no property in the land or emblements is carried to the obligee; but the former is in the heir, the latter in the ex[ecuto]rs; and they, by using their property, do no wrong, and so work no forfeiture of the obligation. this case therefore is not in point, nor can the pl[aintiff]'s counsel show it so, unless he be allowed to supply this circumstance, that there were emblements on the land at the time of executing the lease. but this would be to make an authority.

Objection. Viner. Emblem'. pa. 373. pl. 82.[299]

Ans. A. only devised his <u>rem[ainde]r</u>, to B. now a <u>rem[ainde]r</u>, as to the quantity of the estate, is the same with a <u>reversion</u>. and, said the court in Wrotesly v. Adams Plowd. 196.[300] '"reversio terrae," is in English "the returning of the land," which is the same in sense with "the land returning." wherefore reversio terrae est terra revertens, which is the land in a certain degree, to wit, when it is

298. Id.: quote at 685.

299. Viner, *General Abridgment,* s.v. "Emblements," 9: 373 ¶ 82.

300. *Wrotesley versus Adams,* 1 Plowden 187–99, 75 E.R. 287–305 (K.B., Trinity 1553 and Michaelmas 1554).

discharged of the particular estate.'[301] and again ibidem, "a devise of the reversion of an acre," and a "demise of the acre when it shall return to me" is of the same sense and substance.'[302] so in the case in Viner, a devise of the rem[ainde]r was no more than a devise of the land when it should remain or return to A. which would not be till after the death of B. to whom an intermediate estate was given. this devise of the rem[ainde]r therefore was to carry nothing to B. till after her death, which was the first instant of the devisor's rem[ainde]r coming into actual existence but, in the mean time, the emblements growing on the land at his death, were a part of his old life estate,[303] which could not pass by a devise of the rem[ainde]r, **{H42}** and therefore would go to his ex[ecuto]rs. and so this authority proves nothing but what we admit, to wit, that where ten[ant] for life dies without having conveied his estate i.e. his life estate, the emblements belonging to that life estate go to his exec[uto]r: it was never said that if a man devises or otherwise conveys lands to be taken into possession 50. years hence, or when B. shall die, that this carries the emblements now growing, or any other present profit. yet that it does not, is all which Viner's case proves.

Obj. pa. 13. of the Argum[ent]. 'The crop, after severance, is not properly emblements which are corn &c growing.'[304]

301. Id.: quote in 75 E.R. at 301.

302. Id.

303. a possessory interest in land the duration of which is limited to the life of the party holding it or of some other specified person.

304. Supra, at H8.

Ans. but the crop before severance is growing, and therefore emblements and the emblements, i.e. the crop which was growing at the instant of the test[ato]r's death is what we claim.

Obj. 'The emblements are as much his separate property, and subject to the regulations which concern personal chattels, as his cattle' &c.

Ans. this is the very point we are contending. you say they are his separate [meaning I suppose, his absolute][305] property: we, that they are only his property, sub modo,[306] i.e. if he does not by his own act part with or determine his estate in the lands. As to their being 'as much subject to the regulations which concern personal chattels as his cattle &c' it is taken too much for granted both here, and thro' the whole argument that emblements are personal chattels. Lord Coke indeed, declaring of what things a larceny may be committed, sais 'tho' goods be personal, yet if they sever[307] any thing of the realty, no larceny can be committed of them. as any kind of corn[308] growing on the ground is a personal chattel, and the ex[ecuto]rs of the owner shall have them tho' they be not severed; but yet no larceny can be committed of them, because they are annexed to the realty. so it is of grass standing on the ground, or of apples, or any other fruits upon trees or bushes, or of woods grow-

305. Brackets in original.

306. under a qualification; subject to a restriction or condition.

307. "savour" in Coke, not "sever."

308. omitted: "or grain."

ing'[309] 3 inst. 109.[310] and all of these he sais, ibidem, are 'not meer personal goods.' here then Lord Coke tho' he calls Emblements 'chattels personal,' yet sais they are not meerly so, they are only so in the same sense **{H43}** in which grass, fruits, woods growing &c. are called so. by others these things are said to be chattels real. thus Cowel's Interpreter, voce Catalls[311] 'Chattels real be such as either do not appertain to the person, but to some other thing by way of dependency, as a box with charters of land, the body of a ward, apples upon a tree, or a tree itself growing on the ground.' cites Crompton's justice. fol. 32. b.[312] Terms de la ley. verbo Chattel.[313] so also sais Cuningham. Law. Dict. voce 'Chattels.'[314] and Ro. abr'

309. omitted: "but if the owner cut the grass, or gather the fruit, or cut the wood, then larceny may be committed of them."

310. Sir Edward Coke, *The Third Part of the Institutes of the Laws of England: Concerning High Treason, and Other Pleas of the Crown, and Criminall Causes* (London: Printed by M. Flesher, 1644), 109.

311. John Cowell (or Cowel) (1554–1611), *The Interpreter of Words and Terms, Used either in the Common or Statute Laws of this Realm, and in Tenures and Jocular Customs...* (London: J. Place, A. & J. Churchill, and R. Sare, 1701), s.v. "Catalls" (unpaged).

312. This citation apparently is to Sir Anthony Fitzherbert and Richard Crompton, *L'Office et authoritie de Justices de peace...* (London: Richard Tottell, 1584; reprint, London: Professional Books Limited, 1972), a manual written in Law French, principally by Richard Crompton (fl. 1553–1606), Middle Temple, J.P. (1577–1595). The cited page of the 1584 edition does not mention chattels.

313. John Rastell [or William Rastell?], *Les Termes De La Ley: or, Certain Difficult and Obscure Words and Terms of the Common and Statute Laws of this Realm Now in Use, Expanded and Explained* (London: Printed by W. Rawlins,, S. Roycroft and M. Flesher..., 1685), 115–116 (s.v. "Catals"). John Rastell (d. 1536), printer and lawyer, Lincoln's Inn. On William Rastell, see infra, note 352.

314. T[imothy] Cunningham, Esq. [d. 1789], *A New and Complete Law-Dictionary or General Abridgment of the Law, on A more Extensive Plan than any Law-Dictionary hitherto*

727.[315] sais 'corn committed to the ground is a chattel real, which is annexed and belonging to the freehold; and not a chattel personal.' Gilb. l. Evdce.[316] and Swinb. who in a passage cited on the other side calls emblements 'mobilia' says they are 'immobilia'[317] in Part VII. §. 10. near the end.[318] between these authorities Blackstone seems unwilling to decide. he therefore steers a mean, which I think will be found the true course. 'emblements[319] are subject to many, tho' not to all the incidents attending personal chattels. they were deviseable by testament before the stat[ute] of wills,[320] and at the death of the owner shall vest in his ex[ecuto]r, and not his heir &c. [therefore tho' the emblements are assets in the hands of the ex[ecuto]r,][321] are forfeitable on outlawry,[322] and distreinable[323] for rent, they are not in other respects considered as personal chattels;

*published; containing, not only the Explanation of the Terms, but also the LAW itself, both with Regard to Theory and Practice*, 2d ed. in 2 vols. (London: Printed by his Majesty's Law Printers, 1771), 1: [480–481], s. v. "Chattels or Catals." This edition lacks pagination; citations here use the penciled pagination supplied by the New York University Law Library.

315. Rolle, *Abridgment*, 1: 727 ¶ 17.

316. Gilbert, *Law of Evidence*, 249 (emphasis added).

317. immovable things; land or buildings.

318. Swinburne, *Treatise on Testaments and Last Wills*, Part VII, at 420–421.

319. omitted: "are distinct from the real estate in the land and"

320. 32 Hen. VIII, c. 1 (1540).

321. Brackets in original. The words in brackets are not in Blackstone. The sentence in Blackstone begins immediately after this note with the word "They".

322. process by which a defendant or another person in contempt of criminal or civil process was declared an outlaw.

323. seizable, usually by a landlord upon default of a tenant; detaining personal property, whether lawful or unlawful, for any purpose.

and particularly they are not the object of larceny, before they are severed from the ground.' 2. Bl. 404.[324] they seem in truth to be chattels of a mixt nature, partly personal, partly real. Lord Coke himself sais they are not 'meerly personal but savor of the realty' i.e. they partake of the nature of the realty to which they are annexed. these instances prove they do. 1. if the estate be held in jointenancy [i.e., joint tenancy]: 2. if in severalty, and it be aliened without reserving the emblements: 3. if it be held at will and the will determined by the ten[ant]. 4. if it be conditional and forfeited by breach of the cond[itio]n: 5. if it be of certain duration, as that of ten[ant] for years: 6. if the emblements were not sowed by the claimant, or some body in posses[sio]n for him: 7. if the estate be held wrongfully; in all these instances the emblements go not as chattels personal, but with the realty: and in the four last, if he in rem[ainde]r be living, the emblements go to him; if he be dead, they go to the heir, as parcel of the inheritance. on the other **{H44}** hand they go to the ex[ecuto]rs in the instances so often before mentioned, to wit, where the estate was wrongful, joint, of certain duration &c. and they may be taken in execution. this shews then that my Lord Coke and Blackstone are properly cautious when they consider them as not meerly personal, since it is apparent they are as often subject to the regulations which govern real, as to those which govern personal estate. and therefore the conclusions do not hold which are drawn every where thro' the argument for the pl[aintiff] [see pa. 1. 13. 7. 8.][325] on a supposition

324. Blackstone, *Commentaries*, 2: 404.

325. Supra, at H4, H8–H9, H11. Brackets in original.

that they are 'mere personal chattels.'

Objection. the test[ato]r died on the 18th. of Aug. when some plants of tobacco were cut. these cannot be distinguished from those which were unsevered, and so Rob[ert] Bolling having intermixed his plants with those of Archib. Bolling without his consent, the whole mass becomes Archib[ald] Bolling's.

Ans. 1. Place this objection before the eye of reason. A[rchibald] Boll[ing] has a few plants on the lands of R[obert] Boll[ing] to prevent their perishing R[obert] Boll[ing] concludes to take care of them. not having a separate house to spare for their cure, he puts them into that wherein were his own plants. he cures them for A[rchibald] Boll[ing] and, as, in the process of that cure, they have unavoidably become intermixed with his own, so that the individual plants cannot be distinguished, he is ready to return them pari numero.[326] what is that equal number is easily discoverable[.] the overseer, before auditors, can state how many plants he tended. he knows how many nearly were cut at the death of his emploier: indeed the season and climate [to wit, of Amherst][327] shew it could have been very few. this then gives the proportion to which A[rchibald] Boll[ing] is entitled. but no, sais A[rchibald] Boll[ing]; you intermixed them without my consent, and so the whole mass is become mine.

2. Place this objection in a legal point of view. If Titius confuses his own property with that of Caius, <u>in the possession of Caius</u>, as if he throws his gold into the crucible where Caius has

326. of the same number or quantity.

327. Brackets in original.

fused his own gold, the whole mass belongs to the latter. I admit it. for Titius thereby expressly abandons his right, and Caius acquires it as first occupant. 2. Bl. 9.[328] when any person does an 'act which shews an intention to abandon his property, it then becomes, naturally speaking, **{H45}** publici juris,[329] once more, and is liable to be again appropriated by the next occupant. so if one is poss[esse]d of a jewel, and cast it into the sea or a public highway, this is such an express dereliction. that a property will be vested in the first fortunate finder, that will seize it to his own use.' here it is put into the occupancy of Caius, and so operates like a transfer. but if Titius, having property of his own in his own poss[essio]n, takes the property of Caius, and confuses it there with, Caius cannot claim the whole mass. for here is no act declaring Titius's intention to abandon his own property, but the reverse; he still retains the poss[essio]n. nor is there any occupancy in Caius, upon which his right was founded in the former instance. his only remedy is then to bring an action of Trespass against Titius for the wrong done him. accordingly if one man takes a sheep from another and puts [it] with his own flock so that it cannot be distinguished, or if he takes a guinea from another and puts into his own purse, or if he takes the corn of another and puts into his own barn, he is a trespasser, and on an action brought, the enquiry is, not how many sheep, or guineas, or how much corn the trespasser has of his own, that the whole value of that may be given in damages, but how much he took from the sufferer. his loss is the measure of the dam-

328. Blackstone, *Commentaries,* 2: 9.

329. public right; when a thing is common property so that anyone can make use of it.

age done him, not the possessions of the trespasser. to apply this to our case: R[obert] Boll[ing] having a number of plants of his own, mixes therewith the plants of A[rchibald] Boll[ing]. he has not thereby abandoned his own, nor given A[rchibald] Boll[ing] any occupancy of them. A[rchibald] Boll[ing] is therefore entitled only to what was taken from him. but it is well worthy consideration that A[rchibald] Boll[ing] had property in no plants. the property thereof was vested in the ex[ecuto]r, that is, in R[obert] Boll[ing] who might therefore mix them with his own, or sell, or do any thing else with them. he is indeed obliged to answer for their value; but this is no abridgement of his <u>absolute property</u> in the plants themselves. so that in truth R[obert] Boll[ing] has not intermixed any property of A[rchibald] Boll[ing]'s with his own unless perhaps the guineas for which these plants sold. yet this will not entitle him to all R[obert] Boll[ing]'s guineas, or in other words to all his estate; but he must prove how many he lost, and retribution will thereby be estimated. an ex[ecuto]r on any other terms would be in a fine situation.

**{H46}** Having now gone thro' all the objections stated on the part of the pl[aintiff] I shall only repeat and apply the conclusion formerly drawn, and unimpeached by any of these objections. it is that 'Emblements go to the ex[ecuto]r of the sower, if his estate was rightful, not joint, of incertain continuance, and determined by the act of god or of the law: but if it was wrongful, or joint, or of certain continuance, or determined by his own act, as by desertion, forfeiture, alienation without reserve &c. they go with the lands.' to apply it. E[dward] Bolling's estate was indeed rightful, not joint, and of incertain continuance. but it was determined by his own act, i.e. by devise without reserving the emblements when he had opportunity to reserve them if he had meant to do so. they therefore return to their natural channel and pass with the land to Robert Bolling.

Thus stood the law in the year 1711. when as yet no act of assembly had been made on the subject. but our legislature at that time,[330] took up into consideration, that tho' for the encoragement of agriculture, the law in certain instances had given the emblements to the sower, and in others to the owner of the lands, yet it had in neither case given them reapers: that in England indeed no inconvenience was thereby produced, because any number of reapers may be there hired on short warning; but that this could not be done in our country, where the lands are cultivated by slaves alone, and he who has them not of his own cannot hire them, more especially in those seasons of the year wherein they would be most wanting. they therefore, to save the emblements to the community as well as to the individual, determine to give him reapers also; and enact 'that where any person or persons shall die intestate, whilst his crop of Indian corn, wheat, or other grain, or tobacco is on the ground, unfinished; or dying testate, shall not have otherwise directed, all and every servant and slave, emploied in the said crop at the time of such decease, shall be continued on the plantations

330. 9 Anne, c. 2 (Virginia 1711): *An Act directing the manner of granting Probate of Wills, and Administration of Intestates Estates,* in Hening, ed., *Statutes at Large,* 4: 12–25: quote at 21–22, from § 27.

and emploied in the crop or crops respectively until the 25th. of December. then next coming: and that then the said crop {**H47**} shall be deemed and taken to be assets in the ex[ecuto]rs or adm[inistrato]rs hands, to be valued by appraisers to be appointed in the same manner as they shall be for the other part of the deceased person's estate.'[331] here then they direct that the same hands shall finish the crop; and, when finished, they do not remove the property, which, as I before observed, was sometimes in the sower, sometimes in the owner of the soil. they do not take from him his emblements, but they annex to them the labor of the slaves till the 25th. of December. hereby putting the labor of slaves on precisely the same footing with the emblements, or rather making that labor the dependant or accessary, of which the emblement is the principal, and to go with that in every case. so that the Argument sais truly that 'this act meddles not with the profits of lands, leaving them as they were at the common law' and 'that by the confusion of the emblements of land with the profits of slaves, the legislature has declared them to be homogeneous.' but what follows is inconsistent with this, and with the law, 'and the former [emblements][332] consequently to be personal chattels, and then they must go as all other personal chattels go.' and in the sentence preceeding 'this act has resolved the question, whether emblements pass by a devise of the land, in the negative.' it is inconsistent with the sentence first cited which said that 'the act had not meddled with them': because if it did not meddle with them, it could not resolve any question

331. Id.

332. Brackets in original.

about them, nor declare or make them to be any thing but what they were before. it is inconsistent with the law; because as we have before seen, emblements are not meer personal chattels; but are, sui generis,[333] of a mixed nature, and go sometimes as personal, sometimes as real estate. the legislature have not given the emblements to the labor of the slave, for then they would go to legatees, but the labor of the slave to the emblement. to express our conclusion therefore from this act of assembly in terms accurately true, we must say 'this act has annexed the labor of slaves to the Emblements, declared it homogeneous with them, and given it to him (whether sower or owner of the soil) who can entitle himself to the Emblements.' whether the **{H48}** declaring the crops assets contradicts this rule will be hereafter considered to avoid interruption at present. it must be observed that under this act the owner of the emblements could only finish what was actually in the ground; he could not put in a single new seed. therefore it would often happen that a person dying between the months of Aug. and of Feb. i.e. the times for sowing of wheat, and of tobacco seed, his ex[ecuto]r was to keep the plantations and slaves till July which would be 12. months, only to finish the wheat he had sowed, without being at liberty to put in either tobacco or Indian corn. this was a great imperfection in an act which went on the principle of saving both to the community and individual. another imperfection was that it had made the whole crop assets, without deducting the incidental charges. a third, that it entitled an ex[ecuto]r sometimes to keep out the owner of the soil a whole twelvemonth, which was much

333. of its own kind or class, unique.

too long. the act of 1730. c.8. s.10. 11.[334] therefore, to remedy these three inconveniencies, after reciting the old law verbatim, and that 'whereupon it may be questioned whether the same shall extend to the whole crop, when only some part of it is planted or sown, and whether the whole crop shall be assets, without deducting the charges that are incident to the making the same; for making the same more clear'[335] enacts 'that where any person shall die between the 1st. day of March and the 25th. day of Dec.' [this restricted the too long detention of the land][336] 'the servants and slaves which such person was poss[esse]d of, at the time of his or her death, shall be continued and emploied upon the several plantations held and occupied by the deceased person until the 25th. day of Dec. in that year, for the making and finishing a crop of tobacco, corn, or other grain' [the words 'making a crop' gave leave to plant other things][337] 'and such crop so made and finished shall be deemed assets as aforesaid, after the charges of clothing and feeding the servants and slaves so emploied therein; and also the expense of tools and utensils for them to work with, and the quitrents[338] of the land whereon

334. 3 & 4 Geo. II, c. 8, §§ 10, 11 (Virginia 1730): *An Act to prevent losses to Executors and Administrators by the sale of Negroes, Goods, and Chattels, taken in Execution; for amending the Law, in relation to Executors and Administrators; for maintaining actions of account against Executors and Administrators; and by one Joint Tenant, and Tenant in Common, their Executors and Administrators; for impowering Fathers to dispose of the Custody and Tuition of their Children; and for the better managing and securing Orphans Estates*, in Hening, ed., *Statutes at Large*, 4: 281–87: quote from §§ 10, 11 at 284.

335. Id.

336. Brackets in original.

337. Brackets in original.

338. rent paid by tenant of freehold by which he is discharged from any other rent.

they work, and other incident charges shall be deducted.'[339] **{H49}** the last words remedied the other imperfection. Now this law greatly enlarged the privilege of him who owned the Emblements. it not only continued his right to the labor of the slaves for finishing the emblements he had put in the ground, but gave him leave to put in, and with the same slaves to tend, new Emblements, provided he could finish them by the 25th. of Dec. and still the right to the original Emblements was what drew all the rest after it, and assimilated their nature to it's own. it drew a right to the labor of the slaves requisite to finish them; then it drew a right to put in new emblements; and lastly a right to the labor of the same slaves requisite to finish the new.

One only imperfection remained still to be remedied. the law, tho' it had taken from an heir or legatee the use of his slaves till the 25th. of Dec. had not even directed that they should then be delivered clothed. for this purpose the act of 1748. c.5. s.30.[340] provides that this shall be done, and does not in another tittle alter the clause cited above from the law of 1730.[341] So that it appears from a view of these three acts that the act of 1711.[342] meddled not with the right to the Emblements, but annexed thereto the Labor of the slaves till Dec[ember] 25. — that the act of 1730.[343] made a new

339. 3 & 4 Geo. II, c. 8, §§ 10, 11 (Virginia 1730), in Hening, ed., *Statutes at Large*, 4: 284.

340. 22 Geo. II, c. 5, § 30 (Virginia 1748).

341. 3 & 4 Geo. II, c. 8, §§ 10, 11 (Virginia 1730).

342. 9 Anne, c. 2 (Virginia 1711).

343. 3 & 4 Geo. II, c. 8, §§ 10, 11 (Virginia 1730).

annexation of a right to sow or plant more emblements, and the labor of the same slaves to finish them. and the act of 1748.[344] as to this matter made no alteration. the conclusion then is still what it was before 'that the labor of slaves is by the laws annexed to the Emblements, is homogeneous with them, and goes to him who can entitle himself to the emblements.' that right then being determined, this follows of course.

Objection. all the acts declare the crop so made shall be *Assets* in the hands of ex[ecuto]rs and adm[inistrato]rs, which makes them personal chattels, & then they must go as personal chattels do; that is, I suppose, to the residuary legatee, where there is one, and where none, to the distributees.

Answer. '*Assets*, from the French *Assez*, i.e. *satis.* signifies '*goods enough* to discharge that burthen which is cast upon the ex[ecuto]r or heir in satisfying the test[ato]r's *debts* and *legacies.*' Cowel's Interp. voce *Assets.*[345] **{H50}** the testator's goods and chattels 'shall be *assets* (from the French *assez.* enough) 'or *sufficient* goods and chattels to make the ex[ecuto]r chargeable[346] to a creditor or *legatee.*' Cun. L. dict. voce *Assets.*[347] cites Termes de la ley.[348] 'whatever is so recovered, that is of a saleable nature, and may be converted into ready money is called *assets,* in the hands of the ex[ecuto]r or adm[inistrato]r, that is, *sufficient,* or *enough* (from the French *assez*)

344. 22 Geo. II, c. 5, § 30 (Virginia 1748).

345. Cowell, *Interpreter of Words and Terms,* s.v. "Asset" (unpaged).

346. omitted: "as far as the said goods and chattels extend"

347. Cunningham, *New and Complete Law-Dictionary,* 1: [181].

348. Rastell, *Les Termes De La Ley,* 63–64.

to make him chargeable to a *creditor* or *legatee*.' 2. Bl. 510.[349] and Cowel ubi supra[350] sais 'and altho' this word *Assets* wear the vizard of a substantive, yet is it in truth but an adverb, and signifies goods *enough* to discharge that burthen &c.' as before.[351] *Assets*, then signifies in English *Enough*, and this calls for two other questions, to wit, *Of what?* answer. of *goods* and *chattels*. *For what?* answer. to satisfy *debts* and *legacies*. so that tho', in common speech, we say *assets*, shortly, yet these words are constantly understood and make a part of the idea, to wit, 'of *goods* and *chattels* to pay *debts* and *legacies*.' by use we have made the adverb *assez*, or *assets* or *assetz*, as it was spelt in old French, to carry in it the whole idea of 'goods and chattels *enough* to pay debts and legacies.' but in pleadings where we express our sense fully, we are to this day obliged to use the word *assez*, or *satis*, or *enough*, adverbially, and to join with it the other words beforementioned. thus in the declaration we say 'post cujus quidam mortem licet *satis*, et *sufficiens* de *bonis* et *catallis* ipsius W. ad solvendum omnia *debita* et *legata*' &c see Rast. 40. c.[352] and in the Plea 'dicit quod ipsa plene administravit omnia bona et catalla

349. Blackstone, *Commentaries*, 2: 510.

350. where above mentioned.

351. Cowell, *Interpreter of Words and Terms*, s.v. "Asset" (unpaged). Emphasis added in the manuscript.

352. The citation is to William Rastell, *A Collection of Entries of Declarations, Barres, Replications, Rejoynders, Issues, Verdicts, Judgements, Executions, Proces, Continuances, Essoynes, and divers other matters*... (London: Printed by John Streater, James Flesher, and Henry Twyford, assigns of Richard Atkins and Edward Atkins..., 1670). The quotation does not appear at fol. 40. William Rastell (1508?–1563), judge and author of legal commentaries, Lincoln's Inn (1539), serjeant-at-law (1555), J. Q.B. (1558–1563).

&c' ib. 323. a. [b][353] he does not say 'administravit omnia assets' or in Eng[lish] 'has administered all the *enough.*' for that would be nonsense. again in the verdict the jurors say 'habuit diversa *bona* et *catalla* ad *sufficientiam* pro satisfactione *debiti* predicti' &c.[354] and in the Judgment the court say it is to be levied, not of the *enough* of his test[ato]r, but '*de bonis* et *catallis* &c.' ib. 323.b.[355] this is to shew that the word *assets,* like it's significate *enough,* is a complex term, when used alone, and has the other words understood 'of *goods* and *chattels* to pay *debts* and *legacies*;' and constantly denotes that portion of the personal estate which is *sufficient* for the paiment of *debts* and *legacies*: and this may be more or less, as the debts and legacies are great or small. and this being **{H51}** understood when we use the word *assets,* we may so translate it in the act of assembly which will then stand thus 'which crop shall be *goods* and *chattels* for the paiment of *debts* and *legacies.*' and this removes all ambiguity. we cannot indeed at first distinguish which individual goods and chattels will be applied to the paiment of debts and legacies; but when they are all paid, what remains is not called *assets*; because the term being relative, to wit, to debts and legacies, there is nothing left to which it may relate. therefore what remains assumes now another name, and is called 'the *surplus* or *residuum.*' thus 2. Bl. 514.[356] 'when all the *debts* and *particular legacies* are discharged,

353. Rastell, *Collection of Entries...*, fol. 323, col. b (s.v. "Executors").

354. Only the first five words of the quotation are in Rastell, *Collection of Entries*, fol. 323.

355. Ibid., fol. 328 col. b: "of goods and chattels."

356. Blackstone, *Commentaries*, 2: 514. The quotation follows this citation.

the *surplus* or *residuum*,' not the *assets*, 'must be paid to the residuary legatee.' there can be no instance of authority produced where this term is used to denote the *personal estate* in general, abstracted from the idea of paying debts and legacies, or in other words, it is never used to denote the *distributable* or *residuary surplus*. what I infer from all this is, that the word *assets* denotes that part of the personal estate which will actually be applied to the paiment of debts and legacies, and that as soon as these are paid there are no such things as *assets* in existence. so that where an act of assembly directs that any thing 'shall be *assets* in the hands of ex[ecuto]rs and adm[inistrato]rs,' it means only that 'it shall be considered as a *chattel* for the purpose of paying *debts* and *legacies*, if there be a deficiency without it' but if not, it remains in the hands in which it would have remained had such act never been made. so that this is my position. a thing by being made *assets*, is only subjected to the paiment of *debts* and *legacies*, if necessary, in favor of creditors and legatees: but if not so applied, it remains as it would have done, had no act been made. on the other hand, is it said That it becomes thereby not only subject to paiment of *debts* and *legacies*, but, if not so applied, is made a part of the *residuum*, and shall go to the residuary legatee, or if there be none, to the distributees? if this is said, I deny it, and in support of that negation, produce these proofs.

1. the Slave act of 1705.[357] has a proviso 'that slaves shall be liable to the paiment of debts' which I conceive has the same effect

357. 4 Anne, c. 23, *An act declaring the Negro, Mulatto, and Indian slaves within this dominion, to be real estate* (Virginia 1705), in Hening, ed., *Statutes at Large*, 3: 333–35: the quotation following this citation is from § 4, at 334.

as if it had said they should **{H52}** be *assets* in the hands of ex[ecuto]rs and adm[inistrato]rs, for the paiment of *debts.* yet if there be no necessity to apply the whole or any part of the slaves to the paiment of debts, what is so unapplied does not become a part of the distributable or residuary surplus, but retains it's real nature and descends to the heir at law. it is farther remarkable that this act does not make slaves *assets generally*; which would, I expect, have subjected them to both *debts* and *legacies*; but only *specially*, for the purpose of paying debts. they cannot therefore be sold to pay legacies: as little can they be thrown into the *residuum*, for the residuary legatee, or distributees; these being purposes to which the act has not given them. to state my meaning, in a clearer light, I observe, that *Personal estate* is put into the hands of an ex[ecuto]r or adm[inistrato]r for three purposes. 1. it is *assets* to pay *debts.* 2. it is *assets* to pay particular *legacies.* 3. what is unapplied to these purposes is a *residuary*, or *distributable surplus.* now when an act subjects any new matter to be applied to any of these purposes, if necessary, the direction of the act is attended to strictly, and the new matter not applied to any of the three purposes not mentioned in the act. slaves are made *special assets*, that is, *assets* for the *special* purpose of paying *debts.* therefore they are applied to no other of the three purposes abovementioned. they are not *assets* to pay *legacies*, nor does what is unapplied become a part of the *residuary* or *distributable surplus.*

2. The act of parl[iament] 5. G.2. c.7.[358] declares that

358. 5 Geo. II, c. 7 (1732): *An Act for the more easy recovery of debts in His Majesty's plantations and colonies in America,* in *Statutes at Large* (Pickering), 16: 272–74. The quotation following this citation is from § 4, at 274.

American lands 'shall be chargeable with all just debts whatsoever.' this is making them special *assets* in the hands of the heir for the purpose of paying *debts.* now if the declaring any subject *assets* not only makes them liable to *debts* and *legacies*, but converts what is not applied to these purposes into a *personal residuum*, and so carries it to the residuary legatee, then is there no such thing left in America as inheritable property; and so our lands themselves are meer personal estates. once admit such a postulatum, and I defy the most subtle casuist to avoid the consequence.

3. By the stat[ute] of frauds 29. Car. 2. c.3.[359] a Trust estate in fee-simple is made *assets* in the hands of the heir, for the debt of his ancestor cestuy que trust,[360] in the **{H53}** same manner as lands in possession are. yet will any person say such a trust estate is applicable to any other the purposes of personal estate? that it may be sold to pay *pecuniary legacies*? that what is not sold shall go to the *residuary legatee*? and yet if declaring a thing '*assets* in the hands of ex[ecuto]rs, adm[inistrato]rs or heirs' makes that thing <u>merely personal estate</u>, and what is unapplied thereof to *debts* and *legacies*, transmissible to the *residuary* legatee or distributees, then would all trust estates of inheritance be meer personal estates, and go to such legatee or distributees, and not to the heir.

359. 29 Car. II, c. 3 (1676 [1677]): *An Act for prevention of frauds and perjuries*, in *Statutes at Large* (Pickering), 8: 405–10.

360. variant of *cestui que trust*: He who has a right to a beneficial interest in and out of a legal estate the title to which is vested in another; the person who possesses the equitable right to property and receives the rents, issues, and profits generated by that property, legal possession of which is vested in the trustee; the beneficiary of a trust.

4. the same stat[ute] enacts that an estate pur autre vie[361] shall be deviseable, and if not devised 'it shall be chargeable in the hands of the heir if it shall come to him by reason of a special occupancy as *assets* by descent, as in case of lands in fee-simple; and in case there be no special occupant thereof it shall go to the ex[ecuto]rs or adm[inistrato]rs of the party that had the estate thereof by virtue of the grant and shall be *assets* in their hands.'[362] here then an estate pur autre vie, which before this stat[ute] went to the general occupant, is now, if not limited to the heir, given to the ex[ecuto]r or adm[inistrato]r, and, like the emblements in our case, made '*assets* in the hands of the ex[ecuto]r or adm[inistrato]r.' if therefore, by making emblements *assets*, what of them is unapplied to debts and legacies, becomes a part of the residuary or distributable surplus, as is urged on the other side, then an estate pur autre vie, being in like manner made *assets*, will in like manner, become a part of the residuary or distributable surplus. so econtra,[363] if an estate pur autre vie tho made *assets*, is by force of that term only applicable to the paiment of debts, to which the stat[ute] points it, and shall not go into the *residuum*: pari ratione,[364] Emblements, tho made *assets*, are by force of that term only applicable, as general assets are, to paiment of *debts* and *legacies*, and shall *not go* into the residuum; but

361. literally, an estate for another life: a possessory interest in land the duration of which is limited by the life of a person not the holder.

362. 29 Car. II, c. 3, § 12, cl. 2–4 (1676 [1677]), in *Statutes at Large* (Pickering), 8: 407–408.

363. variant of *e contra*: from the opposite; on the contrary.

364. for the like reason; by the like mode of reasoning.

be, if unapplied, as if no such act had ever been made. and that by such conversion of an estate pur autre vie into *assets*, what is unapplied of it does not go into the distributable residuum is a point adjudged.

**{H54}**

2. Salkeld. 464. 'Oldham v. Pickering. Mich. 8. W.3. B.R.'[365]

'In attachment sur prohibition[366] the case was briefly thus: Thomas Oldham being seised of a messuage[367] in the county of Chester, to him and his assigns for three lives died intestate without children, leaving only Anne Pickering his sister: administr[atio]n was committed to Mary Oldham the pl[aintiff] whom the def[endant] now sues in the spiritual court of Chester for distribution, and to exhibit an inventory, which she exhibited and omitted there out the Estate pur autre vie; whereupon the simple question was this[:] whether an estate pur autre vie be not distributable in like manner, as intestates goods and chattels are, according to 22. &

365. *Oldham versus Pickering*, 2 Salkeld 464–65, 91 E.R. 400–401 (K.B., Michaelmas 1696). See also Holt 503, 90 E.R. 1176; Holt 504, 20 E.R. 1177; 3 Salkeld 138, 91 E.R. 738; 1 Ld. Raymond 96, 91 E.R. 960 (case name reported as *Olderoon vers. Pickering*). William Salkeld (1671–1715), barrister, Middle Temple (1698); serjeant-at-law (1715); published reports of cases and other legal writings.

366. Taking or seizing persons or property under or by virtue of a writ of prohibition, by which a superior court directs the judge and parties of a suit in an inferior court to cease proceedings, on the suggestion that the suit itself or an issue arising therein lies outside the inferior court's jurisdiction.

367. dwelling-house with the adjacent buildings and curtilage (enclosed space of ground).

23. Car. 2.[368] by force of 29. Car.2. c.3.[369] which enacts for the amendment of the law, <<That an estate pur autre vie shall be deviseable,[370] and if no such devise thereof be made, the same shall be chargeable in the hands of the heir, if it shall come to him by reason of a special occupancy, as *assets* by descent; as in case of lands in feesimple; and in case there be no special occupant thereof, it shall go to the ex[ecuto]rs or adm[inistrato]rs of the party that had the estate thereof by virtue of the grant, and shall be *assets* in their hands.>> And after a long argument by Cheshire for the pl[aintiff] and by Ward for the def[endant] the whole court, viz. Holt, Rokeby,[371] Turton and Eyre,[372] unanimously gave judgment 'that the prohibition should stand, and that an estate pur autre vie, belonging to an intestate was not distributable; for notwithstanding this alteration by the stat[ute] it remains a freehold still; and the amendment of the law in this particular, was only designed for the relief of Creditors; that if it came to the heir by reason of a special occupancy, it should be in his hands assets by descent, that is liable to the paiment of those *debts* where the heir is chargeable, and of

368. 22 & 23 Car. II, c. 10 (1670): *An Act for the better settling of intestates estates*, in *Statutes at Large* (Pickering), 8: 347–50.

369. 29 Car. II, c. 3, § 12, cl. 2–4 (1676 [1677]), in *Statutes at Large* (Pickering), 8: 407–408. The quotation follows this citation; emphasis added in the manuscript.

370. omitted: "by a will in writing, signed by the party so devising the same, or by some other person in his presence and by his express directions, attested and subscribed in the presence of the devisor by three or more witnesses;"

371. Sir Thomas Rokeby (1631?–1699), barrister, Gray's Inn, serjeant-at-law; J. C.P. (1689–1695), J. K.B. (1695–1699).

372. Sir Samuel Eyre (1633–1698), barrister at Lincoln's Inn (1661), serjeant (1692), J.K.B. (1694–1698).

those only; but if there was no special occupant, then it should go to the ex[ecuto]rs or adm[inistrato]rs, i.e. they shall be in the room of the occupant, and it shall be *assets* in their hands, i.e. they shall be bound to pay the *debts* of the deceased to the value thereof; so that it is not so much as *assets* to pay *legacies*, except such as are devised particularly thereout, the stat[ute] making it *assets* only for this particular intent, to pay creditors; and no debts appearing in this case, the adm[inistrato]r is as it were the occupant, and shall not **{H55}** be compelled to make any distribution thereof, as he shall of goods and chattels according to 22. & 23. Car. 2.'[373]

here then the judges declare that the act having made an estate pur autre vie *assets* to pay debts, and expressed no other purpose, it shall be applied to no other, not even to the paiment of *legacies*, much *less* to that of increasing the personal *residuum*. and this was in favor of an adm[inistrato]r who had no other claim but that he was occupant, against a sister who demanded distribution. [Note the reasoning of the judges in this case might perhaps render it questionable whether Emblements, by being made *assets*, are subject to anything but *debts*. that they are subjected thereby to particular *legacies* as well as *debts* I have all along supposed, but whether right or wrong is totally immaterial in our question, and therefore not worth the trouble of a present enquiry.][374] it is almost unnecessary to observe that a residuary legatee and distributee stand on the same footing. that surplus which goes to the residuary legatee, if a person

373. 22 & 23 Car. II, c. 10 (1670), cited in *Oldham versus Pickering* (Salkeld), 91 E.R. 400–401: quotation at 400–401.

374. Brackets in original.

appoints one, goes, if he does not, to persons whom the statute appoints, and who are called distributees. so that the quantum[375] passing to them is the same, tho' they take under a different conveiance, the residuary legatee taking under a will, the distributee under a statute: but still the thing taken, to wit, the residuum, is the same. so that their rights are perfectly commensurate.

Objection. Argum. pa. 8.[376] it is unjust that the devisee of the land should have the profits of slaves devised to another person.

Ans. to detain the lands from their owner, where the Emblements are given from him in any case, is in some degree unjust. but yet this private injury is made to give way to public good, which is promoted by the encoragement of agriculture. in our instance the legislature had three ways of effecting their purpose. 1. by dividing what was made between the legatee of the slaves, and devisee of the lands. this was rejected as subject to a thousand inconveniencies. 2. to give the profits of the lands to the legatee of the slaves. 3. to give the profits of the slaves to the devisee of the lands. the legislature chose the latter. a justification of their choice is obvious and **{H56}** unnecessary. but 'it is unjust that the slaves of one devisee should work the lands of another for the benefit of that other.' and how is the injustice proposed to be removed? by giving their profits to the devisee of the slaves? no. by giving them, and the profits of the other devisee's land to a third person, the residuary legatee. so instead of amending, you double the injustice. in our case the injury is comparatively small; for six out of the

375. something, a finite quantity.

376. Supra, at H9–H10.

thirteen slaves which finished the crop were given to the devisee of the lands. as to the other seven, they happen indeed in this instance to be given to the person who is residuary legatee; but the rule contended for by him is to be universal. he claims these emblements or profits of both lands and slaves, not as devisee of the slaves, but as residuary legatee. his rule therefore will most frequently take place in cases where the residuary legatee is different from both the devisee of the lands and the slaves, because this most frequently happens. so there will be one person's slaves, working another person's lands, for the benefit of — a third person. and this is to prevent the injustice done the legatee of slaves in working them for the devisee of the lands. but this remedy leaves the old evil as it found it, and makes a new one. in fact there is no way wherein so little injustice will be done individuals, and so much good effected for the state as by annexing the labor of slaves to the Emblements, and making it follow them into whatever hands they go.

I think it is to be wished that now, when questions on this subject are first arising, an end should be put to them, by carrying the Labor of the slaves with the Emblements, and subjecting them at once to the same rules. if that were done, we have a set of rules, already formed, which will apply to every case that can arise; and judges will determine, counsel advise, and even the people themselves proceed, at once with certainty and precision. but on the other hand, if a set of rules is to be now built up express for this particle of property, I fear we shall find that (like the jumble of real and personal rules which our legislature made it necessary to compound when they altered the legal nature of the slaves themselves) it will introduce infinite contest, and time, and expence, **{H57}** before they can be framed consistent with themselves, and with the other parts of the law. Here then I shall wind up this branch of dispute, by bringing together our several conclusions, which are,

That Emblements are *chattels* of a *mixt nature*, subject in some instances to the rules which govern personal, in others to those which govern real estate.

That, *annexation* to the *soil*, being their most distinguishing character, has laid them under this as a primary rule 'quicquid plantatur solo, solo cedit.'

That by way of *exception* to this, a secondary rule has been formed 'he who sows shall reap' 'provided his estate was rightful, not joint, of incertain duration, and determined by the act of god, or of the law': but that each of these circumstances is necessary to entitle him to the exception; insomuch that if his estate was wrongful, or joint, or of certain duration, or determined by his own act, he does not come within the *exception*.

That a conveiance by *deed* or *will*, has, by several adjudications, been declared a determination by the party's *own* act.

That tho' some of these adjudications were on conveiances by *deed*, yet equally with the others they support the position that 'a *devise* of lands passes the emblements,' because a *devise* is considered merely as a *conveiance*. from whence too it follows that a *devisee*, and *alienee* by deed take the same rights; which rights are not commensurate with, nor analogous to, those which descend to an *heir*.

That these adjudications are liable to no just objection, nor are they contradicted at all by those produced on behalf of the pl[aintiff].

By devise of the *lands* therefore to Rob[ert] Boll[ing] the *emblements* also passed to him.

Nor did the *friendly act* of taking care of the plants which were severed, whether considered as *vested* in Arch[ibald] Boll[ing] or in *himself*, intimate a *dereliction* of what were his own, with which they became unavoidably *intermixed*, or give any *occupancy* thereof to Arch[ibald] Boll[ing] but both law and justice are satisfied if Rob[ert] Boll[ing] accounts for their *value*.

**{H58}**

That Rob[ert] Boll[ing] being thus entitled under law to the *Emblements*,

Our acts of assembly have annexed to them the *Labor* of the *slaves* emploied in their culture, have made that labor homogeneous with the emblements, and therefore given it to him who can entitle himself to them: saving to creditors a right to have them applied to the paiment of their *debts*.

The *Rents* of the tenements for the year in which the test[ato]r died, and which were not paiable till days subsequent to his death, are another part of our claim under the devise of the Buffalo lick plantation. these I understand are given up by the other party. they are not mentioned in the Argument. indeed the rule is settled that Rents go to him to whom the lands belong at the last moment at which they are paiable. Salk. 578.[377] and I only mention them here that they

377. *Lord Rockingham & Al. contra Oxenden & Al.*, 2 Salkeld 578, 91 E.R. 487 (*coram* Trevor, Master of the Rolls, 1711).

may be made a part of the award.

A *Second* general claim is to the tes[tato]r's *Credits*, burthened with his *debts*. the clause on which it is immediately founded is this. 'it is my will and devise that my book be given up to my brother Robert, and that he recieve all the debts due to me, and pay all that I owe.' Arch[ibald] Boll[ing] objects that this is an appointment of Rob[ert] Boll[ing] his ex[ecuto]r, and that what he recieves, he recieves as ex[ecuto]r, and after paiment of debts, shall bring what is left of it into the residuum. on the other hand, Rob[ert] Boll[ing] insists that, to make this clause an appointment of an ex[ecuto]r is merely an artificial construction of the law; and that the test[ato]r intended by it a very different thing, to wit, to transfer to him the right to his credits, paying thereout his debts. that the intention of the test[ato]r in testamentary dispositions is not to be controuled by artificial deductions; and shall be carried into effect altho the words, in which he has happened to express himself, do in law produce an additional effect.

**{H59}** Now that he did intend this legacy beneficial to Rob[ert] Boll[ing] will appear

on the *Face* of the will

from *Parol proof* dehors[378] of the will.

On the *Face* of the will itself.

1. from the '*gift* of the book.' the word *give*, imports a transfer of the *use*, as well as *legal property*, of the thing given: insomuch that when used to transfer real estate, it carries in itself a warranty of the title. the bequest of the book then by the word '*give*' carried

378. out of, without, beyond, foreign to, unconnected with.

both an use and property in the paper and leather of which it was made. but how idle and nugatory would the gift of the paper and leather be, if their appendages, the *Credits*, were not to follow them? no body can suppose the test[ato]r intended to give his brother merely a parcel of waste paper. lest they should however he has taken care to explain it; to declare his intention that the substance shall follow the shadow; for he adds to the '*gift* of the Book' that his brother shall have, or *recieve* his Credits, *paying* his debts. this would have been naturally understood from the *gift* of a Book of accounts. if a man should by will give to another 'his outstanding debts,' no body would doubt the legatary's taking these debts beneficially. — so if he gave his 'debts paying thereout what he owed;' the same right would pass, only infringed a little in it's extent by cutting out a small part. — so if he should give 'his accounts,' every body would percieve his meaning to give him the Credits, paying thereout the Debts associated with them. — so would it be if he gave his 'Book of accounts' or his 'Book,' for their being sowed together in the form of a book can not alter the case. a 'gift of his book' then is synonimous with a 'gift of his debts paying thereout what he owed.' but the adding these words was necessary for another purpose. the testator knew his book was no accurate state of his accounts. that the account of every person with whom he had dealings was not there inserted, and that of those which were, every article of Debtor and Credit was not stated. yet he did not mean to give what was entered to one brother, and what was not entered to another, and so to put each debtor into two different hands. he **{H60}** therefore to the gift of his book adds 'that he shall recieve *all* the debts due to me, and pay *all* that I owe.' these are his express words, and include the Credits and Debts which his book would have omitted. — this answers an objection made on the other side 'that at any rate the gift of the book would not carry the credits which were not entered therein.' yet we are ready to admit this objection. for if the gift of the book did not transfer any credits which were not therein stated, by the same reason it did not transfer any debts not therein stated. this would be a cession of no small value to us.

2. from the import of the word '*recieve*,' which is sufficiently expressive of an intention in the testator that he should have the property. suppose the testator in any other clause had appointed some other person ex[ecuto]r. it cannot be doubted but the word '*recieve*' in this bequest would then have transferred the right to these monies. this proves it proper and sufficient then to carry a legacy. indeed no technical term, no precise form of words is requisite to dispose of property in a will. any expressions, from which the intention of the test[ato]r can soon be collected, shall be effective of that intention. thus 'I leave to my wife &c.' Ro. 478.[379] '200. £ to be at the disposal of my wife' 2. Ves. 181.[380] have been construed a devise to the wife. 'I desire that my wife shall give to

379. Rolle, *Abridgment,* [1?] 478. Volume 1, page 478 addresses confirmations by the dean and chapter of a cathedral. Volume 2, page 478 concerns statutes. Neither page discusses the subject addressed in the manuscript.

380. *Earl of Stafford v. Buckley,* 2 Vesey Senior 171–82, 28 E.R. 111–18 (Ch., 23 Feb. 1760): quote in 28 E.R. at 117. Francis Vesey, Sr. (fl. 1740s–1750s), barrister and Master of Chancery (Ireland); his *Reports* of Chancery cases were published in 1755.

I.S.' Vin. abr. (I.6.) 25.[381] ib (N.b.) 25.[382] 'I give my lands to I. S. to sell' or 'to do what he pleases with' Co. Lit. 9. b.[383] 'I release all my lands to I. S.' Bendl. 34.[384] 'I appoint that £80. thereof shall remain to I. S.' 2. Abr. Eq. 323. 22[385] 'I devise that my heir shall renounce his right in Black acre to I. S.' 1. Ray. 187.[386] these several expressions amount to a devise to I.S. and why? not because they are ipso facto a transfer of property to the devisee: even the words 'I give' 'devise' 'bequeath' have not that effect. the property passes not by any thing in the will, but by the assent of the ex[ecuto]r. but these expressions manifest a desire in the test[ato]r, and so are a direction to his ex[ecuto]r, that the property should be transferred to the person named. so does the expression in our case 'I will that my brother Rob[ert] shall recieve the debts due to me.' Godolph. 281.[387] is express 'if a man by will says, my will, pleasure, or desire is

381. Viner, *General Abridgment*, s.v. "Devise," (I. 6) "Good. And What will amount to a Devise," 8: 72 ¶ 25.

382. Viner, *General Abridgment*, s.v. "Devise," (N.b.) "What passes an Interest and what an Authority. By the Word Until &c. and of what Continuance," 8: 289 ¶ 25.

383. *Coke on Littleton*, 1: 9. b., "Of fee simple."

384. *Case no. 137, Anno 18 Hen. 6*, Benloe 34, 73 E.R. 955 (1440). This is a brief report in Law French.

385. 2 Equity Cases Abridged 323–24 (¶22), 22 E.R. 276 (¶22) (anonymous manuscript report, Ch., Hilary 1718).

386. *Baker vers. Wall*, 1 Ld. Raymond 185–87, 91 E.R. 1019–1021 (K.B., Easter [Paschal] 1698): quote in 91 E.R. at 1021.

387. John Godolphin, *The Orphans Legacy: or A Testamentary Abridgment. In Three Parts.... The Third Edition much augmented and enlarged* (London: Printed by Assigns of Richard and Edward Atkins, 1685), Part III, "Of Legacies and Devises," chap. III, "Of Words and Expressions Sufficient for Legacies," sec. 1, "Any words, whereby the Testators mind or meaning is express'd or implied, are sufficient for Legacies," 281. On Godolphin (1617–1678), see J. H. Baker, "Famous English Canon Lawyers: John Godolphin and Richard Burn," *Ecclesiastical Law Journal* 3 (1994): 214–222.

that he shall have, or *recieve*, or keep, or retain, these or the like words are {**H61**} sufficient to create a good bequest.'[388] the test[ato]r sais his brother Rob[ert] was to recieve his debts. but wherefore was he to recieve? answer. part that he might pay it away again, the other part for the residuary legatee. so in the instances before mentioned 'I leave to my wife' — 'I give to I. S. to sell' — '80.£ to remain to I.S.' you may with equal reason say the legacies were left, given to be sold, or directed to remain with the wife, or with I.S. for the residuary legatee. but in those cases it was understood that being placed with the wife, or with I.S. they were there placed for their own use, and not for the use of others. so here we must believe that the test[ato]r meant to place these *reciepts* with Rob[ert] Boll[ing] for his own use, not for that of another. in a conveiance of lands the presumption is alwais that it is still for the use of the conveior, and it rests with the conveiee to overweigh that presumption by contrary proof, either within or without his deed. but in the case of a will, the presumption goes over to the other side. the benevolence of the test[ato]r is the basis on which every will is formed. it is supposed to actuate every movement of his mind thro' the whole of it. this then, as a presumptive consideration supports every devise for the use of the devisee till the contrary

388. Emphasis in manuscript. Godolphin, *Orphans Legacy*, 281, reads as follows:

> 1. If a man in his Last-Will and Testament says, I do give, bequeath, devise, order or appoint to be paid, given or delivered; or, My Will, Pleasure or desire is, That he shall have or receive, or keep, or retain; or, I dispose, or assign, or leave such a thing to such a one; or Let such a person have such a thing; or any other words whereby the Testators mind or meaning of bequeathing is expressed, or sufficiently implied, shall be significant enough whereby the Legacy shall pass, provided no other legal Obstacle stand in the way…

be proved. and in Leak and Randal's ca. cited 4. Co. 4. a.[389] it was adjudged that this presumption shall not be destroyed by any extraneous evidence, but must be taken away by the will itself. in favor of Rob[ert] Boll[ing] then is that presumption at present. here are monies put into his hands without saying for whose use. that benevolence which is[390] presumed to have actuated the testator in every clause of his will, carries the use also to Rob[ert] Boll[ing], from whom it is not to be taken but on proof[391] that it was not intended for him. the test[ato]r in this instance seems to have extended his bounties to these two brothers, pretty nearly in equal degree. he had given them lands differing little in value: he had given Rob[ert] Boll[ing] six working slaves, and was framing his residuary bequest so as to give seven to Arch[ibald] and lastly he divides his residuum between them, and instead of making them joint legatees of the whole, he gives the one part of it, to wit, his money to the one brother, the other part consisting of horses, clothes &c. to the other in separate rights. so that **{H62}** Rob[ert] Boll[ing] is in some measure a residuary legatee, he being to take the residuum of the credits, after the debts are paid thereout: and Arch[ibald] Boll[ing] is residuary legatee of the other parts of the estate, being to take what remains, when the several parts otherwise disposed of are taken away. but it is objected that 'a *receiver* is from the nature of his substitution, accountable for what he recieves, as a

389. *Leak and Randal's Case* (Court of Wards, 1596), cited in *Vernon's Cases in Chancery*, 4 Coke Reports 1a–5b, 76 E.R. 845–59 (Q.B., Michaelmas 1572): cite in 76 E.R. at 856.

390. <supposed>

391. <drawn from the will itself>

bailiff, factor, ex[ecuto]r &c. ans[wer]. this depends entirely on the nature of his substitution. if he is substituted bailiff, factor, ex[ecuto]r, in express terms, or in words which shew the appointer intended the substitution to be of that and no other nature, then he is accountable. but if the substitution be of another nature, as a conveiance inter vivos[392] for consideration expressed, or a devise or legacy by will which imports in itself a consideration, to wit, the benevolence of the test[ato]r towards the legatee or devisee, then, from the nature of this substitution, the *reciever* is not accountable. for instance a man directs in his will that his daughter shall *recieve* £100. perhaps from the debtor himself, and not the ex[ecuto]r. is she accountable for this? no. and yet she is a *reciever.* but not being a reciever of that kind who are subject to account, she is not accountable. so the directing that Rob[ert] Boll[ing] shall *recieve* his credits, paying thereout his debts, imports a receipt, without being subject to account as much as if he had directed him to recieve £100. or that precise sum which will be left of the credits when the debts are paid. to state what is the law as to those recievers who from the nature of their substitution are accountable over, and thence draw inferences against those who from the nature of their substitution are not accountable, works no conviction. if it can be shewn indeed that this clause did not intend to make Rob[ert] Boll[ing] a legatee of what he *recieved,* but merely an ex[ecuto]r, who from the nature of his substitution is subject to account, something would be done. but that is the point in dispute

392. between the living, from one living person to another; often used to describe property transferred by a conveyance, as distinguished from a case of succession or devise.

between us, and so should be proved from unexceptionable postulata,[393] and not from those which first suppose the thing that is to be proven.

3. from the '*reciept* of the *debts*' being connected or coupled with the '*gift* of the *Book.*' words of doubtful meaning may recieve illustration from others in their neighborhood. for a moment suppose it doubtful whether the **{H63}** '*reciept* of his debts' was intended to be beneficial, or fiduciary. the context, to wit, the '*gift* of the book' explains the doubt and proves a beneficial devise intended.

4. from the manner in which the several parts of this sentence operate. had the test[ato]r only said 'I give to my brother Rob[ert] my Book, and will that he recieve my debts' and there stopped, I think his meaning could not have been doubted. The addition then 'that he pay all I owe' operates only by way of exception. it abridges the bequest pro tanto,[394] but does not destroy it in the whole. it is as if he had said 'I give him my outstanding debts, except so much as is requisite to pay what I owe.'

Obj. that if the debts had exceeded the credits, the residuary legatee must have supplied the deficiency out of his part; and if, in this case, the residuum must have been diminished, that in the contrary event it should be increased is as true, as that 'Quod sentit onus sentire debet et commodum.'

Ans. that if the Credits had been deficient, the residuum must have supplied, is true; that, if both these had been deficient, the specific and other legatees must also have supplied, is equally true.

393. things laid down as facts or postulates.

394. for so much, for as much as may be, as far as it goes.

shall their portions then be increased in the one case, because in the other they would have been diminished? I doubt that by such reasoning you will give every legatee and devisee a right to the whole credits; because the part of every one is subject to be diminished, if the credits and residuum prove deficient. most certainly if Arch[ibald] Boll[ing] may say 'my legacy would have suffered diminution if the Credits had been insufficient; if therefore they are sufficient, it ought to recieve the increase, because Qui sentit onus sentire debet et commodum'[395] so might Sarah Tazewell say with equal reason 'my legacy would have been diminished if both credits and residuum had been insufficient; if therefore they are sufficient, it ought to recieve the increase, because qui sentit onus sentire debet et commodum.' and so might Bolling Eldridge say; and so Richard Kidder Meade; and so in short might one and all say; and thus one and all make right to the selfsame thing. but state the law in it's simple dress, divested of artificial inferences. every person takes his **{H64}** legacy subject to refund in a certain order, if necessary. the residuum first, next the personal, last the real estate. and each is entitled to his whole, if the debts do not take it from him, or to so much as is left, if a part and not the whole is taken; and is not to give up the little left to him who would have been next called on, because it might have happened so that his legacy also would have been broken in upon.

Obj. Nay it is even objected that if this clause is a legacy of the outstanding debts, the def[endant] is not obliged to apply any of them to the paiment of what the test[ato]r owed till the

395. He who sustains the burden shall derive the benefit.

residuum is first exhausted.

Ans. 'my will is that he recieves all the debts due to me, and *pay all that I owe.*' upon what then is this objection founded? is it that the test[ato]r had not power to appropriate the monies due to him as a fund for the paiment of his debts? or is it that he has not, in terms sufficiently explicit, made that appropriation? I think the most learned counsel cannot devise words more explicit to common sense. or is it that a rule of law, which throws the debts on the residuum, shall prevail against the avowed will of the testator? tho' the creditors have a right to lay their hands on any subject chargeable with their debt, yet among legatees the will of the test[ato]r is so far supreme. that he may lay his debts on any fund: and if a creditor, passing by that fund, levies his debt on what was given to another, that other shall come for compensation on the fund which the testator has said shall '*pay all he owes.*'

5. from the *location* or *situation* of this clause. [and here I must beg the will may be turned to and read over; having inserted it verbatim in the state of the case for this purpose principally.][396] observe it comes in a little below the middle of the will. the testator was going on in a full career of donation. to one who attends to the usual operations of the human mind, it is inconcievable that he should all of a sudden fly off from a tract of thought in which he was proceeding, in the midst of his benevolences to erect a barren ex[ecuto]rship, and then again return to giving. reason as well as constant practice has placed the appointment of an ex[ecuto]r after all those purposes are expressed which he is desired to execute. but

396. Brackets in original. Jefferson transcribed the will in full, supra at H16–H17.

here, while the test[ato]r is instantly pursuing an uniform and connected train of purposes, a scrap of **{H65}** a sentence is laid hold of, withdrawn from its context which might alone explain it, and by the subtle reasonings of the law, it is distorted into a circumlocutory form of appointing an ex[ecuto]r, tho capable of another, and a most obvious construction, which would preserve, instead of interrupting that uniform tendency of mind in the test[ato]r.

6. from the most unusual and *circumlocutory* form of this appointment of an ex[ecuto]r, if considered merely as such. the common form of appointment is 'I constitute' 'I nominate' 'I ordain' 'I appoint' &c' 'such an one my ex[ecuto]r.' constant usage has rendered this familiar even to the lowest and most illiterate of the people. it is presumed there is no one a stranger to the name of an *executor.* every person then, when appointing one would describe him by that name, as being the most obvious, the shortest, and most complete description of his charge. no man would chuse to build up an appointment by enumerating the several branches of his duty, as superintending the labor of his slaves, buying clothes and provisions for them, selling his crops or other estate, recieving, paying, &c. when he could do the same thing more completely in three words 'I appoint I.S. my ex[ecuto]r.' had Edward Bolling intended this as the appointment of an ex[ecuto]r, as he was no lawyer, he could not but entertain some doubt it might not be an appointment. is it concievable then that he should hesitate to remove the doubt, when three words writing would do it. he was acquainted with the term '*executor.*' his estate was in the hands of his father's *ex[ecuto]rs.* till he came of age, to these *ex[ecuto]rs* he was

obliged constantly to apply for his clothes, his food, and his pocket expences, and at the hands of these *ex[ecuto]rs* he recieved his estate when he came of age. he could not then have been ignorant of the term '*ex[ecuto]r,*' and, knowing it, he must have preferred it as a more complete and ready appointment, than an enumeration of his duties. but I am persuaded that by the clause now in question he had not a thought of appointing an *ex[ecuto]r,* but totally forgot to do it: and that had he been asked, after writing his will, whom he had appointed ex[ecuto]r? his answer would have been 'I have forgotten to appoint one.' I do not mean by this that the clause now under consideration shall not have the effect of constituting Rob[ert] Bolling his ex[ecuto]r. I know that by a legal **{H66}** construction it is to have that effect. but I contend that the test[ato]r had not then in contemplation the appointment of an ex[ecuto]r, and consequently that his purpose was something else, to wit, to give a legacy. Nor does the objection weigh here that by allowing this clause to have the effect of constituting an ex[ecuto]r, it is thereby satisfied, and so we are under no necessity of ascribing to it any other meaning. the business here is not how to get rid of the several devises in the will by giving to them some other trifling and perfunctory effect, and so heaping all the estate together for the residuary legatee; but it is to investigate the test[ato]rs real view and intention, and not suffer it to be set aside because some other effect, not within his purpose, happens to result from the form in which he has expressed himself. here is a clause the direct import of which is that 'Rob. Boll[ing] shall receive a legacy': it's constructive import is that 'he shall be an ex[ecuto]r.' both are consistent and may well stand together. there is no necessity that the latter should destroy the former; on the contrary were either to prevail against the other, it should seem that the stronger ought, and that a <u>direct</u> is stronger than a <u>constructive</u> purpose. suppose a man, poss[esse]d of personal estate alone, makes a will in these words only 'I leave all my estate to A[rchibald] B[olling] in testimony whereof &c' this will be admitted to pass the estate to A[rchibald] B[olling] as a legatory. yet by Swinb. IV. 4. (3.)[397] these words, and several similar which he there puts, will make him *ex[ecuto]r.* a bequest of the residuam, will, without more saying, make the person to whom given an ex[ecuto]r. Swinb. ib. (4.)[398] yet will it not bar his right as legatory. here then are instances of what I urge; that tho' by construction of law the clause may produce it's secondary effect of appointing an ex[ecuto]r, yet it's primary one shall also take place, to wit, the bequeathing a legacy. Obj. that if Rob[ert] Boll[ing] had renounced the ex[ecuto]rship, he could not have claimed under this clause. answ. Why not? whenever a legacy is given as a satisfaction 'for the trouble of the ex[ecuto]rship', by renouncing the trouble, the legacy is given up; for where no service is performed no reward can be claimed. but if the legacy be given in general terms, so as that it may not be intended in consideration of his trouble, a renunciation of the ex[ecuto]rship does not bar his right to the legacy. see 1. Peere Will. ca. 88. Humberston v. **{H67}**

397. Swinburne, *Treatise on Testaments and Last Wills,* Part IV, "Of a pure or simple assignation of an Executor," 246–53.

398. Id.

Humberston.[399] now in our case the legacy is given in personal terms; so far as from being expressed to be given in consideration of the trouble of the ex[ecuto]rship that it may be doubted whether the test[ato]r intended to make him ex[ecuto]r.

The testimony adduced from the will itself in favor of Arch[ibald] Boll[ing] is the residuary clause. 'the rest of my estate, negroes, horses, clothes, and every other part of my estate not already given I bequeath to my brother Arch[ibald] Bolling.' here then he only bequeaths what he had not before given. this brings back the old question, whether he had before given these monies? which must therefore be determined on the former clause, and cannot recieve aid or illustration from this. so far indeed it seems to throw light on the subject. by enumerating his negroes, horses, clothes, we may infer what classes or species of articles he meant to pass by the devise of 'every other part of his estate' and that his debts being of a different class or species from those mentioned, were not intended to pass. thus 1. Abr. Eq. 201. 14. Trafford v. Berridge[400] a 'devise of all his goods, chattels, household stuff, furniture, and *other things* which then were or should be in his house at the time of his death.' adjudged that £265. in money found in his house did not pass. <<for that by the words 'other things' shall be intended things of the like nature or species, with those before men-

399. *Humberston versus Humberston*, 1 Peere Williams 330–33, 24 E.R. 412–13 (Ch., Hilary 1716); also in Gilbert's Reports 128, 25 E.R. 89–90.

400. *Trafford and Berridge*, 1 Equity Cases Abridged 201 (¶14), 21 E.R. 989 (Ch., Michaelmas 1729).

tioned.>> — so 2. Abr. Eq. 328. 2.[401] S.C. Vin. Devise (O.b.) 7.[402] 'I give the rest of my estate, chattels real and personal, to I.S.' resolved that nothing but his chattels passed, this enumeration restraining the meaning of the word 'estate.' 3. P. W. 112. Woolcomb v. Woolcomb.[403] 'devise of his household goods, and *other goods*, plate and stock within doors and without.'[404] money, cash and bonds, adjudged not to pass: the words 'other goods' signifying things of the like nature with household goods. And so in the present case the test[ato]r enumerating his negroes, horses, and clothes, may shew what kinds of things he had in view, and may serve to restrain the meaning of the words 'every other part of my estate' so as not to include his monies. had he considered them as a part of what he had not yet given, it is probable in the highest degree, he would have named his 'outstanding debts' in the enumeration; more especially as these outstanding debts are stated to have been large. we cannot believe that in enumerating the principal articles of the **{H68}** residuum he was giving he would mention such trifles as his horses and clothes, and omit the capital article of

401. 2 Equity Cases Abridged 328 (¶2), 22 E.R. 280 (¶2) (Ch., 1713):

> 2. A Man seised of Lands in Fee, made his Will, and thereby *gave several Legacies*, and then bequeathed in these Words, "*I give the rest of my Estate, Chattels real and personal,* to J.S." Resolved per Harcourt, C. that nothing but his Chattels passed by the word Estate. Hil. 11 *Ann.* [1713] Anon. 8 Vin. 294, pl. 7. (*MS Rep. S.C. accord.*)

402. Viner, *General Abridgment*, s.v. "Devise," (O.b.) "What passes by the Words, Residue of Estate," 8: 294 ¶ 7. S.C. means "same case."

403. *Woolcomb v. Woolcomb*, 3 Peere Williams 112, 24 E.R. 990 (Ch., 1731).

404. Id.

outstanding debts. so a man who had just made the tour of America, would hardly say 'he had visited the towns of Contocook, Kenderhook, Concord, and all the other towns of America'. Boston, New York, Philadelphia, as being the great and principal objects, would first strike his mind in recollecting and enumerating the places he had visited, and would most certainly be mentioned.

from these several circumstances then it is apprehended the test[ato]r's intention was that his brother Rob[ert] should recieve these debts, in his private right, and that Arch[ibald] should not have them: and that this appears on the *Face* of the *will.*

But we will also enquire Whether that intention may not be ascertained by *Parol proof* dehors of the will.

In these cases the leading caution is that we admit no evidence to <u>contradict</u> the express words of the will, which is directly inhibited, in England by the stat[ute] of frauds,[405] and here by the act of ass[embly] 1748. c.5. s.12.[406] which as to this matter is copied verbatim from the stat[ute] of frauds. with this caution in view, the judges in England have admitted parol evidence in several instances, but particularly to *explain* the test[ato]r's intention where *doubtfully* expressed in the will. instances of this applicable to the present case are as follow

| | |
|---|---|
| 5. Co. 68 Cheyney's case[407]<br>2. Abr' Eq. 416.14 S.C. 2 Barn. 118.[408] | } Parol proof admitted of the person for whom a legacy was intended. |

405. 29 Car. II, c. 3 (1676 [1677]).

406. 22 Geo. II, c. 5, § 12 (Virginia 1748).

407. *The Lord Cheyney's Case,* 5 Coke Reports 68a–68b, 77 E.R. 158–59 (Q.B., Court of Wards, Michaelmas 1598–1599).

408. 2 Equity Cases Abridged 416.14, 22 E.R. 354 refers to the case of *Brown et al'* and

| | |
|---|---|
| 2. Ves. 517 Pendleton v. Grant.[409] | Parol proof of the *thing* intended to be given. |
| 2. Ves. 736. Batchelor v. Searle[410]<br>2. Ves. 252. Gainsborough's case[411]<br>2. Ves. 448. Lady Granville v. Dss. of Beaufort[412]<br>4. Abr' Eq. 245.9. Littlebury v. Buckley[413]<br>2. P.W. 210 D. of Rutland. v. Dss. of Rutland[414] | The ex[ecuto]r was allowed to introduce parol proof that the test[ato]r intended him the surplus in *his private right*, and not in trust for the next of kin: which decisions are percieved to be applicable to the case of a residuary legatee, when we reflect on what was observed before, that he takes those rights which would have passed to the distributees, had the residuary clause been omitted. |

*Longley & Al'*, 2 Barn. K.B. 118, 94 E.R. 394 (K. B., Hillary 1731). Page 448 of that reporter is not revelant to the present context.

409. *Pendleton versus Grant*, 2 *Vernon's Cases in Chancery*, 517, 23 E.R. 931 (Ch.,[1705]). This case was reported by Vernon, not Vesey. A comparison to similar cases appears in 21 E.R. at 1011.

410. *Batchellor et Ux' versus Searl*, 2 *Vernon's Cases in Chancery*, 736–37, 23 E.R. 1081 (Ch., Hilary, 24 January [1716]). For the full text of this case, see Gilbert's Reports 126–27, 25 E.R. 88–89. This case was reported by Vernon, not Vesey. A comparison to similar cases appears in 21 E.R. at 1022.

411. *Gainsborough Comities versus Gainsborough Com'*, 2 *Vernon's Cases in Chancery*, 252–54, 23 E.R. 764–65 (Ch., 27 Feb. [1691]). This case was reported by Vernon, not Vesey. A comparison to similar cases appears in 21 E.R. at 1010.

412. *Lady Granvill & Al' versus Dutchess of Beaufort*, 2 *Vernon's Cases in Chancery* 648–50, 23 E.R. 1023–1024 (Ch., 24 Feb. [1709]). This case was reported by Vernon, not Vesey. Comparisons to similar cases appear in 21 E.R. at 1010 and 22 E.R. at 352.

413. *Littlebury and Buckley*, 1 Equity Cases Abridged, 245 (¶9), 21 E.R. 1022 (Ch., n.d.): cite of case only.

414. *Duke of Rutland & al' versus Duchess of Rutland & al'*, 2 Peere Williams 210–16, 24 E.R. 703–705 (Ch., [1723]).

**{H69}** so that it may be safely laid down that *Parol proof*[415] is admissible and proper here to explain what the test[ato]r is supposed to have expressed doubtfully, vid' the capacity in which Rob[ert] Boll[ing] was to recieve his debts.

What then does our *Parol* testimony prove? 1. both deponents, who are the test[ato]r's overseer and his wife, say they were present when he wrote his will, that after writing it he told them what he had 'left' or 'given' to his brother Rob[ert] in the enumeration he mentions the lands, the slaves by name, and the outstanding debts. so that he speaks of all these as '*left*' or '*given*' in the same sense to his brother; i.e. '*left*' or '*given*' to him in his *private right*. so that we may as well say the *lands* and *slaves* were given him as ex[ecuto]r, as that the *debts* were. 2. the deponents say that tho' they often after in other conversations heard him repeat the same thing yet he never spoke a word of his brother Rob[ert] being his ex[ecuto]r. a strong proof that he viewed him as a *legatee*, and not as an *ex[ecuto]r*. 3. that on the contrary from these conversations they both understood his meaning to be that Rob[ert] Boll[ing] should take as a *legacy* what was left of his credits after paying his debts. this part of the testimony I take to be conclusive. for who can best judge of the test[ato]r's intention: we who see nothing but the written letter? or those who saw him write it; to whom he repeated and explained the substance of what he wrote; and with whom he often conversed on the subject? surely the latter can best tell us the meaning of an expression on which we are doubting.

415. parol (oral) evidence taking the form of testimony by a witness (whether presented orally or by deposition).

This general question then being discussed, Whether the def[endant] is entitled to the Credits paying the Debts, as a beneficial devise? we proceed to enquire 1. What are the Credits, and 2. What the Debts, included in these general terms?

1. We say we are entitled, as one of his Credits, to *£500. due from Buchanan* for the warehouses at Pocahontas. That these warehouses were in the will devised to the pl[aintiff] we admit: but his counsel will admit on the other hand that the sale of them afterwards was a revocation or an ademption of the devise. passing by a thousand other authorities this will suffice. 5. Bac. 527. Sparrow v. Hardcastle.[416] Lord Hardwicke sais 'if one, seised in fee, devises, then infeoffs[417] another to the use of himself in fee: tho' it is the old use that remains, yet it is a *revocation*,[418] tho' it is his on **{H70}** the feoffment.[419] so of a bargain and sale without inrollment.'[420] that the alienation of the warehouses then subsequent to the devise of them, was a total revocation of that devise, cannot be denied: and if the devise was totally revoked, the pl[aintiff] cannot, under that,

416. *Sparrow v. Hardcastle* (Ch., 6 May 1754), in Bacon, *A New Abridgment of the Law*, 5: 527. The quotation follows this citation. See also 3 Atkyns 798–806, 26 E.R. 1256–1260; Ambler 224–28, 27 E.R. 148–50.

417. to perform an act or execute an instrument giving a freehold interest in land accom panied by *livery of seisin*, an act symbolically transferring actual possession of the land.

418. emphasis added in manuscript.

419. The act or instrument giving a freehold interest in land accompanied by *livery of seisin* (see supra note 417).

420. Inrollment (variant of *enrollment*) is the act of recording, enrolling, or registering.

claim the money for which they sold. — It is remarkeable too in the present case that the test[ato]r, on the sale of the warehouses, bought slaves and other things to a somewhat greater amount, relying on the reciept of this money to pay for them. these very purchases go to Arch[ibald] Boll[ing] as part of the residuum. so that not satisfied with the *things bought*, he wants also the money which was *the price* of them. but surely as Rob[ert] Boll[ing] is to pay for these negroes &c. it is highly reasonable he should have what was to have been applied to that purpose. as the sale therefore was a *revocation* of Arch[ibald] Boll[ing]'s title to either land or money; as he actually has the *fruits* of the sale in slaves &c. bought with the money; there can be no reason for withdrawing these £500. due from Buchanan to the test[ato]r, from the Credits which he has bequeathed to Rob[ert] Boll[ing].

2. Among the *Debts*, to the paiment whereof the will subjects Rob[ert] Boll[ing] ought not to be reckoned the *test[ato]r's proportion of his father's debts.* because it was neither *his debt*, nor, under his father's will, *chargeable* on his estate; but was the debt of his father, and, at the time the will was written, was chargeable and impending on Arch[ibald] Boll[ing]'s estate: and so does not come within the words of the will. he recieved his estate expressly exempted from the paiment of those debts. if he considered the original size of that debt, the very great estate his father left which, except his elder brother's part, was all put into the hands of the ex[ecuto]r for the paiment of the debt, and the length of time the ex[ecuto]r had held the several dividends of that estate; he had every imaginable reason to believe it was long ago paid, and that he

should never be called on for a shilling of it. he could not therefore have it in contemplation when he directed that his brother Rob[ert] should pay all that *he owed.* the words of the clause shew he only meant his own private debts: for he bequeaths his Book, which contained none but his private accounts, and directs that his brother should receive what **{H71}** was due to him, and pay what he owed; still meaning *debts ejusdem generis*[421] with those in his book, i.e., his private debts. But what most of all evinces that he did not include *his father's*, within the idea of *his own debts*, is that by this bequest he meant to give his brother something. now only cast an eye on the account annexed to the answer. add £550 to the debtor side and instead of leaving a balance of about £200. in favor of Rob[ert] Boll[ing] it brings him £350. in debt. this plainly evinces that, as his words do not include his *father's* debts, so neither did his intention. or, in other words, this unexpected call from his father's ex[ecuto]r, was not under his contemplation when he wrote the will. now the object which the test[ato]r had in his view, is what we are to pursue. he had given to his brother Robert his Credits. he excepted thereout as much as would pay his debts. this then must be the extent of the exception to be decreed. I have said he could not mean to enlarge the *exception* by the addition of his father's debts 1. bec[ause] he did not know of such a debt. 2. because had

421. of the same kind, class, or nature. In interpreting wills and other instruments, the *ejusdem generis* rule provides that, where general words follow an enumeration of persons or things, by words of a particular and specific meaning, such general words are not to be construed in their widest extent, but are to be held as applying only to persons or things of the same general kind or class as those specifically mentioned.

he known it the exception would have become larger than the thing out of which it was excepted. 3. because the context explains his meaning to be only debts ejusdem generis with those in his Book. to shew nothing shall be included by the words of the test[ato]r which did not make a part of his idea, I will cite a case from Fortescue. 184. 'Roe v Fludd. 2. G.2. C.P.,[422] 'This was a devise of lands to R. Bishop and his heirs for ever.'[423] 'and as to all the rest and residue of my real & personal estate whatever, not before herein bequeathed, I give and bequeath to Elizabeth Fludd and her heirs. the devisee R. Bishop died before the devisor, so it was a lapsed legacy.'[424] 'and the court held that Eliz[abeth] Fludd could not take it by the said words, tho' a lapsed legacy, for it must be expounded the rest and residue of the lands undevised at the time of making the will, and not at his death; and so judgment was given for the pl[aintiff].'[425] there were other facts relating to other points in the case,[426] which are here omitted. 2. Cun. L. Dict. voce *Legacies*[427] is this original case. 'if A. gives all his goods, plate and furniture at F. to A. his wife for life, and declares that he will dispose thereof after the death of A. by a codicil, and makes A. residuary legatee of all other his personal estate, then makes two codicils, but takes **{H72}**

422. *Roe and Fludd*, Fortescue 184, 92 E.R. 811 (C.P., Paschal 1729).

423. Id.

424. Id.

425. Id.

426. <but>

427. Cunningham, *New and Complete Law-Dictionary*, 2: [368–373], s.v. "Legacy."

no notice of the goods, plate and furniture at F. and makes his wife one of his ex[ecuto]rs, that then the wife not have the absolute interest in the goods, plate, and furniture at F. but that it should be distributed after her death as an indisposed interest, and she to have her widow's part thereof only.' Pasch. 1730. Davers v. Gibbs[428] decreed.' if then the father's debt were not meant by the test[ato]r to be a part of what his brother Rob[ert] was to pay; the residuum, being the natural fund for the paiment of all debts not expressly charged on any other, must be answerable for this which is not charged on any other fund. however, had it been otherwise, the award would only be that the father's debts should be paid with the test[ato]r's own debt, not of the Credits <u>so far as they should go</u>. that their excess might not make this bequest of the Book a charge on Rob[ert] Boll[ing].

For the same reason the residuum must pay the legacy of £100. to Sarah Tazewell, as it must have paid other pecuniary legacies had there been others. this was no *debt*; because a *debt* and a *legacy* are distinct things. had the test[ato]r charged his lands with the paiment of his *debts*, they would not have been subject to the paiment of *legacies*. thus sais Lord Talbot 3. P.W. 323.[429] 'where one gives a specific or even a pecuniary legacy, and devises lands to pay his *debts*, if a simple contract creditor comes upon the personal estate, and exhausts it so far as to break in upon the specific or pecuniary

428. *Davers v. Gibbs* (n.c., Paschal 1730), in Cunningham, *Law Dictionary*, at 2: [369] col. 2.

429. *Haslewood v. Pope*, 3 Peere Williams 323, 24 E.R. 1084–1086 (Ch., 1734). The quotation following this citation is from 24 E.R. at 1085.

*legacy*, these legatees shall stand in the place of the creditors to recieve their satisfaction out of the fund raised by the test[ato]r for the paiment of their debts.' so that if a *legatee* comes on the fund raised for the paiment of *debts*, it must only be in the place of, or as representing a creditor, not on any right he has as legatee. suppose for instance the legatee's demand was of £1000. and the creditor had taken from the personal fund only £100. The legatee could only have the £100. replaced out of the real fund, and the remaining £900. is chargeable on the personalty alone. if then the charging his lands with the paiment of *debts* does not subject them to *legacies*, by the same rule, the charging his Credits with the paiment of *debts*, does not subject them to *legacies*. but the credits given to Rob[ert] Boll[ing] are only charged with 'what the test[ato]r owed,' i.e. 'his debts'. the *legacies* therefore are not included within this **{H73}** charge, and so must resort to the residuum, which is the fund the law provides for them. this may be stated in another light. this bequest to Arch[ibald] Boll[ing] was only of 'the rest of his estate not already given.' but the £100. to Sarah Tazewell was 'already given', and so was to be taken out before the residuum was formed.

To recapitulate what has been said on this *Second* head

That the test[ato]r did intend this a beneficial bequest appears

On the *Face* of the *will* itself, and principally

from the import or efficacy of the word '*give*.'

from that of the word '*receive*.'

from the *location* of this clause, to wit, in the midst of *donations*.

from it's *circumlocution*, which shews the test[ato]r did not mean it as an appointment of an ex[ecuto]r; and therefore that he had another meaning.

from his not *enumerating* it in the *residuary* clause.

From *Parol proof* dehors of the will, which is *admissible*; and is

that the test[ato]r spoke of having '*left*' and '*given*' his lands, slaves, and debts in the same sense.

that he never mentioned that Rob[ert] Boll[ing] was to be his *executor.* but

that he meant his debts as a *legacy.*

Among the *Credits* we are entitled to is to be reckoned Buchanan's £500.

because the sale of the warehouses *revoked* the devise[.]

because Arch[ibald] Boll[ing] has the *fruits* of the sale, in his residuum.

Among the *Debts* we are to pay, are not to be reckoned

the test[ato]rs *proportion* of his *father's debts.*

because not *his debt, nor impending on his estate.*

because the context explains it *debts ejusdem generis* with those in the Book.

because the test[ato]r *knew not* of this debt, so had it *not in view.*

because it would make this bequest a *charge,* not a *legacy.*

nor the *legacy* of £100. to *Sarah Tazewell.*

because a *legacy* is not a *debt,* nor a fund for paying *debts,* liable to *legacies.*

because the *residuum* excludes *what* was *before given.*

**{H74}**

III. But if this was no more than the appointment of Rob[ert] Boll[ing] ex[ecuto]r, it was then an *Extinguishment* of his debt to the test[ato]r.

Plowd. 184.[430] 'if the debtee makes the debtor and another his ex[ecuto]rs, altho the debtor never administers, yet his action is gone for ever, which is agreed to by all the justices according to the report 21 E. 4,[431] and the reason thereof is good; for the other cannot bring an action without naming him who does not administer, notwithstanding his refusal; and they two cannot sue one of themselves as ex[ecuto]rs for a personal thing; and therefore in the same case the action is extinguished, altho the debtor who does not administer, but disagrees, dies first, and the other survives him. for a personal action once in suspense by the act of the party intitled to it, is alwais extinguished.' Woodward v. Lord Darcy. the same law is laid down in Nedham's case 8. Co. 136. a.[432] 'if the obligee maketh the obligor his ex[ecuto]r, it is a release in law of the debt, because it is the act of the obligee himself; and therewith agreeth 8. E.4. 3. 21 E.4. 2.b.'[433] and in the case of Wankford v. Wankford

430. *Woodward versus Lord Darcy*, 1 Plowden 184–186, 75 E.R. 282–87 (Q.B., Trinity 1557–1558). The quotation following this citation is from 75 E.R. at 283.

431. *Les Reports des Cases ... en temps Du Roy Edward le Quart*, "De Termino Paschae Anno xxi. E. IIII.," ¶ 4, at 3.

432. *Sir John Nedham's Case*, 8 Coke Reports 135a–136a, 77 E.R. 678–81 (C.P., Paschal 1604). The quotation following the citation is from 77 E.R. at 680.

433. The citations in the quotation from *Nedham's Case* are to *Les Reports des Cases... en temps Du Roy Edward le Quart*, "De Termino Hillarii Anno viii. E. IIII.," ¶ 3, at 24; and to id., "De Termino Hillarii Anno xxi. E. IIII.," ¶ 2 (b), at 21–22.

Salk. 299.[434] this point is agreed to be settled by all the judges of the King's Bench, to wit, Gould,[435] Powys,[436] Powell,[437] and Holt, in confirmation of a judgment of the Common Bench which had adjudged the same thing. [this case is too long to be* transcribed.[438] but if there by any doubt on this question I beg it may be turned to and read, because I rely on it as decisive.][439] the result of these authorities is That the making a debtor an ex[ecuto]r is an extinguishment of the debt under these restrictions. 1. that it be subject to Debts on a deficiency of assets. 2. to any legacy particularly fixed on it. and both of these restrictions are founded on the same reason, to wit, that the appointment operates by way of legacy. it is subject to debts because it is still part of the test[ato]rs personal estate, and his personal estate tho' given in legacies in express terms, may yet be taken to pay debts: it is subject to any *legacy* particularly fixed on it; because the legacy given out of it, operates as an excep-

434. *Wankford versus Wankford,* 1 Salkeld 299–309, 91 E.R. 265–72 (K.B., Hilary 1702). This case also appears in summary form in Holt's Reports, K.B., 311–14, 90 E.R. 1072–1073; 3 Salkeld 162–64, 91 E.R. 753–54.

435. Sir Henry Gould (1644–1710), barrister, Middle Temple (1667); J. K.B. (1699–1710).

436. Sir Littleton Powys (1648?–1732), barrister, Lincoln's Inn (1671); Baron, Exch. (1695–1701); J. K.B. (1701–1726).

437. Sir John Powell (1645–1713), barrister, Inner Temple (1671); J. C.P. (1686–1687); Baron, Exch. (1691–1695); J. K.B. (1702–1713).

438. "Since transcribed and to be found at pa. 63." —This is Jefferson's marginal note, indicated by the asterisk in the manuscript before the word "transcribed." The transcription of *Wankford,* in the handwriting of Anderson Bryant, appears infra, at H78–H90, following the end of the first argument for the defendant.

439. Brackets in original.

tion. it is as if he said 'I give my ex[ecuto]r the debt he owes me, excepting so much thereof, which I give to I.S.' Lord Holt indeed considers the operation of this appointment rather as a paiment and release, than as a **{H75}** legacy. but agrees expressly with Powell and the other judges as to the point of law then and now in dispute. let Powell's reason however speak for itself. he cited 21. E.4. 4.[440] and said 'if the debtee makes the debtor and another his ex[ecuto]rs, altho' the debtor never administers yet the action is lost for ever, and said it was agreed on all hands that if the ex[ecuto]r had proved the will, the action had been gone: and that the case 21. E. 4.[441] had been confirmed since by many authorities.'[442] and again he said 'that this extinguishment was not wrought by way of actual release, because then the debt could not be assets; but by way of legacy or gift of the debt by the will; and where that debt or any part of it is expressly devised by the will to pay a legacy, it will be assets to pay such legacy; because the test[ato]r did not intend to extinguish the whole debt; and so is the case in Yelverton. 160.[443] but <u>where there is no such special devise</u> the debt shall be extinguished, notwithstanding any other legacies. in 1. Ro. 920. 921.[444]

440. *Les Reports des Cases... en temps Du Roy Edward le Quart*, "De Termino Paschae Anno xxi. E. IIII.," ¶ 4, at 3.

441. Id.

442. *Wankford versus Wankford* (1 Salkeld), 91 E.R. 265–72: quote at 267.

443. *Flud versus Rumsey*, Yelverton 160, 80 E.R. 127 (K.B., Trinity 1610).

444. Rolle, *Abridgment*, 1: 920–921 (s.v. "Executors, (G) Que serra dit assets").

it is given as the reason why the debt remains assets in the hands of the ex[ecuto]r, and that it is extinct only by the will.'[445]

Objection. Brown v. Selwin. Ca. temp. Talb. 240.[446]

Ans. this is no contradiction of the rule before laid down; because it comes in under one of the exceptions, the ex[ecuto]r's debt being described and expressly given away. the Chancellor's words, if attended to, will shew the difference between that case and ours. 'it will appear clearly from the general words of devising the residue i.e. "all his real and personal estate which he had not *thereby before* given to the residuary legatees" that this debt which at that time was part of the personal estate falls within the description: the test[ato]r was entitled to this debt when he made his will, and at the time of his death; he had not before disposed of it, nor had he appointed mr Selwin ex[ecuto]r.'[447] here he gives explicitly the reason on which he grounds his decree, to wit, that the ex[ecuto]r's debt was particularly described and given away. for sais he 'the test[ato]r devises all which he had not thereby before given' &c now sais he 'this debt falls within the description'[448] for 'he had not given it *before*, the appointment of mr Selwyn ex[ecuto]r comes afterward.' and so the case states it. at the time when he writes his residuary clause then, **{H76}** he had not thereby *before* given it, and

445. *Wankford versus Wankford* (1 Salkeld), 91 E.R. 265–72: quote at 268.

446. *Brown v. Selwin et contra*, 25 E.R. 756–58.

447. Id.: quote at 757 (emphasis in manuscript).

448. Id.

so that clause describes and gives it away; and the subsequent appointment of Selwyn his ex[ecuto]r will not extinguish it against the express gift. but compare this with our case, and see how remarkeably they differ in that very circumstance which the Chancellor [Talbot] gives as his ratio decidendi.[449] Edw[ard] Boll[ing] first constitutes Rob[ert] Boll[ing] his ex[ecuto]r, which is a legacy of the debt. then comes the bequest to Bolling Eldridge, and then the residuary devise in these words 'the rest of my estate &c not *already* given, I give to my brother Arch[ibald].' now the debt of R[obert] B[olling] was *already* given by having *already* appointed him ex[ecuto]r, and so this residuary clause does not describe it nor carry it to A[rchibald] B[olling]. we cannot say then here with the Chancellor in Brown v. Selwyn[450] that 'he had not *before* disposed of it, nor had he appointed the def[endant] ex[ecuto]r.'[451] for here he had *before* appointed him ex[ecuto]r, and so had *already* disposed of it. this case then comes in under the rule 'that the making a debtor ex[ecuto]r, is an extinguishment of the debt, where there are other assets sufficient for debts, and where neither the whole nor any part of it is particularly given away.' and accordingly, notwithstanding this case which had been determined before Blackstone wrote, he lays down the law to be thus still 'if a creditor constitutes his debtor his ex[ecuto]r, this is a release or discharge of the debt, whether the ex[ecuto]r acts or no; provided

449. ground or reason of decision; the point in a case that determines the judgment.

450. *Brown v. Selwin et contra,* 25 E.R. 756–58.

451. Id.: quote at 757.

there be assets sufficient to pay the test[ato]r's debts: for tho' this discharge of the debt shall take place of all legacies, yet it were unfair to defraud the test[ato]r's creditors of their just debts by a release which is absolutely voluntary.' 2. Bl. 512.[452] and in 1. Atk. 461. Hudson v. Hudson.[453] Lord Hardwicke lays it down as law at this day. his words are 'if a creditor makes his debtor his ex[ecuto]r, the debt is totally extinguished and cannot be revived, tho' the ex[ecuto]r should afterwards die intestate, and administration de bonis non[454] of the first test[ato]r should be granted.'[455]

To apply the result of this to our case '1. there are other assets sufficient to pay the testator's debts. 2. he has not given away this debt on any part of it either by name or any description which will take it in. It is therefore a *legacy* or *extinguishment* of the *debt*.'

**{H77** — blank}

452. Blackstone, *Commentaries*, 2: 512: quote at 511–12.

453. *Hudson v. Hudson*, 1 Atkyns 460–62, 26 E.R. 292–94 (Ch., 7 Nov. 1737).

454. *administration de bonis non administratis*: administration of the estate of someone who has died without a will by a person appointed by the court of probate to administer on the effects of a decedent that have not been included in a former administration.

455. *Hudson v. Hudson*, 26 E.R. 292–94: quote in 26 E.R. at 293.

**{H78}**[456]

Wankford versus Wankford. Intr. in C.B.[457] Mich. II. Will. III. Rot.[458] 311. 312. &. Intr. in B.R.[459] Hill. I. Ann. Rot. 484.[460]

In an action of debt upon two bonds, one for 240 £. dated 1 November. 24. Car. 2.[461] and the other for 800 £. dated the 10th day of January the same year, by Elizabeth Wankford, widow, administratrix with the will annexed of Thomas Shelley, against Robert Wankford, son and heir of Robert Wankford the obligor, by which bonds the obligor bound himself and his heirs, &c. The defendant prayed oyer[462] of the letters of administration, and therein appeared the will of Thomas Shelley, in which was this clause: And I do hereby ordain and make the said Robert Wankford my son in law (who was the obligor) full and sole executor of this my last will, to pay my debts and legacies; And after the oyer of the letters of administration pleaded in bar, that Thomas Shelley the obligee, the 13th. of July. 30. Car. 2.[463] made his will, and Robert Wankford, the obligor in the said Bonds, his executor, and afterwards, viz. the 20th. of July the same year died, after

456. The transcript of *Wankford v. Wankford* is in Anderson Bryant's handwriting.

457. C.B. — Court of Common Pleas. Note that all reports of this case are to proceedings in King's Bench.

458. in rotulurus: in the rolls.

459. B.R. — *Banco Regius*, or Court of King's Bench.

460. *Wankford versus Wankford* (1 Salkeld), 91 E.R. 265–72.

461. 1673.

462. hearing or examination in court.

463. 1679.

whose death Robert the obligor took upon him the burden of the execution of the said will, and administred divers goods and chattels which were the testator's at the time of his death, and afterwards, the 17th. of August 1686. Robert the father made his will, and made the plaintiff his executrix, and afterwards the same day died, after whose death the plaintiff took upon her the burden of the execution of the last mentioned will, and proved it long before the grant of administration above set forth; the plaintiff replied protestando,[464] that the defendants plea is insufficient for want of alledging that Robert the obligor proved Shelley's will, or that Elizabeth the plaintiff proved it, and that it does not traverse or deny Nisi argumentative,[465] that Shelley died intestate; pro placito[466] she says that Robert the obligor never proved the will of Shelley, but died soon after him without proving the will; and that it is true, that the plaintiff was made executor of the will of Robert the obligor, and after his death proved it, and took upon her the execution thereof; and further says, that before the proving of the will of Robert the obligor by her, as aforesaid, or the administration of the goods of Shelley to her committed, viz. the 31st. of **{H79}** July 1689. she refused before the ordinary to prove Shelley's will; or to administer as executrix to him, whereby Shelley died intestate, and administration of his goods and chattels was committed to the plaintiff, and

464. protesting; emphatic word formerly used in pleading by way of protestation (the indirect affirmation or denial of the truth of some matter which cannot with propriety or safety be positively affirmed, denied, or entirely passed over; the exclusion of a conclusion).

465. except argumentatively.

466. for her plea.

that Thomas Shelley left no goods and chattels sufficient ad satisfaciend. ejus. debita et separales denar. summas per ipsum diversis personis debit. & solubiles et adhuc insolut. existen. praeter debitum praedict. superius petit. ac ci debit. per et super scripta obligatoria praedict.[467] To this replication[468] the defendant demurred generally,[469] and the plaintiff joined in demurrer, and Judgment was given in C.B. for the defendant, and the plaintiff brought a writ of error[470] upon that Judgment in B.R. and assigned the general errors, and after the cause had been several times argued, the court delivered their opinions seriatim, that the Judgment ought to be

**Gould** affirmed: *Gould, J.* said, that the case was in short, Shelley the obligee makes his will, and makes Robert Wankford the obligor his executor, who dies without proving his will, and makes his wife the daughter of Shelley his executrix, who proves the will, and also takes administration to Shelley her father with his will annexed, and whether this be a release of the bond, was the question: he said that if R.W. had proved the will, then that had been clearly a release, for

467. to satisfy his debts and the several sums of money owed by him to various persons and payable and still unpaid, except for the aforesaid debt claimed above and owed to him by and upon the aforesaid writings obligatory.

468. in common-law pleading, plaintiff's reply to defendant's plea; in chancery, plaintiff's reply to defendant's answer.

469. a defendant's initial plea that, taking as true the plaintiff's allegations of fact, denies they are a sufficient legal basis to allow the plaintiff to proceed or to require the defendant to answer.

470. an appellate court's writ, directed to a lower court of record, requiring it to remit to the appellate court the records of an action before it in which a final judgment has been entered, to permit the appellate court to examine errors alleged to have been committed in adjudicating the action and, if necessary, reverse, correct, or affirm the lower court's judgment.

it was agreed, that if the obligee makes the obligor his executor, and the obligor proves the will, it is a release; but the question is, Whether the obligor's not proving the will, will alter the case: and he said that he thought it did not: he put the cases of. 20. E. 4. 17. a.[471] *Br. exer.* 114.[472] 21. E. 4. 3. 81.[473] *Plowd.* 184.[474] That if several obligors are bound jointly and severally, and the obligee makes one of them his executor, it is a release of the debt, and the executor cannot sue the other obligor: So if the obligee makes the obligor and I.S. his executors, altho' the obligor never administers, yet the action is gone forever; and altho' the obligor dies and makes an executor, the other co-executor of the first testator who survives, shall not have an action against the executor of the obligor; he said that this case was stronger; that it appeared here that tho' the executor had not proved the will, yet he had administred, and by that means had put it out of his **{H80}** power to refuse the executorship; and that the proving the will was only to signify to the spiritual Court that there was a will, because, in case there was none, then there was a dying intestate, and the commission of administration belongs to them. he said, that an executor is a compleat executor to

471. *Les Reports des Cases... en temps Du Roy Edward le Quart,* either "De Termino Paschae Anno xx. Edwardi. IIII.," ¶ 17, at 3–4; or "De Termino Michaelis Anno xx. Edwardi IIII.," ¶ 17, at 13–16.

472. Brooke, *La Graunde Abridgement,* s.v. "Executors," ¶ 114, at fol. 308a.

473. *Les Reports des Cases... en temps Du Roy Edward le Quart,* "De Termino Hillarii Anno xxi. Edwardi IIII.," ¶ 2, at 21–22. Holt's opinion cites ¶ 3, but no case in this year numbered ¶ 3 or ¶ 81 seems relevant to this point. The citation provided here is an editorial conjecture.

474. *Woodward versus Lord Darcy,* 75 E.R. 282–87.

all purposes but bringing of actions, before probate; that before probate he may release an action, may be sued, may alien, or give away the goods or otherwise intermeddle with them; and for this he cited *Plowd.* 280.[475] 5 *Co.* 28. a.[476] 1. *Mod.* 213.[477] and he said that this would be the diversity. That if the executor refused the executorship, then he refused to accept the appointing him executor as a release, and by consequence the making him executor will have no operation; but if he does not refuse the executorship, but administers the goods, then that will be a release; and he cited also the case of Abram versus Cunningham, 2. *Lev.* 182. I. *Ven.* 303.[478] where it was resolved, that administration committed where there was a will and an executor, tho' the will was concealed, was void, and that it was all one, tho' the executor of the will, when it did appear, refused to intermeddle. he said, that if there were several executors, and all died before a notice of the will; yet this making the obligor executor would amount to a release: that there was no case express in point, viz. that it is a release where the executor never proves the will, but that it is cited, being put generally without mentioning whether the will was proved or not, and that upon such a general pulling and agreeing it to be a release, it is to be concluded that there is no diversity. That where the executor does administer,

475. *Graysbrook against Fox*, 1 Plowden 275–83, 75 E.R. 419–34 (K.B., Michaelmas 1561–1562).

476. *Russel's Case*, 5 Coke Reports 27a–28a, 77 E.R. 91–93 (Q.B., Hilary 1584).

477. *Parten and Baseden's Case*, 1 Modern 213–14, 86 E.R. 836–37 (K.B., Paschal 1677).

478. *Abram v. Cunningham*, 2 Levinz 182–84, 83 E.R. 508–509 (K.B., 1677–1678); 1 Ventris 303–304, 86 E.R. 195–96 (K.B., Hilary 1677–1678).

which he appears to have done in this case, and by that has put it out of his power to renounce, it will be a release, like the case in 3. Co. 26. b.[479] <<A. makes an obligation to B. and delivers to C. to the use of B. 'tis the deed of A. immediately, but B. may refuse it, and by that the bond will lose it's force; so of a gift of goods and chattels, if a deed be delivered to the use of the Donee, the goods and chattels are in the Donee immediately before notice or agreement; but the Donee may refuse, and by that the property and interest shall be devested.>>

*Powys J.* said, that an executor is a compleat executor as to every **{H81}** intent but bringing of actions before probate, so that he may release a debt due to the testator, assent to a legacy, intermeddle with the goods of the testator and he cited, besides the books already cited, 36. H. 6. 7.[480] *Dy.* 367.[481] and argued from the form of the probate of the will; but an administrator cannot act before letters of administration granted to him: he said, the executor by acting would become liable to the suits of all the creditors of the testator before probate, which R.W. the executor in the present case had made himself liable to by administring the goods of the testator, and therefore according to the known maxim of the law, qui sentit onus sentire debit et commodum, that this would amount to a release of

479. *Butler and Baker's Case*, 3 Coke Reports 25a–36b, 76 E.R. 684–713 (Q.B., Michaelmas 1591): The quotation following this citation is in 76 E.R. at 689.

480. *La Premiere Part des Ans du Roy Henry Le VI....* (London: Printed by George Sawbridge, William Rawlins, and Samuel Roycroft, Assigns of Richard and Edward Atkins Esquires, 1679), "Anno. xxxvi. Henrici VI.," ¶ 7, at 13.

481. *Fowler against Clayton, and others*, 3 Dyer 366a–367a, 73 E.R. 821–23 (Q.B., 1579–1580).

the debt without probate; he cited the case of Abram versus Cunningham, and the opinion of *Twysdon*[482] (which he remembred in the report of that case in I. *Ven.* 303.)[483] which opinion was also cited by *Gould. J.* in his argument, that tho' the executor debtor refuses, yet the action is gone, and the administrator cannot sue him; but he seemed not to rely upon it, but said it differed much from this case: That here H. should have a burden, such as an executor is put upon, whether he would or no: he said, that the diversity would be where the executor did actually refuse, before the ordinary,[484] and where he did not actually refuse, but only did not intermeddle with the administration; in the first case it would be no release, but it cannot be otherwise in the second, and more clearly so, where the executor did intermeddle with the administration, as he did in the present case.

**Powell** *Powell. J.* said, that the case was, the obligee makes the obligor his executor, who dies before he proves the will; and the question is, whether the debt be extinct, or the administrator of the obligee may sue the heir: he cited the case 21. *E. 4. 4.*[485] if the debtee makes the debtor and another his executors, altho' the debtor never administers, yet the action is lost for ever, and said it was agreed on all heads, that if the executor had proved the will, the action had been gone;

482. Sir Thomas Twysdon (Twisdon) (1602–1683), barrister, Inner Temple (1626); serjeant-at-law; J. K.B. (1660–1678).

483. *Abram v. Cunningham* (Ventris), 86 E.R. 195–96.

484. at common law, one who had exempt and immediate jurisdiction in ecclesiastical causes.

485. *Les Reports des Cases ... en temps Du Roy Edward le Quart*, "De Termino Paschae Anno xxi. E. IIII.," ¶ 4, at 3.

and that the case 21 *E. 4.*[486] had been confirmed since by many authorities, and that none of these authorities take any notice of the probate of the will; and if there were any such diversity it could not but have been taken notice of in some of them: but the reason that they go upon is that a personal action once suspended **{H82}** by the act of the party, is gone for ever, and tho' in some cases it may be suspended and revive again, yet never where the suspension is from the act of the party. he said that some books say the action is gone, some say the debt is gone, and some say the debt remains; but they will be all reconciled by this, that the debt will be assets; he said he could not see how the probate of the will altered the case; for the executor has assented to the executorship by intermeddling with the goods, and the act of the Ordinary has no effect; because the Ordinary has no right in any case where there is an executor, and all the executor's right is under the will, and all that right that he hath, he has by the will. he is in possession of all the testator's goods before probate, and may bring Trover[487] or Detinue;[488] so he may avow for rent where a reversion for years comes to him from his testator. but tho' he may commence an action before probate, yet he cannot indeed go on with the action; for when he comes to declare,

486. Id.

487. in common law, an action to recover damages against a person who found another's goods and wrongfully converted them to his own use.

488. in common law, an action for the recovery, in specie (hard cash), of the value of per sonal chattels from one who acquired possession of them lawfully but retains possession without right, together with damages for the wrongful detention.

he must produce in court the letters testamentary;[489] but now if probate were necessary to make him an executor, he could not bring the action without probate, as is evident in the case of an administrator, in which case there is no right till administration committed; for till then the administrator cannot bring an action; but in the case of an executor, the not proving the will is only an impediment to the action; but the right of action is the same before probate as after; and the reason why an executor cannot go on before probate is for the inforcing of probates, as is said in *Hutton.* 21.[490] because upon probates there are Inventories exhibited and other acts done by the executor, which are for the benefit of the creditors of the testator. he said, that if administration of the goods, &c. of the obligee was committed to the obligor, that was but a suspension of the action, and no extinguishment of the debt; but the reason of that is, because the commission of administration is not the act of the obligee, and so is 8 *Co.* 136. Sir John Needham's case;[491] he said, that unless the executor proved the will, he could not continue the executorship, and so is *Dy.* 372.[492] That in such case, administration de bonis non must be committed; but that case was the first

489. a formal instrument of authority and appointment given to an executor by the proper court, upon the admission of the will to probate, empowering the executor to enter on the discharge of that office.

490. *Wolfe versus Heydon,* Hutton 30–31, 123 E.R. 1078–1079 (C.P., Trinity 1619). Bryant miscopied the cite as Hutton 21.

491. *Sir John Nedham's Case,* 77 E.R. 678–81.

492. *Sir Rowland Heyward's Case,* 3 Dyer 372a, 73 E.R. 833–34 (Q.B., Michaelmas 1580–1581).

case of it, and it appears by the case in I. *Leon.* 275.[493] (where debt was brought against one as executor or in such a case, and the defendant pleaded in abatement[494] of the writ, that **{H83}** he was an executor of an executor, and therefore ought to have been so sued, and not as an immediate executor, and the plaintiff replied that the first executor died before probate, and the writ was awarded to be good) that there was no notice taken amongst the lawyers of that opinion, and indeed the opinion deemed to have proceeded rather from a compliance with the usage of the spiritual court, than from any ground in the reason and nature of the thing; for the power the executor has of making an executor to the first testator is by the will of the first testator, and not at all from the act of the ordinary, and it is by an implied power given to the first executor by the will of his testator and so is *Plowd.* 290a.[495] All the interest of the administrator is, from the ordinary, but all an executor's interest is from the testator. he said, that this extinguishment was not wrought by way of actual release, because then the debt could not be assets, but by way of legacy or gift of the debt by the will; and where that debt, or any part of it, is expressly devised by the will to pay a legacy, it will be assets to pay such legacy, because the testator did not intend to extinguish the whole debt, and so is the case in *Yelv.* 160.[496] but where there is no such special devise, the debt

493. *Powley and Siers Case,* 1 Leonard 275, 74 E.R. 250 (Q.B., Michaelmas 1584).

494. an entire overthrow or destruction of the suit so that it is quashed and ended.

495. *Chapman against Dalton,* 1 Plowden 284–92, 75 E.R. 434–47 (Q.B., Trinity 1564).

496. *Flud versus Rumsey,* 80 E.R. 127.

shall be extinguished notwithstanding any other legacies. in I. *Ro.* 920, 921.[497] it is given as the reason why the debt remains assets in the hands of the executor, and that it is extinct only by the will. a man cannot in strictness make a release by will, but the debt will be extinguished in such case with the diversity before taken: he said, that there would be a great diversity where the obligee made the obligor executor, and where the obligor made the obligee his executor; for in the last case the debt is not extinct, but only upon supposal that the executor has assets, which he may retain to pay himself; for tho' the obligee may give the obligor the debt, yet that will not hold vice versa, but in case of failure of assets the executor may sue the heir: Indeed where the executor has assets, the debt is gone, but that is because he may retain and pay himself, and so is 12. *H. 4.* 21.[498] *Plowd.* 185. b.[499] But if he has no assets, the action is never so much as suspended, for the executor may sue the heir, at the very day, and so it is not within the rule of a personal action once suspended, &c. he said, that there had been an objection made from the form of the **{H84}** letters of administration[500] in this case; that the court does indeed take notice of the forms used in

497. Rolle, *Abridgment,* 1: 920–21 (s.v. "Executors, (G) Que serra dit assets").

498. *Les Reports del Cases en Ley, Que furent argues en le temps de tres Haut & Puissant Princes Les Roys Henry le IV. & Henry le V. Ore Novelment Imprimes, Corriges, & Amendes, avec le Notations & References al Brook, Fitzherbert & Statham.* (London: Printed by George Sawbridge, William Rawlins, and Samuel Roycroft, Assigns of Richard and Edward Atkins Esquires, 1679), "De Termino Michaelis Anno xii. Henrici IIII.," ¶ 21, at 11.

499. *Woodward versus Lord Darcy,* 75 E.R. 282–87.

500. a formal instrument of authority and appointment given to an administrator by the proper court empowering the administrator to enter on the discharge of that office.

the spiritual court, and where there is no probate of the will (as in this case) they grant an immediate administration, and not an administration de bonis non administratis, which is done where the executor has actually administred the goods of the testator; but this form has not been constant, and adminstrations de bonis non administratis by the executor have been granted in the former case, and so it was done in the case of Heydon and Wolfe. *Palm.* 153. 2. *Cro.* 614. *Hutt.* 30.[501] he said, that if the making the obligee executor did extinguish the debt by way of release then it would work Nolens volens:[502] But if it took effect as a legacy, then the obligor refusing the executorship does also lose the benefit of what he would have had by being executor, and consequently the debt will not be extinguished: but he said he would not determine that point, because it appeared upon the pleading, that the executor administred goods of the testator, which is an agreement of the executorship, and so strong an one that he could not afterwards refuse it; and so the want of probate would not alter the case.

*Holt, C.J.* The pleadings in this case are perplexed; but upon the whole matter the case is but this, viz. R.W. is bound to S.S. who makes R.W. his executor, and dies; R.W. administers several goods, but dies before probate, the plaintiff takes administration to S.S. and brings an action on the bond against the heir of R.W. and the question is, the obligee having made the obligor executor, and

501. *Heden vers Wolfe,* Palmer 153–56, 81 E.R. 1023–1025 (report in Law French); *Hayton against Wolfe,* Croke, Jac. 614, 79 E.R. 524 (K.B., Michaelmas 1622); *Wolfe versus Heydon,* 123 E.R. 1078–1079.

502. whether willing or unwilling, consenting or not.

he having administered some of the goods, tho' not proved the will, whether that will amount to a release? And I agree it is a good release as this case stands.

There have been three objections occurred which render this point considerable[:]

1st. That when a will is made, and H. executor thereof, if the executor does administer, but dies before probate of the will, an immediate administration is committed; whereas, if the will had been proved, the administration must be de bonis non administrat' by the executor.

2dly, that the constant course of the spiritual court is, where the **{H85}** executor dies before probate, to make the ground and foundation of their granting administration to be, because the executor died ante onus executionis testamenti super se susceptum.[503]

3dly, That tho' the executor was administrator, yet if he dies before probate, his executor cannot be executor to the first testator. But notwithstanding these objections, I hold that the obligee's making the obligor his executor is a release in that case, and that for these reasons:

1st. Because by being made executor he is the person, that is intitled to receive the money due upon the bond before probate, and as he is the person that is intitled to receive it, he is also the person that is to pay it, and the same hand being to receive and pay, that amounts to an extinguishment: The rule does not indeed always hold, but is liable to these limitations:

503. before the burden of executing the testament taken upon him.

1st. If the obligor makes the obligee, or the executor of the obligee, his executor, this alone is no extinguishment tho' there be the same hand to receive and pay; but if the executor has assets of the obligor, it is an extinguishment, because then it is within the rule, that the person who is to receive the money, is the person who ought to pay it; but if he has no assets, then he is not the person that ought to pay, tho' he is the person that is to receive it; and to that purpose is the case of 11. H. 4. 83.[504] and the case of Dorchester versus Webb, I. *Cro.* 372. 1 Jo. 345.[505] where the obligee makes the executor of one of the obligors his executor, who has no assets, this is no discharge of the debt; because, tho' this executor, as executor of the obligee, is the person to receive; yet having no assets of the obligor, he is not the person who ought to pay: But if the executor of the obligee is made executor to one of the obligors, and has assets of the obligor, the debt is extinct, and the executor cannot sue the other obligor, for the having assets amounts to payment, and the same point was again resolved, *Hill.* 24. & 25. Car. 2. B.R. in the case of Lock and Crosse,[506] where the obligee was made executor to one of the obligors, and in an action by him against the other,

504. In the reports of 11 Henry IV consulted, no case bears the paragraph number 83. See, however, *Les Reports del Cases en Ley... en le temps de... Les Roys Henry le IV. & Henry le V.*, "De Termino Trinitatis Anno xi. Henrici IIII.," ¶ 32, at 83–84.

505. *Dorchester against Webb*, Croke Jac. 372–73, 79 E.R. 924–25 (K.B., Michaelmas 1634); W. Jones 345, 82 E.R. 182. The report of W. Jones is a summary in Law French. Sir William Jones, (1566–1640), barrister, Lincoln's Inn (1595), serjeant (1617), C.J. K.B. (Ireland) (1617); J. C.P. (1621), J. K.B. (1624); author of *Reports of Cases from 18 James I to 15 Charles I* (1675).

506. *Crosse and Corke Administrator of Redman*, 3 Keble 117, 84 E.R. 626 (K.B., Trinity 1673). The case was decided in Trinity, not Hilary Term.

where the matter was pleaded, the plea was held to be naught, because he did not shew to what value the assets were **{H86}** that he administred; but if the defendant had shewn that he administred goods to the value of the debt in demand, it had been a good plea.

2dly. Suppose the obligor takes administration to the obligee, in that case the same person has a right to receive the money, and is to pay it, and yet that will be no extinguishment, and so is 8. Co. 136. Sir John Needham's case;[507] but the reason of the diversity is, because the administration is made such by act of law, but the executor by the act of the testator, and for that reason it is no extinguishment; but if the administrator having no assets pays a debt of the Intestate to the value of the bond, out of his own money, that will be a release; tho' I do not know that it has ever been adjudged so.

3dly. If the executrix of the obligee takes the obligor to husband, that is no extinguishment of the debt, and so is the case of Crossman and Read. *Co. Lit.* 264. 1. *Leon.* 320. *Moor.* 236.[508] But if the obligee herself takes the obligor to husband, that is an extinguishment of the debt, because it would be a vain thing for the husband to pay the wife money in her own right; but he may pay money to her as executrix, because if she lays the money so paid to her by itself, the administrator de bonis non of her testator (if she dies intestate) shall have that money as well as any other goods that were her testator's; for if the goods of the testator remain in specie, they shall go to the administrator de bonis non, because in that case

507. *Sir John Nedham's Case*, 77 E.R. 678–81.

508. *Crossman against Reade*, Croke Elizabeth 114, 78 E.R. 371 (Q.B., n.d.). No report of or reference to this case appears in Leonard, Moore, or Coke.

it is notorious which were the goods of the testator, and they are distinguishable; and there is the same reason where money is kept by itself, and the husband permits it so to be; but if the husband seizes it, it will be his, and will be a devastavit.[509] In case of a feme covert[510] made executor, the husband has a great power: he may administer and bind her tho' she refuses, and may release the debts of the testator; so is 33. H. 6. 31.[511] But the wife cannot do any thing to the prejudice of the husband, without his consent.

My second reason is, That when the obligee makes the obligor his executor, tho' it is a discharge of the action, yet the debt is assets, and the making him executor does not amount to a legacy, but to payment and a release. If H. be bound to I.S. in a bond of 100. £. **{H87}** and then I.S. makes H. his executor; H. has actually received so much money, and is answerable for it, and if he does not administer so much, it is a devastavit.

3dly. By administring the executor has accepted of and taken upon him the whole administration, and is a compleat executor. he is before probate intitled to receive all debts due to the testator, and all payments made to him are good, and shall not be defeated, tho' he dies and never proves the will. All the testator's goods are actually in his possession, tho' at what distance soever, and he may maintain Trover for them; and as he may maintain a

509. literally, "he has wasted": the act of an executor or administrator in wasting the goods of the dedecent; mismanagement of the estate by which a loss occurs.

510. a married woman.

511. *La Premiere Part des Ans du Roy Henry Le VI...*, "De Termino Michaelis Anno. xxxiii. Henrici VI.," ¶ 31, at 47.

possessory action, so he may avow for rent where a reversion of a term comes to him; and for such rent as has accrued after the death of the testator, he may avow before probate, because the reversion is vested in him by the will; but for such arrears as accrued due in the testator's life time, he cannot avow without probate: he may bring an action of debt for a debt due to the testator before probate, so that tho' the teste of the original appears to be before the probate, yet it is well; so is I. *Ro.* 917.[512] Now the executor having all these advantages before probate, and the law taking notice of him, and he having actually administred, which is such an acceptance of the executorship that he cannot refuse it afterwards, this is a release. Indeed if he had not administred, but had refused in the ecclesiastical court to be executor, that making him executor had not been a release; for you shall no more force a man to accept of a release against his will, than of a deed of grant; and the subsequent refusal makes the deed void ab initio,[513] as if a deed of release were delivered to B. to the use of the obligor, if the obligor refuses to accept it, it is not the deed of the obligee, and he may plead non est factum[514] to it. 5. Co. 119. b.[515] and besides, if the obligor were never executor, then was he never the person intitled to receive the money, and consequently not within the reason of the rule of extinguishment.

512. Rolle, *Abridgment,* 1: 917 ¶ 2 (s.v. "Executors (A) Le power del Executors devant probate").

513. from the beginning.

514. in common law, a plea denying execution of an instrument that is the basis of plaintiff's action.

515. *Whelpdale's Case,* 5 Coke Reports 119a–119b, 77 E.R. 239–43 (K.B., Trinity 1605).

It is said, that H. who is made executor, is executor till actual refusal, and that was the resolution of the case of Abram versus Cunningham; and if so, then his adminstring in this case having put it out of his power to refuse, he has by administring accepted the executorship, which is that which makes the release: If H. makes **{H88}** his debtor and I.S. his executors, if I.S. administers, tho' the debtor never does, this is a release; so is 20. *E. 4.* 17.[516] 21. *E. 4.* 3.[517] And where H. makes his will and several executors, if one of them refuses and the rest administer, that makes his refusal void, and the refusing executor may notwithstanding release any debt. 5. *Co.* 28. a.[518] And in actions brought by them the refusing executor must be named. 9. *Co.* 97.[519] And if the refusing executor survives, he may take the executorship upon him. The case indeed in *Dy.* 160.[520] is contrary, and holds that the refusing executor must come in and act during the life of the acting executor; But the 21. *E. 4.* 23.[521] is contrary to Dyer, and according to the preceding

516. *Les Reports des Cases... en temps Du Roy Edward le Quart,* either "De Termino Paschae Anno xx. Edwardi IIII.," ¶ 17, at 3–4; or "De Termino Michaelis Anno xx. Edwardi IIII.," ¶ 17, at 13–16.

517. *Les Reports des Cases... en temps Du Roy Edward le Quart,* "De Termino Hillarii Anno xxi. Edwardi IIII.," ¶ 2, at 21–22. Holt cites ¶ 3, but no case decided in this regnal year numbered ¶ 3 seems relevant to this point. The citation provided here is an editorial conjecture.

518. *Russel's Case,* 77 E.R. 91–93.

519. *Sir George Reynel's Case,* 9 Coke Reports 95a–99b, 77 E.R. 871–78 (Ch., Hilary 1612).

520. *Water de Chirton's Case,* 2 Dyer 160b, 73 E.R. 349–50 (K.B., Trinity 1557–1558).

521. None of the cases numbered ¶ 23 in 21 Edward IV seems relevant to the text. See, however, *Les Reports des Cases... en temps Du Roy Edward le Quart,* "De Termino Paschae Anno xxi. E. IIII.," ¶ 8, at 23–24.

position; and in *Hardr.* 111. Pawlett versus Freke,[522] it is resolved, that where the refusing executor survives, administration committed during his life is void. In my Lord Petre's case,[523] which was before a commission of Delegates at Serjeants Inn;[524] where the case was, that several executors were named in the will, and one refused, and the other acted, and those that acted died, and the administration was committed before any refusal by the surviving executor to I.S. the administration was held to be void, because the refusing executor surviving, might, notwithstanding his former refusal, have taken upon him the executorship; and afterwards on another refusal of the surviving executor before the Ordinary, administration was committed to the Lord Petre, and was held to be good; and upon that title he maintained in this court an action of Trover for a Jewel.

If H. makes the obligor and others his executors, and the obligor refuses, but the others administer, and the obligor dies first, yet the debt is released; and the only reason of that must be, that the refusal was void, and the obligor might have come in and administred notwithstanding; for the probate by the other executors is for his benefit.

Now I come to answer the objections, and as to the first, That tho' an executor has administred, yet an immediate administration is committed, if he die before probate, and not an administration de

522. *Pawlet versus Freak,* Hardres 111, 145 E.R. 406 (Exchequer, n.d.). Sir Thomas Hardres (1610–1681), serjeant-at-law; barrister, Gray's Inn (1669); author, *Reports of Cases in the Exchequer 1655–1670* (published in 1693).

523. *Lord Petre vers. Heneage,* 1 Lord Raymond 728, 91 E.R. 1386 (K.B., Trinity 1701). See also *Lord Petre against Heneage,* 12 Modern 520, 88 E.R. 1491 (K.B., [1701]).

524. one of the Inns of Court where barristers and solicitors were trained.

bonis non. I answer, That the reason of this is, because the administring is an act in pais, of which the spiritual court cannot take **{H89}** notice, and they must commit administration according as it appears to them Judicially, and not according to the fact, and yet the acts done by the executor are good.

As to the second, That the administration in this case is grounded upon this, that the executor died ante onus executionis testamenti super se susceptum: I answer, that these words are to be understood in a limited sense, viz. that the executor died ante onus, &c., super se susceptum in the ecclesiastical court.

3dly, And which is the most considerable objection, That the executor dying in this case before probate, his executor is not executor to the first testator, but administration must be granted cum testamento annex',[525] tho' he did administer. To this I answer, that the executor by administring has take upon him the executorship, and has put it out of his power to refuse. 9. Co. 33. b. [36. b.] Hensloes case:[526] And where an executor administers, tho' he refuses afterwards before the Ordinary, yet administration cannot be committed during his life; and if administration be granted, it is void, and so is I. Mod. 213. Parten's case.[527] Now tho' the executorship ceases by the death of the administring executor in this case; yet he being executor by his own administring, that has by consequence had its operation of a release already. But then it may be said, what is the reason why, the executor dying before probate, tho' after admin-

525. with the will attached.

526. *Hensloe's Case*, 9 Coke Reports 36b–41b, 77 E.R. 784–93 (Q.B., Trinity 1600).

527. *Parten and Baseden's Case*, 86 E.R. 836–37.

istring, his executor shall not be executor to the first testator? why? it is because his executor cannot prove the will of the first testator, and consequently is incapable of recovering his debts, and consequently of being his executor: the administring executor may prove his testator's will, because he is the person named in the will; and if he does so, his executor shall be executor to the first testator, because there needs no new probate; but where the executor dies after administring and before probate, his executor cannot prove the will of the first testator, because he is not named executor to him in the will; and no one can prove the will but who is named executor in the will; the executor of an executor may renounce being executor to the first testator; but if he does not renounce, he is executor of course. I. *Cro.* 614.[528] And so it was held in the case of Abram and **{H90}** Cunningham. the executor's not proving the will, does upon his death determine the executorship, but not avoid it. If an executor obligor proves the will, and afterwards dies intestate, (which is a parellel case to the present case) his administrator is not executor of the will of the first testator. But yet the debt having been extinguished by his being compleatly executor and proving the will, tho' his administrator cannot continue the executorship, that will not revive the debt; so here, the administring executor not proving the will, and so his executor not being executor to the first testator, (if he were justly executor by administring to extinguish the debt) this inability of continuing the executorship will not alter the case.

The Judgment of C.B. was affirmed.

528. *Hewer against Bartholomew*, Croke, Elizabeth 614, 78 E.R. 855–56 (Q.B., Trinity 1587).

{**H91** — blank}

# {H92}[529] A. Bolling versus R. Bolling

1. <<General rule, where a man hath an incertain interest in land and sows the land, and his estate determines, yet he hath a title to the corn that he hath sown on the land, tho' the property of the land is altered.>> Gilbert's law of Evidence.[530]

The reasons are

<<First because it is a public benefit that the lands should be sown and cultivated, and all things that tend to plenty and increase ought to have the uttermost security that the law can give it; for hence it is fit that they should suppose a property in the corn distinct from that of the soil, and that this property should be at the intire disposal of the owner distinct and separate from the land, that all incouragement possible might be given to tillage, and that no man might decline cultivation under this fear, lest the profits should be swallowed by any person that he disliked.>> Gilbert's law of Evidence.[531]

<<Secondly, when any person hath sown, he hath gained a special property in the corn by his labor and industry, and therefore, tho' the property in the soil changes, yet the property of his labor remains; and this arises from the natural consideration of property which was at first derived from labor, for a man's own actions are most properly his own, and from thence all ownership begins, for

529. This part of the transcript, the second argument by George Wythe for the plaintiff, Archibald Bolling, is in Anderson Bryant's handwriting.

530. Gilbert, *Law of Evidence*, 243.

531. Id.

the very value of the soil is not more from the natural product than from the labor and industry that men have employed in their cultivation, which will very plainly appear by considering the difference between that in England and that in the West Indies. If also over and above the natural product of a cultivated soil, corn still adds a further value to the land, that the value of the land producing corn surmounts the value of a natural product from another cultivated soil, as much as that doth the product of a waste and barren soil, it follows that there ought to be another property in the corn distinct from that of land, in as much as there is a labor in the acquiring and sowing the corn distinct from the labor whereby the land was at first occupied and gotten; also there is a distinct charge in sowing the corn from the money whereby the land was purchased; **{H93}** from thence the law in following nature doth erect a distinct property in the corn different from the soil[.]>> *Gilb. law of Evidence.*[532]

<<Thirdly, there is a property in the corn distinct from the soil before the corn is committed to the earth, and that property is not lost by sowing it in a man's own soil: for I cannot lose the property of what is my own by putting it into a place which is my own also: but if I sow my corn in another man's soil, it ceases to be mine, in as much as I set it in the place of the natural product of his soil, and therefore it must belong to the owner as the natural product of the soil did; and were it otherwise men would break in upon other peoples grounds and sow them, and keep men out of the disposal of their own estates, and thereby they would raise a property to them-

532. Id., 243–44.

selves from another's estate, and put the owner to the trouble of controverting it; because a man expects a yearly return of the corn which he sows, it is reckoned part of his personal estate as the corn itself was before it was sown. But otherwise of timber trees planted, for they must be supposed to be annexed to the soil, since they were planted with the prospect that they could not come to be of use till many generations afterwards.>>

*C. Baron Gilbert* law of Evidence pa. 243. 4. 5.[533]

But there are several exceptions to the general rule.

1. <<If a tenant at will determine the will by any act of his own, he shall not have the corn sown; for when he determines his will, the interest is in another, and therefore he can no more reap the increase of his corn than if he had sown in another man's ground, the corn growing in the mean time, hindering the owner from all natural increase. and therefore to determine the will is to relinquish the corn, for to leave the land is to leave the profits of it.>> *Gilb.* law of Evidence pa. 246.[534]

2. If a tenant for life commit waste,[535] whereby his estate is forfeited, he shall not have the corn growing at the time he is evicted, because his estate is determined by a wrongful act of his own.[536]

3. <<Two joint tenants, one of them dies, the corn goes to the

533. Id., 244–45.

534. Id., 246.

535. an abuse or destructive use of property by one in rightful possession.

536. Gilbert, *Law of Evidence*, 247: "But if a Lease were made till the Tenant did Waste, and the Tenant doth Waste, he shall not afterwards have the Corn sown, for here he determines his Lease by a voluntary Act of his own."

survivor, and the moiety[537] shall not go to the executors of the deceased, for they are supposed to carry on the **{H94}** cultivation of the soil by a joint stock, and in all joint stocks, besides merchants, there is a survivorship.>> *Gilb.* law of Evidence. 248.[538]

4. <<If a woman seised in fee or for life sows the land and then takes a husband, and he dies before the severance the wife shall have the profits, and not the executors of the husband; for the corn committed to the ground is a chattel real that is annexed and belonging to the Freehold, and not a chattel personal,[539] and therefore, without the husband's disposition of it during his life, it belongs to the wife, and not to the husband.>> *Gilb.* law of Evidence. 249.[540]

5. If a man seised in fee of land sows it, and then conveys it, the purchaser or donee shall have the corn. The reason why the corn passeth to the donee as appertaining to the soil, when the property of the soil altereth and yet shall not descend to the heir when the property of the soil remains in the first owner, it is said by Gilbert to be this: <<every man's donation being taken most strongly against himself shall pass not only the land itself, but the chattels that belong to the land, but no chattels can descend to the heir, they go to the executor.>> *Gilb.* law of Evidence. 250.[541]

So if one seised in fee sows land, and devises it, the devisee shall

537. the half of everything; joint tenants are said to hold by moieties.

538. Gilbert, *Law of Evidence*, 248.

539. omitted: "annexed to and transferred"

540. Gilbert, *Law of Evidence*, 249.

541. Id., 250.

have the corn, and not the executors of the devisor, for the devisee in relation to the chattels belonging to the land, is put in the place of the executors by the words of the will. *Gilb.* law of Evidence. 251.[542]

According to the distinction in this last exception, by the common law, Robert Bolling would have been entitled to the crop growing upon Buffalo-lick plantation when the testator died, as it was at that time.

But it seems that this distinction is abolished, and the common law altered by act of general assembly. 22. Geo. II. cap. III. [5] Sect. 30.[543] which enacts

'That where any person shall die between the first day of March, and the twenty fifth day of December the servants and slaves which such person was possessed of at the time of his or her death shall be continued and employed upon the plantation and plantations held and occupied by the deceased person, **{H95}** until the twenty fifth day of December then next following, for the making and finishing, a crop of tobacco, corn, or other grain, which crop, so made and finished, shall be assets in the hands of the executors or administrators, after the charges of cloathing, and feeding such servants and slaves, and the expence of tools and utensils for them to work with, and also the quitrents of the land whereon they work, levies and other incident charges, shall be deducted.' For now by the act,

542. Id., 251.

543. 22 Geo. II, c. 5, § 30 (Virginia 1748), in Hening, ed., *Statutes at Large*, 5: 464. The quotation appears in the paragraph following this citation.

1. The crop is not annexed and belonging to the freehold, but is annexed to and incorporated with the profits of slaves, not a freehold, but a mere chattel interest.

The crop to be thus finished, is to be thrown into the ordinary fund for payment of debts, and is not distinguished from any other ingredient of that fund.

So that an executor may apply, or a creditor may levy an execution upon a crop that grew upon land devised before any other part of the estate, in satisfaction of a debt, or a Judgment. And if he should do so, it is apprehended the devisee of the land could not be reimbursed the value of the crop out of the rest of the estate.

He certainly could have no right to the labor of slaves employed in finishing the crop, if they were given to others, either by the common law, or by any words in the act; for by the former the legatees would have had an immediate right to possess their slaves, and by the other, altho' the legatees have no right to possess their slaves before the time allowed for finishing the crop be passed, their labor in the meantime is not given to the devisee of the land, neither ought the act to have such intendment; because it is unequitable:

For then, if in this case Edward Bolling had died intestate, as to all his estate, except Buffalo-lick plantation, so that the other lands would have descended to the heir at law; with the slaves, and, among them, such as were employed upon Buffalo-lick, the crops upon all the other plantations must have been distributed among the next of kin, and Robert Bolling, besides having the crop of Buffalo-lick, and the advantage of the heir's slaves to finish it, would have come in for a share of all the other crops too.

**{H96}** 2. The crop is not only separated from the freehold, and annexed to another kind of interest, but is expressly directed to go to a different person from him who takes the land; this going to the devisee, that to the executor or administrator.

The act, in relation to the crop, hath put the executor or administrator in the place, to use the language of Judge Gilbert, of the devisee of the land.

3. The executors and administrators are empowered not only to take the growing crop, but to employ all the testators or intestate's servants and slaves in making and finishing a crop.

So that if the testator or intestate die after the first day of March, and before the crop is begun, the executor or administrator may begin and finish the crop.

Now if Edward Bolling had died the second of March, before a plant or grain of corn was in the ground, by the devise of Buffalo-lick plantation, Robert Bolling, it is supposed, could not have claimed the crop which should be made and finished afterwards; for it was not emblements.

And the act has made no difference between the crop begun and not begun when the testator died; and it is apprehended to be impossible to assign a reason why there should be such a difference.

Again, by the act, all the crop is to go together, as well that part of the tobacco which was cut when Edward Bolling died the eighteenth of August, as what remained growing; and both are considered as his estate.

4. By the act the executors and administrators having power to

continue and employ all the decedents servants and slaves upon his plantations until the twenty fifth of December, for making and finishing a crop, &c. it seems the right of the person, to whom the land is devised, is suspended, as to the exercise of that right, until that time; so that the crop is severed before his right to take the profits of the land commences.

The executors and administrators have a right to hold the land, at least all that part of it which is or may be planted, until the crop is finished; how **{H97}** then can the crop, as emblements, belong to him, who has no right to take possession of the land till after the crop is finished, and actually severed?

The act having declared, that the crop, when finished, shall be assets in the hands of executors and administrators, it becomes, as it is apprehended, of consequence subject to distribution among next of kin, or to a residuary bequest. For,

1. The crop in it's nature is personal estate

Before this act emblements were chattels, some authors call them chattels personal, which savor of the realty, others say they are chattels real.

But every one admits them to be chattels, and all chattels, whether real or personal, are personal estate.

A term of years, which is undoubtedly a chattel real, is yet a part of the personal estate.

And growing corn, before this act, was to be put into the Inventory by the executor. *Swinburne* VI. 7. (8.)[544]

544. Swinburne, *Treatise on Testaments and Last Wills*, Part VI, at 420.

By the act the whole crop is certainly as much a personal estate as emblements were before the act.

2. The common law supposed the owner of the soil to have a right to emblements distinct from the right to the soil.

This Judge Gilbert repeatedly says in the passages before quoted.

And it is proved by this, that before a man could by law devise lands he might devise the crop growing upon it, or emblements. *Perkins.* 512.[545]

By the act the owner of the soil's right to the crop is as distinct from his right to the soil as his right to emblements was before the act.

Now all chattels, or, in other words, all personal estate, to which a decedent has a sole right, and which goes to his executors and administrators, is subject to distribution and to residuary bequests.

The case of Oldham v. Pickering. 2. Salkeld. 464.[546] so far from contradicting this position, as the defendant's counsel thinks, seems plainly to admit it.

**{H98}** 'In Attachment sur prohibition the case was briefly thus, Thomas Oldham being seised of a messuage in the county of Chester, to him and his assigns for three lives, died intestate without children, leaving only Anne Pickering his sister: administration

545. Perkins, *A Profitable Booke... Treating of the Lawes of England...*, chap. 8, "Devises," ¶ 512, at 224–25.

546. *Oldham versus Pickering* (Salkeld), 91 E.R. 400–401. The report is quoted in the paragraph following this citation.

was committed to Mary Oldham the plaintiff whom the defendant now sues in the spiritual court of Chester[547] for distribution, and to exhibit an Inventory, which she exhibited, and omitted thereout the estate pur autre vie, whereupon the single question was this. Whether an estate pur autre vie be not distributable in like manner, as intestates goods and chattels are, according to 22. and 23. Car. 2.[548] by force of 29. Car. 2. cap. 3.[549] which, enacts for amendment of the law, <<That an estate pur autre vie shall be deviseable, and if no such devise thereof be made, the same shall be chargeable in the hands of the heir, if it shall come to him by reason of a special occupancy,[550] as assetts by descent; as in case of lands in fee simple; and in case there be no special occupant thereof, it shall go to the executors or administrators of the party that had the estate thereof by virtue of the grant, and shall be assetts in their hands.>> And after a long argument by Cheshire for the plaintiff and Ward for the defendant the whole court, viz. Holt, Rokeby, Turton, and Eyre, unanimously gave Judgment, that the prohibition should stand, and that an estate pur autre vie, belonging to an intestate, was not distributable; for notwithstanding this alteration by the statute, it remains a freehold still and the amendment of the law in this particular, was only designed for the relief of creditors; that if it came to the heirs

547. one of the English local courts devoted principally to ecclesiastical cases.

548. 22 & 23 Car. II, c. 10 (1670).

549. 29 Car. II, c. 3, § 12, cl. 2–4 (1676 [1677]), in *Statutes at Large* (Pickering), 8: 407–408. The quotation follows this citation.

550. entry into lands held for the life of another under the original grant, or as heir of the tenant.

by reason of a special occupancy, it should be in his hands assetts by descent, that is liable to the payment of those debts where the heir is chargeable, and of those only; but if there was no special occupancy, then it should go to the executors or administrators, i.e. they shall be in the room of the occupant, and it shall be assetts in their hands. i.e[.] they shall be bound to pay the debts of the deceased to the value thereof; so that it is not so much as assetts to pay legacies, except such as are devised particularly thereout, the statute[551] making it assetts only for this particular intent, to pay creditors: and no debts appearing in this case, the administrator is as it were the occupant, and shall not be compelled to make any distribution thereof, as **{H99}** he shall of goods and chattels according to 22. and 23. Car. 2.'[552]

Now why was the estate pur autre vie, belonging to an intestate, not distributable?

Because, notwithstanding the alteration by the statute, it remained a Freehold still.

And a freehold is not an estate distributable by the statute of distributions,[553] which, like our act for that purpose, directs 'goods chattels and personal estate' only to be distributed.

But if the act of Parliament[554] had declared the estate pur autre vie to be a 'chattel' of the intestate, and assetts in the hands of

551. 29 Car. II, c. 3, § 12 (1676 [1677]).

552. 22 & 23 Car. II, c. 10 (1670).

553. Id.

554. Id.

executors and administrators, then the reasoning in the case would have been inverted thus:

'An estate pur autre vie belonging to an intestate is distributable, for since this alteration by the statute the estate no longer remains a freehold, but is part of the personal estate, and consequently within the statute of distribution.'

Our act does not indeed declare a crop to be chattels, because emblements were unquestionably chattels before, and the legislature hath not made them less chattels by connecting them with the profits of slaves, and throwing them confusedly into a fund, which consists wholly of chattels.

But, emblements being chattels, and this act declaring them to be assetts, they are therefore distributable.

But notwithstanding the case of Oldham v. Pickering it was far from being a settled point that, so in an estate pur autre vie, altho' a freehold, [it] should not be distributed as appears by what follows.

Hilary Vacation 1730.

Witter versus Witter. 3 Peer Williams. pa. 99.[555]

'Robert Witter possessed of a term for ninety nine years of lands in the county of Chester, if three lives, or any of them, should so long live, held of the late Earl Rivers, made A. his executor, and by his will devised the term to his **{H100}** infant Nephew, John Witter, and died, his own life one of the three lives. the executor applied to the Earl Rivers to renew, by adding a third life, and there was some slight proof that the Earl had refused to make any more

555. *Witter v. Witter,* 3 Peere Williams 99–102, 24 E.R. 985–86 (Ch., Hilary 1730). The quoted report follows this citation.

leases for years of his Tenements[556] in lease, but had changed them to lives, in order to make votes in chusing members of Parliament when he was in the administration. so that in the present case the executor of Robert Witter the lessee took a new lease in the name of a trustee to him and his heirs for three lives (viz.) that of the infant and the two old lives; and this was in trust for the infant and his heirs.

'The infant died above the age of fourteen and under twenty one, unmarried, and intestate: Whereupon the question was, who should be entitled to this lease, his heir or administrator.

'It was insisted, that the administrator of the infant was entitled; and that it should not be in the breast of any executor or trustee to alter the nature of the trust-estate, any more than it was in the election of a Guardian to change the personal estate by investing it in lands: since this would be to give an absolute power of disposing of and altering the right and property of the lease, to one who was but a bare trustee; that if the court had been applied to for leave to do this, they would never have granted it, without a provision, that in case the infant should die during his infancy, the purchase should not turn to the prejudice of the representatives of his personal estate: also that this would be injurious to the infant himself who, if it had continued, as originally it was a lease for years, might have devised it at fourteen; whereas being turned into a freehold

556. everything that may be held or possessed, provided it be of a permanent nature, whether of a substantial and sensible, or of an insubstantial, ideal kind. At common law, "tenements" includes lands, other inheritances, capable of held in freehold, and rents. *Tenemental land* is land distributed by a lord among his tenants, as opposed to the demesnes, which he and his servants occupied.

descendible, it would not be devised by him until his age of twenty one.

'On the other side it was represented as likely to prove very detrimental to an infant, if in case where the Lord would not renew but for lives, the executor should not be enabled to comply with this; because the other two lives might drop during the infants life; and the case would be the same if there were but one life in being; and then the infant, instead of being deprived of the power of devising (as had been objected) **{H101}** might have no estate to devise; that the putting the infants life in the lease must be for the benefit of the infant and of him only, and as to what had been mentioned of turning an infants personal into a real estate, that seemed to be a thing not necessary, but the renewal of the lease was a matter of absolute necessity.

'*Lord Chancellor* [King]:[557] This renewal lease, tho' for lives, shall follow the nature of the original one, and go to the executors as administrators of the infant as that should have done. If the fact had been (which has not been fully proved) that the Lord Rivers would not have made any other than a descendible lease for three lives, this might and ought to have been declared in trust for the benefit of the executors and administrators of the infant, if he should die during his infancy. Now tho' this trust be not declared yet it is in equity implied, since the renewal lease tho' for lives, comes in the place and stead of the original lease, which was for years. In consequence of which his Lordship declared that the same

557. Peter, Baron King (1669–1734), barrister, Middle Temple, 1698; C.J. C.P. (1714–1725); Lord Chancellor (1725–1733).

should be liable to a distribution according to the statute,[558] saying that tho' the spiritual court cannot intermeddle with a Freehold to distribute it, yet it doth not follow but that this court may inforce such a distribution.'

De term. S. Hilary 1732.

Sir Samuel Marwood v. Cholmley Turner Esqr. 3 *Peer Williams.* 163.[559]

Sir Henry Marwood, seised of an estate for three lives, held of the archbishop of York, and having among other things, devised that leasehold estate, after making his will, surrendered his lease for lives and took a new lease for three lives to him and his heirs.

<<Upon the back of the will these words were written (and as supposed) by the testator's own hand, 'this is my will,' afterwards these words were written 'But not now so intended to be.'

<<The spiritual court having construed the indorsation as a revocation of the will, and thereupon granted administration as if sir Henry Marwood had died intestate; the lord chancellor, prima facie[560] inclined to think that this estate **{H102}** pur autre vie was since the statute of frauds, to be taken in as *Personal estate.*

<<It was answered (and the court allowed the answer) that the lease being granted to sir Henry *and his heirs this was a descendible*

558. 22 & 23 Car. II, c. 10 (1670).

559. *Sir Samuel Marwood, Bart. v. Cholmley Turner, Esq.*, 3 Peere Williams 163–72, 24 E.R. 1013–1017 (Ch., Hilary 1732). The paragraphs following this citation indicated as quotations come from this report.

560. at first sight; on the first appearance.

*freehold and a real estate.*>>[561]

So that if the estate pur autre vie had been a chattel no body ever questioned but when it was made assets it would have been subject to the statute of distribution;[562] and in this case it seemed admitted if a limitation had not been to the heirs, the estate should have been distributed.

The doubt was, notwithstanding the case of Oldham v. Pickering, whether such an estate remained a freehold, or became a personal estate after the statute of frauds; And this doubt continued till 14. *Geo. II.* cap. 20.[563]

Whereby reciting that 'by an act made in the 29th year of the reign of King Charles the second, intituled, an act for prevention of frauds and perjuries,[564] amongst other things, it was enacted, that estates pur autre vie, whereof no devises should be made, should[,] in case there should be no special occupant thereof, go to the executors or administrators of the party that had the estate thereof by virtue of the grant and should be assets in their hands; and reciting further that doubts had arisen, where no devisee[565] had been made

561. *Sir Samuel Marwood, Bart. v. Cholmley Turner, Esq.*, 24 E.R. 1013–1017: quote in 24 E.R. at 1014.

562. 22 & 23 Car. II, c. 10 (1670).

563. 14 Geo. II, c. 20 (1741): *An Act to amend the law concerning common recoveries, and to explain and amend an act made in the twenty ninth year of the reign of King Charles the Second, intituled, An act for prevention of frauds and perjuries, so far as the same relates to estates pur autre vie,* in *Statutes at Large* (Pickering), 17: 435–38. The provision quoted (with slight alterations of tenses) in the following paragraph is from § 9, at 438.

564. 29 Car. II, c. 3 (1676 [1677]).

565. "devise" in the statute.

of such estates, to whom the surplus of such estates, after the debts of such deceased owners thereof were fully satisfied, should belong: it is enacted, that such estates pur autre vie, in case there be no special occupant thereof, of which no devise shall have been made, according to the said act for prevention of frauds and perjuries, or so much thereof as should not have been so devised, shall go[,] be applied[,] and distributed[,] in the same manner as the personal estate of the testator, or intestate.[']

It will be objected, that the law, by declaring the crop to be assets, hath only subjected it to the payment of debts and legacies.

Supposing this, which however is not admitted, to be true; why is not the crop applied to the payment of debts and legacies?

**{H103}** Does not the law, by declaring the crop to be assets, take the emblements, which in that case were not assets before, from the devisee? and what right can he have to them? and if he had a right to the crop, as it was at the testator's death, what right had he to employ the slaves bequeathed to other persons for his benefit?

If any other person besides Robert Bolling had been executor, and made the crop, could he, as devisee of the land, have recovered the crop; or, if it had been applied in discharging a debt or legacy, been reimbursed the value of it?

If then the law, by declaring the crop to be assets, only subjected it to the payment of debts and legacies; it is not discerned how it will follow, that the devisee of the land can claim them.

Again, if Edward Bolling had died the second of March, before the crop was planted, and the executor had begun and finished a crop, this by law would have been assets; but could the devisee of the land have claimed them? would he call that emblements which was not sown? or would he say that a devisee of land is entitled to assets?

Lastly the whole crop, as well what was severed, as what was growing when the testator died, is made assets; if the devisee of the land has a right to the one why not to the other too under this law?

But let this objection be examined further.

The word assets is said to be derived from the French assez an adverb signifying enough.

In its original and proper application it signified goods enough to discharge that burthen which is cast upon the executor or heir in satisfying the debts and legacies of the testator or ancestor.

In this sense it was used when the quantity of the goods was compared with the amount of the demands chargeable upon them.

Afterwards it was understood, and is now most frequently used in an improper sense, to signify, not the comparative quantity, but the nature of **{H104}** the goods, with respect to their being subject to debts or legacies, generally or particularly.

Assets are real or personal, where a man hath lands in fee simple, and dieth seised thereof, the lands, which come to his heirs, are assets real; and where he dies possessed of any personal estate, the goods, which come to the executors, are assets personal. Terms de ley.[566]

Assets enter mains,[567] <<is when a man indebted makes execu-

566. Rastell, *Les Termes De La Ley*, 63.

567. assets in hand; assets in the hands of executors or administrators applicable for the payment of debts.

tors, and leaves them sufficient to pay>> his debts and legacies, <<or some Commodity or profit is come to them in right of their testator[,] this is called assets in their hands.>> Cow. interp. Assets[568] Off. Ex. 307.[569]

<<Damages recovered by the executor in an action of trespass shall be assets.>> 1. Inst. 124.[570] Off. Ex. 308.[571]

Per Murray Sollicitor general. 2. Fr. Atk. 206.[572] 'tho the law says that a reversion after an estate tail[573] is not assets, yet it is a gross and inaccurate expression, and is only sub modo, for there is a *liableness* which makes it assets in futuro,[574] or in other words, a quality to be *liable* to the debt in futuro.'

The word assets is not used in this act of general assembly in it's proper sense. 'Where any person shall die between the first day of March and the 25th day of December the servants and slaves which such person was possessed of &.c. shall be continued and employed

568. Cowell, *Interpreter of Words and Terms*, s.v. "Asset" (unpaged), from which the language preceding the citation is drawn.

569. Wentworth, *Office and Duty of Executors*, 307 (Curson, "Supplement: Of Executors").

570. *Coke on Littleton*, 1: 124, "Of Villeinage."

571. Wentworth, *Office and Duty of Executors*, 308 (Curson, "Supplement: Of Executors").

572. *Kinaston versus Clark*, 2 Atkyns 204–206, 26 E.R. 526–28 (Ch., Trinity vacation 1741): The quotation following the citation is in 26 E.R. at 527.

573. a possessory interest in land subject to a condition defining the class of heirs who may take possession of the property — most often, heirs directly descended by blood from the current owner so long as the owner's posterity endures in a regular order and course of descent.

574. in future.

upon the plantation and plantations held and occupied by the deceased person until &c. for the making a crop &c. which crop, so made and finished, shall be assets in the hands of the executors and administrators.' &c.

If we understood the words thus: 'which crop shall be enough' of goods in the hands of executors and administrators to discharge the debts of the testator or intestate, it would be very indifferent english, and, if at all intelligible, often not true in fact.

But the meaning is, 'which crop shall be such an estate in the hands of the executors and administrators as is liable for payment of the **{H105}** decedents debts and legacies.' What estate is it that in the hands of executors and administrators is liable for payment of his debts and legacies? or in other words, what are assets in the hands of executors and administrators.

Answer. 'all the personal estate whereof the testator died possessed, whether it consists in chattels real, as leases for years, mortgages, &c. or chattels personal as household goods, money, cattle, &c. the first of which the civil law distinguishes by the name of immoveable goods, the latter into moveable, belong to the executors, and are <u>assets</u> in their hands for payment of the testators debts and legacies.' Office of executor 52.[575] Bacon's Abr. 2. vol. pa. 416.[576]

Hence it seems that all a man's personal estate is assets, because

575. Wentworth, *Office and Duty of Executors*, 52.

576. Bacon, *A New Abridgment of the Law*, 2: 416 ("Executors and Administrators: (H) What shall be deemed the Testator's Personal Estate, or Assets in the Hands of the Executor"). The quoted part of this paragraph is from Bacon.

all is liable to pay debts and legacies, whether it exceed, or is exceeded by, the debts and legacies:

For his personal estate is called assets, even if it do not amount to so much as his debts.

By 4. Ann. cap. 7. [33] sect. 2.[577] 'after debts &c. the surplusage, i.e. the remainder, of all and singular the goods, chattels, and personal estate of every person dying intestate &.c. i.e. of all that estate which was liable to the payment of debts, or, in other words, of the assets in the hands of administrators, shall be distributed &c.'

If that be not the true meaning of assets it must be this:
'That the word assets denotes that part of the personal estate, not which is liable but which will actually be applied to the payment of the debts and legacies,' and this seems to be the opinion of the defendant's counsel.

But, not to insist that this a novelty, and that it is contradictory to the act, according to which the crop shall be assets, not: when it is paid away for that might sometimes not happen, but when, i.e. so soon as it is made and finished;

If no part of the estate be assets but what will actually be applied **{H106}** in payment of debts and legacies; and if consequently, it is not assets before it be so applied; it seems there is no such thing as assets.

For the moment it is paid away it is not the testator's or intestates assets, but the creditors or legatees property.

577. 4 Anne, c. 33 (Virginia 1705): *An act for the distribution of intestates estates, declaring widows rights to their deceased husbands estates; and for securing orphans estates,* in Hening, ed., *Statutes at Large,* 3: 371–76. The quotation from § 2, at 371–72, follows this citation.

If the estate be not assets before or after it be paid away it is not assets at all.

In truth that the nameing of an executor in a will is a gift in law of all the testator's personal estate to the executor, and that a commission of administration vests the property of all the intestates personal estate in the administrator, is founded in this, that all that estate is assets.

That the legal property of the whole is in them is indisputable. Yet they are but trustees as to the surplus for residuary legatees and next of kin.

If all the personal estate be assets the act of distribution operates upon the remainder of the assets after the debts &c. paid.

Accordingly it will not perhaps be disputed that the surplusage of the crop, which one act calls assets, would, by the other act, have been distributed in the following instances:

I. If Edward Bolling had died intestate.

The heir, it is agreed, could not take the crop.

There was no devisee to claim it.

The administrator might take it by the act.

But he has no right to retain any part of what he takes, as administrator, to his own use.

He must then distribute it.

Yet it is assets.

II. If Edward Bolling had died the second of March before the crop was begun, and made no disposition of the surplus, and the executor had, after his death, made and finished a crop.

**{H107}** The devisee of the land could not take it as emblements, for it was not in the ground when the testator died[.]

He could not claim it as assets, for a devisee of the land, as such, has nothing to do with assets.

The executor might have taken it.

But then he would have taken it as a trustee for the next of kin.

Yet the crop would have been assets.

III. That part of the crop which was severed when the testator died, if he had not bequeathed the surplus, is admitted to be distributable.

Yet the whole crop is assets.

If in these instances, the crop would have been distributable; there can, it is presumed, be no doubt, that in the present case the crop was given by the bequest of the residue to Archibald Bolling: for

As, by the act of distribution, after debts, funerals, and just expences of every sort, first paid and allowed, the surplusage of all and singular the goods, and chattels, and personal estate of every person dying intestate shall be distributed:

So a residuary legatee after debts and legacies paid is entitled: to the surplage [i.e., surplusage] of the testator's estate.

II [IV?]. By the words of Edward Bollings will, 'It is my will and desire that my book be given up to my brother Robert, and that he receive all the debts due to me and pay all that I owe.' Archibald Bolling insists, that the outstanding debts are not bequeathed to Robert Bolling, but are part of the residuum bequeathed to Archibald Bolling.

'That my Book be given up,' do not import a gift of the debts thereby appearing to be due to the testator.

To 'give up' signifies not always 'parting with or transferring a right,' but sometimes 'the putting a thing into ones possession for another purpose **{H108}** than that of enjoyment, and that he receive all the debts due to me' in themselves, mean no more than a power to receive those debts, not that the receiver should apply them to his own use[.]

And these words and those that follow, 'and pay all that I owe' seem to explain the purpose for which the book should be given up to be, that the person it was to be given up to might from thence discover partly who were indebted to the testator, and to whom he was indebted.

So that the words altogether may mean no more than this, 'let my book be put into the possession of my brother Robert, and let him receive what is due to me, and pay what I owe', and might be intended only as the appointment of an executor.

It is true this is not the form of words ordinarily used in the appointment of an executor; and it is not improbable that the testator might be acquainted with the ordinary form.

But if this be a proper form of appointment, (as it is admitted to be, for it is under that, and no other appointment, that Robert Bolling has acted as an executor, and claims the benefit of an extinguishment of his debt,) altho' it be by a circumlocution, that, it is presumed, will not warrant us to ramble into the field of conjecture and probability to find another meaning.

Obj. Godolph. 281.[578] 'If a man, by will, says, my will,

578. Godolphin, *Orphans Legacy*, 281. The words in the manuscript are a paraphrase of Godolphin; only "My Will, Pleasure or desire is, That he shall have or receive, or keep, or retain" is a direct quote.

pleasure or desire is that he shall have, or receive, or keep, or retain, these, or the like words, are sufficient to create a good bequest.'

Ans. It is apprehended that this authority, as to the word receive, is to be understood of things in the testators possession; and then it seems not applicable.

If a man says, my desire is that Titius receive my slave Demetrius, or that Caius receive my horse Argus: if we do not expound the term receive in the same sense as the word 'have', which indeed is sometimes, but not always, **{H109}** one of it's proper senses, we must suppose the testator had no meaning or a very idle one.

For otherwise, the legatary might take the horse or slave into his possession indeed, but must restore him the same moment to some other.

But it is not so, when a person says, 'my desire is that Lucius receive all the debts due to me, or collect that money which belongs to me, but is in the hands of other people.'

This indeed may be giving Lucius some trouble, and so will every other part of the executor's office.

But, without being a bequest of the money, when received, to the receiver, the words would be very significant, and answer a very useful purpose, if the debts were applied to the payment of the testator's debts and legacies.

That the clause we are considering is to be so expounded will appear, it is imagined, when we contemplate it in another view.

The testator appointed his brother Robert not only his receiver, but his Bursar.

He was to pay what the testator owed, as well as to receive what others owed to him.

Every one, it is expected, will grant, that from the words, 'shall receive what is due to me and pay all that I owe' the person who is to execute the two offices must sustain the same character in both.

He must either act for himself, or for the testator in both.

If he received for himself, he must pay for himself; if he paid for the testator he must receive for the testator.

Suppose then the testator had died when he made his will, at which time he owed more than was due to him; for it was from the sale of Pocahontas that the balance is now on the other side;

Or suppose by bankruptcy or other accidents the creditor had fallen short **{H110}** of the debts;

Must Robert Bolling have made good the deficiency out of his own, or might he do it out of the testator's estate?

If out of the latter, which it is affirmed he might, it will follow that he received the debts for, and as representative of, the testator, and consequently is accountable for them to the residuary legatee.

The defendants counsel to avoid this objection would have the words, 'It is my will and desire that my book be given up to my brother Robert, and that he receive all the debts due to me and pay all that I owe,' understood sometimes in this sense.

'I give to my brother Robert all my credits; he paying thereout my debts;' inserting the words, 'thereout,' by way of supplement, and making words conditional which the testator used absolutely.

Sometimes the clause is to be understood thus: 'I give to my brother Robert all my credits, except so much as will discharge what I owe'; supplying the word 'except' and giving a different sense to the words from what they import.

And why is the clause to be thus tortured, perverted, interpolated, when it is intelligible, it is satisfied, by being considered as the appointment of an executor?

Because that it should be so it is now, by an event unexpected when the will was made, for the interest of R. Bolling; for it is not doubted he would have rejected the interpretation he contends for if his brother had not sold Pokahontas.

If the words of the will are not sufficient to give the debts to Robert Bolling; the attempt to establish the gift by parol proof, it is hoped, will be fruitless.

Parol proof has been admitted to ascertain a person to whom a legacy was intended.

**{HIII}** As if a legacy be given to John, the son of Thomas, and Thomas has two sons, both named John; proof is allowed to ascertain which of the sons the testator meant.

Parol proof has been admitted to ascertain a thing given.

As if a man bequeaths his trunk, when he has three trunks; proof may be made to ascertain which of the three was intended.

Parol proof is allowable in another instance to rebut an equity.

For example.

If a man appoints an executor, and does not dispose of the surplus of his estate, the appointment of the executor is in law a gift of the surplus to him.

Yet where the executor has a particular legacy, the court of Chancery generally makes him a trustee for the next of kin, as to the surplus, altho' he has the legal title.

But if he can prove that the testator intended the surplus for him, he is allowed to do it by parol evidence, in support of his legal title, and to rebut the equitable title of the next of kin.

But neither of these instances will justify the admission of parol evidence in this case.

In the two final instances it was no question but that something or other was given, and there was some person or other to whom the thing was given. But the question being in one, to whom of several persons, and, in the other, which of several things was intended; there is no possible inconvenience in allowing the proof, and on the other hand, if the proof was not allowed, the will would be void, which would manifestly be doing injustice to some body.

In the clause under consideration the question is not, to whom of several persons, the thing was given, nor what of several things was given.

We admit, if the clause imports a gift, that Robert Bolling is certainly the person, to whom the gift was made, and that the debts is the thing given.

{**H112**} But the question is, admitting Robert Bolling to be the person, and the debts to be the thing intended, whether the words 'it is my will and desire, that my book be given up to my brother Robert, and that he receive all the debts due to me, and pay all that I owe', import a gift of any thing to any person? and surely authorities proving that where, in a legacy, it is incertain which of several things, or who of several persons, was intended, proof is admissible to ascertain the person or thing, cannot be pertinent in this question.

The third and only other instance where a parol proof is allowed seems not more applicable.

Parol proof is admitted of a testator's intention, that his executor should have an undisposed surplus, because this proof stands with the will.

The appointment of an executor is a gift to him in law of all the testator's personal estate. 3. Fr. Atk. 228.[579]

But if there be a particular legacy to the executor it is presumed the testator did not intend him the surplus, because if he had intended him the surplus, it was unnecessary to give that particular legacy, which would otherwise have been included in the surplus; and therefore the court of chancery, upon that presumption, declares the executor a trustee of the surplus, and the next of kin to have a right to the surplus, by the equity of the statute of distribution.

Now if the executor can prove the testator did intend him the surplus, he is allowed to do it, because the foundation of the next of

579. *Southcot versus Watson,* 3 Atkyns 227–34, 26 E.R. 932–36 (Ch., June 1745).

kin's right is only a presumption that altho' the surplus was indeed given to the executor, yet the testator did not intend it for him, which may, with great propriety, be opposed and contradicted by parol evidence, at the same time that it destroys that presumption and rebuts the equity of the next of kin, concurring with the will itself to support a legal title conveyed by it.

But in this case the residuary legatees right is not founded in a presumption that altho' the debts were indeed given to Robert Bolling, yet the testator did not intend them for him.

**{H113}** We say directly the contrary, that by the words, 'my desire is that my book be given up to my brother Robert, and that he receive all the debts due to me, and pay all that I owe', the debts were not given.

If they were the dispute is at an end, and Robert Bolling has both the legal and equitable title to them.

But if they were not given by that clause then we claim the debts, as part of the residuum, undeniably, as we think, comprehended by, and included in the words, 'the rest of my estate, negroes, horses, cloaths, and every other part of my estate not already given, I give and bequeath unto my brother Archibald Bolling for him and his heirs for ever.'

If the former clause is not a gift of the debts, and the other does comprehend them, parol proof of the testator's intending them for Robert Bolling instead of standing with and supporting the will, contradicts the residuary clause, which surely there is not authority to warrant.

De. Term. S. Michaelis. 8. Geo. II. In curia cancellaria[580]

Rep. temp. Talbot. 240.

Brown versus Selwin, et contra.[581]

[']John Brown, on the 23d. of June 1732. made his will and thereby bequeathed to the plaintiff a legacy of £500. and all his plate; to the defendant he give all his leasehold messuages; and after several other legacies, and bequests as well as devising some freehold and copyhold lands he devised as follows. ["]And as for the rest residue and remainder of my estate, whether real or personal whereof I am seised or possessed, or which I am any ways entitled to, which I have not herein and hereby devised given &c. I give and bequeath the same, and every part thereof, and all my right, title, and interest herein and thereto, unto such my executor or executors herein after named, as shall duly take on him or them the execution of this my will, according to the true intent and meaning thereof, his or their heirs, executors administrators and assigns, as tenants in **{H114}** common[582] and not as joint tenants"; and afterwards appointed the plaintiff and defendant his executors and soon after died; and the plaintiff and defendant proved the will. the defendant was at the time of the testator's death indebted to the testator in £3000. principal money besides interest and for securing thereof

580. Court of Chancery.

581. *Brown v. Selwin et contra*, 25 E.R. 756–58. The long quotation following this citation is from this report.

582. in common law, a form of ownership of real property in which two or more persons hold real property. Each tenant in common has an undivided interest in the property; if a tenant dies, his or her interest does not pass to the surviving tenant or tenants, but instead goes to the deceased tenant's heir.

had given a bond to the testator, dated the 20th. of June 1732. in £6000. penalty. the bill was brought that the defendant might account with the plaintiff for the testator's residuary estate, and pay him a moiety of the said £3000. and interest; and the cross bill was to have the bond delivered to be cancelled.

[']It appeared by the answer of the defendant in the original cause, and by the proofs in both causes, that the testator designed to give this money to the defendant, and gave one Viner,[583] the attorney concerned in drawing the will, instructions in writing accordingly; but Viner refused to make mention of it in the will, insisting that the bond would be extinguished and released of course by Mr. Selwin's being appointed executor; but the testator appearing dissatisfied with Viner's opinion, a case was stated for counsels opinion who confirmed what Viner said. in confidence of which the testator signed and published his will with full persuasion that the bond would be extinguished; and this appeared clearly to be the testators intention.

[']*Lord Chancellor* [Talbot]. The question is, whether £3000. which was due to the testator from Mr. Selwin, shall pass to Mr. Selwin by his being made executor? or, whether it passed by the devise of the residue to the two executors? the written instructions for drawing the will directs the £3000. all to Mr. Selwin. The attorney who was to draw the will says it was the testator's intention it should go so. But that he apprehending that making the obligor executor was an extinguishment of the debt, hindred it from being

583. Possibly a reference to Charles Viner (1678–1756), author of *General Abridgment of Law and Equity*— but this identification is uncertain. See supra, note 275.

particularly mentioned. It was never doubted but a debt due from an executor to a testator shall be assets in the executors hands to pay debts; for if the testator had expressly given it away, even that could not have screened it from debts: so the testator may give a legacy out of a debt due **{H115}** to him, as in the case in Yelv. Phillips v. Phillips,[584] which authority is right; the implied gift by making the debtor executor, may be controlled by an express gift or by a devise of all his debts.

[']It hath been questioned whether such a debt be assets to pay legacies in general;[585] but that not being the present case, it is not necessary to be determined. I am at present inclined to think it may; but shall not bind myself by giving my opinion 'til the case happens. If this be considered upon the will, without the parol evidence, it will appear from the general words of devising the residue, i.e. all his real and personal estate which he had not thereby before given to the residuary legatees; that this debt, which at that time was part of the personal estate, falls within the description: The testator was entitled to this debt when he made his will and at the time of his death; he had not before disposed of it, nor had he appointed Mr. Selwin executor. a devise of the residue after payment of debts and legacies plainly comprehends this debt, and the only doubt is with regard to Mr. Viner's evidence who wrote the will. I privately

584. Bryant made an error in transcribing this case. The original report — 25 E.R. 757 — cites "the case in Yelv. 160, *Flud v. Rumsey*," 80 E.R. 107. For *Philips v. Philips*, also cited in *Brown v. Selwin*, see infra, note 585.

585. Bryant omitted a citation from the original report — "(vide *Phillips v. Phillips*, 1 Chanc. Cas. 192, also 3 *Chan. Cas.* 89)." *Brown v. Selwin*, 25 E.R. at 757. The omitted citation is to *Philips v. Philips*, 1 Chan. Cas. 292, 22 E.R. 806–807 (Ch., 1676).

think it was intended the £3000. should go to Mr. Selwin. privately I think so. but I am not at liberty, by private opinion to make a construction against the plain words of a will. None of the cases where parol evidence has been admitted have gone so far as the present case; the farthest they go is to rebut an equity or resulting trust; the parol evidence in those cases tended to support the intention of the testator consistent with the written will, and did not contradict the express words of the will, as in the present case it is better to suffer a particular mischief than a general inconvenience, and so reversed the decree and ordered Mr. Selwin to account with the plaintiff Brown for the said £3000. but no costs. (a) This was, &c.[']

(a) [']This was upon an appeal from the Rolls. This case the 26th of March 1735. came before the house of lords upon an appeal and the lord chancellor's decree was affirmed: and the lords would not allow the parol evidence, to be read, nor even the respondents answer as to these matters.[''][586]

The position which is laid down for the defendant, 'that parol proof is admissible and proper to explain what the testator is supposed to have expressed doubtfully, viz. the capacity in which Robert Bolling was to receive his debts,' must be denied, as it is thought utterly groundless, **{H116}** inconsistent with any resolution that is recollected, and introductive of the numberless mischiefs which courts have been ever guarding against from the

586. *William Selwin v. John Brown*, 3 Brown 607–13, 1 E.R. 1527–1531 (House of Lords, 25 March 1735). Anderson Bryant inserted this last paragraph of the original report in the manuscript as marginal note (a).

admission of parol evidence to controul deeds and wills.

In Vezey's cases second part pa. 217.[587] Sir John Strange[588] master of the rolls[589] said 'the distinction, as to parol evidence, I have always taken to be that in no instance it shall be admitted in contradiction to the words of the will: but if the words of the will are doubtful and ambiguous and unless some reasonable light is let in to determine that, the will will fall to the ground. any thing to explain, not to contradict the will is always admitted.'[590]

But if the parol evidence be admitted what does it amount to?

Edward Bolling told the witnesses that his brother (Robert) was to pay all his debts, and receive what was due to him.

This is no more than what the will says.

The witnesses indeed add 'from his conversation they always understood and verily believe that the debts due Edward Bolling was by him intended as a legacy to Robert.[']

In the case of Tuckers and others against Tuckers executors,[591] upon these words of a will: 'all the residue of my estate I

587. *Hampshire v. Peirce*, 2 Vesey Senior 216–19, 28 E.R. 140–42 (Ch., 7 March 1750).

588. Sir John Strange (1696–1754), barrister, Middle Temple (1718); S.G. (1737); Master of the Rolls (1750); author of *Reports* (published in 1755).

589. an assistant judge of the Court of Chancery, who held a separate court ranking next to that of the Lord Chancellor, and had the keeping of the rolls and grants which passed the Great Seal, and the Chancery records.

590. *Hampshire v. Peirce*, 28 E.R. 140–42: quote in 28 E.R. at 140.

591. *Tucker &c. vs. Tucker's Exors* (April Court, 1740), in R. T. Barton, ed., *Virginia Colonial Decisions, II: The Reports by Sir John Randolph and by Edward Barradall of Decisions of the General Court of Virginia 1728–1748* (Boston: Boston Book Co., 1909), B100–B105: paraphrase of quotation at B100.

give to be equally divided among Robert Tucker, John Tucker, John Cook, and Robert Cook, and Jacob Walker's children;' the question was whether Mr. Walker's children should share only one-fifth part among them, or every one be entitled to an eighth (for there were four of them) of the surplus?

Col. Samuel Boush, who was not only one of the executors, but was the writer of the will, and undoubtedly as capable of understanding and as well qualified to explain his testator's intention as an overseer and his wife their employers, declared it to be his opinion that only a fifth part was intended for Mr. Walker's children. The general court adjudged it so; but their decree was reversed.

**{H117}** The question upon the clause of the will in that case is conceived to be not less doubtful than the question upon the clause now under consideration in this case.

Which ever way this point be determined it will introduce another question.

If the debts be not given to Robert Bolling, he insists that a debt of about £285. due from himself to his testator is extinguished in consequence of the appointment of Robert Bolling as executor of the will.

It is admitted that if the obligee make the obligor executor the debt by operation of law, is extinguished.

When the creditor makes the debtor executor, and dies, the executor who is the only person that can maintain an action in right of the testator cannot sue himself so that no action can be brought in his life time; and it is a maxim in law, that a personal action once suspended, by act of the party, is gone forever.

On the other hand it will be agreed, first, that the debt shall be subject to pay the testator's debts if his other estate be deficient; secondly that, if the debt be given to a legatee, it is not extinguished, but the executor is bound to pay it.

The question between the parties then is, whether the debt in this case is bequeathed to Archibald Bolling or not?

For him it is insisted, that this debt, at the time of Edward Bolling's death, was part of his estate and given by the words 'the rest of my estate negroes, horses, cloathes and every other part of my estate not already given, I give and bequeath to my brother Archibald Bolling.['] and the case of Brown versus Selwin before quoted upon another occasion, is here in this question relied upon as an authority in point.

Against which it is objected for Robert Bolling, first, that the executors debt will be extinguished, and not pass, unless it be <u>specially</u> bequeathed to some other.

This is chiefly grounded upon these words of Justice Powell in the **{H118}** case of Wankford v. Wankford Salk. 303.[592] 'Where the debt or any part of it is expressly devised by the will to pay a legacy, it will be assets to pay such legacy, and so is the case in Yelv. 160.[593] but where there is no such special devise the debt shall be extinguished notwithstanding any other legacies.'

But first this opinion of Powell's was an extrajudicial opin-

592. *Wankford versus Wankford* (1 Salkeld), 91 E.R. 265–72: quote in 91 E.R. at 268. The quotation follows this citation.

593. *Flud versus Rumsey*, 80 E.R. 127.

ion, the question in the principal case being, not how far the executors debt was assets to pay legacies, but whether the debt of an executor, who had administered the estate, without proving the will, was extinguished?

2. The opinion is not warranted by the case in Yelv.[594] which seems to be vouched for it and was thus. Trin. 7. Jac. B.R.

Flud versus Rumsey.[595]

'The suggestion was, that whereas he was indebted to I.S. in £30. which I.S. afterwards in his life time by his deed gave all his goods and chattels to A. and after made the plaintiff and B. his executors, and devised that the plaintiff should pay out of the £30. that he owed £10. to the defendant for a legacy. the defendant had drawn the plaintiff into the spiritual court for the legacy, where by the law the £30. debt is extinguished by making the plaintiff executor: and shewed that he proved the will &c. and per curiam,[596] the defendant shall have a consultation, for, altho' the joint executor has no remedy to recover this £30. against the plaintiff, his co-executor, nor no action can be sued for it in the plaintiffs life, yet the debt is not extinguished, but remains as assets to any other creditor, as 8. E.4.[597] is, and by the same reason that such debt shall satisfy a debt, it shall also satisfy a legacy; and the rather because the

594. Id.

595. Id. The quoted report follow this citation.

596. for the court.

597. *Les Reports des Cases… en temps Du Roy Edward le Quart,* "De Termino Paschae Anno viii. Edwardi. IIII.," ¶ 4, at 3.

testators express intent was so, having precisely limited the legacy to be paid out of the debt.

'Quod nota; per totam curiam.[598] And a consultation was awarded accordingly. *Yelverton* was of counsel with the plaintiff.'

It is true in this case part of the debt was specially bequeathed, but that does not appear to have been the reason of the Judgment which the **{H119}** reporter explains in these words: 'for altho' the joint executor has no remedy to recover this £30. against the plaintiff, his co-executor, nor no action can be sued for it in the plaintiffs life yet the debt is not extinguished but remains as assets to any other creditor, as 8. E. 4.[599] is: and by the same reason that such debt shall satisfy a debt, it shall also satisfy a legacy.' There is indeed this additional reason subjoined, 'and the rather because the testator's express intent, was so, having precisely limitted the legacy to be paid out of the debt.' But the former reason is a better ground to assert the debt to be assets for payment of legacies in general, which Lord Talbot in the case of Selwin v. Brown[600] confesses him self inclined to, then it was for Powell to say, that where there is no special devise the debt shall be extinguished notwithstanding any other legacies.

3. Powell is single in that opinion, at least it does not appear that any one of his brethren concurred with him in it.

598. which note, by the whole court. This note was usually inserted by the reporter in older case reports.

599. *Les Reports des Cases... en temps Du Roy Edward le Quart,* "De Termino Paschae Anno viii. Edwardi. IIII.," ¶ 4, at 3.

600. *Brown v. Selwin et contra,* 25 E.R. 756–58. For the appeal of this case to the House of Lords, see *William Selwin v. John Brown,* 1 E.R. 1527–1531.

4. The opinion, if we are to understand, that such a debt will not pass by a general residuary bequest, not only seems absurd, for the debt being part of the testator's estate, to say that a bequest of all his estate does not include it, is saying, in other words, that the whole of any thing may be less than all it's parts, but is contradicted by Lord Talbot in the case of Brown and Selwin, for there it is resolved, that a debt due from an executor will pass by a general bequest of 'all the real and personal estate not before given'.

But if a debt owing by an executor may pass without a special bequest.

Secondly, it is objected, that this debt does not fall within the description of 'every other part of my estate not already given.'

Because it is alledged that the clause by which Robert Bolling is appointed executor, operates as a gift of the debt he owed the testator; and precedes the residuary bequest; and consequently is no part of the 'estate **{H120}** not already given.'

In the same case Wankford versus Wankford, the same Justice Powell, says. pa. 303. 'the extinguishment was not wrought by way of actual release, because then the debt could not be assets, but by way of *legacy* or *gift* of the debt by the will.'[601]

But in this opinion, he is not only single as in the other, but contradicted by Sir John Holt whose words pa. 306 are, 'when the obligee makes the obligor his executor, tho' it is a discharge of the action, yet the debt is assets, and the making him executor does not amount to a legacy.'[602]

601. *Wankford versus Wankford* (1 Salkeld), 91 E.R. 265–72: quote in 91 E.R. at 268.

602. Id., 270 (opinion of Holt, C.J.).

And yet this dictum of Justice Powell, both unsupported by cases, and denied in the same case by authority beyond comparison superior to him, is supposed to be the chief foundation of this objection.

In the case of Brown v. Selwin, the chancellor explaining the reasons of his decree, after saying, 'the testator was entitled to this debt when he made his will, and at the time of his death, he had not before disposed of it,' adds 'nor had he appointed Mr. Selwin executor,'[603] from which last expression Robert Bollings counsel seems to think it is implied, that if the appointment of Mr. Selwin executor had preceded the residuary bequest, it would not have passed the debt. But it is apprehended by the other side to be exceedingly plain, that the principle he grounded his opinion upon is this: 'that the residuary bequest disposed of every thing the testator was entitled to <u>when</u> he <u>made his will</u>, and <u>at the time of his death</u>.' and if so the case is an authority in point.

It is conceived to be intirely immaterial as to this point in what order the clauses were inserted.

For let us suppose Edward Bolling to have begun his will in this manner: 'all my estate, except what I shall hereafter give to others, I give and bequeath to my brother Archibald Bolling'; and then the other clauses had followed as they now stand;

**{H121}** Would not the will have been expounded as it must now?

In the case of Carter versus Carter. *Vezey*. 2d. part. pa. 169.[604]

603. *Brown v. Selwin et contra*, 25 E.R. 756–58: quote in 25 E.R. at 757.

604. *Carter v. Carter*, 1 Vesey Senior 168–69, 27 E.R. 961–62 (Ch., 26 Nov. and 5 Dec. 1748); 2 Vesey Senior, supp. 95; 28 E.R. 467. The quotation, in 27 E.R. at 961–62, follows this citation.

per *Lord Chancellor Hardwicke.* 'the general rule is, that the construction must be made on the tenor of the whole will taken together; and it is not material in what order the clause is.'

Let us then briefly inquire what reason there is for considering the appointment of a debtor executor as a gift of the debt.

Do these words 'I constitute Robert Bolling my executor,' in a proper sense mean the same thing, as, 'I give and bequeath to Robert Bolling the money he owes me.'

It is expected every one will answer *no.*

Do they mean so in a legal sense?

Chief Justice Holt answers *no.*

Is the doctrine founded in the testator's intention?

Few testators, besides those who have studied law, know that there is any difference between appointing a debtor, and any other, an executor: and any man who does know the difference, except an obstinate and conceited Viner, if he designed to give the debt his executors owed him would rather say, 'I give such an one the debt he owes me,' than 'I appoint such an one executor.'

Is it founded in the principles of Justice and natural equity?

It is only a deduction from a maxim in law.

The court of chancery regarding it as such seems disposed to confine it to the single instance where there are neither debts nor legacies.

Talb. 242.[605] By lord Chancellor [Talbot], 'It hath been ques-

605. *Brown v. Selwin et contra,* 25 E.R. 756–58: quote in 25 E.R. at 757. The quotation follows this citation.

tioned whether such a debt be assets to pay legacies in general, but that not being the present case, it is not necessary to be determined. I am inclined to think it may.'

1. Fr. Atk. 463. Michaelmas term 1737.[606]

**{H122}** Fox versus Fox.

'A. mortgaged his estate to the defendant who paid no money in consideration of the mortgage, but gave A. a bond for £130. A. afterwards makes the defendant his executor: the heir of A. brings his bill to have the real estate exonerated, considering this bond as assets in the hands of the defendant.

'*Lord Chancellor* [Hardwicke]. Notwithstanding at common law the making an obligor executor extinguishes his debt, yet in this case the bond shall be considered as assets in the hand of the defendant the executor, and applied after the payment of funeral expences and *legacies*, to the exoneration of the real estate in favor of the heir.'

In the former of these two cases one Chancellor [Talbot] inclines to throw the executor's debt into the general fund for payment of legacies, and his successor in the other case [Hardwicke] actually does throw it into that fund, making it liable, tho' not specially given, for payment of legacies, and even beyond that.

If such a debt be assets to pay legacies in general, which it could not be if it was given or bequeathed to the executor;

From thence it follows, that the appointment of an executor is not a gift of what he owes the testator;

606. *Fox v. Fox*, 1 Atkyns 463, 26 E.R. 294 (Ch., Michaelmas 1737). The report is transcribed in the two paragraphs following this citation.

Consequently that what Robert Bolling owed his brother Edward not being '*already given,*' was included in the residuary bequest to Archibald Bolling.

If it be determined that by the words, 'it is my will and desire, that my book be given up to my brother Robert, and that he receive all the debts due to me, and pay all that I owe,' that the outstanding debts are bequeathed to Robert Bolling, but that he is to pay out of them what the testator owed then the question is,

Whether Robert Bolling must pay the testators proportion of the debts which are due from his father, and which were by his will charged on his son's estates?

**{H123}**

The defendant in his answer says, 'he conceives the testator's proportion of the debt due from their father John Bolling to Messrs. Hyndman Lancaster and company was not chargeable on the said Edward Bolling at the time of his death, that by the will of his father he was under express exemption therefrom, and that it only became due from his estate after the said Archibald, the complainant (*whose estate till then was charged therewith*) attained to his age of one and twenty years, so that it was under no contemplation of the defendants testator at the time of making his will, nor any part of his idea, when he required the defendant to pay what he owed.'

What were the subjects of the testators contemplation, or what ideas were in his mind whilst he was making his will we pretend to no skill in discovering further than by his words, which cannot be denied to comprehend the debt, if it appear to be a debt that he the testator owed.

A man may owe a debt which he did not contract.

It may devolve upon him with an estate, which is liable to pay the debt.

He must take the estate in his own right indeed; for otherwise he will not be debtor in his own person.

Thus an executor or an administrator, as he takes the estate in trust for others, is not said to owe the debts the decedent had contracted, and therefore when he is sued, the declaration charges him not with *owing*, but only with detaining the debt.

But when lands descend to an heir whose ancestor had bound himself and his heirs in a bond or other specialty, as he takes the lands in his own right, he is answerable as debtor in his own person.

'If any action is brought against the heir upon the bond of his ancestor, and in which the heir is bound, it must be in the debt and distinct[607] because he hath the assets in his own right and therefore is to be sued as if it were his own proper bond.'

**{H124}** Bacons abridg. Heir and Ancestor (G.)[608]

He is indeed not answerable for the debt further than the value of the inheritance he succeeds to, unless he makes himself so, as he may, by his false pleading.

607. "detinet" in Bacon. See infra, notes 608, 610.

608. Bacon, *A New Abridgment of the Law*, 3: 29 ("Heir and Ancestor: (G) How to be proceed against where he is bound"). This citation gives the source for the preceding quotation.

Case of devisees, since the statute against fraudulent devisees is the same.

Now Edward Bolling taking his estate from his father in his own right, if that estate be liable to pay his proportion of the debt, it is his debt, or in the language of his will, it was 'what he owed.'

It is objected that the debt was not chargeable on Edward Bolling, at the time of his death, that by the will of his father he was under express exemption therefrom, and that it only became due from his estate after Archibald Bolling, whose estate until then was charged therewith, attained to his age of twenty one years.

But first, it is denied, Edward Bolling, by the will of his father, was under express or any other exemption from his debt.

Col. Bolling, the father, after making provision for his wife, devising his lands to his sons Thomas, John, Robert, and Edward, and giving legacies to his daughters, declared it to be his will and desire, 'that the slaves given to his wife for life should at her death, be divided among his said sons, and that when the first of said sons should come to the age of twenty one years, all his other slaves should be then equally divided into as many parts as he should have sons living, and the eldest should have one part thereof allotted to him for his own use, and the other parts of the slaves should be delivered unto his said other sons as they should arrive at the same age, respectively, and if any of his said sons should happen to die before he should come to such age, then his part of all the slaves should be equally divided among the surviving sons.'

And after declaring the devises to Thomas Bolling to be in

satisfaction **{H125}** of a legacy he was entitled to by the will of his Aunt Mrs. Whiting, the testator declares it to be his 'will, that the profits of his estate given to his children be applied toward the payment of his debts and their education and maintenance until they should have a right to receive their parts thereof respectively; and that all his stocks and personal estate, after payment of his debts and legacies should be equally divided among his sons in the same manner and at the same time and times as the slaves were before directed to be divided and allotted to them.'

By a Codicil,[609] after devising some land in Bedford to his son Archibald (who was unprovided for by the will, perhaps not being born when that was made) devising other lands to a nephew and some of his friends and divising to his son Archibald part of Buffalo-lick land, all which by the will had been devised to his own son Edward Bolling, the testator declared it to be his 'will and desire that his said son Archibald come in with his other sons for an equal division of his slaves at the same time and times, and under the same regulations, limitations and restrictions as in his said will were mentioned and directed for each of his other sons respectively.[']

By the will and codicil it is 'conceived that Edward Bollings proportion of the debts due from his father was chargeable upon him at the time of his death: that by the will of his father, so far from being under express exemption therefrom, his estate, and consequently himself was under express obligation thereto, and that it became due from his estate so soon as he became entitled to the estate i.e. so soon as his father died; or at furthest so soon as he

609. supplement or addition to a will.

came of age; and that Archibald Bolling's estate charged only with his own never was charged with Edward Bollings proportion of their father's debts.'

Whether this or the defendants opposite conception be more justifiable is submitted.

**{H126}** 2. Col. Bolling could not exempt any part of his estate from the payment of his debts.

His lands indeed were not subject to his debts in general.

But even they were subject to Hyndman's, because it was a British debt; and the creditor might have maintained an action against Edward Bolling and the other devisees declaring in the debet and detinet,[610] in the same manner as a bond creditor may maintain an action against an heir and devisees by the statute against fraudulent devises.

3. Edward Bolling's estate either was exempt from the payment of his father's debts, or it was not.

If it was the determination of this question can be of no consequence either way.

If it was not, Edward Bolling in respect of the estate, was the debtor; and his proportion was a debt 'that he owed.'

4. If any debts due to Col. Bolling had not been recovered when Edward Bolling died, it is imagined, supposing the clause under consideration to be a legacy, his proportion of those debts would have passed by it.

610. originally *debet et detinet*— "He owes and detains": the phrase denoting a writ in the common law in an action of debt brought by an original contracting party who gave credit, against the party who incurred the debt, or his heirs.

And if his legatee could have claimed in one instance surely he ought to be bound in the other.

It is pretended, that Edward Bolling knew nothing of this debt of Hyndman's and therefore had it not in his contemplation.

This may be true; and so may its contrary, both are but conjectures, and one, for any thing that appears, as probable as the other.

It is said if the clause we are considering be a bequest, the testator meant by it to give his brother Robert something; but if you make him liable for the debt, in consideration of the debts he should receive instead of being a gainer he would lose by the legacy. 'but cast an eye on the account annexed to the answer add £500. to the debitor side, and instead of **{H127}** leaving a balance in favor of Robert Bolling, it brings him considerably in debt.'

But let us see, if this argument will not apply more strongly against expounding this clause as a legacy at all; after premising that Edward Bolling meant the same by it at the time he made his will, as when he died.

Let it be remembered that he did not sell his warehouse till after the date of his will.

'Now cast an eye on the account annexed to the answer, deduct £500. the price of the warehouse from the creditor side, and instead of leaving a balance in favor of Robert Bolling, it brings him considerably in debt.' And if Edward Bolling had not parted with the warehouse, and Archibald Bolling had insisted that Robert Bolling should pay all the debts, because all the credits were given to him, it is suspected he himself would have pleaded, 'if this clause be a legacy the testator meant to give me something, but if I am to pay all the debts instead being a gainer, I shall lose by it.' and that he would have thought it a very well warranted conclusion, 'that the clause was merely fiduciary, and intended only an appointment of me executor.'

This elegant hand writing is by Anderson Bryant of Albermarle.[611]

'leaving a balance in favor of Robert Bolling, it brings him considerably 'in debt.'

But let us see, if this argument will not apply more strongly against expounding this clause as a legacy at all; after premising that Edward Bolling meant the same by it at the time he made his will, as when he died.

Let it be remembered that he did not sell his warehouse till after the date of his will.

'Now cast an eye on the account annexed to the answer, deduct '£500. the price of the warehouse from the creditor side, and instead of 'leaving a balance in favor of Robert Bolling, it brings him considerably in 'debt.' and if Edward Bolling had not parted with the warehouse, and Archibald Bolling had insisted that Robert Bolling should pay all the debts, because all the credits were given to him, it is suspected he himself would have pleaded. 'if this clause be a legacy the testator meant to 'give me something, but if I am to pay all the debts instead of being a gainer, 'I shall lose by it.' and that he would have thought it a very well warranted conclusion, 'that the clause was merely fiduciary, and intended only an 'appointment of me executor.'

N.B. This elegant hand writing is by Anderson Bryant of Albermarle

HEH 127, *Bolling v. Bolling* manuscript, from second argument for plaintiff in Anderson Bryant's handwriting

611. This sentence is in Thomas Jefferson's handwriting.

{H128}

# Rob[ert] Bolling ads. Arch[ibald] Bolling. 2d argum[ent] for def[endant][612]

I. Under the devise of the Buffalo lick plantation was claimed in the argument for the def[endant] and not opposed by the pl[aintiff]'s counsel the Rents for a part of the said plantation, growing, and not paiable till after the testator's death.

But there was also claimed under the same devise the *Emblements* unsevered at the time of the testator's death: and in support of that claim these propositions were advanced

1. that at the Common law by the devise of these lands the emblements would have passed to Rob[ert] Bolling.

2. that our acts of assembly had not taken these emblements from him, but had *annexed thereto* the *labor* of the *slaves*, had made that labor homogeneous with the emblements, and of consequence had given it to him who could entitle himself to them: saving only to creditors a right to have them applied to the paiment of their demands.

1. the first of these propositions the adverse counsel now admits, to wit, that, putting our acts of assembly out of the question, Rob[ert] Bolling would be entitled to the emblements growing on the land at the testator's death. But

2. the second he denies, asserting on the contrary that our acts of assembly have taken these emblements from the devisee. in sup-

612. This part of the manuscript, Thomas Jefferson's second argment for the defendant, Robert Bolling, continues in Jefferson's handwriting.

port of this assertion he advances the following argumentative positions

1. that the emblements are annexed to, & incorporated with the labor of the slaves, not a freehold but a mere chattel interest.

2. that the act expressly directs them to go to a different person from him who takes the land, to wit, to the ex[ecuto]r if not to the devisee.

3. that the ex[ecuto]r or adm[inistrato]r is empowered to employ all the slaves in making and finishing a crop.

**{H129}** 4. that the right of the devisee is suspended as to the exercise of it till Dec. 25, and so the emblements become severed before the time at which his right commences.

5. that the act declaring the emblements *Assets* has thereby made them part of the *distributable* or *residuary surplus.*

These positions shall be considered in the order in which the pl[aintiff]'s counsel has thought proper to arrange them, endeavoring under each of them as much as possible to avoid a repetition of any thing contained in the former argument for the def[endant].

1. that the emblements are annexed to & incorporated with the labor of the slaves, not a freehold, but a mere chattel interest.

turn to the words of the act of 1711.[613] [transcribed in the 1st. arg[ument] for the def[endant]. pa. 31.][614] & to those of the act of 1748.[615] [transcribed in the 2d. arg[ument] for the pl[aintiff]. pa.

613. 9 Anne, c. 2 (Virginia 1711).

614. Brackets in original. The cite is to H46–H47, supra.

615. 22 Geo. II, c. 5, § 30 (Virginia 1748).

5.][616] and you will not find a syllable expressing that the emblements are to be taken from the devisee; nor yet that they are given to any other person. (except where it is declared they shall be assets, the effect of which will be investigated when we come to consider the 5th. position.) the acts say simply that where a person dies under the circumstances there pointed out, the slaves on the plantation shall be continued there till Dec. 25. for the making and finishing a crop; or in other words to bring his emblements to maturity & to sever them, and also to put in such other emblements as may be brought to maturity and severed by the 25th. day of December, the time before which it was thought those put into the ground before the test[ato]r's death could not be removed. here then no person, either devisee of land, legatee of slaves, or ex[ecuto]r being named, I ask, Who from the nature of things is to have these emblements thus brought to maturity? in their unripe state, at the instant of the testator's death, it is yeilded they belonged to the devisee of the lands. what then has taken his property from him? not the ex{**H130**}press words of the acts just now referred to; because they are silent, as was before observed. it must then be the Accession to the emblements, to wit, the labor of the slaves. this Accession being made by the legislature without the consent of the proprietor, let us consider if the laws relating to the acquisition of property by Accession in cases too where the Accession is voluntary as to the proprietor, take from him his property whether he will or not. 'by the Roman law if any given corporeal substance received afterwards

616. Brackets in original. The cite is to H94–H95, supra.

an accession by natural or by artificial means, as by the growth of vegetables, the pregnancy of animals, the embroidering of cloth, or the conversion of wood or metal into vessels and utensils, the original owner of the thing was entitled by his right of possession to the property of it under such it's state of improvement: but if the thing itself by such operation was changed into a different species, as by making wine, oil, or bread, out of another's grapes, olives, or wheat, it belonged to the new operator; who was only to make a satisfaction to the former proprietor for the materials which he had so converted. and these doctrines are implicitly copied and adopted by our Bracton, in the reign of king H. 3.[617] and have since been confirmed by many resolutions of the courts. it hath even been held that if one takes away another's wife or son, and cloaths them, and afterwards the husband or father retakes them back, the garments shall cease to be the property of him who provided them, being now annexed to the person of the child or woman.' 2. Blackst. 404.[618] perhaps Doctor Blackstone instead of founding the authority of this part of our law on the adoption of a Bracton and subsequent resolutions of our courts of law, would have done better to have adverted to the laws of nature which tell us that 'whosoever is owner of a thing, to him likewise belong the Accessions of it' to have considered this as the great original from which our Saxon ancestors as well as the Roman lawyers copied their several institutions, and to have proved that it **{H131}** was very antiently a part of our law by the testimony of Bracton and Fleta and by several adju-

617. 1216–1272.

618. Blackstone, *Commentaries,* 2: 404: quotation at 404–405.

dications of our law judges deriving their knolege not merely from Bracton and Fleta, but from immemorial tradition, the only evidence of our unwritten or Common law. 'Mich. 2. El.[619] In a writ of Trespass the def[endant] justifies by reason that one I.S. was seised of an acre of land and leased it to him for a term of 10. years; and then one A. enters into the said land so leased & cut up certain trees there growing and of them made timber & then carried it into the land where the trespass is supposed and then gives the timber to the pl[aintiff]. wherefore the def[endant] enters into the said land and retakes his timber as well to him was lawful. and the writ was Quare clausum fregit ac mearemiumorum suum cepit.[620] Benlows[:] it seems to me that the plea is not good for two reasons, the one for this that when he took the trees and made timber of them; now he has destroyed the knolege [a perde le notice][621] of them, and so the property of them is altered. the other is for this that the def[endant] has confessed an entry which he cannot justify. And as to the first point the justices think the plea good enough, for by the seisure of the trees, the knolege [le notice][622] of them is not taken away, but the property yet remains. in all cases where a thing is taken tortiously and altered in form, if yet that which remains is the principal part of the substance, then is not the knolege [le

619. 1559.

620. "wherefore he broke the close and took the timber"; in common law, a species of the action of trespass.

621. Brackets in original.

622. Brackets in original.

notice][623] lost. as if a man takes my cloak, and makes of this a doublet, yet I may retake this. so if a man takes from me a peice of cloth, and then he embroiders in this a peice of gold, yet I may retake this, and if a man takes certain trees, and then he makes boards of them yet the owner may retake them, because the greater part of the substance remains. but if the trees are fixed in the earth, or if a house be made of the timber, it is otherwise. Quaere[624] the house now is the principal substance.' Moore. 19.[625]

'Trespass of shoes and boots taken. the def[endant] sais that he was possessed of thirty hides [3. dikers][626] of leather and bailed[627] them to W.S. **{H132}** who gave them to the pl[aintiff] who made shoes and boots of them, & the def[endant] retook them. and by the court where grain is taken and made into malt, or money taken and made into a cup, or a cup made into money, these cannot be taken; for grain cannot be known one from another, nor one penny from another; and if a man takes timber and makes of it a house this cannot be retaken, for the nature is altered into freehold. but where a thing can be known the owner may retake this, altho' that another thing be mixed with it: as a man takes cloth and makes it

623. Brackets in original.

624. wherefore, for what reason, on what account.

625. Moore 19–20, 72 E.R. 411–12 (K.B.?, n.d.). ¶ 67, translated in the manuscript from Moore's Law French, refers to no named case, but is titled "Trespass".

626. Brackets in original.

627. created a bailment; delivered goods or personal property to another person, either for a specific use or upon deposit, under an express or implied contract under which the bailed property shall be returned to the original possessor once the use or the purpose of the deposit has been achieved.

into a robe the owner may retake this, for the nature is not changed: and if a man takes my tree and squares it into timber, yett the owner may retake this, for this may be known: and the same of iron made into a bar: & so the retaking of the shoes and boots is good & lawful, for the nature remains: and by some, if a man takes a white peice & makes it to be gilt the owner cannot retake it. 5. H.7. 15.'[628] Bro. abr. Propertie & proprietate probanda. pl. 23.[629] 'Literae, lici sint aurere, perinde membranis chartisae cedunt, sicut ea solo cedere solent quore aedificantur vel insemintur, sed in picturis erit contrarium, ridiculosum erim esset preciosam picturam in per accessionem cedere vicissimae turbulae; et ideo tabula cedit picturae.' Bracton. L.2. c.2. §5.[630] in this instance of a painting made on the canvass of another, we lose sight of the canvas when we con-

628. No case reported in 5 Hen. VII bears the paragraph number 15, nor does any case appearing at page 15 of the reported cases for that year fit this context. *Les Reports des Cases en les Ans des Roys Edward v. Richard iii. Henrie vii. & Henrie viii. Touts qui par cy devant ont este Publies....* (London: Printed by George Sawbridge, William Rawlins, and Samuel Roycroft, Assigns of Richard and Edward Atkins, Esquires, 1679).

629. Sir Robert Brooke, *La Secounde part du Graunde Abridgement, Collecte & escrie per le Judge tresreverend Syr Robert Brooke Chivalier...* (London: Richard Tottell, 1576), "Propertie & proprietate probanda," ¶ 23, at fol. 161b. The quotation in the manuscript, translated from the Law French, immediately precedes this citation. The phrase means "property and the proving of property;" the section of Brooke describes the legal methods by which a person would establish a claim to property.

630. For writing, though in letters of gold, becomes part of parchment and charters exactly as things built upon land or crops sown become part of the soil. But a contrary rule will apply to paintings. It would be ridiculous if by accession a valuable painting became part of a worthless panel. Thus the panel cedes to the painting.

[Henry de] Bracton (Samuel E. Thorne, ed., with revisions and notes, of Charles Woodbine trans.), *On the Laws and Customs of England*, 4 vols. (Cambridge, Mass.: Belknap Press of Harvard University Press in association with Selden Society, 1968–1977), 2: 46.

template what is displayed on it, the greatest efforts perhaps of the genius of an Apelles[631] or Parrhasius.[632] this accession put into balance against the insignificance of the principal substance is allowed to carry both to the wrong-doer. again, grain made into malt or bread, grapes into wine, olives into oil, money into a cup, cannot be retaken by the owner, because sais the book one grain, one grape, one olive, or one peice of money cannot be distinguished from another. timber built into a house on the ground of another cannot be retaken because it is become a part of the freehold. but in all other instances the subject draws to it the accession. Thus **{H133}**

1. Where the Accession is by the addition of another substance, as
   a female animal of one person is made pregnant by the male of another.
   the wife, son, or servant of one has clothes annexed by another.
   embroidery is put by one on the cloth of another.
   letters are written by one on the paper or parchment of another.
2. where the Accession is to any moveable subject by Labor.
   my iron is wrought into bars.
   my timbers into squares or boards.
   my cloak into a doublet, or my cloth into any other form.
   my leather into shoes or boots.

631. Apelles (*fl.* 4th cent. B.C.), Greek painter known for portraits of Philip of Macedon and Alexander the Great and other works, and author of a (lost) book on painting.

632. Parrhasius (*fl.* 5th cent. B.C.), Greek painter and writer on painting.

3. where the Accession is to an immoveable subject by Labor, or by Addition of another subject.
    a house is built on my land by the Labor, or with the Timber, of another.
    a vegetable is transplanted there from the lands, or cultivated by the Labor, of another.

in all these instances the person who originally had property in the subject, having done nothing to relinquish his property, shall not lose it by the wrong of another, but the subject shall draw to it the Accession. the words of Bracton ubi supra are explicit as to the last which has most of the ingredients of our case. 'si Ticius suam plantam in Menii solo posuerit, Menii planta erit.'[633] so also Fleta L.3. c.2. §.13. [§ 8][634] if property in the soil then will draw to it property in the plant, where both the plant & the labor are accessions, much rather shall a property in the soil and plants (as Rob[ert] Bolling had) draw to them the accession of labor alone. I have a feild of corn; my neighbor comes and tends it; does not the corn continue mine? Rob[ert] Bolling had feilds of corn and tobacco; the slaves of A. Boll[ing] assisted those of R. Boll[ing] in tending them by direction of the act of assembly;[635] they continue still the

633. "If Titius plants his own shrub in soil belonging to Maevius, it will belong to Maevius…." Bracton, *On the Laws and Customs of England,* 2: 46. Jefferson mistranscribed Titius as Ticius and Maevii as Menii.

634. H. G. Richardson and G. O. Sayles, ed. and trans., *Fleta,* 3 vols. of 4 expected (London: Selden Society, 1953–1983), Book III, chap. 2, § 8, "Of Accessions," at 4.

635. 3 & 4 Geo. II, ch. 8, § 11 (Virginia 1730).

property of R. Bolling. if the act of assembly indeed has said that this Accession of culture shall draw to it a property in the principal, that **{H134}** is, in the plants, it's efficacy is omnipotent and cannot be withstood. but if it has not decided, as I hope to prove it has not, to whom the plants thus improved shall belong, then Justice and Analogy with the fabric of the law in similar cases carry it to the proprietor of the soil, and authorize my position that the labor of the slaves is annexed, or is an accession to the Emblements, is become homogeneous with them, and consequently is the property of him who can entitle himself to them: i.e. of the devisee of the lands in the present case: and consequently contradict the position of the pl[aintiff]'s counsel 'that the emblements are annexed to, & incorporated with the labor of the slaves.' this answers what is said pa. 6. in the support of this first position 'he certainly could have no right to the labor of slaves emploied in finishing the crop if they were given to others, either by the common law, or by any words in the act, for by the former, the legatees would have had an immediate right to possess their slaves and by the other altho' the legatees have no right to possess their slaves before the time allowed for finishing the crop be passed their labor in the mean time is not given to the devisee of the land.' And as to the case invented to shew that this construction of the act would in that instance work injustice; I answer that it furnishes us with the proof of the wisdom of this act, since the pl[aintiff]'s counsel in order to find a case in which it's operation would be productive of inequality, has been oblige[d] to go out of the circle of nature and reason: for I think I may say his case is framed so extravagantly, that either it never can have happened, or, if ever it did, the test[ato]r must have designed the inequality. if he designed it, the injustice, if any, is not to be charged on this act, but on the statutes giving a man a power of making a will: or it may furnish an objection to the act of distribution for not having obliged the devisee in such a case to bring his devise into hotchpot.[636] no law can be so framed as to produce equality in every case, unless it takes from a proprietor the power of disposing of his property. for certainly as long as he retains that **{H135}** power and has unequal affections for his relations, he will dispose of his property unequally. it suffices if the laws make an equal and just distribution in those cases where accident has prevented the proprietor from making any disposition at all. but where he devises a part (as this case supposes) and leaves the rest of his estate to the disposition of the law, it is evident he means the devisee shall have so much more than his legal part.

pa. 6.[637] 'so that an ex[ecuto]r may apply, or a creditor may levy an execution upon a crop that grew upon land devised before any other part of the estate in satisfaction of a debt or a judgment. and if he should do so it is apprehended the devisee of the land could not be reimbursed the value of the crop out of the rest of the estate.' this shall be answered under the 5'th position.

2. 'that the act expressly directs the emblements to go to a different person from him who takes the land, to wit, to the ex[ecuto]r & not to the devisee.'

636. the combining of properties into a common lot to ensure equality of division among heirs.

637. Supra, at H95. The quotations follow this citation.

I have before observed the act does not expressly direct this except where it sais they shall 'be deemed assets in the hands of the ex[ecuto]r.' and whether by saying this it has put the ex[ecuto]r in the place of the devisee of the land in all cases, is what will be discussed, when we come to the fifth position, from which this is not distinguishable.

3. 'the ex[ecuto]rs and adm[inistrato]rs are empowered not only to take the growing crop, but to employ all the test[ato]r's or intestate's servants & slaves in making & finishing a crop.' and again 'if E[dward] Boll[ing] had died the 2'd of March before a plant or grain of corn was in the ground Rob[ert] Boll[ing] could not have claimed the crop which should be made and finished afterwards; for it was not emblements.' pa. 7.[638]

this objection was obviated in our answer to the first. for in whose lands are these new plants set? in the lands of the devisee. Then 'si Ticius suam plantam in Menii solo posuerit, Menii planta erit.' or in plain English if an act of assembly set **{H136}** plants in the soil of Rob[ert] Boll[ing] they are the plants of Rob[ert] Boll[ing].' so that as to the plants growing at the time of the testator's death they passed to the devisee as included in the property of the soil which passed to him; and they drew to them the accession of labor bestowed on them after they became the property of the devisee. And by the same reasoning, the property in the soil drew to it the Accession of new plants put into it after the death of the test[ato]r, & then drew[639] also the labor bestowed on these new

638. Supra, at H96.

639. <to it the accession>

plants. it will be observed that I still consider the case in it's simple state, as it would have been if the act had omitted the words making them 'assets in the hands of ex[ecuto]rs' because after I shall have proved that, exclusive of these words, the plants would belong to Rob[ert] Boll[ing] I shall endeavor to shew separately that these words do not effect an appropriation but in a single event.

4. 'that the right of the devisee is suspended as to the exercise of it till Dec. 25. and so the emblements become severed before the time at which his right commences.'

does the pl[aintiff]'s counsel mean by this that the Right to the land or the Possession of it only is suspended? not the Right surely; because it was shewn pa. 8. 9. 10. of the former argum[ent] for def[endant][640] that a devise of lands operates as a conveiance & consequently transfers the immediate right. the devisee may vote for a representative at an election. if he dies before the 25'th of Dec. the lands would go to his heir and not revert to the heir of the devisor. his widow would be entitled to dower.[641] his creditors by specialty might levy their executions on these lands. all of which shew that the full fee-simple right passes absolutely and instantaneously to the devisee & is not suspended till Dec. 25. it must be meant then that the Possession of the land is suspended, and further that a suspension of the Possession of the land is an extinction of the right to their profits. whether **{H137}** the act of ass[embly],[642] by giving

640. Supra, at H23–H25.

641. at common law, the doctrine by which a widow may secure financial support for herself and the nurture of her children out of the lands and tenements of her deceased husband.

642. 3 & 4 Geo. II, ch. 8, § 11 (Virginia 1730).

the ex[ecuto]r or adm[inistrato]r a right to consider the profits as applicable to the paiment of debts, has suspended that right of possession which the stat[ute] of wills[643] had given the devisee, is a question not clear enough to give up, nor, in the present case, important enough to deny & to contest. do what you will with the shell while our right to the kernel remains unimpaired. the right to the profits is the useful right, and that alone I am concerned to support. by suspending the right of the devisee to call for his emblements till it be seen whether they may not be wanting to pay debts, it cannot be supposed that his right to them is altogether taken away. or in other words, the bare suspension of the use of a right is no extinguishment of it. if it is, then no distributee can recover his distributory part, because his use of it is suspended for a year by the stat[ute] of distributions[644] that the adm[inistrato]r may have time to see that there is enough besides to pay his test[ato]r's debts. But then it is asked pa. 8. 'can the crop as emblements belong to him who has no right to take possession of the land till they be severed?' I answer, if the possession of these plants which is in the ex[ecuto]r be a trust-possession, to wit, for the use of creditors if requisite for them, otherwise for the use of the devisee, then the devisee, when it is found they are not wanting for creditors will have as good a right to them, tho' he is out of possession, as any cestuy que trust has to the profits of his trust-estate. and whether this be a possession in trust will depend on the justice of the principal position, to wit,

5. that by declaring the crop *assets* in the hands of the

643. 32 Hen. VIII, c. 1 (1540).

644. 22 & 23 Car. II, c. 10 (1670).

ex[ecuto]r or adm[inistrato]r they become a part of the residuary or distributable surplus.

For the literal & proper, as well as modern, meaning of the word *assets*, I must refer to the argum[ent] for def[endant] pa. 34. & sequent.[645] and to the authorities there cited: only begging leave to correct a citation in pa. 18. of pl[aintiff]'s argum[ent] which is said to be from the Termes de ley.[646] it is in these **{H138}** words 'Assets are real or personal; where a man hath lands in fee-simple and dieth seised thereof, the lands which come to his heirs are assets real; and where he dies possessed of any personal estate, the goods which come to the ex[ecuto]rs are assets personal. Terms de ley.'[647] this citation is premised in order to found an objection to my explanation of the word *assets*, viz. that it means '*enough* of the goods and chattels to pay debts.' but unluckily the book has not a word of this citation, but on the contrary gives the very explanation of the word which it is here cited to contradict. the words taken from the book itself are 'Assets is in two sorts; the one called assets per descent,[648] the other assets enter maines.[649] assets per descent is where a man is bound in an obligation & dies seised of land in fee-simple which descend to his heir, then his land shall be called assets, that is

645. Supra, at H49–H55.

646. Rastell, *Les Termes De La Ley*, 63–64 (s.v. "Assets").

647. Supra, at H104.

648. that portion of the ancestor's estate which descends to the heir, and which is sufficient to charge him, as far as it goes, with the specialty debts of his ancestors.

649. assets in hand; assets in the hands of executors or administrators applicable for the payment of debts.

*enough* or *sufficient* to pay the same debt; and by that means the heir shall be charged as far as the land to him descended will stretch.' Termes de ley. verb. assets.[650] to which I will add from Blount's law-dict.[651] 'whoever charges another with *assets*, charges him with having *enough* descended or come to his hands to discharge that which is in demand.' Blount. verb. assets.[652] when we call that fund which is in the ex[ecuto]r's hands for the paiment of debts by the name of *assets*, we do not mean to affirm that it is in every case '*enough* for the paiment of debts' which it is said would be often untrue, but that '*enough*' of that fund shall be taken to pay the debts if it will so far stretch as the book subjoins. this enou*gh, or if* you please this *tantum,* is called *assets* shortly, and by use is made to include the whole idea originally expressed by these words '*enough* of goods & chattels to pay debts' or 'so much of the goods & chattels as will pay the debts.' it is observable too that the Termes de ley in the passage before cited and also in the one cited by the pl[aintiff]'s counsel from Cowel[653] & Off. ex[ecuto]r 307.[654] (by whom it is taken verbatim from the Termes de ley) sais that 'Assets are

650. Rastell, *Les Termes De La Ley*, 63 (s.v. "Assets").

651. Thomas Blount, *Nomo-Lexikon: A law dictionary, Interpreting such difficult and obscure Words and Terms, As are found either in Our Common or Statute, Ancient or Modern Lawes. With References to the several Statutes, Records, Registers, Law-Books, Charters, Ancient Deeds, and Manuscripts, wherein the Words are used: And Etymologies, where they properly occur* ([London] In the Savoy: Printed by Tho. Newcomb for John Martin and Henry Herringman, 1670). Blount (1618–1679) was a barrister of the Inner Temple.

652. Blount, *Nomo-Lexikon*, s.v. "Assets" (unpaged).

653. Cowell, *Interpreter of Words and Terms*, s.v. "Asset" (unpaged).

654. Wentworth, *Office and Duty of Executors*, 307 (Curson, "Supplement: Of Executors").

where a man dies **{H139}** *indebted* &c.' intimating that if he owed no debt, or in other words when all the debts he owed were paid, there would be no assets.

Yet as it is thought that this substitution of the word *enough* for *assets* produces indifferent English, I have no objection to the adoption of the more elegant one furnished from 2. Atk. 206.[655] 'per Murray Sollicitor general[656] tho' the law sais that a reversion after an estate tail is not *assets*, yet it is a gross and inaccurate expression, and is only sub modo, for there is a *liableness* which makes it assets in futuro, or in other words a quality to be *liable* to the debt in futuro.' those things are *assets* then which are *liable* to the test[ato]r's debts. but when all the debts are paid, the emblements of Rob[ert] Boll[ing] are no longer *liable* to debts, because there are no debts for them to be *liable* to. so that if after all the debts are paid you still say they are *liable* to *debts*, it is the same as to say they are *liable* to *nothing*, or have no *liableness*; and consequently are no longer *assets*, because they have lost that quality of *liableness* which is essential in the definition of *assets*. this amounts to the same thing which the def[endant]'s counsel had said pa. 36. 'that as soon as debts and legacies are paid there are no such things as assets in existence'[657]

Obj. pa. 19.[658] where the act sais the crop shall be assets in the

655. *Kinaston versus Clark*, 26 E.R. 526–28: quotation in 26 E.R. at 527. The quotation follows this citation.

656. William Murray, later Lord Mansfield. See supra note 169.

657. Supra, at H51.

658. Supra, at H104–H105.

hands of ex[ecuto]rs & adm[inistrato]rs it means 'that it shall be such an estate in the hands of ex[ecuto]rs & adm[inistrato]rs as is *liable* for paiment of the decedent's debts & legacies, or in other words "all the personal estate whereof the test[ato]r died possessed which belong to the ex[ecuto]rs & are *assets* in their hands for the paiment of *debts & legacies.*" and cites 2. Bac' abr' 416.[659] Ans. the estate in the adm[inistrato]r's hands has several properties. 1. a liableness to debts. 2. a submission to legacies. 3. to distributions. now if the act had meant to give it all these properties it would have said it should be liable to debts **{H140}** and legacies, and the residuum to be distributed. but when it singles out one of these properties only, to wit, a liableness for debts it clearly remains as it was as to the other two, to wit, not liable to pecuniary legacies, nor to be thrown into the residuum. by giving it this quality of liableness to debts it puts it on a footing with every other specific legacy which has this same quality of being *assets*, or being *liable* to the test[ato]r's debts; and yet no body ever supposed of other specific legacies that because they are *assets* they are therefore taken from the specific, and given to the residuary legatee. I suppose it will not be denied that these plants were a specific legacy to Rob[ert] Boll[ing] if the test[ato]r had said in express words 'I give to Rob[ert] Boll[ing] my Buffalo-lick lands with the emblements now growing thereon',[660] the emblements would have been admitted to be as much a specific legacy as the lands themselves, but when he sais 'I give to Rob[ert] Boll[ing] my Buffalo lick lands' this in law includes

659. Bacon, *A New Abridgment of the Law*, 2: 416.

660. <and all the future plants which>

a bequest of the emblements then growing as perfectly as if he had expressed himself in the first form. the words therefore used in the first form 'with the emblements now growing thereon' would have been surplusage; & it is a maxim in law that 'the omission of that which would have been surplusage shall not vitiate.' the latter form therefore carries them clearly as a specific legacy. indeed Gilbert in the place before cited[661] sais expressly that as to the corn growing 'the devisee[662] is put into the place of the ex[ecuto]r by the words of the will' that is, they are bequeathed to him. when therefore the pl[aintiff]'s counsel concludes that the personal estate which has a *liableness* to debts has also a *liableness* to fall into the residuum, he concludes too hastily; for then all other specific legacies, being *assets*, or having a *liableness* for the paiment of debts would also have a *liableness* to fall into the residuum, which is not true. tho' the act of ass[embly][663] has put this specific legacy on the footing of all others by making it *assets* for debts, yet it no more meant thereby to take it from the specific legatee if not requisite for the paiment of debts, than **{H141}** the former laws, by making all specific legacies assets, meant to take them from the legatees and throw them into the residuum. on the contrary we know that tho' a specific legacy is liable to debts if requisite, yet it is so far privileged that it is to be the last called on. while the ex[ecuto]r is directed to abate equally from the pecuniary legacies, or even to use the whole of them till the debts be paid. the specific legacies are still to be kept unabated &

661. Gilbert, *Law of Evidence*, 251.

662. omitted: "in relation to the chattels belonging to the land"

663. 3 & 4 Geo. II, ch. 8, § 11 (Virginia 1730).

untouched as the last resort. and if a creditor using his privilege of levying his debt on any part of the estate should levy it on a specific legacy while there is any part of that fund left which is to pay pecuniary legacies, the specific legatee may come on that fund for reimbursement. so says the Chancellor [Macclesfield][664] in the case of Bowaman & Reeve. Pr. Ch. 578.[665] 3. Bac' abr' 482.[666] 'if creditors bring an action or take out execution on a horse &c. specifically devised, which they may do notwithstanding the specific devise thereof, yet most certainly the ex[ecuto]r or residuary legatee shall be obliged in equity to make them a recompence; for they are to have nothing to their own use but the residue after the debts and legacies paid.' this answers, by denying, what was said pa. 6.[667] which I promised should be answered here, to wit, 'that if an ex[ecuto]r should apply, or a creditor levy execution on the crop, it is apprehended the devisee of the land could not be reimbursed the value of the crop out of the rest of the estate.'

664. Thomas Parker, later Lord Macclesfield (1666?–1732), barrister, Inner Temple (1691); C.J. Q.B. (1710–1718); Lord Chancellor (1718–1725).

665. *Bowaman versus Reeve,* Precedents in Chancery 577–80, 24 E.R. 259–60 (Ch., Michaelmas 1721): quotation in 24 E.R. at 260. The heading of *Bowaman versus Reeve* indicates the year as 1712; the reporter inserted the bracketed year 1721 without acknowledging the contradiction.

666. Bacon, *A New Abridgment of the Law,* 3: 482. The quotation follows the citation; it differs from the actual paragraph in Bacon:

> If a Horse, or Term for Years, which is specifically devised to another be taken in Execution by Creditors on a Judgment obtained, (as they may be) the Specific Legatee shall have Recompence in Equity against the Executors, or Residuary Legatees, for the Value, who are to have nothing till after the Debts and Legacies are paid.

667. Supra, at H95.

Again when it is said that the act meant to make the crop such an estate in the hands of ex[ecuto]rs as is liable for debts which he sais is 'all the personal estate whereof the test[ato]r died possessed whether chattels real or personal', let it be recollected that this includes the test[ato]r's slaves, who are not distributable. so that a part of the estate subject to debts being distributable, and a part not, it was impossible the act could intend to make the crop in all it's qualities such an estate as both of these parts, **{H142}** or to resemble both, for then it must have resembled contrary things, to wit, things distributable and things not distributable. it could therefore only mean to make it such an estate in that single quality in which they resembled, to wit, a liableness to debts.

Obj. pa. 20.[668] 'By 4. Ann. c.7. [33] s.2.[669] after debts &c. the surplusage i.e. the remainder of all and singular the goods chattels & personal estate of every person dying intestate, i.e. of all that estate which was liable to the paiment of debts, or in other words, of the assets in the hands of adm[inistrato]rs shall be distributed &c'

Ans. let the act 'untortured, unperverted, uninterpolated' speak for itself, & it sais no such thing. 'after debts, funerals & just expences paid the *surplusage* of all and singular the goods, chattels, & personal estate of every person dying intestate shall be distributed &c.' now here the act instead of calling the residue by the name of *assets*, as the pl[aintiff]'s counsel would torture it to do, calls it by that very term '*surplusage*' which it was said before alwais to assume

668. Supra, at H105.

669. 4 Anne, c. 33 (Virginia 1705).

after debts & legacies paid. and yet in pa. 21.[670] we are told that this act (I suppose this is the one meant, if not, let it be shewn what other) 'has called the surplusage of the crop *assets*.'

Obj. 'that the naming an ex[ecuto]r in a will is a gift in law of all the test[ato]r's personal estate to the ex[ecuto]r, and that a commission of administration vests the property of all the intestate's personal estate in the adm[inistrato]r is founded in this that all that estate is *assets*.'

Ans. if the sole foundation of this transfer of the personal estate to the ex[ecuto]r or adm[inistrato]r is it's being *assets*, or possessing a quality of *liableness* to debts, then the lands, slaves, & all other the estate of the test[ato]r or intestate are also transferred to the ex[ecuto]r or adm[inistrato]r, because they are also *assets*. so that this, proving too much, proves nothing. this foundation therefore is too restricted. it's foundation at large is this. that all that estate is destined by the law 1. to paiment of debts. 2. to be deliv{**H143**}ered to legatees if there be any. 3. to the distributees if there be none. and it is necessary some person should be appointed to do all this. accord[ing]ly the test[ato]r appoints a person, called an ex[ecuto]r, and transfers to him all his personal estate to perform all these offices: or if there be no will, the law appoints a person, called an adm[inistrato]r, and to him transfers the estate for the same purposes. so that the personal estate is transferred to him, not because it is called *assets*, but because the test[ato]r in one case, & the law in another has thought proper to transfer it to him 1. as

670. Supra, at H106.

*assets.* 2. as a legatory depositum.[671] 3. as a distributable or residuary surplus.

pa. 21.[672] 'if all the personal estate be assets, the act of distribution operates upon the remainder of the assets after the debts paid' & to prove this it is said 'the *surplusage*' (using the proper term) 'would have been distributed in the following instances.[']

'1. if Edw[ard] Boll[ing] had died intestate.' ans. the emblements growing at the time of the death of the intestate would indeed have been distributed; not because they were assets; no man upon earth ever thought of assigning such a reason; but because for the encoragement of tillage the law has in certain instances, already often enumerated, of which this would have been one, given the emblement to him who sowed it. but the plants put in afterwards would not have been distributed, but, if not required for the paiment of debts, would have gone to the heir as an Accession to the land after his title commenced, under the general rule 'si Ticius suam plantam in Menii solo posuerit, Menii planta erit.'

2. it is said it would have been distributed 'if Edw[ard] Boll[ing] had died the 2'd of March before any plants were put into the ground, had omitted in his will to dispose of the residuum, and his ex[ecuto]r had planted and finished a crop.' ans. reasoning on legal principles only I am at a loss to conjecture a foundation for this opinion. the com{**H144**}mon law would have give the plants

671. A depositum is one of the four real contracts specified by Justinian, under which the depositee is not liable for negligence but only for fraud, yet the depository has only possession of the deposit, legal title to which remains in the depositor. A legatory depositum is a depositum of money created by a will.

672. Supra, at H106.

to Rob[ert] Boll[ing] the devisee as an Accession to the soil. the act of ass[embly][673] only takes them from him in favor of creditors when necessary for the paiment of debts, that is, it only makes them *assets*, or goods *liable to debts* as Murray explains it. but all debts are supposed to be paid before the ex[ecuto]r proceeds to distribute the unbequeathed residuum. when therefore all debts are paid these plants lose their quality and name of *assets*, or of *liableness* to debts because there are no longer any to be *liable* to, & consequently resume their former nature of an Accession to the soil, and go with that to the devisee. if indeed Murray had said that *assets*, as such, besides a quality of *liableness* to *debts*, have also a second quality of *liableness* to *distribution*, it would have been something: but he cautiously said that *assets* are those things which have a *liableness* to *debts*. if he had gone further as the pl[aintiff]'s counsel does & said they were also those things which have a liableness to *distribution*, the very instance, to wit, of a reversion of which he was then speaking would have contradicted him. for he knew well that a reversion tho' an *asset*, that is, *liable* to *debts*, is *not liable* to *distribution*. so that the only inherent quality of an asset is liableness to debts. this is of it's essence, without which it cannot exist, that is, it can no longer be an asset. when it loses it's liableness to debts, which it does when there are no debts, or in other words when all debts are paid, it loses it's name and nature. indeed it sometimes happens that the thing which is an asset, or which has a liableness to debts, has also a liableness to distribution. but sometimes it has not. a thing merely personal is an asset, and, when not called for to pay a

673. 3 & 4 Geo. II, ch. 8, § 11 (Virginia 1730).

debt, is also distributable. but lands and slaves are also assets, that is, have a quality of liableness to debts, yet if they escape the call of debts they retain their nature of discending to heirs or going to devisees. so also emblements growing in lands devised are assets; but if they escape the call of debts they retain their former quality of passing with the land to the devisee.

**{H145}** Place this matter in another light. the act of distribution gives title to the distributees in no case but where there is a total or partial intestacy, and then gives title only to the unbequeathed estate. in like manner the residuary legatee takes only the estate unbequeathed in any other part of the will. but plants growing in the lands at the time of the testator's death were bequeathed to Rob[ert] Boll[ing] because like the houses & trees they were included in the bequest of the lands. so also plants put in after his death, were bequeathed to Rob[ert] Boll[ing] because, like all other accessions or future profits, they are included in the bequest of the land. if therefore there had been no bequest of the residuum, they would not have been distributed with the <u>unbequeathed</u> residuum, nor in the present case can they pass to Arch[ibald] Boll[ing] the residuary legatee, because they are <u>bequeathed</u> specifically.

3. it is said 'that part of the crop which was severed before the testator's death would have been distributed had it been undisposed of by the will.'

ans. certainly it would. for the severed crop was neither an emblement nor a subsequent accession; but was to all intents and purposes a part of the merely personal estate of the test[ato]r. we therefore never claimed a plant severed before the test[ato]r's death;

but only those growing at the time of his death, which the law calls emblements & includes in the devise of the land: and say also that had any been planted after (tho' in truth none were) they would have been ours as an Accession to our soil, in like manner included in the devise of the land. so that it is easy to assign the reason why the part of the crop severed before the test[ato]r's death would have been distributed if he had omitted the residuary clause in his will; and yet that part which was not severed shall not be distributed; to wit because the former would in that case have been undisposed of by the will, & the latter was disposed of to Rob[ert] Bolling.

**{H146}** I have now gone through the plaintiff's observations on this head, except so far as they relate to a case which I had produced, and to some other cases newly produced by himself. to these therefore I shall now proceed. but in order to keep in view the purpose for which they are introduced, let it be remembered that I had laid down this position pa. 36.[674] 'that a thing by being made *assets* is only subjected to the paiment of debts in favor of creditors; but, if not so applied, remains as it would have done had no act been made.' in support of this I produced 4 proofs under which the case before mentioned will come to be considered.

1. that *slaves* are by our act of ass[embly][675] made *assets* for the paiment of debts, & yet if the debts can be paid without them, they do not become a part of the *residuary* surplus, but go to the devisees. I suppose the pl[aintiff]'s counsel sees this in a different light from what I do, or he would have thought it worth an answer.

674. Supra, at H51.

675. 3 & 4 Geo. II, ch. 8, § 11 (Virginia 1730).

to me it seems so strictly parallel in the case of a person dying testate, that I am at a loss to preconceive what will be said to distinguish it. it's points of resemblance are these. 1. before the act of 1727,[676] slaves being a real estate passed to the devisee immediately in the same manner as lands: & like them were assets in his hands. so before the act of 1711.[677] Emblements being a chattel annexed to lands & so of a mixt nature, passed to the devisee of the land immediately & in his hands were assets as were the lands themselves. 2. after the act of 1727.[678] which directed that a bequest of a slave should transfer the property in the same manner as if it were a chattel, the property of the slave passed by the will to the ex[ecuto]r (because that was the manner in which property in a chattel passed) and, if not called for to pay debts was by his assent alone to be transferred to the devisee. thus it's nature of being assets in the hands of the devisee was so far altered as to become assets in the hands of the ex[ecuto]r. in like manner after the act of 1711.[679] which made the Emblements assets in the hands of ex[ecuto]rs, their nature under the old law of being assets in the hands of the devisee were **{H147}** now (according to the doctrine of the pl[aintiff]'s counsel which I am not concerned to controvert) so far altered as that they became

676. 1 Geo. II, c. 11 (Virginia 1727): *An Act to explain and amend the Act, For declaring the Negro, Mulatto, and Indian Slaves, within this Dominion, to be Real Estate; and part of one other Act, intituled, An Act for the distribution of Intestates Estates, declaring Widows Rights to these deceased Husbands Estates; and for securing Orphans Estates,* in Hening, ed. *Statutes at Large*, 4: 222–28.

677. 9 Anne, c. 2 (Virginia 1711).

678. 1 Geo. II, c. 11 (Virginia 1727).

679. 9 Anne, c. 2 (Virginia 1711).

assets in the hands of the ex[ecuto]r. 3. slaves if not applied to the paiment of debts retain their former nature of passing to the devisee, and do not become a part of the residuary surplus. so I urge that Emblements if not applied to the paiment of debts retain their former nature of passing to the devisee & do not become a part of the residuary surplus. It may be observed that this overthrows a fundamental position of the pl[aintiff]'s counsel pa. 9. it is this that 'all personal estate to which a decedent had a sole right & which goes to his ex[ecuto]rs & adm[inistrato]rs is subject to *distribution & residuary bequests.*' for by the construction of our slave acts I think it has been alwais admitted that the exceptions in the act of 1705.[680] & 1727.[681] destroy the efficacy of the enacting clause of 1705, which declared them real estate, in every instance except those of descent & dower, & render them in all other cases Personal estate. particularly the clause of 1705.[682] which makes them assets, & that of 1727.[683] which makes them pass to the devisee in the same manner as a chattel make them in these instances a personal estate. then here is 'a personal estate to which the decedent had a sole right & which goes to his ex[ecuto]r' and yet is not subject to distribution[684] or to the residuary bequest. the instance also of a specific legacy contradicts his position, because this is a 'personal estate to which the decedent had a sole right, which goes to his

680. 4 Anne, c. 23 (Virginia 1705).

681. 1 Geo. II, c. 11 (Virginia 1727).

682. 4 Anne, c. 23 (Virginia 1705).

683. 1 Geo. II, c. 11 (Virginia 1727).

684. <&>

ex[ecuto]r' & yet is not subject to distribution[685] or to the residuary bequest. if it be objected that in the case of the specific legacy, and also of the slave as stated above, the testator has otherwise expressly disposed of them & so taken them out of the residuary clause or undisposed residuum: I answer that in like manner the Emblements of the lands, as Baron Gilbert sais, & all their future Accessions or profits pass to the devisee by the devise of the lands: <<the devisee in relation to>> that being <<put in the place of the ex[ecuto]r by the words of the will.>>[686] now as the property in the crop, had the lands been left undisposed of, would have passed to the ex[ecuto]r by the will, tho' not expressly men**{H148}**tioned, so the devisee, being put by the will in his place, must take them by the will. then they are equally with the slave, or other specific legacy beforementioned, otherwise disposed of by the test[ato]r and, & so taken out of the residuary clause.

2. the second proof I produced to shew that a thing by being made assets did not become a part of the residuary or distributable surplus if not applied to debts was that of American lands, which by a stat[ute] of G. 2.[687] are so far as a British parliament may do it made assets for the paiment of British debts, and as is the opinion in the other colonies & in Great Britain of every kind of debt. this also remains unanswered.

3. the same may be said of the third proof, to wit, a trust

685. <&>

686. Gilbert, *Law of Evidence*, 251.

687. 5 Geo. II, c. 7 (1732).

estate[688] which by the stat[ute] of frauds[689] is made assets for the paiment of debts, & yet is not therefore distributable if not applied to the paiment of debts.

4. the fourth was the case of an estate pur autre vie which by a statute is transferred to ex[ecuto]rs & adm[inistrato]rs & declared to be *assets* in their hands. the stat[ute] transferring it to the ex[ecuto]r & adm[inistrato]r & not saying for what purpose they should hold it if it were not requisite for the paiment of debts, it became a question whether by being made *assets,* it was not of course distributable? this was the question in Oldham v. Pickering, to which cited in my former argument pa. 39.[690] & to the observations pa. 40.[691] as well as to the observations of the pl[aintiff]'s counsel in his argum[ent] pa. 11. 12.[692] I shall refer. but I shall beg leave to transcribe the same case from two other books, which collated with the report of it in 2. Salk. will give us perhaps more explicitly the ground of decision.

Holt's rep. 503. 'Oldham v. Pickering. Pasch. 8 W. 3. Rot. 87.[693]
'In prohibition upon demurrer to the declaration the case was A. (who had lands limited to him during the life of B.) died intestate,

688. a trust, all or part of the income from which is to be accumulated during the surviving spouse's life and added to the corpus of the trust, all such funds (corpus and accumulated income) to be paid to the estate of the surviving spouse at that person's death.

689. 29 Car. II, c. 3 (1676 [1677]).

690. Supra, H54.

691. Supra, H55.

692. Supra, H97–H99.

693. *Oldham versus Pickering* (Holt), 90 E.R. 1176. The quoted report follows this citation.

& the pl[aintiff] took out administration, B. the cestuy que vie being still living; there were assets sufficient besides this estate pur autre vie to pay all debts. &c. the next of kin to the intestate libelled in the Spiritual court **{H149}** against the adm[inistrato]r to have this estate pur autre vie distributed.

'Per curiam. such an estate still remains a freehold & the adm[inistrato]r is tenant of such freehold, against whom the praecipe[694] must be brought if a common recovery should be had of the lands; the design of this statute was only in respect to *creditors*, to make an estate pur autre vie *assets for paiment of debts*, and *for that end only* the adm[inistrato]r is made an Occupant but *in all other respects* the quality of the estate remains the same as it was before at Common law; and the Spiritual court never had any *jurisdiction* in cases of freehold.'

3. Salk. 137. Oldison [Oldham] v. Pickering. Mich. 8. W.3.[695]

'In this case it was adjudged that tho' an estate pur autre vie is made assets by the stat[ute] 29. Car. 2.[696] yet 'tis not distributable within the stat[ute] 22. Car. 2.[697] for distribution of intestates estates, because *distribution* is a quality not necessarily included in the notion of *assets* as paiment of *debts* is; now an estate pur autre vie

694. In common-law practice, an original writ drawn up in the alternative, commanding the defendant to do the thing required, or show the reason why he had not done it.

695. *Oldham versus Pickering* (3 Salkeld) 91 E.R. 738. The quoted report follows this citation.

696. 29 Car. II, c. 3 (1676 [1677]).

697. 22 & 23 Car. II, c. 10 (1670).

is not properly goods or chattels, but remains a freehold[698] tho' 'tis assets by the first statute.'[699]

An estate pur autre vie having by a statute, like our emblements, been made *assets* in the hands of ex[ecuto]rs & adm[inistrato]rs, the def[endant] Pickering had libelled in the Spiritual court to have distribution of it. the court of King's bench was therefore now moved for a Prohibition to restrain the Ecclesiastical court from meddling with a *freehold* estate. the court, to wit, Holt, Rokeby, Turton & Eyre, unanimously gave judgment that the Spiritual court should be prohibited & that this was not a distributable estate. their reasons as expressed in one book (2. Salk.)[700] are 'that notwithstanding this alteration by the stat[ute][701] it remains a freehold still; and the amendment of the law in this particular was only designed for the relief of Creditors.'[702] in another book (Holt)[703] 'such an estate still remains a freehold,[704] the design of the stat[ute][705] being only in respect to *creditors*; but in *all other respects the quality of the estate re* **{H150}** *mains the same as it was before at Common law*: & the Spiritual court never had any jurisdiction in

698. <still>

699. The "first statute" is 22 & 23 Car. II, c. 10 (1670).

700. *Oldham v. Pickering* (2 Salkeld) 91 E.R. 400–401.

701. 29 Car. II, c. 3 (1676 [1677]).

702. *Oldham v. Pickering* (2 Salkeld) 91 E.R. 400–401: quotation at 400.

703. *Oldham versus Pickering* (Holt), 90 E.R. 1176–1177.

704. omitted: "and the administrator is tenant of such freehold, against whom the praecipe must be brought if a common recovery should be had of the lands;"

705. 29 Car. II, c. 3 (1676 [1677]).

cases of *freehold*.'[706] in a third (3. Salk.)[707] it is 'tho an estate pur autre vie is made assets by the stat[ute][708] yet 'tis not *distributable*,[709] because *distribution is a quality not necessarily included in the notion of assets, as paiment of debts is*.' Now what is the amount of this? 'that an estate when made *assets* by statute has only it's *unliable* quality altered & converted into a *liable* quality in favor of *creditors*. that in all other respects it's qualities (that is, it's other qualities) remain the same as they were before at Common law & particularly that it is not distributable because distribution is a quality not necessarily included in the notion of *assets* as paiment of debts is.' let us then analyse the qualities of the estate pur autre vie which was made assets by the statute of frauds,[710] & was the subject of debate in Oldham v. Pickering, as they stood before that stat[ute]. & then do the same by Emblements which have been made assets by our act of ass[embly] and are the subject of debate here, & see which of these qualities are altered in both cases.

An estate pur autre vie, when not limited to the heirs (in which case only the stat[ute] gives it to ex[ecuto]rs & adm[inistrato]rs) was

1. of a real & freehold nature.

706. *Oldham v. Pickering* (Holt), 90 E.R. 1176–1177: quotation at 1177.

707. *Oldham versus Pickering* (3 Salkeld), 91 E.R. 738: quotation at 738. The quotation follows this citation.

708. 29 Car. II, c. 3 (1676–1677). The manuscript's quotation from *Oldham v. Pickering*, which resumes following this note, omits this citation.

709. omitted: "within the statute of 22 Car. 2." The statute is 22 & 23 Car. II, c. 10 (1670).

710. 29 Car. II, c. 3 (1676 [1677]).

2. it was indeviseable.

3. indescendible.

4. indistributable.

5. open to any occupant who should first take possession.

6. not assets, i.e. not *liable* to debts

but by the statutes the 2d. 5th. & 6th. qualities were altered. to wit,

2. it was made deviseable expressly.

5. it was taken from the prime occupant & given to the ex[ecuto]r or adm[inistrato]r.

6. it was made *assets*, i.e. *liable* to debts.

the 1st. 3d. & 4th. qualities therefore remained as they did before at Com{**H151**}mon law, that is, it continued 1. a freehold. 3. indescendible. 4. indistributable as was expressly determined in the case of Oldham v. Pickering, till the stat[ute] 14. G.2. c.20.[711] when it's 4th. quality also was altered, & it was made to be distributable in England, tho' to this day it is apprehended not to be so in this country.

An Emblement before the act of 1711.[712] was

1. of a chattel nature.
2. it was not descendible.
3. it was deviseable.
4. if devised, it was not liable to debts in the hands of the ex[ecuto]r.
5. if devised, it was not distributable

711. 14 Geo. II, c. 20 (1741).

712. 9 Anne, c. 2 (Virginia 1711).

6. if not devised, it was liable to debts in the hands of the ex[ecuto]r.
7. if not devised, it was distributable

by the act of ass[embly] it's 4th. quality only was altered, to wit, it's *un-liable* nature was converted into a *liable* one; but as the judges say in the case of Oldham v. Pickering 'all it's other qualities remained the same as they were before at the Common law. particularly it is not distributable, because distribution is not a quality necessarily included in the notion of assets, as paiment of debts is.' so that it still remains the same in it's other qualities, to wit, 1. a chattel 2. not descendible. 3. deviseable. — 5. if devised, not distributable. 6. if not devised, liable to debts. 7. if not devised, distributable.

An Accession (i.e. plants put in after the death of the test[ato]r) was

1. perfectly & absolutely the property of the devisee. consequently
2. it was not liable to the test[ato]r's debts, but as the land itself was.

but the act has altered this & made it liable to the test[ato]r's debts.

But the pl[aintiff]'s counsel seems to think there is some magick quality in a freehold estate which will exempt that from being made distributable by words which would at the same time make any other estate, not possessing that particular magic quality, liable to **{H152}** distribution; and that this was the ground of the judgment in Oldham v. Pickering. whereas the only reason why the judges so particularly single out the *freehold* quality as being unaltered, was, not from any thing particularly sacred & exempt from legislative alteration in that quality, but because the question then before the court, to wit, Whether they should prohibit the Ecclesiastical court from proceeding or not? arose from that particular quality of the estate, which, if unaltered by the act, withdrew it from Ecclesiastical cognisance. and I must appeal to an inspection of the case, as stated in the three books, whether the ground of decision was not this in general terms 'that an act introducing new alterations in the nature of any estate, shall not be intended to reverse the whole nature of that estate in every point, but only to alter those qualities particularly expressed to be altered.' and consequently that in the present case the act of ass[embly] by making emblements liable to *debts*, has not taken away their deviseable quality, nor yet given them a distributable one where they had it not before.

Or to state this reasoning in the pl[aintiff]'s own form pa. 11.[713] where he sais 'Now why was the estate pur autre vie belonging to an intestate not distributable? because notwithstanding the stat[ute] it remained a *freehold* still; and a *freehold* is not an estate distributable by the stat[ute] of distribution,[714] which directs goods, chattels, & personal estate only to be distributed.' 'but if the act of parl[iament] had declared the estate pur autre vie to be a chattel of the intestate & assets in the hands of ex[ecuto]rs & adm[inistrato]rs, then the reasoning in that case would have been inverted thus "an estate pur autre vie belonging to an intestate is distributable; for since this

713. Supra, H99.

714. 22 & 23 Car. II, c. 10 (1670).

alteration by the statute the estate no longer remains a freehold but is part of the personal estate and consequently within the stat[ute] of distributions."[715] I will say in like manner Now why are devised Emblements belonging to a test[ato]r **{H153}** not distributable? because notwithstanding the act of ass[embly][716] they remain a *devised estate* still, and a devised estate is not an estate distributable by the stat[ute] of distributions which directs the goods chattels & personal estate of an intestate only, that is, only the untestated or undevised goods chattels & personal estate to be distributed. and tho' these devised emblements are of a chattel nature & by the act are made assets in the hands of ex[ecuto]rs & adm[inistrato]rs, yet notwithstanding this alteration by the act they remain a devised estate and consequently are not within the stat[ute] of distribution.'[717]

But the pl[aintiff]'s counsel seems to think that in the cases of Witter & Witter,[718] & Marwood v. Turner[719] the decision in Oldham v. Pickering was unsettled by the Chancellor [King]. let us therefore review these cases and see if they affect this.

Witter v. Witter. 3. P.W. 90. pl[aintiff]'s argum[ent] pa. 12.[720]

In this case an ex[ecuto]r held an estate for 99 years, if three lives so long lived, in trust for an infant, which estate, if unaltered,

715. Id.

716. 3 & 4 Geo. II, ch. 8, § 11 (Virginia 1730).

717. 22 & 23 Car. II, c. 10 (1670).

718. *Witter v. Witter*, 24 E.R. 985–986.

719. *Sir Samuel Marwood, Bart. v. Cholmley Turner, Esq.*, 24 E.R. 1013–1017.

720. *Witter v. Witter*, 24 E.R. 985–986.

would on the death of the infant have gone to his adm[inistrato]r, & been distributable among his next of kin. the ex[ecuto]r however takes on him to surrender this estate & to take back a new lease for three lives absolutely to the infant & his heirs which, by the limitation to the heirs, would on the death of the infant go, not to his distributees, but to his heir. the infant dies. & the question was, between the heir claiming under this new lease & the adm[inistrato]r claiming under the old one, not whether the estate pur autres vies taken back by the ex[ecuto]r was made distributable by having been made assets, but, whether the ex[ecuto]r should have it in his power, by altering the nature of an estate of his own head, to alter the course of it's passage from one set of claimants to another? or in other words to take from the distributees & give to the heir at-law? the Chancellor [King] determined in this, as he has ever done in every similar case, that an ex[ecuto]r should have no **{H154}** such power of sacrificing one set of representatives in favor of another. Therefore sais he 'this renewed lease shall follow the nature of the old one' (that is it shall be distributable as that would have been & not indistributable as the new one would of itself be) 'though for lives'[721] (and so in it's proper nature indistributable) 'it comes in the place and stead of the original lease which was for years'[722] (and distributable) now here the Chancellor [King] is express that he grounds his decree on the nature of the former estate which was distributable & the inability of the ex[ecuto]r to alter that nature, and not on the nature of the new estate which was indistributable. his

721. *Witter v. Witter*, 24 E.R. 985–986: quotation at 986.

722. Id.

words, & the very question before the court, clearly imply that had this new estate pur autres vies been standing on it's own bottom it would not have been distributable. for if it had been distributable as standing on the bottom of the lease for years, & if it would also have been distributable as a lease pur autres vies,[723] then it was distributable in all events, & how could any other parties than the distributees be introduced, or any question arise, or the Chancellor [King] proceed to argue it? yet the pl[aintiff]'s counsel cites it to shew that 'notwithstanding the case of Oldham v. Pickering it was far from being a settled point that even an estate pur autre vie should not be distributed.' whereas even the counsel for the distributees never so much as hint that this estate would have been distributable if it had stood on any other bottom but that of a distributable one. they claim it on no other principle but that the ex[ecuto]r had transgressed his duty in changing a distributable estate into an indistributable one which they admit this to be when they say that 'the court if applied to for leave to convert this estate for years into an estate pur autres vies would not have granted it without a provision that in case the def[endant] should die during his infancy the purchase should **{H155}** not turn to the prejudice of the <u>representatives of his personal estate</u>.' and the Lord Chancellor [King] implies the same where he sais he would have directed the new lease to be in trust for the distributees, plainly intimating it would not be so without such direction. but the pl[aintiff]'s counsel seems to lay some stress on these words 'tho' the Spiritual court cannot intermeddle with a *freehold* to distribute it, yet it doth not

723. for the lives of others.

follow but that this court may inforce such a distribution.' but for what reason could not the Spiritual court do this? because this estate, however tortiously, was now converted into a *freehold*; & the Spiritual court has no jurisdiction in cases of freehold, nor power to determine on them, nor process to lay hold of them. and on what principle would the court of Chancery inforce the distribution of a *freehold?* because it was in it's nature distributable? no: because in this instance it had by a breach of trust been substituted in the room of a distributable estate, & it is the Chancellor's proper province to redress all breaches of trust, let them concern *freehold*, or what they will. so that this case is so far from unsettling that of Oldham v. Pickering that it is all along an admission of it, the Chancellor & counsel taking constantly for granted that the estate pur autres vies, independant of other circumstances would have been indistributable as was determined in Oldham v. Pickering.

Marwood v. Turner 3. P.W. 163,[724] abridged. pl[aintiff]'s arg[ument] pa. 15.[725]

[take notice that the parties here were the devisee of Sir. Samuel pl[aintiff] & his heir def[endant].][726]

Now what were the questions which arose & were determined in this case? 1. Whether this estate was of such a nature, viz. freehold or chattel; as that a determination by the Spiritual court that the will of Sir. Samuel Marwood was revoked should preclude the court of Chancery from entering into the same question? **{H156}**

724. *Sir Samuel Marwood, Bart. v. Cholmley Turner, Esq.*, 24 E.R. 1013–1017.

725. Supra, H101–H102.

726. Brackets in original.

for if it was a freehold the Spiritual court had nothing to do with it, & their determination had been coram non judice[727] and void: but if a chattel, then it was within the bounds of their jurisdiction & their decision conclusive. the Chancellor determined it was a freehold estate & that the Spiritual court, having no jurisdiction where a freehold estate is concerned, he might proceed to the 2d. question which was Whether this will was revoked or not? he did so, & determined it was revoked, in consequence of which it fell to the ground, & the estate pur autres vies having been limited to Sir Samuel & his heirs, went to the def[endant] who was his heir. now here no distributees, nor any persons for them were before the court, nor could be; the limitation to the heir having excluded every one else, if the will was set aside; and if it was not set aside, the devisee who was the pl[aintiff] had right to it. this case then determined nothing more than what I insist on as well as the pl[aintiff]'s counsel, that notwithstanding the estate pur autres vies is by the act of parl[iament][728] made assets, yet it still continues a freehold estate; that is, no more of it's former nature is taken away or altered than the act expressly takes away or alters. before the act it was not liable to debts; the act declaring it assets, takes away that quality & makes it liable to debts. but the act, not going further, does not take away it's freehold nature, does not alter it's descendible nature, does not affect it's indistributable nature. yet at the end of this case the pl[aintiff]'s counsel sais 'so that if the estate pur autre vie had

727. literally, "in the presence of a person not a judge": a judgment rendered by a court lacking jurisdiction to hear and decide a case, and thus deemed void.

728. 22 & 23 Car. II, c. 10 (1670).

been a *chattel* no body ever questioned but when it was made assets, it would have been subject to the stat[ute] of distribution;[729] and in this case it seemed admitted if a limitation had not been to the heirs the estate should have been distributed.' I could wish the particular passage had been pointed out in which this 'seems to be admitted.' if there is the word 'distributee' or 'distribution' in the whole case, if there is a sentence which in the most distant manner looks towards the distributee or his interest, or any body represent**{H157}**ing him or his interest, if there is a word of reasoning which leads towards any body but the heir or the devisee, the only parties then before the court or who could be before it, I might venture to give up the question. does the pl[aintiff]'s counsel mean (as I conjecture from the words he expresses in Roman characters) that because the limitation was to Sir. H. and his *heirs*, this was a *descendible freehold* & *real estate?* the book sais 'because the grant was to Sir. H. and his heirs for three lives it was a descendible freehold & real estate[.]' the grant for *three lives* made it a freehold & real estate; the limitation to *his heirs* made it a descendible one. but suppose the limitation to his heirs left out, still it would have been a freehold & real estate, and would not have been thereby rendered a chattel. and there is not a word implying to whom it would have gone in that case. indeed it must be admitted that it's real, it's freehold, & it's descendible nature is mentioned for no other purpose than to shew it was such an estate as the Spiritual court could take no cognisance of. that was the question then under discussion, & to elucidate that alone it is mentioned, & not to settle or to intimate to whom the

729. Id.

estate would have gone if the limitation to the heirs had been left out. in one part of the case it is allowed that if by the stat[ute] of frauds,[730] which made it assets, it was also made a personal estate, the will would have fallen to the ground. but what then? does the book say it would have gone to distributees? no, it does not say to whom, & it is plain enough it would have gone to the def[endant] who was heir by virtue of the limitation.

Lastly the stat[ute] 14. G.2. c.20.[731] is introduced to prove that notwithstanding the case of Oldham v. Pickering it still remained a doubt whether this estate pur autre vie was not become personal estate & consequently distributable after the statute of frauds.

**{H158}** ans. 1. observe the stat[ute] sais 'that *doubts* had arisen &c' in the past tense. which was true; because the doubt had certainly arisen and produced the decision of Oldham v. Pickering. but it does not appear judicially that after that decision any doubt was entertained on the question. that case settled the law to be that an estate pur autre vie was not distributable. and as it was thought more equitable that the law should be otherwise, it became necessary to alter it by an act of the legislature. so that the passing the act of 14. G.2.[732] to make it distributable is rather evidence that it was not so before.

2. nothing is less to be depended on than the allegations in the preambles of modern statutes. the facts set forth in them, are most commonly mere creatures of the brain of the penman, & which

730. 29 Car. II, c.3 (1676 [1677]).

731. 14 Geo. II, c. 20 (1741).

732. Id.

never existed but in his brain. that this is true with respect to our own acts of ass[embly] we all know too well to require instances of proof. that it is also true with respect to the English acts take the testimony of one who seems to have bestowed much more than ordinary attention on that part of the law. 'it is frequently said that the preamble to a statute is the best key to it's construction; it often however dwells upon a pretence which was not the real occasion of the law, when perhaps the proposer had very different views in contemplation. the most common recital for the introduction of any new regulation is to set forth that "doubts had arisen at Common law" which frequently never existed; & such preambles have therefore much weakened the force of the Common law, in many different instances. the 12th. chapt. of the 18th. H.6.[733] furnishes us with the proof of this, as well as many other statutes. by the 9th. H.5.[734] it had been enacted that malicious indictments supposing crimes to have been committed in places not to be found in any part of the county should be utterly void. this stat[ute] by express words was only to continue **{H159}** till "the next parliament after the return of that king from France"[735] & yet in the 18th. year of his successor it is recited to be a doubt whether the stat[ute] was then in force "par opinion de ascuns est expirè par opinion des autres nient

733. 18 Hen. VI, c. 12 (1439): *Appeals or Indictments of Felony, committed in a Place where there is none such,* in *Statutes at Large* (Pickering), 3: 234–35.

734. 9 Hen. V, c. 1 (1421): *A Continuance of the Statutes of 7 Hen. 5 touching Indictments,* in *Statutes at Large* (Pickering), 3: 590.

735. The statute reads: "till the next Parliament to be holden after the King's Return from beyond the Sea into England."

expirè.'"[736] Barrington[737] on the stat[ute] 18. H.6. c.12. the truth is it was become necessary to supply a defect in the stat[ute] of frauds,[738] which had omitted to give a valuable part of a man's estate to his relations; and the drawer of the act which was intended to effect that alteration of the law recites currente calamo[739] 'that doubts had arisen' which probably he well knew to have also subsided.

pa. 17.[740] it is asked 'if the law by declaring the crop to be assets hath only subjected it to the paiment of debts, why is it not applied to the paiment of debts?'

Ans. 1. because as an ex[ecuto]r is privileged to pay his own debt before any other of only equal dignity, so he is privileged to exempt his own fund from the paiment of debts, & to throw them on any other equally liable. thus if one specific legacy be given to the ex[ecuto]r & others to others & it be necessary that some of them be applied to the paiment of debts, he may apply those of the other specific legatees & exempt his own. 2. this devise to Rob[ert] Boll[ing] was a specific devise, & specific legacies are never to be broken into till all the personal fund not specifically bequeathed be

736. Daines Barrington, *Observations on the More Ancient Statutes, from Magna Charta to the Twenty-First of James I. Cap. XXVII. With an Appendix, being a proposal for new modelling the statutes* (London: Printed by W. Bowyer and J. Nichols, 1769), 353–354. The manuscript adds emphasis to the word "doubt." See infra, note 737.

737. Daines Barrington (1727–1800), barrister, Inner Temple, and Justice of the Counties of Merioneth, Carnarvon, and Anglesey.

738. 29 Car. II, c. 3 (1676 [1677]).

739. literally, "the pen of the time": the words of the day, usage at that time.

740. Supra, H102.

exhausted. but in the present case it has not been exhausted. 3. justice did not require that the ex[ecuto]r should apply the crop devised to him to the paiment of debts, because the test[ato]r had provided & expressly charged another fund with the paiment of his debts.

pa. 17.[741] 'if the def[endant] had a right to the crop as it was at the test[ato]r's death, what right had he to employ the slaves bequeathed to other persons, for his benefit?'

Ans. the best of all rights; a right founded on an express **{H160}** act of ass[embly][742] which empowered, nay obliged him to employ the slaves of other persons in finishing the crop, lest there might be a deficiency for the paiment of debts. if there happened no such deficiency the act permitted the law to take it's course, & to carry to the owner of the plants the melioration of them. and this eventual gain was but an equivalent for the loss which he might eventually sustain by the application of his plants to the paiment of debts. it is true indeed that the devisee of the slaves by this provision loses part of the benefit of his bequest. but if this is a wrong, the legislature are authors of the wrong. they thought that it was proper to enlarge the fund for paiment of debts. they found that by taking from the devisee the labor of his slaves the remnant of a year (during which they would be of little use to him, as he was supposed to have no crop prepared for them to finish) they might make a great addition to that fund, to wit, of the whole crop in the

741. Supra, H103.

742. 3 & 4 Geo. II, ch. 8, § 11 (Virginia 1730).

ground which otherwise would be lost to every body by taking away the hands who were to have finished it: and that by suffering the property of the plants in their improved state to remain with their owner if not requisite for paiment of debts they would avoid doing injustice to him. these reasons satisfied them I suppose when they were fixing a small loss on the devisee of the slaves to save a much greater to the estate in general. and at any rate this may satisfy us, that the legislature have chosen to fix the loss on him & we have no right to ask wherefore.

Here then I shall sum up what has been said in reply on this head. That the Common law having, as is admitted, declared that the plants growing

passed by the devise of the land to Rob[ert] Boll[ing], it follows that the labor of the slaves, which was annexed to these plants by our act of ass[embly],[743] was given to the subject to which it was annexed (unless required for paiment of debts) by this general rule of law that 'Accessions follow their principal.' And by the same rule new plants (had there been any) set in after the test[ato]r's death would also have accrued to the owner of the soil in which they were set, that is, in the present case to Rob[ert] Boll[ing].'

**{H161}**

That the right of the devisee to the land, notwithstanding this act of ass[embly] is not suspended a moment, but is conveied to him by

the will at the instant of the test[ato]r's death: & that if his possession be suspended (which I neither deny nor admit) yet it is

743. 1 Geo. II, c. 11 (Virginia 1727).

no extinguishment of his right, because in the mean time it remains in the ex[ecuto]r in trust for creditors & for himself.

That the Common law having thus given these plants to Rob[ert] Bolling and the act of ass[embly] not taken them from him in express words, they must be still his unless the making them *assets in the hands of ex[ecuto]rs & adm[inistrato]rs* shall be thought to devest his right <u>in every event</u>.

But that this cannot be for the following reasons.

The term *assets* or *enough* is merely a <u>relative</u> term, to which *debts* is the constant and only <u>correlative</u>: and by declaring these plants *assets,* the act only means that *enough* of them, if they will so far stretch, shall be taken for paiment of (their correlative) *debts*

*Assets,* in their abstract nature, have one & one only primary and essential quality, to wit, *liableness* to debts; but when all debts are paid the things which had that liableness have now lost it, there being no debts to be liable to, & having lost their primary & essential quality, they cease to exist as assets, & with the nature lose also the name.

Emblements, i.e. the plants growing, pass to the devisee by the will as a specific devise, and when by an act of ass[embly] they are made liable to debts, they are only put on a footing with other specific legacies, which are also liable to debts, but, if not requisite for them, still go to the legatee, & do not fall into the distributable or residuary surplus.

The making of a thing assets does not of course transfer it to ex[ecuto]rs or adm[inistrato]rs for the use of a distributory or residuary claimant; for then lands and slaves would also be so transferred as they are made assets by several acts.

**{H162}**

It is no objection that the plants growing would have been distributed in case of Edw[ard] Boll[ing]'s death intestate, that being one of the instances of exception to the general rule 'Satum cedit solo'[744] explained before when treating of emblements. And plants put in after his death, would not in the like case have gone to his adm[inistrato]r for the purpose of distribution, but would have belonged to the heir (if not requisite for debts) as an Accession to his soil.

Neither is it true if E[dward] B[olling] had died the 2d. of March intestate only as to the residuum, & the crop had been planted & finished by his ex[ecuto]r that that crop would have been distributed: because the land belonging to the devisee, any subsequent Accession to it will belong to him also, this being one of the rights inherent in ownership of the soil.

Slaves, American lands, & trust estates are by several acts[745] made *assets*, yet if not applied to the paiment of debts they do not fall into the distributable surplus.

An estate pur autres vies made *assets* by a stat[ute] has been solemnly determined not to be thereby made distributable, which adjudication confirms the rule 'that a statute altering any quality in

744. Crops accede to the soil.

745. 3 & 4 Geo. II, ch. 8, § 11 (Virginia 1730) (slaves); 5 Geo. II, c. 7 (1732) (American lands); and 29 Car. II, c. 3 (1676 [1677]) (trust estates).

any kind of estate does not effect a total reversal of all the qualities of that estate, but only of the particular one expressly mentioned to be altered.' and more particularly that the 'making a thing assets does not make it distributable, because distribution is a quality not included in the notion of assets.[']

This is not confined to any mystical quality supposed to be in a freehold estate, but, from the reason of things, and the authority of this decision, extends to every quality of the estate altered.

No subsequent determination or stat[ute] has shaken the authority of this decision.

And finally the act making the crop assets has not thereby made it distributable, this being not included in the notion of assets: or in other words the giving to the crop a quality of liableness to debts, has not give it the distributable quality, which is not included in the other nor necessarily connected with it.

**{H163}**

II. Under the bequest of the testator's *book* of accounts was claimed to the proper use of the def[endant].

His Credits burthened with his Debts, but

1. in the Credits were meant to be included Buchanan's debt of £500. &
2. among the Debts was not reckoned

One fifth part of the debts of I. [i.e., John] Bolling, father of the test[ato]r: nor the legacy of £100. to Sarah Tazewell.

If Rob[ert] Boll[ing] took the test[ato]r's book of accounts to, his own proper use, it seems now to be admitted that Buchanan's debt did not pass to him as one of the Credits, & that his subjection to the test[ato]r's debts did not oblige him to pay the legacy to Sarah Tazewell. so that nothing remains now in question but

1. Whether the test[ato]r's book was bequeathed to Rob[ert] Boll[ing] for his proper use, or only for the purpose of making him ex[ecuto]r?

2. if for his proper use, Whether with the debts of Edward Boll[ing] he is to pay also one fifth of the debts of John Bolling.

1. that the legacy of the book to Rob[ert] Boll[ing] was intended for his proper use was urged to be apparent from the Face of the will.

That it does so appear I shall still rest on what was said in the argument for the def[endant]. which does not appear to be shaken by any thing advanced on the other part. on this head therefore I shall do nothing more than give short answers to some passages in the argum[ent] of the pl[aintiff]'s counsel.

Godolphin. 281.[746] had been cited for the def[endant] to prove that the word *receive* in a will imports a legacy. that author sais 'if a man by will sais my will pleasure or desire is that he shall have, or *receive*, or keep or retain, these or the like words are sufficient to create a good bequest.' the answer of the pl[aintiff]'s counsel is 'it is apprehended that this authority as to the word *receive*, is to be understood of things in the testator's possession & then it seems applicable.' Now this is answering an authority not from any circumstance found or even hinted in the book, **{H164}** but from one

746. The manuscript presents a paraphrase of Godolphin, *Orphans Legacy*, 281, following this citation. Only "My Will, Pleaure or desire is, That he shall have or receive, or keep, or retain" is quoted.

picked up 'in the feild of conjecture,' a liberty by the Leys [i.e., laws] of which, as was observed before, any authority whatever may be disarmed & even pointed in its opposite direction. in the present instance the words of the authority are general, & there is nothing to establish the conjecture of the pl[aintiff]'s counsel that they were not intended to be taken generally. let us suppose in the case he puts that the slave Demetrius, or the horse Argus, instead of being in the test[ato]r's possession at the time of his death, had been in the possession of some other person. would not the words 'I desire that Titius may receive my slave Demetrius, or that Caius receive my horse Argus' give them to Titius or to Caius as a legacy? if they would, then it follows that the circumstance of possession is altogether immaterial, and that Godolphin has been proper in stating in general terms that 'the words have[,] *receive*, keep, or retain, are sufficient to create a good bequest.'[747]

It is then affirmed pa. 26.[748] that as Robert Boll[ing] paid, so likewise he received debts as representative of the test[ato]r. I admit it. but what he adds is controvertible, 'and consequently is accountable for them to the residuary legatee.' for by 'being accountable for them' I suppose it is meant they are to be delivered over to the residuary legatee as his property. now this I deny. Robert Bolling (for instance) as representative of the test[ato]r received possession of the negroes Jane bequeathed to mrs Bland, Louisa bequeathed to Anne Bolling, Jack bequeathed to mr Meade, & Bob to Bolling Eldridge. yet he was not accountable for them to the residuary lega-

747. This "quotation" is a close paraphrase of Godolphin, *Orphans Legacy*, 281.

748. Supra, H110.

tee, but to the several legatees to whom they were specifically bequeathed. he received possession of the negroes bequeathed to himself as representative of the test[ato]r. yet for them he was not accountable to Arch[ibald] Bolling. he received the £100. given to mrs Tazewell as representative of the test[ato]r, yet he was not accountable for it to the residuary legatee, but to mrs Tazewell. in truth the conclusion drawn that because he was to **{H165}** receive the debts as representative of the test[ato]r he was of consequence to be answerable for their surplus to the residuary legatee, is much too large. for what he receives as representative of the test[ato]r he is to account to the particular persons to whom the will directs him to account, that is, to the respective legatees. now if Arch[ibald] Bolling is the legatee of this surplus of Debts, R[obert] Boll[ing] is accountable to him for it. but if it is bequeathed to Rob[ert] Boll[ing] then he is not. & this is the very question between us. so that to affirm him accountable to the residuary legatee is but an affirmation of the point in dispute.

The charge of 'interpolating' a clause in the will in order to avoid this objection the pl[aintiff]'s counsel will, I imagine withdraw on a review of the expressions to which he objects. in pa. 44.[749] I had said "a gift of his book" is synonimous with a "gift of his debts paying thereout what he owed." and again pa. 48.[750] 'it is as if he had said "I give him my outstanding debts except so much as is requisite to pay what I owe."' these expressions were in both instances intended to be paraphrastical on the testator's words: for I

749. Supra, H59.

750. Supra, H63.

take that to be paraphrase where you professedly use words of your own to explain more at large what you conceive the writer to have expressed shortly. whereas an interpolation is a wilful substitution of words in the writer's text with design that they shall pass as the words of the writer. let him only for a moment then attend to the expressions objected to and say whether they are offered to the reader as the identical words of the test[ato]r, or as my own paraphrase on his words.

And as the objection had too little weight to induce such a method of avoiding it, so was the purpose for which it was supposed to be done too unreal to be seriously aimed at. it is thus evolved by the pl[aintiff]'s counsel, pa. 27.[751] 'And why is the clause to be thus tortured, perverted, interpolated &c.? Because that it should be as, it is now, by an event unexpected when the will was made, for the interest of **{H166}** Rob[ert] Bolling: for it is not doubted he would have rejected the interpretation he contends for if his brother had not sold Pokahontas.' & in the page before[752] it was said that when the test[ato]r 'made his will he owed more than was due to him, for it was from the sale of Pokahontas that the balance is now on the other side'. but there seems to be no authority for this assertion. the answer of the def[endant] expressly deposes 'that the test[ato]r sold the warehouses at Pokahontas after making his will & in contemplation of that sale made purchases to a greater amount than the sum for which they sold.' so that the balance against the testator, instead of being lessened, seems to have been

751. Supra, H110.

752. Supra, H109.

increased in consequence of this sale.

I must now proceed to the last page[753] to pick up an argument on this head which to me appears to be dropped there somewhat out of place. 'Let it be remembered,['] sais the pl[aintiff]'s counsel, [']that Edw[ard] Boll[ing] did not sell his warehouse till after the date of his will. now cast an eye on the acc[oun]t annexed to the answer, deduct £500. the price of the warehouse from the creditor side & instead of leaving a balance in favor of Rob[ert] Boll[ing] it leaves him considerably in debt.' but if the memento premised had been of the whole truth, the reasoning must have stood thus 'Let it be remembered that Edw[ard] Boll[ing] did not sell his warehouse till after the date of his will, <u>& that in consequence of that sale he made new purchases to a yet greater amount</u>. Now cast an eye on the account annexed to the answer, deduct £500. the price of the warehouse from the creditor side, <u>and a yet greater sum from the debtor side</u>; and a valuable balance will still remain in favor of Rob[ert] Bolling, which shews the legacy might be beneficial as it is urged the test[ato]r intended it.'

Besides the evidence in favor of the def[endant] arising from the face of the will, the same thing was supposed to be proved by parol testimony, which it was insisted was admissible in this case. but here I **{H167}** shall readily acknolege I was under an error; and that while considering this part of the subject I did not sufficiently attend to the effect produced by a residuary clause. the rules for the admission of parol evidence I believe I laid down rightly enough. but the adverse counsel has convinced me that our case, is not with-

753. Supra, H127.

in them. upon the will alone therefore that question is to rest.

2. Among the debts to which Robert Boll[ing] was subjected by this bequest was not reckoned one fifth part of the debts of I. Boll[ing] father of Edw[ard]. with respect to this point the following was the general reasoning of the def[endant]'s counsel. 'that E[dward] B[olling] having given to Rob[ert] Boll[ing] his credits, excepting thereout enough to pay his debts, the extent of that exception must be determined by the testator's intention, the objects which he had in view at the time of writing the will forming it's true limits. and it was urged. ['] he could not have this debt in contemplation 1. because he did not know of it. 2. because had he known of it he could never have meant to make it a part of the exception, since that would have made the exception larger than the thing out of which it was excepted, or in other words, a part greater than the whole. 3. because from the context, the gift of the book being connected with the words "that he receive all the debts due to me and pay all that I owe" explain what debts he meant, to wit, his proper debts, there being no others entered in his book; whereas this was not his proper debt but a debt of his father's.' Whether therefore this was so far his debt as to bring it literally within the words of the will is not the proper question, but whether or not it was within his intention? here again I must refer to my former argum[ent] for the support of this reasoning adding in this place a very few words only.

pa. 49.[754] Obj. 'if any debts due to Col. Bolling had not been recovered when Edw[ard] Boll[ing] died it is imagined, supposing

754. Supra, H126.

the clause under consideration to be a legacy, his proportion of those debts **{H168}** would have passed by it.[']

Ans. not if as good circumstances could be produced to prove he did not intend Rob[ert] Boll[ing] should receive any part of his father's debts, as are produced to prove he did not intend he should pay any part of them.

It had been said in the argument for the def[endant] that the test[ato]r by this bequest meant to give Rob[ert] Bolling something. that casting an eye on the account annexed to the answer & adding 550£ to the Debtor side, instead of leaving a balance in favor of Rob[ert] Boll[ing] it brings him considerably in debt. instead of giving an answer to this reasoning as applicable to the point for which it was urged and which was then under the pen of the pl[aintiff]'s counsel, he only tells us it may be turned against us on another question handled some pages before, to wit, the question Whether the bequest of the book was intended beneficially to Rob[ert] Boll[ing] or not. but this is avoiding, not answering an objection.

III. We come now to the 3d. and last question Whether, if the bequest of the book produced nothing more than an appointment of Robert Bolling to be ex[ecuto]r, it was not then an extinguishment of his debt to the test[ato]r?

It is agreed that if the debtee make the debtor his ex[ecuto]r the debt is extinguished. to prove this the case of Wankford v. Wankford[755] was cited and relied on as decisive. the judges indeed in that case, tho' they agreed in the effect of the will, to wit, that it

755. *Wankford versus Wankford* (1 Salkeld), 91 E.R. 265–72.

extinguished the debt, yet differed as to the manner in which this effect was operated; Judge Powell thinking it was by way of legacy; while Holt thought it by way of actual paiment and release. to the former, as a more simple method of accounting for and explaining the rule of law with it's exceptions, the def[endant]'s counsel had inclined, and therefore alone had introduced it. yet this preference of Powell's hypothesis, adopted for the sole purpose of explanation, has been thought important enough to subject his opinion minutely to be scrutinized and finally condemned as extrajudicial, unwarranted by his **{H169}** authorities, singular and absurd, pa. 38. 39. 40.[756] and the pl[aintiff]'s counsel in order to create a variance between Judge Powell and his authority cited from Yelv. 160.[757] reverses the method he had before put in practice pa. 25.[758] to get rid of a quotation from Godolphin. for as in that case, in order to adapt the authority to the cause of his client, he would have general words restrained to a special meaning: so here on the contrary he would enlarge a special decision (that so much of a debt as was particularly bequeathed should remain unextinguished) to a general one (that the whole debt should be unextinguished.)[.] but this trouble was unnecessary. for the def[endant]'s counsel was far from relying on the peculiar mode of operation argued from by Justice Powell, as the chief foundation of his objection, as is supposed pa. 41.[759] on the contrary he is so well assured that it is immaterial

756. Supra, H117–H120.

757. *Flud versus Rumsey,* 80 E.R. 127.

758. Supra, H108–H109.

759. Supra, H120.

whether this operation is by way of legacy, or of paiment & release, that without losing time in defending Powell's or examining Holt's hypothesis, he is willing to rest it on the latter. Let it be then that the appointment of a debtor ex[ecuto]r 'amounts to a paiment and release' or in other words that it is as if the debtor had made paiment to the debtee in his life and the debtee had given him a release. now I cannot see what the pl[aintiff] gains by this. for applying it to our case, it will stand thus. Rob[ert] Boll[ing] being indebted to Edw[ard] Boll[ing] in the sum of £235. the latter made his will wherein he gives several legacies to others, makes Rob[ert] Boll[ing] his ex[ecuto]r, and bequeaths the residuum of his estate to Arch[ibald] Boll[ing]. now this appointment of Rob[ert] Boll[ing] ex[ecuto]r, sais Lord Holt, amounts to a paiment of his debt & release; that is, it is as if Rob[ert] Boll[ing] had paid the debt to Edw[ard] Boll[ing] and Edw[ard] Boll[ing] had given him a release. the debt then being paid & released was become no debt at all, consequently it was no longer Edw[ard] Boll[ing]'s estate, nor can pass by a bequest of the residuum of <u>his estate</u>.

The case of Brown v. Selwin is still relied on for the pl[aintiff] as prov**{H170}**ing that in all cases where there is a residuary bequest in a will, this shall prevent so much of the operation of the same will as would make the appointment of it's ex[ecuto]r amount to a paiment & release of the *debt.* thus again enlarging a special decision, founded upon the particular words and situation of the residuary clause, to a general one which shall govern every case where there is a residuary clause, let it's terms or situation be what it will. and it is further thought 'exceeding plain that the principle on which the

Chancellor [King] grounded his opinion was this "that the residuary bequest disposed of every thing the test[ato]r was entitled to when he made his will and at the time of his death." if this was really the Chancellor's [King's] principle, it was so extravagant as totally to destroy the authority of his decision. for upon that principle the £500. & the plate bequeathed to Brown and the leasehold messuages given to Selwin, together with all the legacies given to others, become void, and these things should have been equally divided between Brown and Selwin under the residuary bequest, because 'the test[ato]r was entitled to them when he made his will and at the time of his death.' so in our case Edward Bolling being 'deceased he made his will and at the time of his death' entitled to the several things bequeathed to his other brothers and sisters, to Meade and to Eldridge, all these bequests are made void by his residuary devise, that being a 'disposition of everything he was entitled to when he made his will and at the time of his death.' a bequest of the residuum of an estate then is a bequest of the whole estate. thus is this Chancellor made to decree that a residuary clause swallows up all the rest of the will, and that the relative expression 'all the rest of my estate not before disposed of,' includes it's correlative 'the estate before disposed of.' but the Chancellor is so far from being liable to this absurdity that no such principle can be found or inferred from his words. they are 'if this be considered {H**171**} upon the will, it will appear from the general words of devising the residue i.e. "all his real and personal estate which he had not thereby before given" to the residuary legatees, that this debt which at that time was part of the personal estate falls within the *description.* the test[ato]r was entitled to this debt when he made his will and at the time of his death; he had not before disposed of it, nor had he appointed mr Selwin ex[ecuto]r.' here he makes the *description* the foundation of his decision expressly. for he sais this debt falls within the *description* of his estate not *before* given, for not having appointed mr Selwin ex[ecuto]r he had not *before* disposed of it. but in our case the test[ato]r when he wrote his residuary clause had *already* appointed Rob[ert] Boll[ing] his ex[ecuto]r, & so had released this debt; consequently it did not fall within the description of 'the rest of his estate not *already* given.' so that there is this difference between the case of Brown v. Selwin & ours, that in that the debt was particularly described and bequeathed away, and so was not released according to the general rule before laid down; but in ours, it was not particularly described & bequeathed, & so was released by the same rule.

But it is said to be 'entirely immaterial in what order the clauses were inserted. for let us suppose Edw[ard] Boll[ing] to have begun his will in this manner "all my estate what I shall hereafter give to others I give and bequeath to my brother Arch[ibald] Boll[ing].["] and then the other clauses had followed as they now stand. would not the will have been expounded as it must now'? I answer, it would. because the word 'hereafter' placed at the head of the will in that case would have performed the office of the words 'already' or 'before' placed at the end usually. that is, it would have taken the debt of Rob[ert] Boll[ing] which would have been 'thereafter.' otherwise disposed of out of the description of the residuary clause which gives only 'all the estate not "thereafter" given to others.'

**{H172}** Obj: Vezey 2d. part. pa. 169.[760] per Lord Ch[ancel-lo]r Hardwicke 'the general rule is that the construction must be made on the tenor of the whole will taken together, & it is not material in what order the clause is.'

Ans. this might be true in cases resembling the one then before the Chancellor[.] what that was I know not, as I do not possess the book. but this I may assert that Lord Hardwicke would never say that where the relative terms 'before' & 'hereafter' are used descriptively, it is not material in what order clauses stand. let us try it. A man possessed of six slaves A. B. C. D. E. & F. makes his will in the following words. "I give to my friend I.S. my slaves A. & B. for his life. I give to my friend I.N. my slaves. C. & D. for his life. the remainder in the slaves *before* given I bequeath to X. I give to my friend Z. my slaves E. & F. for his Life. in testimony whereof &c.' now the bequest to X. as it stands here entitles him to a remainder in 4. slaves. if it stood next after the clause of bequest to I.S. it would entitle him to a rem[ainde]r in but two. if it stood as the last clause in the will it would entitle him to a rem[ainde]r in six. and can any body suppose Lord Hardwicke would say in this case that 'it is not material in what order the clauses stand?'

pa. 42.[761] 'Do these words ["]I constitute Rob[ert] Boll[ing] my ex[ecuto]r["] in a legal sense mean the same thing as "I give and bequeath to Rob[ert] Boll[ing] the money he owes me?"['] Justice Powell sais Yes. Justice Holt, No. but both say it extinguishes the

760. *Carter v. Carter* (1 Vesey Senior), 27 E.R. 961–62. The quotation from Hardwicke, at 961–62, follows this citation.

761. Supra, H121.

debt, and that is enough for Rob[ert] Boll[ing] who, if he is entitled to retain the money, will not be very anxious whether it be by way of legacy, or of release.

pa. 43.[762] Talb. 242.[763] Lord Talbot sais 'it hath been questioned if such a debt be assets to pay legacies in general, but that not being the present case it is not necessary to be determined. I am inclined to think it may, but shall not bind myself by giving my opinion till the case happens.' All delicacy about authorities seems now to have subsided. here is the <u>inclination</u> of a Chan{**H173**}cellor on a point which had not been argued, which was not in question, which could never come but incidentally before the court of which he was judge but belonged properly to the department of the Common law, and on which he does not pronounce even an obiter dictum, but expressly reserves his opinion till the case should happen; this I say is produced to contradict a judge within whose proper province the question lay, who declared it to be his opinion, not merely his inclination, who supported this opinion by authorities, & whose judgment on a question of Common law (tho' perhaps it might give way to that of a Holt, as would the opinion of any judge who has lived since the days of Lord Coke, yet) surely is not to be controlled by that of a Lord Chancellor Talbot. on the same side too we find D[octo]r Blackstone arranging himself in the place cited. pa. 61.[764] where he sais that tho' such a discharge of a debt

762. Supra, H121.

763. *Brown v. Selwin et contra* (Talbot), 25 E.R. 756–58: quotation at 757. The quotation follows this citation.

764. Supra, H76.

being voluntary shall not defraud creditors yet it shall take place of all legacies.[765]

But this inclination of Lord Chancellor Talbot's is said to have been confirmed by the decision of Lord Hardwicke in the case of Fox v. Fox. 1. Atk. 463.[766] transcribed in the pl[aintiff]'s argum[ent] pa. 43.[767] where it is said the Chancellor [Hardwicke] has actually made the ex[ecuto]r's debt liable to the paiment of legacies in general. yet this case on a nearer examination will appear to be nothing more than the common case of marshalling assets; where, whether the ex[ecuto]r's debt should be subject to legacies in general was no part of the question. the ex[ecuto]r was indebted to his test[ato]r by bond in £130. that this was subject to debts has all along been admitted. he had at the same time a demand against the estate for the same sum, for which the lands of the heir were under mortgage to him. by fixing therefore his demand upon his own debt, which was strictly justifiable in a court of Chancery, & peculiarly so in the present case the one debt had actually been contracted for the other, the lands of the heir were exonerated, the personal fund left unimpaired for the paiment of **{H174}** legacies, and thus justice done to all parties, and the maxims of the Chancery strictly observed. the decision indeed is expressed so shortly, and the word 'legacies' (on which alone the pl[aintiff]'s counsel relies for his authority) is dropt in so unexpectedly and impertinently as might induce an imputation of carelessness on the reporter. his words are

765. Blackstone, *Commentaries*, 2: 511–12.

766. *Fox v. Fox*, 26 E.R. 294.

767. Supra, H121–H122.

that this debt shall be <<applied after the paiment of funeral expenses and *legacies* to the exoneration of the real estate in favor of the heir.'>>[768] from which one might conclude it was a certain position in law that legacies were alwais to be paid before the lands of the heir should be exonerated from their burthen. but that legacies are to be so preferred seems far from being a settled point. the decisions have been contradictory as may be seen by turning to the following cases. Cope v. Cope 2. Salk. 449.[769] Anon. 2. Ca. Ch. 4.[770] Anon. Freem. Ch. R. 204.[771] Hawes v. Warner Freem. Ch. rep. 277.[772] in favor of the legatee. Meynell v. Howard. Pr. Ch. 61.[773] Clifton v. Burt 1. P.W. 195.[774] in favor of the heir. White v. White. 2. Ves.[775] dubitatur.[776] nor do I recollect any later case which may be considered as a settlement of the law either way: for surely we are not to consider as such this side-stroke of Lord

768. *Fox v. Fox,* 26 E.R. 294: quotation at 294.

769. *Cope contra Cope,* 2 Salkeld 449–50, 91 E.R. 389–90 (Ch., n.d.). A comparison with other cases appears in 1 Equity Cases Abridged 270, 21 E.R. 1038.

770. *Anonymus* [*sic*], 2 Chancery Cases 4, 22 E.R. 818 (Ch., 27 Nov. 1679).

771. *Anonymus* [*sic*], 2 Freeman's Chancery Cases 204, 22 E.R. 1161 (Ch., Trinity 1695).

772. *Hawes v. Warner,* 2 Freeman's Chancery Cases 277–78, 22 E.R. 1208–1209 (Ch., Hilary [1704]).

773. *Meynell versus Howard,* Precedents in Chancery 61, 24 E.R. 30 (Ch., Trinity 1696).

774. *Clifton v. Burt,* 1 Peere Williams 678–82, 24 E.R. 566–69 (Ch., 1720).

775. *White versus White,* 2 Vernon's Cases in Chancery 43–44, 23 E.R. 638–39 (Ch., 25 Jan. 1688). This case was reported by Vernon, not Vesey.

776. doubtful, wavering, uncertain.

Hardwicke's. considering this as a 'quaestio diu vexata'[777] had he meant to decide upon it, he would certainly have paid to the understandings of mankind the compliment of a little reasoning. but it is evident from another consideration he could not mean to give this as a judicial opinion on the question on mature deliberation; because there was no such question then before him. the parties in court were the heir & debtor. the claim of the one was exactly commensurate with the debt of the other. none of it therefore would remain to pay legacies or any thing else. and in fact no legatee appears in the case. we may therefore well say that Lord Hardwicke has in this case decided no other point but this, that, the ex[ecuto]r's own debt being confessedly assets for the paiment of debts, his own demand should be fixed on it, that by thus marshalling the assets, the lands might be exon**{H175}**erated and the personal fund kept entire for the paiment of legacies. and this is agreeable to the settled rule for marshalling of assets, which to use the words of the Chancellor [Nottingham][778] in the case before cited from 2. Ca. Ch. 4.[779] 'that where mortgage debts & legacies can be satisfied by marshalling the assets, both shall be satisfied.' this is precisely what Lord Hardwicke here did. he fixed the mortgage demand on the debt of the ex[ecuto]r whose privilege exempted it from an application to the paiment of legacies, and by thus

777. a vexed question or mooted point; a question often agitated or discussed but not determined; a question or point which has been differently decided, and so left doubtful.

778. Sir Heneage Finch, Lord Nottingham (1621–1682), barrister, Inner Temple; S.G.; A.G. (1670); Lord Chancellor (1673–1682).

779. *Anonymus* [*sic*], 22 E.R. 818: quotation at 818, following this citation.

marshalling the assets he contrived that both should be satisfied. now this is by no means settling the law to be as the pl[aintiff]'s counsel supposes that the appointment of a debtor ex[ecuto]r is no longer an extinguishment of the debt, but that it shall be liable to legacies generally as well as debts.

But after all what inference could be drawn to the prejudice of the def[endant] if his debt could have been proved subject to legacies? this could only have been to legacies of some specific sum. a residuary legacy is a thing of no determinate size. it is as absolutely satisfied by one pound as one hundred. to fulfil it's intent no other legacy need be sacrificed, no operation of law controlled. it is only a bequest of what remains when all other donations whether expressed in words or implied by law, are made good. all mortgage monies or other charges on real estate are to be first taken off, all debts, all pecuniary legacies to be paid, retribution made for specific legacies if a creditor happen to have levied his debt on them, and all charges of administration are to be borne, before the residuary legatee can claim any thing as his. had the law therefore been that such a debt should be subject to legacies, yet this would of course be intended but of specific or pecuniary legacies. thus in the case beforementioned tho' it is doubtful whether an heir shall be entitled to an exoneration of his lands against a specific pecuniary legatee, yet it never was doubted but that he should **{H176}** against a residuary legatee. see the cases White v. White. 2. Ves.[780] Lord Gray v.

780. *White versus White*, 23 E.R. 638–39.

Lady Gray 1. Ca. Ch. 296.[781] Hawes v. Warner Freem. Ch. rep. 277.[782] Howel v. Price 2. Vern. 624. S.C. 1 P.W. 291. S.C. Pr. Ch. 477.[783] King v. King 3. P.W. 98.[784]

Again it would in any event only be subject to legacies as it is to debts, that is, on a deficiency of other assets. so lands and slaves are subject to debts, but only in case of a deficiency of other assets. specific legacies in like manner if other assets fail must be applied to pay debts. but in our case no such deficiency happens. there is enough to pay debts, enough to satisfy legacies specific and pecuniary, enough to comply with the operations of law, and then a good residuum for the pl[aintiff].

To close this point therefore, & with it this long dispute

The appointment of a debtor ex[ecuto]r is an extinguishment of the debt.

but it still continues liable to debts, and to any legacy particularly fixed on it.

in our case no legacy is particularly fixed on it.

the case of Brown v. Selwin is in our favor because it confines the residuary legatee to the articles *described* in the

781. *Lord Grey against the Lady Grey and others*, 1 Chancery Cases 296–97, 22 E.R. 809–10 (Ch., [1677]). A comparison to similar cases appears in 21 E.R. at 1039.

782. *Hawes v. Warner*, 22 E.R. 1208–1209.

783. *Howell versus Price & ux e con'*, 2 Vernon's Cases in Chancery 701–702, 23 E.R. 1055–1056; 1 Peere Williams 292–96, 24 E.R. 394–96; Precedents in Chancery 477–78, 24 E.R. 214 (Ch., 1717). The manuscript's reference to Vernon 624 is incorrect; 624 is the case number rather than the page cite. This case is also reported in Precedents in Chancery 423–25, 24 E.R. 189–90.

784. *King v. King and Ennis*, 3 Peere Williams 358–61, 24 E.R. 1100–1101 (Ch., [1735]).

residuary clause, & our debt is not within that *description.*

but it is not subject to any legacy not particularly fixed on it.

Powell's opinion is expressly so.

Lord Talbot gave no opinion, & declared he would give none till the case happened.

Lord Hardwicke has only determined, what never was denied, that such a debt, being assets for the paiment of debts, it shall in the general marshalling of assets take it's arrangement as a debt.

if it were subject to legacies in general as the pl[aintiff] would have it would only be to specific and pecuniary ones. and even then, only on a deficiency of other assets, which does not happen here.

For all these reasons the debt of Rob[ert] Boll[ing] to E[dward] Bolling is in the present case extinguished by the appointment of him ex[ecuto]r.

{**H177** — blank}

{H178}

# A. Bolling versus Robert Bolling.[785]

[I.] It having been said, 'that the emblements are annexed to, and incorporated with, the labour of the slaves,' the defendants counsel, in considering this position, observes, 'there is not a syllable in the act expressing that the emblements are to be taken from the devisee, nor yet that against this it is insisted, that by these words in the act[786] 'the servants and slaves of any person dying between 1 March and 25 December shall be continued and employed upon his plantations for making a crop,' the emblements, if not taken from, do not belong to, the devisee, as shall be hereafter explained; and that it is equally true, that there is not a syllable expressing that the labor of the slaves is to be taken from the legatee, and given to the devisee of the land. the defendants counsel, after reciting some of the words of the act, and by a proper explication referring them to the crop both growing at, and planted after, the testators death, stating the case thus: 'here then no person, either devisee of land, legatee of slaves, or executor, being named (it must be noted he considers the case here as if the words, 'which crop shall be assets in the hands of executors and administrators,' had not been in the act) 'asks who, from the nature of things, is to have the emblements or crop thus brought to maturity?' 'in their simple state, at the instant of the testator's death, it is yielded,['] says he, [']that they belonged to the devisee of the land' this is extending

785. This last part of the manuscript, George Wythe's concluding reply for the plaintiff, Archibald Bolling, is in Anderson Bryant's handwriting.

786. 3 & 4 Geo. II, ch. 8, § 11 (Virginia 1730), in Hening, ed., *Statutes at Large*, 4: 284. The quotation follows this citation.

the concession alluded to farther than the terms of it will warrant, all that hath been yielded was, that, if the act of assembly had not been made, 'by the common law, the devisee of land would have been intitled to the crop growing upon it when the testator died, as it was at that time.' it was not ever, it is not now yielded, that, when the act directed the testators slaves upon the plantation to be continued there, and employed in making and finishing a crop, such crop, in it's ripe or unripe state at the instant of the testators death, belonged to the devisee of the land. the contrary is affirmed, and, in some measure to prove it, one argument, among others, relied upon is, that, by the act, the emblements are annexed to, and incorporated with, the **{H179}** other subjects, to wit, the labor of the slaves, and the crop unfinished at, and begun after, the testators death; from which the proposition of the defendant's counsel. 'that the act had annexed to emblements the labor of the slaves, and made that labor homogeneous with the emblements,' seems not materially variant, unless it be in this, that the latter supposes the emblements still to belong notwithstanding the act to the devisee of the land, and does not include the crop begun after the testators death. at least we agree in, for we both insist upon, this: that the right to the emblements and the right to the labor of the slaves shall go together. The defendant's counsel supposing the emblements to belong to the devisee of the land asserts, passim, that they drew to them the accession of labor bestowed on them. on the other side, as no more reason is discovered for attributing this power of attraction to the emblements, than to the labor of slaves, the legatee's right to the latter by the will being as unquestionable, and commencing as early, as the devisee's right to the former by the common law; so it is not admitted, that the books and cases, concerning acquisition of property by accession, referred to by defendant's counsel, maintain the point they are quoted for.

Whilst they are under consideration it should be remembered, that the question here is, not only 'whether the laws relating to acquisition of property by accession take from the proprietor (devisee of the land) his property,' as it is called, but also, whether those laws, in such a case as this *give* the accession to the proprietor? for Robert Bolling claims, and this argument of his counsel is urged to assert his right to, both the crop, as it was at the testator's death, and the labor of the slaves employed in bringing it to maturity, and severing it.

Where a thing belonging to one, taken by another, is changed into a different species, it becomes the property of the latter; as wine, oil, bread, made of grapes, olives, wheat.

Where a thing belonging to one, taken by another, is wrought upon, but not so as to change its species, it doth not generally become the property of the operator; thus the original owner of cloth, or of wood and **{H180}** metal, retains his title after the first is embroidred, or the others are fabricated into vessels and utensils. to this the instance of an elegant picture is an exception. this privilege granted by Justinian,[787] whose words Bracton transcribes,[788] was an eulogy worthy a roman emperor to bestow upon one 'in omnibus cujus (Parrhasii) operibus intelligitur plus semper, quam pingitur; et

787. *Institutes of Justinian*, Lib. II, Tit. I, §§ 31–32, at 107, 108.

788. Bracton, *On the Laws and Customs of England*, 2: 46.

cum ars summa sit, ingenium tamen ultra artem est:'[789] and upon another (Apelles) than whom a conqueror of the world 'ab alio pingi se vetuit edicto[']?[790]

With respect to a foetus in the womb the roman law, from which our law adopted the doctrine, was thus: 'partum ancillae matris conditionem, nec statum patris in hac specie considerari, explorati juris est.['] C.3. t.32.[791] [']Pomponius scribit, si equam meam equus tuus praegnantum facerit, non esse tuum, sed meum, quod natum vizt.[792] D. lib. 6. fib.. 1. c.5. §2.[793] [']cum praegnans mulier, legata, aut usucapta, aliove quo modo, pariat, ejus ficert partus, cujus est ea cui concretur, non cujus tunc fuisset, sum conciperat.['] D. lib. 41. t.1. c. 66.[794]

789. "in all his works, more is always to be understood than is painted, and although art is everything, nevertheless genius is above art." The source of this quotation has not been identified; it is neither in Bracton's *On the Laws and Customs of England* nor in Justinian's *Institutes, Code, or Digest.* This quotation and that following disprove the assertion that "throughout the *Bolling* case, Wythe refrained from indulging in quotations from classical writers." Dumbauld, *Thomas Jefferson and the Law,* 227n261.

790. "forbade that he be painted by anyone else." The source of this quotation has not been identified; it is neither in Bracton nor in Justinian.

791. *The Code of Justinian,* Book III, Tit. 32, c. 7: "It has been established by law that the offspring of a female slave follows the condition of its mother, and in a case of this kind the condition of the father should not be taken into consideration." S. P. Scott, ed., *The Civil Law,* 17 vols. (Cincinnati: Central Trust Company, 1932; New York: AMS Press, 1973), 12: 313.

792. "est" transcribed as "vizt."

793. *The Digest of Justinian* (Latin text ed. Theodor Mommsen with Paul Krueger; trans. and ed. Alan Watson), 4 vols. (Philadelphia: University of Pennsylvania Press, 1985), Book VI, I. *Vindicatio of Property,*" at 1: 202: "Pomponius also states that if your stallion has made my mare pregnant, the resulting foal will not be yours but mine."

794. *Digest of Justinian,* Book XLI, "Ownership of Things,", I, 66, at 4: 501: "If a preg-

The defendant's counsel, thinks Doctor Blackstone instead of 'founding the authority of this part of our law on the adaption of a Bracton and subsequent resolutions of our courts of law, would perhaps have done better to have adverted to the laws of nature'. against this nothing is objected; but when he teaches as one of those laws, 'that who soever is owner of a thing, to him belong the accessions of it,' one, who does not pretend to be deeply read in the great volume of nature, will, however, venture to say, if this be found among her laws, it must be understood with some qualification wherein he is the more confident, because Puffendorf having lib. 4. c.7. §.2.[795] delivered the same rule, and in the same words, another learned author makes this stricture upon it: 'this rule is very uncertain and imperfect, and we may better put these two instead of it, 1. if the addition made to a thing belonging to us proceed from the thing itself, or from any act of our own, and if coming other ways it belongs to nobody, it is naturally our acquirement, or at least we can't be deprived of it upon the account of any other. 2. but if the thing or work which is added to our possession belongs **{H181}** wholly or in part to another, it naturally follows that there must be a kind of community in relation to the whole between us and him, so that one of us must transfer his right to the other, tho' this does not often happen, for this community ends, and consequently the additional acquirement is then made, either by the mutual agreement of

nant woman be bequeathed or usucapted or alienated in some other manner and then gives birth, her issue will belong to her owner at the time of the birth, not to him who then owned her when she conceived."

795. Pufendorf, *Law of Nature and Nations*, Book 4, chap. 7, sec. 2, at 398.

the parties, or by the settlement of some positive law, which ends the difference according to the nature of the circumstances, and maxims of equity.['] Barbeyrac's[796] notes[797] on Puffendorf cites Titius's observations. 298.[798] this community, according to the proportion of materials and labor contributed by the parties, seems more rational, with a distinction to be mentioned presently than the acquirement to one, unless it be in the pregnancy of animals; where the male of the human species, if a freeman, can seldom have any other motive for coition with a slave but gratification of appetite, and if a servant, owes no services of this kind to his master: and what a male of the brute species, suffered to range abroad, and not kept at expence purposely for admissure, deserves for his owner, in consideration of any loss sustained by the act of generation, is too trifling to have been ever seriously claimed. this instance, and others, if there be others, analogous, excepted then; when I, with your consent, have wrought upon your subject, by which it is become more beneficial to you; the laws of nature tell me, 'that, until I shall have agreed to give you my labor, or shall have received a satisfaction for it, the accession you possess i.e. the work of my hands, is my property.' in this judge Gilbert concurs, who says, treating of the origin of property, 'that it was at first derived from labor, for a

796. Jean Barbeyrac (1674–1744), French jurist, known chiefly for his preface and notes to his translation of Pufendorf's *De Jure Naturae et Gentium.*

797. Pufendorf, *Law of Nature and Nations,* Book IV, chap. 7, sec. 2, at 398n1: note by Barbeyrac.

798. Gottlieb Gerhard Titius (1661–1714), Dutch legal commentator and author of *Observationes ad Puffendorfum De officio hominis ac civis* (Rheims: Johannem Broedelet, 1728).

man's own actions are most properly his own, and from thence all ownership begins, for the very value of the soil is not more from the natural product than from the labor and industry that men have employed in their cultivation.'[799] it is therefore conceived that Robert Bolling's claim to the accessions in this case is not better supported by the natural law, than his claim to the subject they are annexed to is by the civil law of the country, as will appear hereafter. if indeed accession be without consent of the proprietor, or accompanied or preceeded by some wrongful act, the operator shall loose his labor and accession. thus, the prior who took **{H182}** the child, and the adulterer who took the wife, of other men, and cloathed them, after the father reclaimed the one, and the husband the other, which cases are alluded to by Blackstone II. 405,[800] as the author there cited shews, could not recover the garments. what therefore, the defendant's counsel, after reiterating the instances wherein the property of materials is transferred if there be an essential, and retained if only a formal change and adding that of timber built into a house on the ground of another (is not this last out of place here?) subjoins, 'but in all other instances the subject draws to it the accession,' is denied, if the assertion be intended to comprehend instances where the accessions are by consent and not unlawful. but perhaps he did not design to comprehend them: for having arranged accessions in three classes where they are 1, by addition of another substance, 2, to any moveable subject by labor, 3, to an immoveable subject by labor, or by addition of another subject; he

799. Gilbert, *Law of Evidence*, 244.

800. Blackstone, *Commentaries*, 2: 405.

says 'in all these instances, the person who originally had property in the subject having done nothing to relinquish his property shall not loose it by the *wrong of another*, but the subject shall draw to it the accession.' now his hypothesis being extended to instances of accessions by the *Wrong* of another, there will no controversy until the question, whether the accession in this case was by the *Wrong* of another, or not? comes to be discussed; but if it be extended to all cases, without regard to that distinction, it is not allowed to be maintainable by the laws of nature, or by his quotations, which compared together are apprehended, some expressly to prove, and all to recognize or suppose that distinction.

Where the defendant's counsel, after citing from Bracton who transcribes verbatim out of Justinian's institutes. lib. 2. tit. 1 § 31[801] (except that the former writes Menii for Maevii) 'si Titius suam plantam in Maevii solo posuerit, Maevii planta erit,'[802] and referring to Fleta, adds 'if property in the soil then will draw to it property in the plant, where both plant and labor are accessions, much rather shall property in the soil and plants (as Robert Bolling had) draw to them the accession alone,' let him be reminded 1st that it is not admitted or proved, that Robert Bolling, notwithstanding the act of assembly, had such a *Property* in the soil as would draw to it property in the plant; and secondly, that it is not admitted, or proved, that property in the soil will draw the plant unless it be put there by *wrong*; but that both are denied.

801. *Institutes of Justinian*, Lib. II, Tit. I, § 31, at 107.

802. "[I]f Titius places his own plant in the ground of Maevius, the plant will belong to Maevius..." Id.

**{H183}** When he states this case: 'I have a feild of corn; my neighbor comes and tends it,' (to which however the principal case cannot be admitted to be properly resembled, until the feild of corn is proved to be Robert Bollings, and without supposing the neighbor to come and tend it by wrong) and asks 'does not the corn continue mine?' it is answered, yes; not because you have any positive right to the labor which the corn is indebted to for it's growth, but because, as baron Gilbert saith, 'were it otherwise, men would break in upon other peoples grounds and sow them, and keep men out of the disposal of their own estates, and thereby they would raise a property to themselves from another's estate, and put the owner to the trouble of controverting it.'[803]

How the case next stated by the defendant's counsel, 'Robert Bolling had feilds of corn and tobacco; the slaves of A[rchibald] Bolling assisted those of R[obert] Bolling intending them, *by direction of the act of assembly*,' differs from the preceding, if in that the neighbor came and tended the crop by wrong, and here unwarrantably it is affirmed 'the fields of corn and tobacco continued still the property of R[obert] Bolling,' shall be shewn hereafter.

It was not pretended by plaintiff's counsel, 'that the accession of culture shall draw to it a property in the principal, i.e. in the plants.' he said that 'the crop was annexed to, and incorporated with, the profits of slaves'; and that the act of assembly had directed them to go together, or if you will, had *drawn* both a different way from what they would otherwise have gone in and this position he does not consent to discard, nor does he allow it to be contradicted

803. Gilbert, *Law of Evidence*, 245.

by the principles of justice or law, as the defendant's counsel insists. neither can the plaintiff's counsel admit, that the objection 'that the devisee of the land could have no right to the labor of slaves employed in finishing the crop, either by the common law, or by any words in the act,' is answered. it is not proved that he could by the former, unless it be an accessory right, which is reprobated, if the accession be not by wrong; nor is it proved that he could by the other, unless 'the words, "a crop, made and finished upon a man's plantation, by his slaves, the year in which he dies, shall be assets in the hands of executors and administrators," mean, 'that the crop shall belong to the devisee of the land, after the debts are paid,' which **{H184}** is affirmed to be equally untrue.

That such a construction of the act would work injustice, as often as lands and the slaves upon them are disposed of to different persons, is obvious; and therefore the case, said to have been sought for 'out of the circle of nature and reason' (is not this hyperbole? surely it is not an 'extravagant' supposition that a man may devise part of his estate only; a case which, so far from it's being true, that 'it never can have happened,' doth frequently happen) was not 'invented or framed' to shew, that, in 'that' single 'instance,' the act, according to the exposition of the defendant's counsel, [']would in its operation be productive of inequality,' but was supposed, in order to exhibit, in one point, a view of that inequality, which might be extended by discerning judges, to every other point in the 'circle' they would naturally describe, to include all the cases where the inequality was visible, altho in a fainter light in some of these, than in that. so that if the injustice which one exposition of an act would produce be a reason for preferring another exposition, not liable to any such objection, of which the text is, at least equally capable, the plaintiff's counsel cannot allow himself to be disarmed of that argument, or the force of it to be at all weakened, by the strictures made upon it.

The act doth not indeed say, totidem verbis,[804] 'that the emblements shall go to a different person from him who takes the land,' neither doth it as the defendant's counsel makes it, say 'they shall be deemed assets in the hands of executors.' the act of 1711.[805] uses the words '*deemed and taken,*' but that act is repealed by the other. the words of the latter are 'which crop, so made and finished shall be assets in the hands of the executors or administrators,' and the plaintiff's counsel thinks the discrepancy between '*go* to the executors or administrators' and 'be in the hands of executors or administrators' (for what purpose is another question) so unimportant, that, altho' he would not dispair of vindicating his diction, if the dispute were of consequence enough to deserve a criticism, he is willing to reform the position by the correction, and consents that it may stand thus: The act 'expressly directs the crop to be in the hands of a different person from him who takes the land,' which he concieves to be equivalent to what he meant by **{H185}** the other, and to answer its purpose. yea, he does not object to considering the latter act as if it had retained the phraseology of the other, '*deemed and taken to be.*'

804. in so many words.

805. 9 Anne, c. 2, § 17 (Virginia 1711), in Hening, ed., *Statutes at Large,* 4: 22. The quotation follows this citation.

The objection 'that the executors and administrators are impowered, not only to take the growing crop, but to employ all the testators or intestate's servants and slaves in making and finishing a crop; so that if the testator or intestate die after the 1 of March and before the crop is begun, the executor or administrator may begin and finish the crop: and if Edward Bolling had died the 2. March, before a plant or grain of corn was in the ground, Robert Bolling could not have claimed the crop, which should be made and finished afterwards; for it was not emblements,' is said to have been obviated before; for the defendant's counsel asks, 'in whose lands are these new plants set?' and answers 'in the lands of the devisee. then' says he 'si Titius suam plantam in Maevii solo posuerit, Maevii planta erit.' or, in plain english, 'if an act of assembly set plants in the soil of Robert Bolling, they are the plants of Robert Bolling' and the surprising progress and magical operations of some occult qualities in the soil and emblements are investigated, whence we learn how 'the plants growing at the time of the testator's death passed to the devisee as included in the property of the soil, which passed to him;' how 'they draw to them the accession of labor bestowed on them after they became the property of the devisee,' how 'by the same reasoning, the property in the soil drew to it the accession of new plants put into it after the death of the testator, and then drew also the labor bestowed on these new plants.'

Let the foundation of the reasoning by which our property is to be thus drawn from us be examined, after premising that the new plants and the old are to go together; so that Robert Bolling, if not intitled to both, can have neither, which seems not controverted.

It is denied then that "si Titius suam plantam in Maevii solo posuerit, Maevii planta erit,' is well rendered into english by, 'if an act of assembly set plants in the soil of Robert Bolling, they are the plants of Robert Bolling.' for whatever propriety there may be for putting Robert Bolling for Maevius. (there is none in putting an act of assembly for Titius; it must be supposed that Titius set his plants in the soil without consent of Maevius.) the defendant's counsel makes it one part **{H186}** of the case he states, where an accession shall not be taken from the proprietor of the subject, that 'the accession is *involuntary* as to the proprietor; and after observing that 'in all the instances,' he had collected, 'the person who originally had property in the subject, having done nothing to relinquish his property, shall not lose it by the wrong of another, but the subject shall draw to it the accession;' when he says 'the words of Bracton are explicit as to the land, i.e. when a vegetable is transplanted into my land from the lands, or cultivated by the labor, of another, which has most of the ingredients of our case, si Titius suam plantam in Maevii solo posuerit, Maevii planta erit;' he applies the character of *wrong* to the accession; and his meaning must be this: if Titius set his plant, by *wrong*, in the soil of Maevius, it is the plant of Maevius. in truth nothing else can be meant. for where by right, or by my consent, vegetables are transplanted into my land by another, and cultivated by his labor, he, who thus plants and cultivates is at least my tenant at will;[806] and although either of us may, at any time, determine the will, and when the tenant doth it

806. one who holds possession of premises by permission of a landlord or owner, but without a fixed term.

he loseth his vegetable and labor, yet, if I do it, he not only is intitled to the emblements, but hath right of ingress, egress, and regress, for the purposes of cutting and carrying away. the plants set and cultivated by Titius in the soil of Maevius being, therefore, the plants of Maevius *only where they are set and cultivated by wrong, or without the consent of Maevius*; if an act of assembly set plants in the soil of Rob[ert] Bolling, they are not the plants of Rob[ert] Bolling; unless the act of assembly set them there by *wrong*, or w*ithout* the *consent of* Rob[ert] Bolling. but an act of assembly can not work injustice or wrong, whereas in such a case as this, it violates no divine or moral precept; neither can it be said to will or do a thing without consent of any, for 'an act of parliament hath every man's consent present and to come.' Hob. 256.[807] so that it is still conceived to be true, that Rob[ert] Bolling could not have claimed the crop, 'if Edward Bolling had died the 2 March, afterwards begun and made by his executors;' and that a combination of rights to the crops begun and not begun at the testator's death being effected by the act of assembly consequently Rob[ert] Bolling is not intitled to the former because he would not have been intitled to both.

**{H187}** By the act the executors and administrators being impowered to continue and employ the servants and slaves upon the plantation until the 25 Dec. it seemed to the plaintiff's counsel, 'that the right of the person to whom the land is devised is suspended, as to the exercise of it, until that time, so that the crop is severed before his right to take the profits of the land commences,' the

807. *Duncombe versus Wingfield*, Hobart 256, 80 E.R. 400–409 (K.B., Trinity 1618): quotation in 80 E.R. at 402.

defendant's counsel asks, 'if by this be meant, 'that the right to the land or the possession of it only is suspended,' perhaps over-looking the last sentence of the paragraph which clears it of the amphibology[808] this question supposeth. it is not denied, that a devise of land, operating as a conveyance, transfers some immediate right to the land; and so will a devise of a reversion, but it is denied, that a devise of land, since the act, if the testator survive the first of March, transfers a right to *take the profits*, or crop either growing, or which may be made and finished, before the 25 Dec. it is admitted, that the devisee, his estate being a freehold, may vote for representatives in general assembly; that his estate being an inheritance his heir may succeed him and his widow may be endowed, and that creditors may subject his land to their debts; but it is insisted that none of these have any right to possession of the land, at least any part of it that is or may be in culture for a crop to be finished that year, before the 25. Dec. or, in other words, that the right of the devisee &c. as to the exercise of it, i.e. the right to the possession, or to take the profits, is suspended until that time: and that it is by his *right of possession* the original owner of a thing becomes intitled to it's accession, the defendant's counsel must admit, or reject the authority quoted by himself. whether therefore the act of assembly (not, as he states it, 'by giving the executor or administrator a right to *consider* the profit as *applicable to the payment of* debts' but) by enacting that 'the servants and slaves of a person dying after the 1 March and before the 25. Dec. shall be continued and employed upon his plan-

808. ambiguous discourse; a sentence which may be construed in two distinct senses; a quibble.

tation until the last mentioned time for making and finishing a crop, has suspended that right of possession which the statute of wills had given the devisee:' or whether the executor or **{H188}** administrator hath not the right of possession until that time? is a question conceived by plaintiff's counsel to be of such decisive consequence that he is surprised to observe the defendant's counsel pretermitting instead of controverting the point, and resembling the right of possession, which in other places he himself calls the *subject*, to the shell, and the profits, which is but an accession, to the kernel. the acts of parliament authorising dispositions of lands by will, and this act of assembly being, as to this point, in pari materia,[809] are to be considered as forming one system, and to be so construed as that one part be not incompatible with another. according to which canon, where the testator dies between 1 March and 25. Dec. the devise shall not take effect, as to the crop in the ground at his death, or that may be made there the same year, or the right of the devisee to the possession shall not commence, or shall be suspended during that period; in the same manner as if the land had been devised after the 25. Dec. when defendant's counsel supposes, 'by suspending the right of the devisee to *call for his* emblements till it be seen whether they may not be wanting to pay *debts*, that his right to them is not altogether taken away;' it will be granted; but this will not avail until it be proved 1. that since the act of assembly the emblements are *his*; and 2. that they are liable to pay *debts* only; both which are denied. this supposition, therefore, beside the question here treated of, namely, whether 'the crop, can,

809. of the same matter, on the same subject.

as emblements, *belong* to him, or is *his*, who hath no right to the possession of the land, till after the crop is finished and actually severed?' not whether, if the crop *doth belong to him*, or is his, 'by suspending his right to call for it, his right to it be taken away.' it is agreed 'the bare suspension of the use of a right is no extinguishment of it.' the right of a distributee to a share of a surplus is not extinguished, because the act which gave it hath suspended his right to demand it until nine months after the death of the intestate, any more than a debt is extinguished, because by the bond it is not payable until nine or twelve months after the date of it. they are debita in praesentia, solvenda in futuro.[810] but here the crop is not due to the devisee of the land at all, unless **{H189}** he had a right to the possession of the land, whilst the crop was growing, or when it was severed; and he had not any such right, but it was in the executor or administrator. the suspension of a right to demand a debt doth not extinguish or take away the debt, which is the principal subject; but the suspension of a right to the possession of land, will extinguish or take away the right to the crop made during that suspension; the crop being but an accession to that temporary right of possession, and following it as the principal subject. the case then of the distributee intended to illustrate the proposition, 'that the bare suspension of the use of a right is no extinguishment of it,' is not apposite because it does not resemble this case.

That the possession of the executor or administrator is a possession in trust is admitted; and that it is for the use of creditors, is also admitted; but that the possession of the crop, if it be not requisite

810. debts at present, to be paid at a future time.

for creditors, is for the use of the devisee of the land is denied. Before the act, when a man had ploughed and fenced his feilds, and made other preparations for a crop, and died before it was planted or gathered, if without a will, altho' the slaves descended with the lands to the heir, yet where he was the son of the intestate, his younger brothers and sisters being intitled to proportions of the appraised value, might, to raise those proportions, compel a sale, of the slaves; and, if there was a will, made perhaps long before the testator's death, the lands and slaves were often so disposed of, that the one, claimed by legatees immediately, were not employed upon the other, which the devisees could not otherwise till. thus the preparatory labor was thrown away; and the crops perished. hence arose inconveniences to the public, and to creditors and legatees, by diminution of the common stock of the first, and the fund for satisfying the demands of the two others. to remedy these inconveniencies, the legislature seems to have designed to put affairs in the state they would have been in if the testator or intestate had lived to reap the fruits of his industry; and, to effect this, enacts, that where any person shall die between the 1 March, by which time some considerable preparation **{H190}** towards a crop is usually made, and the 25 Dec., by which it might be finished, his servants and slaves on his plantations shall be continued and employed there for making and finishing a crop, which shall be assets in the hands of executors and administrators, after the charges of cloathing and feeding the servants and slaves, and the expences of tools and utensils, quitrents, levies, and other incident charges, deducted in conformity with this supposed design of the act. it is insisted, that the executor or administrator shall have a trust possession of the crop, no otherwise than of every other part of the personal estate, in the same manner, and for the same persons as if the testator or intestate had not died until the 25 Dec. and that the meaning of the words, 'which crop shall be assets in the hands of executors and administrators,' is, which crop shall be liable in the hands of executors and administrators to the payment of the decedent's debts and legacies.

For the meaning of the word assets, the defendants counsel, referring to his former argument, corrects a citation said to be from Terms de ley,[811] and recites such of the words in the book as relate to assets by descent only. the citation was taken by plaintiff's counsel not from the book itself, which he had not, but from Jacob's law dictionary[812] which quoted it, and with which the citation exactly agrees. Terms de ley hath been since recurred to, after the words transcribed by defendant's counsel and some others, it contains these: 'assets enter mains is when a man indebted (as before is said) makes executors and leaves them sufficient to pay, or some *commodity or profit* it is come unto them in right of their testator, this is called assets in their hands.'[813] these and the words of the citation are not indeed the same; but the variation is apprehended to be immaterial; insomuch that the correction might perhaps have passed unnoticed, if an apology for what might else seem worse

811. Rastell, *Les Termes De La Ley*, 63–64.

812. Giles Jacob, *A New Law-Dictionary: Containing the Interpretation and Definition of Words and Terms used in the Law; And also the Whole Law, and the Practice thereof, Under all the Heads and Titles of the same*..., 2d ed. corrected, with large Additions (London: E. and R. Nutt, and R. Gosling, 1732), s.v. "Assets" (unpaged).

813. Rastell, *Les Termes De La Ley*, 63–64.

than plagiarism had not been judged proper. the defendant's counsel, 'when he calls that fund which is in the executors hands for the payment of debts by the name of assets, does not mean,' as he tells us, 'to affirm that it is in every **{H191}** case *enough* for the payment of debts, but that *enough* of that fund shall be taken to pay the debts if it will so far stretch,' he adds 'this *enough*, or this *tantum*[814] is called *assets* shortly, and by use is made to include the whole idea originally expressed by these words *enough of goods* and chattels to pay debts, or so much of the goods as will pay the debts.' instead of the word *assets* in the act then let the words by which he explains his meaning of it be substituted: 'the servants and slaves of any person dying between 1 March and 25 Dec. shall be continued and employed upon the plantations for making and finishing a crop, which crop shall be a *Fund* in the hands of executors and administrators whereof *enough to pay* debts shall be so applied if *it will so far stretch*.' now this is not the sense in which the word *assets* is understood. '*assets* enter mains is where a man indebted makes executors and leaves them sufficient to pay his debts and Legacies or some other *commodity* or *profit* is come to them in right of their testator, *this* is called *assets*.' Cowell[815] and Office executors[816] taken verbatim from Terms de ley.[817] by which it appears 1. that assets are that *Fund* out of which *Legacies* as well as debts shall be satisfied. 2. that

814. such a quantity, so much.

815. Cowell, *Interpreter of Words and Terms*, s.v. "Asset" (unpaged).

816. Wentworth, *Office and Duty of Executors*, 307 (Curson: "Supplement: Of Executors").

817. Rastell, *Les Termes de la Ley*, 63–64 (s.v. "Assets").

any *commodity* or *profit*, coming to the executor in right of the testator, is called *assets*, whether, for anything the book shews to the contrary, it be *enough* to pay the *debts* and *Legacies*, or not, here it may be noted, by the way, that the observation, 'that the word assets are where a man dies *indebted* &c. intimate, that if he owed no debt, or in other words when all the debts he owed were paid, there would be no assets,' is answered by these words 'and *Legacies*,' in the same citation, which do more than *intimate* that something else besides *debts* is chargeable upon *assets*: of which more hereafter. neither doth the word assets seem to have been understood in the sense defendant's counsel explains it in by sir Edw[ard] Coke 1. Inst. 19. 124.[818] and Wentworth, off. executor 308.[819] where is this example, 'damages recovered by the executor in an action of trespass shall be assets.' indeed the explanation involves a contradiction: for goods and chattels in the hands of the executor, where they exceed, where they **{H192}** are equal to, and where they are less than, the debts are in all these instances called assets. this last is admitted by the defendant's counsel in these words: 'when we call that fund which is in the executors hands for the payment of debts by the name of assets we do not mean to affirm that it is in *every case enough* for the payment of debts.' then according to your explanation of the word assets, in the same page above, 'viz. that it means *enough* of the goods and chattels to pay debts,' that word must have opposite meanings, enough, and not enough, and consequently one opinion

818. *Coke on Littleton*, "Of fee tails," 1: 19; "Of Villeinage," 1: 124.

819. Wentworth, *Office and Duty of Executors*, 308 (Curson, "Supplement: Of Executors").

must contradict the explanation in terms. on the other hand lawyers and judges frequently speak of a sufficiency of assets, and a deficiency of assets[.] the defendants counsel uses that language several times in the last page of his argument of which this explanation makes as good english as a sufficiency of a sufficiency and a deficiency of a sufficiency, or enough of enough and not enough of enough. but enough of this logomachy;[820] especially as the defendant's counsel emancipating the word we have so much reason to be tired with, objects not to the adoption of another, to wit, liableness, the effect of which shall be now considered.

He takes it for granted, that the crop, which the act says shall be assets in the hands of executors and administrators, is liable for debts only: thus he tells us, 'the act singles out one of the properties of a personal estate, to wit, a liableness for *debts*;' and the like assertion occurs in many other places; altho' it never hath been admitted and is denied. and upon this ground, 'those things are *assets* then which are liable to the testator's debts,' he argues, 'when all the debts are paid, the emblements of Rob[ert] Bolling are no longer liable to debts, because there are no debts for them to be liable to. so that if, after all the debts are paid, you still say, they are liable to debts, it is the same thing as to say, they are liable to nothing, or have no liableness, and consequently are no longer assets, because they have lost that quality of liableness; which is essential in the definition of assets,' this he acquaints us, amounts to the same thing which he had said before, viz. 'that as soon as debts and *Legacies* are paid, there are no such things as assets in existence.' the inference

820. contention about words.

that **{H193}** in some cases the crop is *not* assets, may at first view be suspected, because it seems a contradiction to the act, by which it is declared, that when any person shall die between March and December the crop made that year by his servants and slaves upon his plantation *shall be assets*; the term *any*, which is capable of universal application, comprehending *all* cases no less than if the words had been 'the crop made by the servants and slaves of *every* person made upon his plantation the year he shall die shall be assets.' but let the reasoning be examined. the principle 'that those things are assets which are liable to the testator's debts,' if the meaning be, as the deduction from it shews it to be, 'that the crop, being assets, is liable to debts only,' is not true. the explanation of assets from Fr. Atk. 206. 19.[821] does not apply to this subject; that being the case of *real assets* or land of inheritance, to wit a reversion after an estate tail, which is not said to be assets but for the payment of debts, or when it bars a writ of formedon,[822] or sur cui in vita;[823] nor is administered as personal assets, unless it be in such a case as 1. Inst. 124. a.[824] 'if an executor hath a villain [i.e., villein] for years, and the villain purchase lands in fee simple, the executor who had the

821. *Kinaston versus Clark*, 26 E.R. 526–28.

822. a writ for the recovery of an estate brought by a person claiming as issue in tail, or by the remainderman or reversioner after the termination of the entail.

823. a writ available to the heir of a woman whose husband had alienated her land in fee, but who had omitted to bring the writ *sur cui in vita* for recovery of that land; the heir might have the writ against the tenant after her decease.

824. *Coke on Littleton*, "Of Villeinage," 1: 124. a.

villain in auter droit,[825] shall have the land in the same right;' whereas the crop, which is the subject here, is *personal assets*; and the act not having 'singled out one of the properties of assets, to wit, a liableness to debts,' as is pretended, but having declared it shall be assets generally, it is liable, not to debts only, but to legacies also. this is proved by Cowell, verb. assets,[826] and by Off. ex[ecuto]r. 307.[827] quoted before; and by this passage, 'all the personal estates, whereof the testator died possessed, whether it consists in chattels real, as leases for years, mortgages, &c. or chattels personal, as household goods, money, cattle &c. the first of which the civil law distinguishes by the name of immoveable goods, the latter into moveable, belong to the executors, and are *assets* in their hands for the payment of the testators debts and *legacies*.' Off. exr. 52.[828] Bac. abr. 2. 416.[829] and the same thing is admitted by implication in these words of the argument for def[endant]. 'this amounts to the same thing which **{H194}** he had said, 'that as soon as debts and *legacies* are paid, there are no "such things as *assets* in existence,"['] in the same page, but a few lines from the place, where the contrary is supposed: and yet this is the cardinal principle upon which his

825. in another's right; as representing another. An executor, administrator, or trustee sues *in auter droit.*

826. Cowell, *Interpreter of Words and Terms*, s.v. "Assets" (unpaged).

827. Wentworth, *Office and Duty of Executors*, 307 (Curson, "Supplement: Of Executors").

828. Wentworth, *Office and Duty of Executors*, 52.

829. The quotation preceding the citations is from Bacon, *A New Abridgment of the Law*, 2: 416, which also cites Wentworth, *Office and Duty of Executors*, 52.

argument depends. so that, besides the quality of 'liableness to debts,' there is at least one other quality essential in the definition of assets, that is personal assets, namely a liableness to *legacies*, and consequently 'the crop being made assets is' *not* 'liable to debts only.' moreover the principle, if it were true, would not warrant the deduction, 'that the emblements, after debts paid, are the emblements of Rob[ert] Bolling,' unless it be proved, which is denied, that he, the devisee of the land, hath a right to the crop put into the ground after the death of the testator, as well as what was growing before, and the labor of other people employed in tilling both; it being agreed that they must go together. this principle therefore, 'that the crop is liable to debts only,' being rejected; we will endeavour to shew the effect of the crops being made assets after answering two things which lead to the discovery and tend to the elucidation of it: 1. what kind of estate the crop is; and 2. whose estate it is.

1. a crop, as hath been said, is a personal estate. the defendant's counsel enumerating the qualities of emblements, admits the subject to be 'of a chattel nature', but when in other places he says 'they are *like houses* and trees,' *annexed* to lands, 'were *assets* in the hands of the devisee before the act of 1711.[830] *as* the *lands* themselves'; his concession becomes a vox et praeterea nihil,[831] empty sound, for *houses* and trees are part of the *freehold*: and the phrase, 'annexed to lands,' in the ordinary and legal sense of it, implies an union with the right of *freehold*; neither of which can be affirmed, but both are denied of that which is of chattel nature; and lands, called assets in

830. 9 Anne, c. 2 (Virginia 1711).

831. empty words and sound.

the hands of an heir, or devisee, are charged with debts by specialty only wherein the heir was bound, whereas chattels are liable to debts of *all kinds*, and that too by different process, and in different modes. we learn then from Swinburn. part VI. sect. 7 (13)[832] that **{H195}** growing corn, or emblements, are to be put into the inventory by the executor, which would not be if the corn were not a personal estate, for that alone is what he can generally intermeddle with. Perkins tells us, that 'if a man be seised of land in fee or in fee tail, and sow the same land, and devise his corn growing upon the land at the time of his death to a stranger, this is a good devise, notwithstanding that the land be not devisable, nor in use' (the author wrote before the statute of wills) 'but if the devisor had devised the trees growing upon the land at the time of his death, this devise, as to the trees, is void, by which[833] the heir as[834] the devisor shall have them and not the executors.' sect. 512.[835] and Gilbert tells us, 'because a man expects a yearly return of the corn which he sows, it is reckoned part of his *personal estate* as the corn itself was before it was sown, but otherwise of timber *trees* planted; for they must be supposed to be annexed to the soil, since they were planted with the prospect, that they could not come to be of use till many generations afterwards.'[836] these authors prove the

832. Swinburne, *Treatise on Testaments and Last Wills*, Part VI, §7, ¶13, at 420.

833. "because" rather than "by which" in Perkins.

834. "of," not "as" in Perkins.

835. Perkins, *Profitable Booke... Treating of the Lawes of England...*, Chapter 8, "Devises," ¶ 512, at 224–25. Wythe modernized Perkins's language.

836. Gilbert, *Law of Evidence*, 245.

crop to be personal estate; and

2. It is the personal estate of the testator. the act having declared that [']it shall be assets in the hands of the executors and administrators, for payment of the debts and legacies of their testator or intestate.' it then must be his estate; for no other estate but his own is liable in the hands of his executors or administrators to pay his debts and legacies. and not only the crop growing at his death, but what was planted afterwards, is, by virtue of this act, as much his, as if he had lived until it was actually severed; in the same manner as the land purchased by the villain [villein] whom the executor had for years 1. Inst. 124.[837] and the damages recovered by the executor, ibidem, altho they were acquisitions posterior to the testator's death, are his estate, and disposed of accordingly.

If then the whole crop be the personal estate of the testator; to whose use, and for what purpose hath the executor the possession of it? let this question be answered by these words in the argument for **{H196}** the defendant: the estate in the administrators (supply, what is supposed, currente calamo, to have been omitted, or 'executors) 'hands has several properties, 1. a liableness to debts, 2. a submission' (or liableness) 'to legacies, 3. to distributions.' it follows then that the crop, like other personal estate, has these properties, and, after debts and legacies paid, must fall into the surplus, and go either to the distributees, or, as in this case, to the residuary legatee, unless it be included in the devise of the land, which is denied. Against this it is urged by the defendant's counsel, 'if the act had meant to give the crop all these properties, it would have said it

837. *Coke on Littleton*, "Of Villeinage," 1: 124.

should be liable to debts and legacies and the residiuum to be distributed.' but the act by declaring the crop shall be assets makes it liable to debts and legacies, and the crop being a personal estate it is subject to distribution; therefore, if the act, after saying the crop shall be assets, had added 'and shall be liable to debts and legacies,' it would have been a tautology; and, if it had said the crop shall be a personal estate, and shall be distributable, it would not have been saying more than what the common law and the act of distribution had said before: so that, 'if the act had said it should be liable to debts and legacies, and the residuum to be distributed,' as the defendant's counsel says it would have done, if it had intended to give the crop those properties, it would have been surplusage: and we are taught 'the omission of that which would have been surplusage shall not vitiate.'[838] if indeed the act had, as is alleged, 'singled out one of these properties, to wit a liableness to debts,' it might have been objected 'that it remained as it was, as to the other two, to wit, not liable to pecuniary legacies, nor to be thrown into the residuum.' but turn to the words of the act, and you will not find a syllable expressing that the crop is to be liable to debts only, except the words 'shall be assets' which applied to personal estate, have been abundantly proved to mean a fund for payment of debts and legacies. it was not pretended 'that specific legacies, because they are assets, are taken from specific, and given to pecuniary legatees.' but it should be remembered, that a specific legacy, altho'

838. The phrase given by Wythe in the manuscript as a quotation is a logical extension of the common-law maxim *Utile per inutile non vitiatur* ("Surplusage shall not vitiate the essentials").

*assets,* is not *assets* generally, but liable to debts only, and therefore {**H197**} cannot with propriety be resembled to a crop — made upon the land of a devisee, unless the latter can be proved to be a specific legacy to him. and how is that grand point proved? even thus: 'I *suppose*' says the defendant's counsel, '*it will not be denied,* that these plants are a specific legacy to Robert Bolling.' after supposing this, why did not you suppose the dispute at an end! for such would have been the consequence, if that were granted. but indeed, sir, it will be denied, it is denied. 'if the testator had said in express words, I give to Rob[ert] Bolling my Buffalo lick lands with the emblements now growing thereon, those emblements would have been admitted as you say to be as much a specific legacy as the lands themselves.' but when he says I give to Robert Bolling my Buffalo lick lands, that 'this in law includes a bequest of the emblements then growing as perfectly as if he had expressed himself in the first form;' or that the words 'in the first form, "with the emblements growing thereon" would have been surplusage,' cannot be agreed. it is indeed admitted that, by the common law Rob[ert] Bolling would have been by virtue of the devise of the land, intitled to the crop growing upon Buffalo lick when the testator died, as it was at that time, and this in nature of a specific legacy but it is contended that the common law is altered by the act of assembly, so as that, now, the devisee of the land is not intitled to the emblements, and an additional reason to prove it is furnished by this very consideration, to wit, that his title to the crop, if any, is by way of specific legacy: for a specific legacy, altho' liable to debts, cannot be taken to satisfy pecuniary legacies, if there be a deficiency of assets: then the act of assembly having, by saying the crop shall be assets, made it liable to pecuniary legacies, the crop ceases to be a specific legacy, and consequently is no legacy, but falls into, and makes part of the residuum, which in this case is bequeathed to Archibald.

The plaintiff's counsel did not conclude that the personal estate, which **{H198}** 'has a liableness to debts only, has also a liableness to fall into the residuum'; his proposition is, that the crop, being in it's nature a personal estate, it would have been subject to distribution or a residuary bequest before the act of assembly declaring it assets, in all cases, as well as every other part of the personal estate, except in the single instance of a devise of the land the crop was growing on, where the devisee would have taken the emblements, in nature of a specific legacy, as an accession to his right of possession of the soil at the time they were severed; but that since the act, which hath declared the crop shall be assets, the effect of which is that it falls into, and is become part of the general fund, the testator's personal estate, that is liable to debts and legacies, it hath every property of all other kinds of personal estate; and consequently the right of the devisee of the land at the common law is gone, because the crop is now charged with the burden it was before exempt from, to wit, payment of pecuniary legacies, which exemption made it a specific legacy. When the defendant's counsel says 'the act of assembly has put this specific legacy on the footing of all others by making it liable for *debts*,' he again takes the word assets in a sense too confined. indeed if this be all, the act did little or nothing; for at common law emblements unquestionably were liable to debts. Whether if the crop be applied to the payment of a debt, the devisee can be reimbursed out of the rest of the estate? is a question the solution of which depends upon another, viz. whether his right to the emblements remains as it was at common law? it was not said, 'that the act meant to make the crop such an estate in the hands of executors as is liable for *debts.*' the words are 'the meaning is which crop shall be such an estate in the hands of executors and administrators as is liable for payment of the decedents *debts* and *legacies.*' to the question, what estate in the hands of executors and administrators is liable for payment of his debts and legacies, or, in other words, what are assets in the hands of executors and administrators? when the plaintiff's counsel repeating from Wentworth's Off. ex[ecuto]r. 52.[839] answers 'all the personal estate whereof the testator died possessed, whether chattels real or personal,' he is required to 'recollect that this includes slaves, who are affirmed **{H199}** to be not *distributable.*' no! what is to be done when the case happens which is mentioned by 4. Ann. cap. [23] sec. 5?[840] 'no such slaves shall be liable to be escheated[841] by reason of the decease of the proprietor of the same, without lawful heirs; but all such slaves shall in that case, be accounted and go as chattels, and other estate personal.' are not slaves then distributable? yes, undoubtedly, if chattels and other estate personal be distributable. and they would have been distributable in the other case too, where

839. Wentworth, *Office and Duty of Executors*, 52.

840. 4 Anne, c. 23, § 5 (Virginia 1705), in Hening, ed., *Statutes at Large*, 3: 334. The quotation follows this citation.

841. An escheat is a reversion of property to the state due to the lack of any person eligible to inherit.

there was an heir, if it had not been enacted sect. 2. 'that slaves shall be held taken and adjudged to be real estate, and not chattels, and shall descend to heirs.' so that 'the act' did 'intend to make the crop, in all it's qualities, such an estate as' even slaves, where the latter are to 'be accounted and go as chattels and estate personal.' And in this case if Edward Bolling had died intestate, and without heir, the crop and slaves too would have been distributed among his next of kin if any. If 'all the personal estates whereof the testator died possessed, whether chattels real or leases &c. or chattels personal, as goods &c. be assets in the hands of executors for payment of debts and legacies,' converting the terms, 'assets in the hands of executors for payment of debts and legacies, are all the personal estate where of the testator died possessed, whether chattels real as leases &c. or chattels personal as goods &c:' then the plaintiff's counsel, when he interpreted (for his language indicates that he was interpreting) the act of 4. Ann. cap. 7. [33] sect. 2.[842] thus: 'after debts, &c. the surplusage, i.e. the remainder, of all and singular the goods, chattels and personal estate of every person dying intestate, &c.['] i.e. of all that estate which was liable to the payment of debts, or, in other words, of the assets in the hands of the administrators, [']shall be distributed &c.' submits it to the judgment of others, whether he tortured the act to import what it doth not mean. the simple words of the act, 'goods, chattels, and personal estate of every person dying intestate shall be distributed, &c.' unquestionably comprehend a crop, if that be 'personal estate, and personal estate of the decedent,'

842. 4 Anne, c. 33, § 2 (Virginia 1705), in Hening, ed., *Statutes at Large*, 3: 371–72. The quotation follows this citation.

which is expected to be satisfactorily proved; and, consequently the crop, which would have been distributed in case of an intestacy {**H200**} shall belong to the residuary legatee, unless the devisee of the land be intitled to it, as an accession by way of specific legacy, which since the act is denied; and is apprehended not to have been capable of being proven.

The notion of the defendant's counsel was thought to be, 'that the word assets denoted that part of the personal estate, not which is liable, but, which will actually be applied to the payment of debts and legacies.' Having glanced at the novelty of this, and it's contradiction to the act, according to which the crop is assets, not when it is paid away, but when, i.e. so soon as it is made and finished; and having observed that if no part of the estate be assets but what will be applied to the payment of debts and legacies, and if consequently it is not assets before it be so applied, there is no such thing as assets at all; for the moment it is paid away it ceases to be assets; the plaintiff's counsel subjoined, 'in truth that the naming an executor in a will is a gift in law of *all* the testators personal estate to the executor, and that a commission of administration vests the property of all the intestates personal estate in the administrator, is founded in this; that *all* that estate is assets: that the legal property of the *whole* is in them is indisputable.' here the question is plainly, whether *all* the personal estate, or only *part*, viz. what is actually applied to the payment of debts and legacies, be assets? instead of discussing which the defendant's counsel diverts us by saying that 'if the sole foundation of the transfer of the personal estate to the executor or administrator is it's being assets, or possessing a quality of liableness to debts, then the lands slaves and all other the estate of the testator or intestate are also transferred to the executor or administrator, because they are also assets, so that this proving too much proves nothing,' as if the question were how many different things, as assets, are the subject of the transfer? whereas it is, how much of the same thing, as assets, is the subject of the transfer, let the foundation of that transfer be what it will. neither do we learn more of this point by what follows concerning the destination of the estate, and the appointment of persons to minister in that destination, and the reason why the estate is transferred to them. for altho' we are indeed informed, that 'the law hath thought proper to transfer the estate, 1, as assets, **{H201}** 2, as a legatory depositum, 3, as a distributable or residuary surplus;' it is not with precision affirmed that only part, or denied that the whole of the personal estate is assets.

The defendant's counsel admits, if Edward Bolling had died intestate, the emblements growing at the time of his death would have been distributed; not because they were assets, but because, to encourage tillage, the law gives them, in this and some other instances, to him who sowed. but the plants put in afterwards, he says, would not have been distributed, but if not required for the payment of debts, would have gone to the heir as an accession to the land after his title commenced, under the rule, 'si Titius suam plantam in Maevii solo poseurit, Maevii planta erit.' all this, if the act of assembly had not been made, would be right enough, supposing the plants to have been put in the ground without the consent of the heir. but the act hath very much altered the case. for as, 1, there seems to be not less reason (or rather a more cogent reason, since it would be an additional encouragement of agriculture) to give the after made crop to him who had toiled, a quarter of a year, and the greater part of the inclement season, in manuring, ploughing, and fencing, the ground and had procured and maintained laborers and teams, furnished instruments and utensils, saved and provided seeds, and raised plants in nurseries, altho' he should die in seed time, or a few days before it, than there is to give the growing emblements to him who sowed them, but died before they are severed; so therefore, 2. the act hath declared the whole crop, both what is growing when he dies, and what is afterwards planted and sown, to be assets in the hands of the administrator; wisely bestowing a retribution, by which the common law in conformity with the principles of natural equity and sound policy incited the industry of the husbandman who sowed the ground, upon him who had been equally provident and diligent; making the same law where there is the same reason; and contravening the illiberal distinction between the emblements and **{H202}** after crop, for both must go together; and consequently the distributees, who it is admitted would have been intitled to the one, must have been intitled to the other. 3, the act doth not mention or warrant another distinction, invented upon this occasion, to authorise the heir to reap where he did not sow, viz. that the crop shall be assets where it is required to pay debts, and not farther or otherwise; but indiscriminately ordaining the business of the farm or plantation of *any* (which is concieved to be equivalent to *every*) person dying between March and December to be prosecuted for the making and finishing a crop, and declaring the crop, so made by the labor of his servants, to be assets, whether the crop may be required to pay debts or not; 4. this after made crop is the estate, not of the heir, but, of his ancestor the intestate. and therefore the reason, why the crop, if Edward Bolling had died intestate would have been distributed, 'because it was assets,' which if it had been applied to the growing emblements only, as they were at the common law, might have been discountenanced by the contempt it was treated with, applied, as it is, to the after crop too, with which the other is by the act involved, repels the censure, and pretends to be a good reason, pregnant of this conclusive argument: if the whole crop be assets, or hath a liableness to pay the debts of the intestate, and consequently is the property, or 'the goods chattels and personal estate of a person dying intestate,' the surplus of it, 'after debts.' &c. paid, shall be distributed by the very words of the act of distribution.

The plaintiff's counsel supposed it would not be disputed that the crop would have been distributed if Edward Bolling had died the 2d. of March before the crop was begun, and made no disposition of the surplus, and the executor had, after his death, made and finished a crop. he refers to the principles before explained and relied upon as the 'foundation for this opinion,' which the defendant's counsel says he is 'at a loss to conjecture;' the observations in answer to it, and the replies to them shall be exhibited below arranged in opposition to one another.

{H203} *Defendant's Counsel*

the common law would have given the plants to Rob[ert] Bolling the devisee, as an accession to the soil.

the act of assembly only takes them from him in favor of *creditors* when necessary for the payment of debts, that is, it only makes them assets, or goods liable to debts, as Murray explains it.[843]

*Plaintiff's counsel*

it would so, if the plants were put there against or without his consent, but not otherwise.

the act of assembly having declared that the crop shall be assets generally, does not make it goods liable to debts only, but makes it, like other personal assets, goods liable to legacies also. Murray's explanation[844] amounts to no more than that what we call assets is something that is liable to certain demands, but does not prove that every kind of assets is liable to the same demands, and no other. the contrary is notoriously true, as appears by the authorities quoted before. he was treating of land, i.e. a reversion after an estate tail, in which, as legal assets, there is a liableness, or a quality to be

843. *Kinaston versus Clark*, 26 E.R. 526–528: quotation at 527.

844. Id.

liable, not to legacies but, to debts, and to that kind of demand his subject led him to apply his explanation. the crop then being liable to debts and legacies, and being moreover a personal estate, and the estate of Edw[ard] Bolling is intirely taken away from the devisee of the land. all legacies too are supposed to be paid before distribution.

all debts are supposed to be paid before the executor proceeds to distribute the unbequeathed residuum.

when therefore all debts are paid those plants lose their quality and name **{H204}** of assets or of liableness to debts because there are no longer any for them to be liable to, and consequently resume their former nature of an accession to the soil, and go with that to the devisee.

when all debts are paid, the crop does not lose the name or quality of assets, **{H204}** because it is still liable to legacies, and when both debts and legacies are paid, that the deviser of the lands since the act is entitled to it, as an accession; is denied; and hath been disproved.

if indeed Murray had said that assets, as such, besides a quality of liableness to debts, have also a second quality of liableness to distribution, it would have been something.

if he had said that a reversion after an estate tail in land, the subject he was then speaking of, had a quality of liableness to distribution, 'it would have been' falsehood.

but he cautiously says that assets are those things which have a liableness to debts.

'he says no such thing' what he says is, speaking of a reversion after an estate tail, which was liable to a debt only, that 'there is a liableness which makes it assets in futuro, or in other words, a quality to be liable to the debt in futuro.'

if he had gone further as the plaintiff's counsel does, and said they were also those things which have a liableness to distribution, the very instance of a reversion, of which he was then speaking would have contradicted him. for he well knows that a reversion tho' an asset, that is liable to debts is not liable to distribution.

the plaintiff's counsel did not say that real assets, have a liableness to distribution, which is the dogma supposed to be ascribed to him; for he well knew that a reversion in fee after an estate tail tho' liable to debts, is not liable to distribution.

so that the only inherent quality of an asset is liableness to debts. this is of it's essence without which it cannot exist, that is, it can no longer **{H205}** be an asset when it loses its liableness to debts, which it does when there are no debts, or in other words when all debts are paid it loses its name and nature.

this, if confined to real assets, is immaterial in this dispute, if intended to include personal assets is pertinaciously denied.

**{H205}**

indeed it sometimes happens that the thing which is an asset or which has a liableness to debts has also a liableness to distribution but sometimes it has not. a thing merely personal is an asset, and when not called for to pay a debt is also distributable. but lands and slaves are also assets, i.e. have a quality of liableness to debts, yet if they escape the call of debts they retain their nature of descending to heirs or going to devisees.

agreed

so also emblements growing on lands devised are assets but if they escape the call of debts, they retain their former quality of passing with the land to the devisee.

utterly denied.

the act of distribution[845] gives title to the distributees in no case but where there is a total or partial intestacy and then gives title only to the unbequeathed estate. in like manner the residuary legatee takes only the estate unbequeathed in any other part of the will.

true.

but plants growing on the land at the time of the testator's death were bequeathed to Robert Bolling because like the houses and trees they were included, **{H206}** in the bequest of the lands. so also plants put in after his death

in the former part of what is here affirmed, as hath been shown 'contrary things' are 'resembled.' before the statute of wills a man might devise emblements **{H206}** but a devise of trees was void. Perk. 9.[846] there is a property in

845. 22 & 23 Car. II, c. 10 (1670).

846. Perkins, *Profitable Booke ... Treating of the Lawes of England*, chapter 8, "Devises," ¶ 512, at 225 (the manuscript's citation to ¶ 9 is incorrect).

were bequeathed to Robert Bolling because like all other accessions or future profits they are included in the bequest of the lands.[847] if therefore there had been no bequest of the residuum, they would not have been distributed with the unbequeathed residuum, nor in the present case can they pass to Archibald Bolling the residuary legatee, because they are bequeathed specifically.

the corn distinct from that of the soil, and corn sown is reckoned part of the personal estate, but otherwise of timber trees. for they are annexed to the soil. Gilb. 1. 3.[848] as to the latter, a devise of the land, if as is affirmed in another place, it transfers instantaneously a right to the soil, can no more include plants put in the ground the day after the death of the testator. those plants put in a century of years after, and cannot be said to include either, unless a cause includes it's effects.

847. This sentence appears in the manuscript as a marginal note, apparently in Jefferson's handwriting.

848. Gilbert, *Law of Evidence*, 245. The manuscript's citation to 1 and 3 is incorrect.

'That part of the crop which was severed when the testator died, if he had not bequeathed the surplus, is admitted to be distributable;' says the defendant's counsel, 'because it was neither an emblement, nor a subsequent accession, but was to all intents and purposes a part of the merely personal estate of the testator, undisposed of by the will': whereas the plants unsevered at the testator's death, and what, if any, were planted afterwards, which is all he claims, were, he tells us, by the will disposed of to Rob[ert] Bolling. according to this doctrine, the wheat, for that was reaped, and such of the tobacco plants as were severed, would have been distributed; but the unripe plants, those which were planted afterwards, and the indian corn Rob[ert] Bolling the devisee of the land would have taken. doth this 'furnish us with the proof of the wisdom of this act?' or, instead of dividing the crop in this manner, and obliging the executor to number the plants that were cut, when the testator died, or, if that should happen in harvest, or time of corn gathering, to number the sheaves and measure the bushels of grain, and distinguish them in the inventory from what were cut and reaped and gathered afterwards; and keep them separate and to perform this troublesome (if not impossible) difficult **{H207}** task, for no reason but to give an advantage to one, in prejudice of others, of the testator's family; is there 'a man upon earth,' besides the devisee of the land, and his counsel, who would not think the act intended rather to consider and dispose of the whole crop as the 'merely personal estate of the testator,' and in the same manner as if he had lived to finish it? which is humbly conceived to be proved to be the design and effect of the act.

The defendant's counsel having gone through the observations of the plaintiff's, except so far as they relate to the case of Oldham v. Pickering, and to some others, proceeds to consider these. but in order to keep in view the purpose for which they were introduced, he desires it may be remembered, that he had laid down this position, 'that a thing by being made assets is *only* subjected to the payment of *debts*, in favor of *creditors*, but, if not so applied, remains as it would have done, had no act been made.' let it be remembered too that this position is laid down on the other side, 'that a *personal* thing, made assets *generally*, is subjected to the payment, not of *debts only*, but of *legacies* also, and, if not so applied, is *distributable*, or goes to the residuary legatee.' the positions are opposite, if by 'a thing' in the former a personal thing be meant: so that if it should be proved, that a *thing*, which is a *real* estate, by being made assets is subject to payment of *debts* only, it would not concern the present question whether a crop, which is a *personal* estate, being declared assets, be subject to *debts only*? let us then examine the four proofs produced by the defendant's counsel as to this point.

'1. That slaves, by our act of assembly,[849] are made assets for the payment of debts, and yet, if the debts can be paid without them, they do not become a part of the residuary surplus, but go to the devisees.' it may be here remarked, that slaves, if without them the personal estate be sufficient to satisfy the debts, shall not be applied to that purpose by 1. Geo. II. cap. 4. [11] sect. 7.[850] repeated

849. 3 & 4 Geo. II, ch. 8, § 11 (Virginia 1730).

850. 1 George II, c. 11, § 7 (Virginia 1727).

by 22. Geo. II. cap. 5. sect. 29.[851] The act of assembly by which slaves are said to be 'made assets for the payment of debts,' is supposed to be 4. Ann. cap. 3 [23].[852] the 4. sect. of which is in these words; 'provided also that all such slaves shall be liable to the payment of debts, and may be taken by execution for that end, as other chattels or personal estate may be.' the word 'assets' is not in the act, **{H208}** as the defendant's counsel supposes. now compare the things, and behold the points of resemblance. '1.' says he, 'before the act of 1727.[853] slaves being a real estate passed to the devisee immediately in the same manner as lands, and, like them, were assets in his hands.' let this be granted. 'so, before the act of 1711.[854] emblements being a chattel *annexed* to land, and so of a *mixt* nature, passed to the devisee of the land immediately, and, in his hands. were assets, as were the lands themselves.' it is granted that emblements are a chattel. and it may be said emphatically that they are annexed to the land, for their roots insinuate themselves into it. but they are not annexed, in a legal sense, in many instances. for, besides that the owner of the soil hath a distinct property in the emblements, and that they are distinguished from trees, because the latter are *annexed* to the soil, as appears by the quotations from baron Gilbert;[855] they were to be put into the inventory by the

851. 22 George II, c. 5, § 29 (Virginia 1748).

852. 4 Anne, c. 23, § 4 (Virginia 1705), in Hening, ed., *Statutes at Large*, 3: 334. The quotation follows this citation.

853. 1 Geo. II, c. 11 (Virginia 1727).

854. 9 Anne, c. 2 (Virginia 1711).

855. Gilbert, *Law of Evidence*, 245.

executor, Swinb.[856] and therefore did not pass to the devisee *immediately*, nor were in his hands assets, but passed immediately to the executor, and were in his hands liable for payment of debts; neither were they liable as the lands themselves; for those were liable to the testator's debts of all kinds, whereas these are only liable to debts by specialty for which the ancestor bound himself and his heirs. 2d. point of resemblance after the act of 1727.[857] which directed that a bequest of 'a slave should transfer the property in the same manner as if it were a chattel, the property of the slave passed by the will to the executor, and, if not called for to pay debts, was by his assent alone to be transferred to the devisee.' this is granted. and what follows viz. 'thus it's nature of being assets in the hands of the devisee was so far altered as to become assets in the hands of the executor,' is also granted, if, instead of the word, 'assets,' the words 'liable to the payment of debts,' be inserted, these, and not that, being the expression in the act 4. Ann.[858] 'in like manner' says he, 'after the act of 1711.[859] which made the emblements assets in the hands of the executors, their nature under the old law of being assets in the hands of the devisee were now' (according to the doctrine of the plaintiff's counsel which I am not concerned to controvert) 'so far altered as that they became assets in the hands of the executor.' according to the doctrine of the plaintiff's counsel the

856. Swinburne, *Treatise on Testaments and Last Wills*, Part VII, at 420–21.

857. 1 Geo. II, c. 11, §§ 3, 7 (Virginia 1727), in Hening, ed. *Statutes at Large*, 4: 223–24. The "quoted" language following the citation paraphrases the statute.

858. 4 Anne, c. 23 (Virginia 1705).

859. 9 Anne, c. 2 (Virginia 1711).

whole crop, including the emblements, for reasons which **{H209}** he hopes have been so explained that a repetition here is not requisite, is liable, not like slaves to debts only, but like all other personal estate, to debts and *legacies*, and subject to distribution, or a residuary bequest. '3d point of resemblance, is slaves, if not applied to the payment of debts, retain their former nature of passing to the devisee, and do not become a part of the residuary surplus.' (why should it be judged necessary to affirm slaves devised, or a legacy, to be no part of the residuary surplus, i.e. to be no part of what remains after the legacy is taken out; or that the surplus does not include that which it excludes?) 'so I urge,['] says the defendant's counsel, [']that the emblements, if not applied to the payment of debts, retain their former nature of passing to the devisee, and, do not become a part of the residuary surplus.' on the contrary we urge for the plaintiff, that by the act the whole crop, that is, what is severed and unfinished, e.g. tobacco plants cut or housed, &c. and what is growing, or emblements when the testator died, and moreover what is sown or planted after his death, do not pass to the devisee of the land (for him you must mean by the '*devisee*' the emblements not being bequeathed to him otherwise than as included in the devise of the land) but being the testators personal estate, is liable to debts and legacies, and may become part of the residuary surplus. The comparison made by the defendant's counsel then seeming very defective and exceptionable, we will attempt a scheme or analysis to present to view the qualities and properties of the things compared, so far as they relate to this question, that what they agree and what they differ in may be more easily perceptible;

from whence perhaps the defendant's counsel himself may see the matter in a different light from what he hath hitherto done.

*Slaves are* liable to the payment of debts, 4. Ann. cap. 3. [23] sect. 4.[860] but shall not be disposed of by the executor for any other purpose, nor even for that, unless the personal estate be insufficient to satisfy the debts; 1. Geo. II. cap. 4. [11] sect. 7.[861] 22. Geo. II. cap. 3. sect. 29.[862]

*are* a real hereditary estate, where the owner dieth intestate, leaving an heir; 4. Ann. cap. 3. [23] sect. 4.[863]

*shall* not escheat where the owner dieth intestate, leaving no heir, but in that case **{H210}** shall be accounted, and go as chattels, and other estate personal, 4. Ann. c. 3. [23] sect. 5.[864] and consequently shall be distributed.

*disposed* of by sale, gift (in writing recorded 32. Geo. II. cap. 1 [5])[865] or testament, shall be transferred in the same manner as if it were a chattel; 1. Geo. II. cap. 4. [11] sect. 3.[866]

*conveied*, given, bequeathed, or descending to a feme covert shall vest in her husband; sect. 4.[867]

860. 4 Anne, c. 23, § 4 (Virginia 1705).

861. 1 Geo. II, c. 11, § 7 (Virginia 1727).

862. 22 Geo. II, c. 5, § 29 (Virginia 1748).

863. 4 Anne, c. 23, § 4 (Virginia 1705).

864. 4 Anne, c. 23, § 5 (Virginia 1705).

865. 32 Geo. II, c. 5 (Virginia 1758): *An Act for preventing fraudulent gifts of Slaves*, in Hening, ed., *Statutes at Large*, 7: 237–39.

866. 1 Geo. II, c. 11, § 3 (Virginia 1727).

867. 1 Geo. II, c. 11, § 4 (Virginia 1727).

*possessed* by a feme sole[868] shall vest in her husband, when she shall marry; ibid.[869]

*may* be bequeathed by an infant above 18 years old; sect. 5.[870]

*shall* not be forfeited except in cases where a forfeiture of lands would be incurred. sect. 6.[871]

A *crop* is Assets, liable to the payment of debts and legacies, must be applied to discharge them before the executors can dispose of a slave;

a merely personal estate, and being liable to the debts and legacies of the testator and consequently his estate,

distributable, or included in a bequest of the residuary surplus; unless it be notwithstanding the act of assembly; included in the devise of the land, which is affirmed by one, and denied by the other party.

From this it appears, so far is the case of slaves from being 'strictly parallel' to that of a crop, that the two things are, in most instances, heterogeneous: and the instances where they have the same qualities and properties, suggest so many objections against the defendant's demand; all which are either too obvious to need particular notice, or have been sufficiently enlarged upon, except this, in answer to which the plaintiff's counsel is 'at a loss to preconceive what will be said.'

868. a single woman, including those divorced, widowed, and judicially separated.

869. 1 Geo. II, c. 11, § 4 (Virginia 1727).

870. 1 Geo. II, c. 11, § 5 (Virginia 1727).

871. 1 Geo. II, c. 11, § 6 (Virginia 1727).

By the act 22. Geo. II. cap. 5. sect. 29.[872] the very next before the one concerning the crop, it is declared and 'provided, that no executor or administrator hath or shall have any power to sell or dispose of any slave or slaves of his testator or intestate, except for the paying and satisfying the just debts of such testator or intestate, and then only where there is not sufficient other personal estate to satisfy, and pay such debts; and in that case it shall be lawful for the executor or adm[inistrato]r to **{H211}** sell, at public auction, such or so many slave or slaves as shall be sufficient to raise so much money as the personal estate falls short of the payment of the debts.' the same clause is in the 1. Geo. II. cap. 4. [11] sect. 7.[873] now if Edward Bolling's personal estate exclusive of this crop, be not sufficient to pay and satisfy his debts, the deficiency must be raised, either by the crop, or the sale of the slaves included in the residuum bequeathed to Archi[bald] Bolling; for the other slaves being specifically bequeathed, it is admitted that, 'altho' they are liable to debts, if requisite, yet they are so far privileged that they are to be last called on.' the act having so far privileged *all* the slaves of the testator, those in the residuary as well as those in the specific bequests, as to disable the executor to sell any of them, except 'then only when there is not sufficient other personal estate to satisfy and pay the debts,' the crop which is a personal estate, must be first applied to discharge them; and if so, it loses the privilege and nature of a specific legacy, and consequently is, in this case, no legacy at all: from

872. 22 Geo. II, c. 5, § 29 (Virginia 1748), in Hening, ed., *Statutes at Large*, 5: 464. The quotation follows this citaiton.

873. 1 Geo. II, c. 11, § 7 (Virginia 1727).

which this corollary will follow, that the crop falls into the residuum bequeathed, by this description, 'the rest of my estate, negros, horses, cloaths, and every other part of my estate not already given,' to Arch[ibald] Bolling.

The position of the plaintiff's counsel 'that all personal estate, to which a decedent has a sole right, and which goes to executors and administrators, is subject to distribution and to residuary bequests,' understood as the context, and subject of disquisition dictate to a candid interpreter it ought to be understood, is not 'overthrown' by the dissertation to prove, that slaves, if the debts 'can be paid without them, do not become a part of the residuary surplus.' the question being whether a crop, which is a personal estate, declared to be assets in the hands of Executors or administrators. be subject to distribution or a residuary bequest? if the position be taken in a sense corresponding with it, that is, 'that all personal estate, to which a decedent has a sole right, and which goes to executors and administrators,' *as general assets,* or which is *assets* in the hands of executors and administrators *generally* is subject 'to distribution and to residuary bequests,' in which sense (and it was not intended, nor is it desired, to be more comprehensive) the truth of it is thought to have been evinced; it is not contradicted by the case of slaves, or that **{H212}** of any specific legacy for slaves, if there be an intestacy, where distribution of personal estate takes place, are, not a personal estate but, a real estate, unless there be no heir, and then they are distributable; and, if there be a testament, the slaves are either specifically bequeathed, and then, like other specific legacies, they are liable to debts only, and to them no further than to supply a deficiency in the general fund of personal estate, whereas personal assets are liable to legacies as well as debts; or the slaves are bequeathed, as part of the surplus, and then, after debts paid, they are by the testament subject to the residuary bequest: so that the case of specific legacy never at all, and the case of slaves in but two instances, come within the position, thus understood, and the latter, in those two instances, viz. where there is an intestacy and no heir, and where the slaves are bequeathed as part of the surplus, instead of contradicting, affirms the position. all that is alleged by the defendants counsel respecting this first proof in support of his position, 'that a thing by being made assets is only subjected to the payment of debts in favor of creditors, but, if not so applied, remains as it would have done had no act been made,' besides what hath been just considered, having been anticipated in former parts of these animadversions, a reference to them must be less disagreeable than repetition, let us then proceed to the

2. proof. 'that American lands, which by a statute of Geo. 2.[874] are (so far as a british parliament may do it) made assets for payment of british (and some think other) debts, are not thereby subject to distribution.'

This statute enacts, [']that the houses, lands, negroes and other hereditaments[875] and real estates in the plantations,[876] belonging to any person indebted, shall be liable to, and chargeable with, all just

874. 5 Geo. II, c. 7 (1732). The quotation in the next paragraph is from § 4, in *Statutes at Large* (Pickering), 16: 273–74.

875. things capable of being inherited.

876. The statute reads: "situate or within any of the said plantations"

debts, duties and demands[877] owing by such person to his majesty or any of his subjects, and shall[878] be assets for satisfaction thereof, in like manner as real estates by the law of England are liable to the satisfaction of debts[879] by bond, or other specialty, and shall be subject to the like remedies[880] in the plantations, for seising extending selling or disposing of any such houses, lands, negroes, and other hereditaments and real estates, towards the satisfaction **{H213}** of such debts, duties and demands, and in like manner as personal estates in the plantations[881] are seised extended sold or disposed of, for the satisfaction of debts.' if making lands liable to debts, and, for satisfaction of them, saleable as a personal estate, effects a total change in the subject, so that it remains no longer a real, but becomes a personal estate; then whatever rule and mode of succession governs this would govern that. but the statute hath made lands and other real estate liable to debts only; and superadded no other property of personal estate, and we have been taught to argue, 'that when the statute singled out one of the properties of a personal estate, to wit, a liableness to debts, the lands and other real estate remain as they were, as to all the other properties,' and therefore as you say, 'indistributable;' for 'there is,' not 'a *magic*' but a legal 'quality in a freehold estate which will exempt that from being made distributable by words which would at the same time make a personal

877. omitted: "of what kind or nature soever"

878. omitted: "and may be"

879. omitted: "due"

880. omitted: "proceedings and process in any court of law or equity, in any of the said"

881. the statute reads: "in any of the said plantations respectively"

estate, not possessing that particular quality, liable to distribution.' the emblements, being as you admit of a chatel nature, and the act having besides, declared the crop shall be assets, by which it becomes liable to the testators debts and legacies, and possesses all the qualities of personal estate, the question is reduced to this: whether the crop, in case of an intestacy, be distributable? what then is it to the purpose, that lands, which are not of a chatel nature, by being made liable to debts only, are not subject to distribution? doth it amount to more than this: that a real estate doth not become a personal estate, when a statute attributes one quality only of the latter to the former? let this be granted. make what you can of the concession. the other proofs are not more pertinent.

The 3d. is, 'that a trust-estate, which by the stat[ute] of frauds[882] is made assets for the payment of debts, yet is not therefore distributable, if not applied to the payment of debts.'

The words of the statute are, 'if any cestuy que trust hereafter shall die, leaving a trust in *fee simple* to descend to his heir, there, and in every such case, such trust shall be deemed and taken, and is hereby declared to be assets by descent, and the heir shall be liable to, and chargeable with the *obligation* of his ancestors, for and by reason of such assets, as fully and amply **{H214}** as he might and ought to have been if the estate in law had descended to him in possession in like manner as the trust descended.' 29. Car. II. cap. 3. sect. 10.[883]

A legal estate of fee simple in lands coming to an heir, by the

882. 29 Car. II, c. 3 (1676 [1677]).

883. 29 Car. II, c. 3, § 10 (1676 [1677]), in *Statutes at Large* (Pickering), 8: 407.

common law is assets by descent, and, in respect of them, he is liable to; and chargeable with the obligation of his ancestor; but the lands, 'if not applied to the payment of the debts,' or if they be partly so applied, are not distributable. a trust-estate in fee simple descending to an heir, by the statute is assets by descent, and, in respect of them he is liable to, and chargeable with, the obligation of his ancestor, as fully and amply as if the trust had been a legal estate, but no further or otherwise. this is called a 'proof that a thing, by being made assets, is only subjected to the payment of debts in favor of creditors; but, if not so applied, remains as it would have done, had no act been made:' and that too in order to shew that a thing of a chatel and distributable nature, made assets, shall not be distributed! if it had been said 'that a legal estate in fee simple descending to an heir, which by the common law is made assets for the payment of the ancestor's debt by obligation, yet is not therefore distributable, if not applied to the payment of the debt,' would it not have been as good a proof? and would it have been resented as a slight if such a proof had 'remained unanswered?'

The last proof produced to shew, 'that a thing, by being made assets, did not become a part of the residuary or distributable surplus, if not applied to debts,' was the case of an estate pur autre vie. by stat[ute] 29. Car. II.[884] it was enacted, 'that an estate pur autre vie shall be deviseable, and if no such devise thereof be made, the same shall be chargeable in the hands of the heir by reason of a special occupancy, as assets by descent, *as in case of lands in fee simple*;

884. 29 Car. II, c. 3, § 12 (1676 [1677]), in *Statutes at Large* (Pickering), 8: 407–408. The quotation follows this citation.

and in case there be no special occupant thereof it shall go to the ex[ecuto]rs or adm[inistrato]rs of the party that had the estate thereof by virtue of the grant, and shall be assets in their hands.' the case of Oldham v. Pickering was, Thomas Oldham, seised of a mesuage [messuage] to him and his assigns, for three lives, **{H215}** died intestate, and without children. administration of his estate was committed to Mary Oldham. a suit was brought in the spiritual court by the next of kin for distribution, and to exhibit an Inventory. the administratrix exhibited an Inventory but omitted out of it the estate pur autre vie. application was made to the court of king's bench for a prohibition[885] to hinder the spiritual court from proceeding to order this estate to be inventoried; because it was suggested, that the estate pur autre vie, remains a freehold, as it was at common law notwithstanding the act had declared it should be assets in the hands of ex[ecuto]rs and adm[inistrato]rs.' and if so the spiritual court, which cannot determine a right of freehold, had not cognisance. on the other hand, if by force of the act the nature of the estate was changed from a freehold to a chatel interest, the spiritual court might lawfully proceed to make distribution. therefore 'the single question in the case was this: whether an estate pur autre vie, be not distributable, in like manner as intestates <u>goods</u> and <u>chatels</u> are according to the 22 and 23. Car. 2.[886] by force of 29. Car. 2. cap. 3?[887] the court gave judgment that the prohibition

885. at common law, a writ by which a superior court directs the judge and parties of a suit in an inferior court to cease proceedings, on the suggestion that the suit itself or an issue arising therein lies outside the inferior court's jurisdiction.

886. 22 & 23 Car. II, c. 10 (1670).

887. 29 Car. II, c. 3 (1676 [1677]).

should stand and that an estate pur autre vie belonging to an intestate was not distributable.' 2. Salk.[888]

The plaintiff's counsel thinks that any man may discover the ground of the judgment in this case to be, 'that the estate pur autre vie, notwithstanding the alteration made by the statute was not a chatel, but remained a freehold still'; these are the very words in 2. Salk.[889] with which agree these words in the book called Holt's rep[orts].[890] 'such an estate still remains a freehold.' and these in 3. Salk.[891] 'it is not distributable because distribution is a quality not necessarily included in the notion of *assets*, as payment of debts is, now an estate pur autre vie is not properly goods or chatels, but remains a freehold.' the reasons why the court adjudged it to remain a freehold were 1. the law designed only to relieve creditors who could not subject the land after it came to the hands of the occupant to the debt of the tenant who died seised of it; which design appeared from hence, 'that if it came to the heir, by reason of a special occupancy, it should be in his hands assets by descent **{H216}** (from the act of parliament add 'as in case of lands in fee simple') that is liable to the payment of those 'debts where the heir is chargeable, and of those only; but if there was no special occupancy then it should go to the ex[ecuto]rs or adm[inistrato]rs, i.e.

888. *Oldham versus Pickering* (2 Salkeld), 91 E.R. 400–401: quotation at 400.

889. Id., quotation at 400.

890. *Oldham versus Pickering* (Holt), 90 E.R. 1176–1177; the quotation following the citation is at 1177.

891. *Oldham versus Pickering* (3 Salkeld), 91 E.R. 738; the quotation following the citation is at 738.

they shall be in the room of the special occupant, and it shall be assets in their hands,' 2. Salk.[892] and be chargeable in the same manner; and as the act designed only the relief of creditors, and no benefit to any other person; so neither 2. by the words 'shall be chargeable in the hands of the heir, if it shall come to him by reason of a special occupancy as assets by descent, as in the case of lands in fee simple, and in case there be no special occupant thereof it shall go to the ex[ecuto]rs or adm[inistrato]rs. and shall be assets in their hands.' is any such change wrought in the estate as that from being a freehold it is become a chatel interest; for in the notion of assets distribution is a quality not necessarily included, as payment of debts is; 3. Salk.[893] nay, this estate pur autre vie when it comes to the heir being 'assets by descent as in case of lands in fee simple,'[894] and when it goes to the ex[ecuto]r or adm[inistrato]r, he being 'in the room of the occupant or heir' and therefore taking the same estate which was a freehold, 'it is not so much as assets, to pay legacies.' Salk.[895]

The case then proves this: that a freehold estate, which in it's nature, is not distributable, does not become so, nor become a part of the residuum or surplus of the personal estate, by being made assets for payment of debts only; but it does not prove that a crop, which is a personal estate, and in its nature distributable, when it is not otherwise disposed of, does not continue distributable, and will

892. *Oldham versus Pickering* (2 Salkeld), 91 E.R. 400–401: quotation at 400.

893. *Oldham versus Pickering* (3 Salkeld), 91 E.R. 738: quotation at 738.

894. *Oldham versus Pickering* (2 Salkeld), 91 E.R. 400–401: quotation at 400.

895. Id.

not fall into the residue, by being made assets for the payment of debts and legacies, which it is insisted annihilates the title of the devisee of the land to the emblements at common law. the position therefore 'that a thing by being made assets is subjected only to the payment of debts in favor of creditors, but, if not so applied, remains as it would have done had no act been made,' if by 'thing' the crop be meant, as it must be to answer the purpose, is **{H217}** not proved, unless a freehold, which is the subject of the case, and a personal estate, can be so resembled as that what is said of the one made assets may be said of the other too. now when you say, speaking of an estate pur autre vie, 'having by a statute, *like* our emblements, been made assets in the hands of executors and administrators,' if you mean that the words in the act of parliament are the same as the words in the act of assembly, it is admitted. but if you mean, that where a freehold, which is exempt from distribution, is made assets, and a personal estate, which is not exempt, is made assets, the word assets is to be understood in the same sense in both cases it is disproved, not by the help of 'magic' but, by the case itself, which contradistinguishes assets per descent coming to an heir as special occupant, or if there be no special occupant going to the ex[ecuto]r or adm[inistrato]r in his room, where the assets are liable to debts only, from assets to pay legacies, to which, as well as debts, the personal estate is subject. the answer you give to the question you propound, 'what is the amount of the judges reasons expressed in the books in which the case is reported'? viz. 'that an *estate*, when made assets by a statute, has only its unliable quality in favor of creditors,' so far is right, if by 'estate' be understood an estate of *freehold*; but is denied to be authorised by the case, if by estate be understood *personal* estate, what you add, 'that in all other respects its qualities (that is its other qualities) remain the same as they were before at common law,' is not exceptionable, otherwise than that either the words, 'common law,' may be left out; or, if they remain, some such words as 'or by statute' ought to follow them; for if the estate had any qualities by statute as well as by common law, it would remain the same as to all those qualities, which the subsequent statute did not take away or alter: for example, the emblements at common law is a personal estate; and by the act of distribution,[896] if not disposed of, was distributable; when a subsequent act made it assets, its qualities remained the same as they were before, that is the emblements continued a personal estate, and were distributable if not disposed of. the last part **{H218}** of the answer, 'and particularly, that it' [an estate made assets by a statute][897] 'is not distributable, because distribution is a quality not necessarily included in the notion of assets as payment of debts is,'[898] if spoken of a real estate, is defective in the reason assigned. for a real estate made assets is not distributable both because distribution is not necessarily included in the notion of assets, that is real assets, and because it is not 'goods and chatels' which are the things that are distributable; and this is part of the reason given in the case 3. Salk.[899] where immediately after the words you transcribe from

896. 22 & 23 Car. II, c. 10 (1670).

897. Brackets in original.

898. *Oldham versus Pickering* (3 Salkeld) 91 E.R. 738: quotation at 738.

899. *Oldham versus Pickering* (3 Salkeld), 91 E.R. 738.

thence into your answer are these, 'now an estate pur autre vie is not properly goods and chatels, but remains a freehold:' and if spoken of emblements is not true, for emblements are personal estate, distributable, if not disposed of; before the act they would have been disposed of as a specific legacy and not otherwise included in a devise of the land; a specific legacy cannot be applied to discharge a money legacy, but the act hath made emblements, with the rest of the crop, assets generally; and personal assets shall be applied to pay pecuniary legacies, as well as debts; therefore emblements upon land devised is no specific legacy, and so not disposed of, and consequently 'distribution is a quality necessarily included in the notion of assets,' when emblements are made assets.

The plaintiff's counsel notwithstanding the case of Oldham v. Pickering thought it far from being a settled point that even an estate pur autre vie, made assets in the hands of ex[ecuto]rs or adm[inistrato]rs should not be distributed, and supposed there was some reason to doubt it, finding it recited in an act of parliament that such a doubt had arisen; but he is so thoroughly convinced that the case proves nothing at all material in the present dispute, he will admit it to be law; and, therefore it will be unecessary for him to observe upon what is said, in six pages in the argument for the defendant to support the authority of that case and in opposition to another case quoted upon the same subject.

**{H219}** What is said concerning the executor's right to retain the crop as a specific legacy has been answered by shewing that it is no legacy to him as devisee of the land; and his claim of a right to employ the slaves bequeathed to other persons in finishing the crop for his benefit hath been shewn to be groundless.

To conclude this point then,

The act hath taken from Robert Bolling the emblements he would, as devisee of the land, otherwise have been entitled to, for,

[I.] 1. The emblements are an accession to the right of possession of the soil, at the time they were severed. but he had no right to the possession of Buffalo-lick until the 25. December, before which they were severed, otherwise than as executor. his possession, in the meantime, therefore, was in right, not of himself, but of the testator, as the possession of any other person appointed ex[ecuto]r, would have been, according to the rule, quand duo jura in una atque eadem persona concurrunt idem est ac si persona diversa essent.[900] and consequently he hath the emblements, as he had the possession, the subject to which they adhere, in the same right, to wit, of the testator, and in the same manner, as if the testator had died the 25th. of December, the act having as it were continued the testator's right to the soil in the executor who personates him for the purpose of making and finishing a crop.

And although emblements were so far the personal estate of the testator at common law

900. Variant of the maxim in 4 Coke Reports 118 — *Quando duo jura concurrent in una persona, aequem est ac si essent in diverso*: "When two rights concur in one person, it is as if they were in separate persons." S. S. Peloubet, *A Collection of Legal Maxims in Law and Equity, With English Translations* (New York: S. S. Peloubet, Law Publisher, 1884), 240 (maxim no. 1995).

as that they were liable, after the other chatels not specifically bequeathed were applied to the payment of debts; yet the act having made them assets generally, by which they become liable to legacies, after debts.

2. The emblements which by the common law would have passed in nature of a specific legacy to the devisee of the land they were upon, now by the act cease to be a specific legacy, and consequently are no legacy at all to him; the foundation upon which only he can claim them being this, that they are by the devise of the lands included with, **{H220}** and 'as much a specific legacy as the lands themselves,' which the defendants counsel insists upon; and which hath been disproved; and therefore the emblements falling into the general fund for payment of debts and legacies are part of the residuum bequeathed to Archi[bald] Bolling.

3. The emblements are not a specific legacy, and so are no legacy to the devisee of the land, because by the act slaves shall not be sold for payment of debts, but to supply a deficiency in the personal estate, so that if in this case the debts cannot be discharged without selling the slaves included in the residuum or surplus bequeathed to Archi[bald] Bolling, or the crop, the latter, being personal estate, must be called on to redeem the former; whereas a specific legacy 'is so far privileged that it is to be the last called on,' of those things that are liable to debts. this

privilege 'is of its essence, without which it cannot exist, that is, it can no longer be a legacy, but loses its name and nature.'

4. The whole crop, what was severed, but unfinished, when the testator died, what was growing at that time, and what was put into the ground afterwards, must be disposed of in the same manner, so that the devisee of the land cannot be intitled to the one unless he be intitled to the others. the severed plants are admitted not to be his; the posthumous plantation was not by wrong, in which case only the possessor of the subject is intitled to the accession; but by authority and direction of the law: and therefore, Robert Bolling, as he could not be intitled to the severed and the after planted parts of the crop, but the whole must go together to Archi[bald] Bolling, the residuary legatee.

II. The defendant's counsel 'urges it to be apparent from the face of the will, that the legacy' (as he calls it) 'of the book to Robert Bolling was for his proper use,' let the features of this face, which we suppose to **{H221}** be the words of the will, be examined separately, and then the whole form, that we may discover whether such was the testator's intention.

If 'it is my will and desire that my book be given up to my brother Robert' import a legacy of the book to the use of Robert, the word '*given-up*' must be understood in a sense the plaintiff's counsel cannot find it to have been ever understood in before.

To give up the ghost is to die. an apostate is said to give up his religion; a woman to give up her virtue, when she becomes a prostitute. to give up a friend is to betray him, to desert him, to have no further connection with him. to give up an author is to discover him. to give up an argument is no longer to continue the dispute; which was the meaning of the defendant's counsel when he said 'I might venture to give up the question.' to give up the town, in a capitulation, is to surrender it, in a treaty, to restore it to them from whom it had been taken. to give up a right is not to assert or not to claim it. to give up his books and effects to his creditors is to deliver them to these to satisfy their demands.

The plaintiff's counsel is not able, and does not pretend to enumerate all the instances, where the word is used. but as in none of those he hath mentioned, which are all he can now recollect, except what may be resembled to one or other of them, so he thinks, that there is not any wherein, the word signifies to part with, and transfer the property of a thing one hath an undisputed right to dispose of to another, which is conceived to be included in the idea of a legacy.

The instance most like the present seems to be that where a man is said to give up his books and effects to his creditors. but in that, as to so much of the effects as is equal to the debts, the giving up is rather a payment than a transfer, a restitution of some right witheld from the owner, not a bestowing of a new right; whereas a legacy is not a praeexistent right, but originates with the testament; and, as to the surplus, the creditors have no more than a fiduciary possession of what was given up, and must account for that to the debtor; so that if **{H222}** the cases may be compared, Robert Bolling must account to some body for the book, unless it be shewn, from some other words in the will, to have been given up to him for 'his proper use.'

Do the following words, 'and that he receive all the debts due to me and pay all that I owe' give the debts to him? does barely desiring one to *receive* my money as vi termini,[901] authorise him to *spend* it? when my property is taken out of the hand of this man, and put into your hand, does it cease to be mine? and how is such an effect produced? is there any other change than that of the holder, unless the owner, besides impowering you to receive the money, by some other act signify a consent that there shall be a change of the property too? is there any 'mystical' meaning in the words, 'receive all the debts due to me,' when they are in a will, which the same words have not in other writings, or when spoken in ordinary discourse?

Godolphin's Orph. leg.[902] was cited for def[endant] to prove, that the word *receive*, in a will, imports a legacy. and his counsel observes that the answer given to it, viz. 'that the authority, as to the word *receive* is to be understood of things in the testator's possession,' is 'answering an authority not from any circumstance found or even hinted in the book, but from one picked up "in the field of conjecture."' surely it is not unusual to answer an authority from a circumstance not found or hinted in the book, if, from the reason of the thing, a doctrine so very general as this author's is here, ought to be confined to particular cases; especially when there are no circumstances mentioned by the author. and the reason alleged

901. the force of the term, the meaning of the expression used.

902. Godolphin, *Orphans Legacy*, 281.

against taking the word *receive* as importing a legacy in this case, is still thought to be a very good one, wherever 'picked up.' in order to illustrate it, the pl[aintiff']s counsel stated a case and argued thus. if a man says, my desire is that Titius receive my slave Dometrius [i.e., Demetrius], or that Cauis [i.e., Caius] receive my horse Argus, unless we expound the word *receive* in the same sense as the word *have*, we must suppose the testator, where he was in possession, had no meaning, or a very idle one. but it is not so, when a man says, my desire is, that Lucius receive all the debts due to me, or collect that money which belongs to me, but is in the hands of other people and it is shewn **{H223}** how the word would be significant in one case, and not in the other. in answer to this, 'let us suppose,' says the def[endant]'s counsel 'that the slave Demetrius or the horse Argus, instead of being in the testator's possession at the time of his death, had been in the possession of some other;' and then he asks, 'would not the testator desire that Titius may receive my slave Demetrius, or that Caius may receive my horse Argus,' give them to Titius or to 'Caius, as a legacy?' now what is this but stating the case and propounding the question over again? and when he adds, 'if they would, then it follows, that the circumstance of possession is altogether immaterial,' if any thing be affirmed, what is it 'but an affirmation of the point in dispute?' Let us add to the case he supposes, what will make it more nearly resemble the principal case, and inquire how it will be then. Edward Bolling having given and bequeathed his lands and several slaves, which were in his possession, to Titius (i.e. Robert Bolling) and others, and being intitled to Demetrius, a slave who was not in his possession, says 'I desire that Titius (R[obert] B[olling]) receive my slave Demetrius;' then gives a slave Bob to B[olling] E[ldridge] and concludes with this clause: 'every other part of my estate *not already given* I give and bequeath to my brother Archi[bald] Bolling.' to whom is Demetrius *given*?

But if the distinction between things in, and things out of, the testator's possession be groundless, the authority is far from proving, that the word *receive* in this will imports a legacy. the whole paragraph in Godolphin is this:[903] 'if a man in his last will and testament says I do give, bequeath,[904] order, or appoint to be paid, given, or delivered; or my will, pleasure, or desire is, that he shall have, or receive, or keep, or retain, or I dispose, or assign, or leave such a thing to such a one,[905] or any other words, whereby the testator's mind or meaning of bequeathing is expressed, or sufficiently emploied,[906] shall be significant enough whereby the legacy shall pass, provided no other legal obstacle stand in the way; because it is not in last wills and testaments as in deeds; for in deeds the words do fall under stricter examination than the intention or the mind: but in wills and testaments the testator's mind and meaning is more valuable and **{H224}** of more efficacy in construction than his words, so long as the interpretation of his mind and meaning hold a conformity with his words, nor is oppugned by any other part of his last will and testament. for a testator is not limited to any form of

903. The remainder of this paragraph quotes Godolphin, *Orphans Legacy*, 281.

904. omitted: "devise"

905. omitted: "or, Let such a person have such a thing;"

906. The word in Godolphin is "implied," not "emploied."

words or phrases in declaring his meaning and intent, so as they be but significant enough to make a discovery thereof, without repugnancy to any other part of his will.'

Hence it appears, that we should interpret the words of a testament, although they may not be such as are strictly proper, so as to effectuate the testator's intention to be discovered from the testament, and so as that one part be not repugnant to another. the word receive is not put down to shew, that whenever it occurs in a testament, 'it is sufficient to create a good bequest.' but as one of those examples, where a word perhaps not proper, 'if the testators mind or meaning of bequeathing is expressed, or sufficiently implied thereby,' shall be significant enough 'whereby the legacy shall pass.' now we object, that by the words, *receive all the debts,* the testator's mind or meaning of bequeathing the debts is not expressed or sufficiently implied in this case. because,

1. the word *receive,* which in any case is but an improper one to convey a right, is less proper in this instance, the subject being debts, by the single act of collecting which its meaning is fully satisfied, and a necessary business is performed, without a transfer of a right to the money, whereas in some other instances the word, if it should not create a bequeast, would have an idle meaning.

2. the testator appears to have understood and to have used the proper words of bequeathing, whenever he designed to give a thing. his testament, besides the preamble, this clause concerning the book and debts, and the conclusion, contains ten devises and legacies, in all which without one exception, he declares his mind or meaning of bequeathing by the terms, 'I give and bequeath.' whence it is

inferred, if it had been his mind or meaning to create a legacy to Robert Bolling of the money to be received by him, the testator would have emploied the same words, 'I give and bequeath.'

**{H225}** 3. Robert Bolling being appointed not only to receive the debts due to the testator, but to pay what he owed, acted in both offices, not for himself, but for the testator. this was thought to be conclusive. what is said by the def[endant]'s counsel in answer to it must therefore be enlarged upon.

'It is affirmed['] says he, 'that as Robert Bolling paid, so likewise he received debts, as representative of the testator.' he adds, 'I admit it.' what is it you admit, sir? the proposition contained in the terms of the concession is an inference from certain premises. you had urged that the legacy, as you call it, of the book to Robert Bolling was intended for his proper use; and that by the words, 'that he receive all the debts due to me, and pay all that I owe,' he had a right to the money he should collect, burthened with the debts. it was objected on the contrary, that the testator had appointed Robert Bolling not only his receiver, but his bursar; that he was to *pay all* the debts the testator owed, as well as *receive all* the debts others owed to him. that he who was to execute the two offices must sustain the same character in both; that he must act either for himself, or for the testator in both; that if he received for himself he must pay for himself; and if he paid for the testator, he must receive for the testator: but it was affirmed, that, if the testator had died when he made his will, at which time (it was supposed) he owed more than was due to him, for it was (thought to be) by the sale of Pokahontas that the balance is now on the other side, or if, by bankruptcy, or any other accident, the credits had fallen short of the debts, Robert Bolling must not have made good the deficiency out of his own, but might have done it out of the testator's estate. now do you admit these premises, and that *from them* 'it will follow, that Robert Bolling received the debts for, and as representative of the testator?' if you do admit them, as you are understood to do (otherwise, why did you not disprove or deny them?) what is added, 'and consequently Robert Bolling is accountable to the residuary legatee,' is conceived to be not 'controvertible' for in like manner, according to what you tell us, as Robert Bolling, representing the testator, when he received possession of the negroes bequeathed to **{H226}** his sisters and Mr. Mead and Mr. Eldridge, and the £100. bequeathed to Mrs. Tazewell, was accountable to those legatees to whom the things were bequeathed; so, representing the testator, when he received the debts, he is accountable for them to the legatee, to whom they were bequeathed. and who is that? the answer is, by the words, 'my will and desire is, that my brother Robert receive all the debts due to me, and pay all that I owe,' Robert Bolling's right to the debts due to, and his obligation to pay the debts due from, the testator, were, not personal but, merely vicarious, or for, and as representative of, the testator; and the money received, not being other wise given, was included in this bequest, 'the rest of my estate, negroes, horses, cloaths, and *every other part of my estate not already given,* I give and bequeath to my brother Archibald Bolling;' and therefore Archi[bald] Bolling, thus succeeding to every right remaining in the testator, or '*not already given,*' is the legatee to whom the debts were bequeathed. so that if, as you say, 'what

Robert Bolling received as representative of the testator, he is to account for to the particular persons to whom the will directs him to account, that is, to the respective legatees;' and if desiring Rob[ert] Bolling to receive all the debts due to the testator, and to pay all that he owed, be not a legacy of the one to him for his own use, since it doth not burthen him with the other out of his *own estate*, the conclusion, that Rob[ert] Bolling is accountable for the debts to Archi[bald] Bolling the residuary legatee, is not 'too large,' nor is it 'an affirmation' only, but is a proof 'of the point in dispute.'

The plaintiff's counsel had said, that, to avoid this objection, the adverse counsel would have the words, 'my will and desire is that my book be given up to my brother Robert, and that he receive all the debts due to me, and pay all that I owe,' *understood* sometimes in this sense: 'I give to my brother Robert all my credits, he paying *thereout* my debts,' inserting the word thereout, by way of supplement, and making words conditional, which the testator used absolutely. and at other times he would have the clause understood thus: '*I give* to my brother Robert all my credits *except so much as will discharge what* I owe,' supplying the word *except*, and giving a different sense to the words from what they import. this **{H227}** is not charging 'a wilful substitution of words in the *writer's text*, with a design [']that they shall pass in the words of the writer,' but only that he would have the writer's text *understood* as if some of his words had been left out, and instead of them other words of a different meaning substituted; for the truth of which the argument in the hands of it's author is appealed to. if this may not be called an interpolation (which may be erased, since it gives offence) it is not allowed to be properly called a paraphrase, unless something else is meant by that term than explanation of the text by fuller and clearer words, of the same signification. for 'my will and desire is that my book be *given up* to my brother Robert, and that he *receive* all the debts due to me, and *pay all* that I owe' are denied to be '*a gift*;' or to be synonymous with '*a gift* of his debts, *paying thereout what* he owed;' or to be the same 'as if he had said "I give him my outstanding debts, *except so much as is requisite to pay what I owe.*"' besides the difference between 'my desire is, that my book be *given up*,' and 'I *give* my book'[,] and between 'my desire is that he *receive* my debts,' and 'I *give* him my debts,' where there is less agreement in sense than in sound; — the words '*paying thereout what he owed*;' or '*except so much as is requisite to pay what I owe*,' would have implied either that he should in all events pay the debts, and depend upon what he could collect to reimburse himself; but this the def[endant]'s counsel rejects, when he admits 'that as Rob[ert] Bolling received so likewise he *paid* debts, as *representative* of the testator': or else the words would have implied, that the debts due to the testator exceeded what were due from him; but there is not a syllable in the will to justify a supposition, that such an idea was in the mind of the testator; nor any thing to countenance it but a labored synonyma,[907] a commentitious 'as if he had said,' or a miscalled paraphrase. after all it will perhaps appear that the debts amounted to more than the credits.

907. a word or phrase having the same sense as another, a synonym. Wythe used the term sarcastically, to make the point that Jefferson offered as a synonym for the language at issue a reading that, in fact, is not synonymous with the language at issue.

With respect to Pokahontas, what Rob[ert] Bolling says in his answer, viz. 'that the testator, in contemplation of the sale of the warehouses, made various purchases to a greater amount than the nominal sum for which they sold, which purchases were devised to the complainant (except **{H228}** one of £80.), in the residuary clause of the will, and increased the debts of the testator,' the plaintiff's counsel can say nothing to. he and his brother, it is supposed, may agree that fact. may not his credits have been increased too? but yet there was a debt of between 5 [500] and 600 £. Edward Bolling was chargeable with for his proportion of his father's debts, as appears by Thomas Bolling's declaration, which would have made the testator's debts exceed his credits, even including what Rob[ert] Bolling owed him. but this proportion of the father's debts it seems, is not allowed to be 'reckoned amongst the debts which Rob[ert] Bolling was subjected to' by the clause in his brother Edward's will.

'It had been said in the argument for the def[endant] that by this bequest' (for his counsel will have it that this clause is a bequest) 'the testator meant to *give* Rob[ert] Bolling something. that casting an eye on the account annexed to the answer, and adding £550. to the debtor side, instead of leaving a balance in favor of Rob[ert] Bolling, it brings him considerably in debt.' the testator tells us he meant 'that his book be given up to his brother Robert, and that he receive all debts due to him, and pay all that he owed.' but that by those words untortured, unperverted, unparaphrased, he appears to have meant to give any thing to Rob[ert] Bolling remains to be proved. certain it is the testator, when he made his will, did not mean to give Pokahontas to Rob[ert] Bolling, because those warehouses are devised to Archi[bald] Bolling. it is confessed indeed he cannot by that devise claim the price for which those houses were sold, the sale being a revocation of the devise. but possibly the testator made no alteration in his will, either because he supposed the price would pass by the devise of the houses, not knowing the sale by operation of law to be an ademption of the legacy, or because he knew that this money would fall into the residue of his estate, and so Archi[bald] Bolling would have it that way.

It is then denied to be apparent from the whole face of the will, or from any part of it, that a legacy was intended of the book or debts to Rob[ert] Bolling for his own use.

**{H229}** The reasons why Edward Bolling's proportion of his father's debts is not to be reckoned amongst those which his brother, Robert as he contends was directed to pay shall now be considered.

It is objected in the answer, that by the will of his father, Edward Bolling was at the time of his death under express exemption from those debts. but being confronted by the will the def[endant] appears to be mistaken; for the profits of the estates given to the sons by an express charge, are to be applied to the payment of their father's debts; and the stocks and personal estate are not to be divided until after they are discharged.

The def[endant]'s counsel upon this point reasons thus:

'Edward Bolling having given to Rob[ert] Bolling his credits *excepting thereout enough* to pay his debts' (is this 'using words of your own to explain *more at large* what you conceive the testator to have expressed *shortly.*' his words without a redundant one, double yours in number) 'the extent of the *exception* must be determined by the testator's intention, the objects which he had in view at the time of writing the will forming it's limits.'

This is founded altogether upon an exception contained, not in the will but, in a paraphrase, as it is called, supposed to be more expressive of the testator's meaning than his own language[,] a dangerous kind of reasoning. two or three paraphrases have been made of this clause, and then the author singling out one of them makes it his thesis for an argument, leaving the will as if we had nothing more to do with it. he then proceeds —

'The testator could not have this debt (viz. of Hyndman and Lancaster) in contemplation for three reasons. 1. because he did not know of it.'

Robert Bolling in his answer tells us 'the debt was under no contemplation of his testator at the time of making his will, nor any part of his idea when he required him to pay what he owed.' but his reason not like his counsel's, 'because he did not know of it,' is because **{H230}** as he unaccountably suggests, Edward Bolling, 'by the will of his father was under express exemption therefrom, and it only became due from his estate after Archi[bald] Bolling (whose estate till then was charged therewith) attained to his age of 21 years.'

When these gentlemen shall have agreed between themselves upon which of these reasons they mean to rely, they are required to shew the 'express exemption' pretended by the one, or how it appears, as the other affirms, that Edward Bolling 'did not know of the debt his father owed to Hyndman and Lancaster.' it cannot be pretended, that he did not know himself to be liable to pay his proportion of his father's debts in general, because his estate is chargeable therewith by the same will as he derived his title to that estate by. so that if he knew of the one, he must know of the other too. and it cannot be now discovered, but by necromancers, that this debt alone had escaped his knowlege. the contrary is rather presumable, the debt being large, and so many of his family being concerned to discharge it, and if he did not know of it, yet it is included with those debts which he declared it to be his desire that his brother, Robert should pay, for it hath been proved in the former argument, to be a debt that he owed.

The def[endant]'s counsel supposing this clause to be a bequest, and that some benefit was intended for Rob[ert] Bolling, both which are denied, and with extraordinary liberty expounding it as if the debts Rob[ert] Bolling was directed to pay, were an exception, a

2d. reason why this debt is said not to have been in contemplation of the testator, is 'because had he known of it he could never have meant to make it a part of the exception, since that would have made the exception larger than the thing out of which it was excepted, or, in other words, a part greater than the whole.' but, if this debt be, as it is proved to be, a debt which the testator owed, and therefore within his words; is not this an unanswerable argument for rejecting a paraphrase with which an absurd sense of the clause, unless half its meaning be taken away, is only considered?

The 3d. reason is, 'because from the context the gift of the book being **{H231}** connected with the words "and that he receive all the debts due to me, and pay all that I owe," explains what debts he meant, to wit, his proper debts, there being no others entered in his book; whereas this was not his proper debt but a debt of his father's. whether therefore this was so far his debt as to bring it literally under the words of the will is not the proper question, but whether or not it was within his intention.' upon this it is observable, 1. that the words, 'my will and desire is that my book be *given up* to my brother Robert,' are supposed to be a gift, which is again denied. 2, it does not appear that all the debts of the testator which are confessedly to be paid by Rob[ert] Bolling are entered in his book. let it be produced. 3, there is no ambiguity in the words, 'pay *all* the debts that I owe,' so as to require an explanation. they are less ambiguous unquestionably than, 'that my book be given up,' so that explaining those by these is explaining per ignotius [ignotus].[908] 4, if the debt of his father 'was so far his debt as to come literally within the words of his will,' which is affirmed, and seems admitted; to exclude this debt would not be explaining but contradicting the will. 5, it is true the intention of a testator is chiefly to be regarded, but that intention is to be discovered from the words, so that what is within his words hath ever been agreed to be within his intention, unless there would be some inconsistence or absurdity, which no man, without a paraphrase, can shew there would be by making the intention equally comprehensive with the words in this case. if indeed the words of the paraphrase had been

908. by the unknown.

in the will instead of what it contains, it would have been inconsistent and absurd to say he should pay out of the debts more than they amounted to; but this is chargeable, not upon the will, but upon the mutilation and metamorphosis it suffers by such a paraphrase. and even in that case why should not the debts be applied as far as they would go; and why should the largest sum the testator owed be picked out and wholly charged upon another fund?

The plaintiff's counsel had said, 'if any debts due to Col. Bolling had not been recovered when Edward Bolling died, it was imagined, supposing the clause under consideration to be a legacy, his proportion of those debts would have passed by it.' this is answered thus: 'not if as good circumstances could be produced to prove he did not intend Rob[ert] Bolling should **{H232}** receive any part of his father's debts, as are produced to prove he did not intend he should pay any part of them.' would he not have done as well in 'avoiding' the objection as in answering it in that manner? these 'good circumstances' are produced by the paraphrase.

It is now apprehended, that the foundations upon which Rob[ert] Bolling claims the debts as bequeathed to him are not only 'shaken' but intirely demolished; it is conceived to be manifest that the words of the clause in question do not in themselves create a legacy; and that it was not the testator's intention they should; and that this clause is no more than an appointment of Rob[ert] Bolling to be executor, which appointment he might express in this manner, because he might suppose the executor would have little or nothing to do in that office besides receiving and paying debts.

III. If the whole clause (not the bequest of the book, as the def[endant]'s counsel states it) be no more than the appointment of Rob[ert] Bolling to the executorship, it was admitted, supposing there had been nothing else in the case, that a debt of about £235. which he owed to the testator would have been extinguished.

But the appointment of a debtor executor not being an extinguishment if the debt is bequeathed to another, and Edward Bolling having given and bequeathed every part of his estate not already given to his brother Archi[bald] Bolling, the debt is claimed, as being included in that residuary devise.

The def[endant]'s counsel had, in his former argument insisted, that the appointment operated as a legacy. now he tells us this, which was an hypothesis of judge Powell in arguing the case Wankford v. Wankford, 'had been adopted for the sole purpose of explanation, and that he was far from relying upon it as the chief foundation of his objection,' as had been supposed; treats it as a point 'not important enough to be minutely scrutinized;' gives it up, as well he may, by saying **{H233}** that, without losing time in defending it, he is willing to rest it on the hypothesis of chief justice Holt, to wit, that the appointment of a debtor executor, amounts to payment and a release'; and he seems so assured that by this Rob[ert] Bolling 'is intitled to retain the money that he thinks he need not be very anxious, it being immaterial whether the extinguishment be by way of legacy or release.'

In this assertion there will be discovered, upon examination, perhaps more of confidence than of soundness, as the plaintiff's counsel will endeavor to shew, after observing that he is not justly chargeable with inconsistency in his method of reasoning upon the quotation from Godolphin,[909] and of shewing that Powell's opinion was not warranted by the case of Flud v. Rumsey which he cited from Yelverton;[910] and observing further, that the opposite counsel is thought to have mistaken the last mentioned case, when he supposes the decision to be 'that *so much* of the debt as was particularly bequeathed should remain unextinguished;' whereas the court's opinion appears by the book to have been, that the *whole* debt remained unextinguished.

It being agreed then that the appointment of a debtor executor operates as an extinguishment of the debt, not because it is a legacy but, because it amounts to payment and a release; the def[endant]'s counsel considers it 'as if the debtor had made payment to the *debtee* (testator) in his *life* and the *debtee* (testator) had given him a release.' and if this be right no wonder 'he cannot see what the plaintiff gains by it.' but

1. the appointment of the executor, like every other part of the testament, having no operation whatever, until after the *death* of the testator, if it should amount to payment and a release by *him* in his *life* of what the executor owed to him, it would not be less preposterous than that an effect should be prior to its cause, or than that a thing should act before it exists.

2. if the appointment of Rob[ert] Bolling executor, according to the def[endant]'s counsel be 'as if Rob[ert] Bolling had paid the debt to Edw[ard] Bolling, and Edward Bolling had given him a

909. Godolphin, *Orphans Legacy*, 281.

910. *Flud versus Rumsey*, 80 E.R. 127.

release;' so that 'the debt, being paid **{H234}** and released, was become no debt at all;' and consequently 'it was no longer Edward Bolling's estate,' it may be added, neither would it be assets to pay Edward Bolling's debts; a consequence equally true. but the def[endant]'s counsel admits 'the debt still continues liable to debts,' which it would not if 'it was no longer Edward Bolling's estate.' does not this reasoning then, 'proving too much, prove nothing'? so

3. if the testator specially bequeath the debt, the appointment of the debtor executor afterwards, being 'as if the debtor had made payment to the debtee in his life, and the debtee had given him a release,' would be a revocation and ademption of the legacy. but this is too gross even for a Powell to admit the contrary.

When therefore to chief justice Holt's expression,[911] 'that the making him (the debtor) executor does not amount to a legacy but to payment and a release,' the def[endant]'s counsel subjoins, 'or, in other words, that it is as if the debtor had made payment to the *debtee in his life*, and the *debtee* had given him a release,' he says more than Holt said, or appears from his argument to have intended.

To prove that when a debtor appointed executor by the creditor administers the goods, but dies before a probate, the debt is extinguished, the learned judge [Holt] gave three reasons, of which the two former only need to be here noticed. 1. 'because by being made executor he is the person that is intitled to *receive* the money due upon the bond before probate, and as he is the person appoint-

911. *Wankford versus Wankford* (1 Salkeld), 91 E.R. 265–71. The quotation from Holt's opinion, id. at 270, follows this citation.

ed to receive it, he is also the person that is to *pay* it, and the *same* person being to *receive* and *pay, that* amounts to an extinguishment. 2. when the obligee makes the obligor his executor, tho' it is a discharge of the action, yet the debt is *assets*, and the making him executor does not amount to a legacy, but to payment and a release. if H. be bound to I.S. in a bond of £100. and then I.S. makes H. his executor, H. has *actually received* so much money, and is *answerable* for it, and if he does not administer so much, it is a devastavit.'

Hence it appears, that he to whom the payment is made, and by whom **{H235}** the release is supposed to be given, is not the debtee or testator, as the def[endant]'s counsel would have it understood, but his executor; he actually *receives* and is afterwards *answerable* for the money: and as he is the person that is intitled to receive, and is also bound to pay it, the action to recover it, which is suspended during his life, for he cannot bring the action against himself, being totally discharged, according to the maxim, a personal action once suspended by act of the party is gone forever, *that* amounts to payment and a release, and 'as if the debtor had made payment to the debtee in his life, and the debtee had given him a release,' but in the same manner as if any other debtor of the testator had made payment to the executor, after the death of the testator, and the executor had given him a release.

But although the action is discharged, the debt remains part of the testators estate, for it is assets to pay his debts, and, bequeathed, must be accounted for by the executor to the legatary.

It is indeed objected, that unless it be expressly, that is, specially bequeathed, the executor is not accountable. to support this distinction the def[endant]'s counsel before relied upon justice Powell's opinion, in refuting which the 'trouble' the plaintiff's counsel was at it seems was 'unnecessary.' what then is the foundation of it? are not the terms '*every other part of my estate not already given*' equally comprehensive as if the particular articles of which the residue consisted had been enumerated; and do they not consequently include this debt, which by the appointment of the debtor executor, is confessedly no legacy, and so was *not already given*? to this an affirmative answer is dictated by common sense; and with that authority will be found to agree.

The plaintiff's counsel, when he said he apprehended it to be exceedingly plain, that the principle the chancellor [Talbot], in the case of Brown v Selwin, grounded his opinion upon was this, 'that the residuary bequest disposed of every thing the testator was intitled to when he made his will, and at the time of his death,' meant every thing that was not given to others; and he is persuaded that this was understood to be his meaning by the def[endant]'s counsel, although **{H236}** he hath amused himself with detecting the absurdity of making the relative expression, 'all the rest of my estate not before disposed of,' to include its cor-relative, 'the estate before disposed of.'

'In order to get rid of' this authority, the def[endant]'s counsel, after rehearsing these words of the chancellor, 'if this be considered upon the will, it will appear from the general words of devising the residue, i.e. 'all his real "and personal estate which he had not thereby before given"' to the residuary legatees, that this debt, which '*at that time* was part of the *personal estate* falls within the description.

the testator was intitled to this debt when he made his will, and at the time of his death; he had not before disposed of it, nor had he made Mr. Selwin executor,' observes, 'here he makes the description the foundation of his decision; for he says this debt falls within the description of his estate not before given' — be it so — but what he adds — '*for* not having appointed Mr. Selwin executor, he had not before disposed of it' — implying an affirmation, that by the appointment of Mr. Selwin executor, if it had preceded the devise of the residue, the debt would have been *before* disposed of — is a misrecital. the chancellor [Talbot] doth not say so. his words are, 'he had not before disposed of it, *nor* had he appointed Mr. Selwin executor.' this is very different from what he is made to say, and will not authorise the proposition, that if the testator had appointed Mr. Selwin executor before devising the residue, he would thereby have disposed of the debt. then the def[endant]'s counsel says, 'the testator, in our case, when he wrote his residuary clause, had *already* appointed Rob[ert] Bolling his executor, and so had' — what? — *already given* or *disposed* of this debt? — no. it is now admitted that the appointment of a debtor executor is not a legacy gift or disposition — but 'had *released* this debt.' two pages before this release is said to be, 'as if the debtor had made payment to the debtee in his life, and the debtee had given him a release;' here payment is dropped altogether, and the release, instead of being given in the life, is supposed to be given by the will, which hath no force till after the death. whereas it hath been shewn, **{H237}** 1. that the payment, actual payment is made to the *executor*: 'if H. be bound to I.S. in a bond of £100. and then I.S. makes H. his executor, H.

has *actually received* so much money,' says Holt.[912] payment then is not made, nor supposed to be made to the testator. neither is it the release of the testator. the release is simultaneous with the payment, being effected by a concurrence of the obligation to pay, and the right to receive in one and the same person, namely the executor; it is by the agency of him that this effect is produced; and therefore the release is his act. 2. the release effected by the appointment of a debtor executor is not the release of the testator, because if it were so, whatever part of the will it occurred in, the release would so far prevail against the devise of the residue, which this case of Brown v Selwin proves to be otherwise. for there the debt due from Mr. Selwin was not extinguished by appointing him one of the executors; when if in place of that appointment, the testator had said, 'I release Mr. Selwin from the £300. he owes me,' the debt would undoubtedly have been extinguished. So that the debt in this case not being released as it were by the testator.

According to the opinion of the chancellor [Talbot] in the case of Brown v Selwin, it appears 'from the general words of devising the residue, i.e. every other part of his estate *not already given*,' that this debt, which 'at that time was part of the estate *not already given*, falls within the description. the testator was intitled to this debt when he made his will, and at the time of his death; he had not before disposed of it;' and altho' he had 'made Rob[ert] Bolling executor,' such an appointment hath been proved, and is now admitted not to be a legacy, and so no gift or disposition. And

912. *Wankford versus Wankford* (Salkeld), 91 E.R. 265–71. The quotation is from Holt's opinion, at id. 270.

therefore this case of Brown v Selwin 'is still relied on for the Plaintiff by his counsel as a case in point.[']

From these words of def[endant]'s counsel, 'there is this difference between the case of Brown v Selwin and ours, that in that the debt was particularly described and bequeathed away' (note the chancellor [Talbot] says *general words of devising the residue*) 'and so was not released, according to the *general rule* before laid down; but in ours, it was not particularly described and bequeathed, and **{H238}** so was released by the same rule.' one would think there was some such general rule as this laid down: 'that where a debtor is appointed executor the debt is *released* if it be not particularly described and bequeathed away.' if that is what the def[endant]'s counsel means, it is asked where he found and how he proved the rule? it is not to be 'picked up' even in Powell's argument, nor is it contained in terms of the like import in the case of Brown v Selwin. it is also required to be shown that, by the words, 'every other part of my estate not already given I give and bequeath to my brother Archi[bald] Bolling.' Rob[ert] Bolling's debt is less 'particularly described and given away,' in this case, than by the words, 'rest residue and remainder of my estate &c. whereof I am seised or possessed, or which I am any ways intitled to, which I have not herein and hereby devised given &c., I give and bequeath the same,' &c. Mr. Selwin's debt was described and bequeathed in the case of Brown v Selwin.

Nor is this the only case in point. that of Philips against

Philips, term. Mich. 28. Car. II. in canc.[913] is another. <<Nicholas Philips, the testator, made his will, and made the defendant executor, and devised divers legacies, and the residue of all his personal estate to the plaintiff. the executor was debtor to the testator in £400. he left sufficient personal estate to pay all his legacies. the question was, whether the £400. being discharged in law to the executor, should be accounted as part of the residue, there being no need of it to pay debts or legacies particularly given; for the testator must not be supposed ignorant, but knowing of the law, that by making his debtor executor, he thereby discharged the debt, and so the £400. became no part of the personal estate, and so no residue thereof. and difference was pressed between legatees and debtor, in which the debt, tho' discharged, should be assets, and where it was between the executor, who is in this case in effect a devisee of the debt. but the lord chancellor [Nottingham] disallowed the difference, and decreed for the plaintiff the residue, &c against the executor, tho' it was objected that this case was different from former precedents.>> 1. Chan. ca. 292. there is not any **{H239}** difference between this case and the principal case, but that, in the latter, which is so far contrary to the other, without the money due from the executor, the testator's debts, his proportion of what his father owed included, and legacies cannot be satisfied otherwise than by breaking in upon the slaves in the residuary bequest to Archi[bald] Bolling, unless the personal estate, of which no inventory is annexed to the answer, be more considerable than is imagined. but

913. *Philips v. Philips*, 22 E.R. 806–807. The quotation following this citation is at 806–807.

does not this difference add strength to the authority? which moreover answers the observation, 'that if the executor's debt be subject to legacies, it could only have been to those of some specific sum.'

It is hoped to be sufficiently proved by this time to be entirely immaterial in what order the clauses appointing the executor, and bequeathing the residue in this will, were inserted, the former being neither a legacy, as is now admitted, nor a release by the testator, so that the debt remaining part of the testator's estate not already given was consequently given and bequeathed to Archi[bald] Bolling.

Interest upon whatever balance may be in Rob[ert] Bolling's hands, it is expected will be thought a reasonable demand.

The plaintiff's counsel had made it a question, whether the emblements before the act of assembly, would have passed by a devise of the land on which they grew. afterwards, finding the point settled by authorities he suppressed his first argument, the material parts of which, as to the other points, were transcribed, with additions, into the second, the figures in the margines of this refer, those on the right hand to the pages of that, and those on the left hand to the pages of the second argument of the defendant's counsel.[914]

914. This edition omits the marginal numbers described in this paragraph.

# Glossary

Note: This glossary includes all legal terms and words or brief phrases (up to ten words) in Latin, Law Latin, and Law French. Any phrase beginning with "in" is listed under the next word in the phrase.

**ab alio pingi se vetuit edicto:** forbade that he be painted by anyone else. (Lat.)

**abatement:** an entire overthrow or destruction of the suit so that it is quashed and ended.

**ab initio:** from the beginning. (Lat.)

**ab intestata:** from an intestate, in case of intestacy. (Lat.)

**act in pais:** an act done out of court, and not a matter of record. (Law Fr.)

**ademption:** extinction or withdrawal of a legacy by testator's act that, by indicating testator's intention to revoke, is equivalent to a revocation.

**administrator:** a person appointed by the court or other legal authority to administer the assets and liabilities of a decedent who has died without making a will, or whose will does not satisfy the legal requirements for a will. (See also *executor.*)

**administration de bonis non administratis:** administration (of the estate of someone who has died without a will) by a person appointed by the court of probate to administer on the effects of a decedent that have not been included in a former administration. (Law Lat.)

**alien:** (also *alienate*) to convey or transfer an item of real or personal property from one person to another. *Alienation* is the action of alienating. An alienor (also *alienator*) is one who alienates.

**alienation inter vivos:** transfer of property from one living person to another, as distinguished from a testamentary gift or a case of succession or devise. (Law Lat.)

**allodial:** free; not holden of any lord or superior; owned without obligation of vassallage or fealty; the opposite of feudal.

**amicus curiae:** friend of the court; one who is invited to submit briefs or arguments to the court to aid in the decision of a case, though not a party in interest before the court. (Law Lat.)

**amphibology:** ambiguous discourse; a sentence which may be construed in two distinct senses; a quibble.

**ante onus executionis testamenti super se susceptum:** before the burden of executing the testament taken upon him. (Law Lat.)

**in articulo temporis:** at that point in time. (Lat.)

**assets entre mains:** assets in hand; assets in the hands of executors or administrators applicable for the payment of debts. (Law Fr.)

**assets per descent:** that portion of the ancestor's estate which descends to the heir, and which is sufficient to charge him, as far as it goes, with the specialty debts of his ancestors. (Law Fr.)

**attachment sur prohibition:** Taking or seizing persons or property under or by virtue of a writ of prohibition, by which a superior court directs the judge and parties of a suit in an inferior court to cease proceedings, on the suggestion that the suit itself or an issue arising therein lies outside the inferior court's jurisdiction. (Law Fr.)

**in auter droit:** in another's right; as representing another. An executor, administrator, or trustee sues *in auter droit.* (Law Fr.)

**bailed:** created a bailment; delivered goods or personal property to another person, either for a specific use or upon deposit, under an express or implied contract under which the bailed property shall be returned to the original possessor once the use or the purpose of the deposit has been achieved.

**baron and feme:** husband and wife. (Law Fr.)

**bequeath:** to give personal property to another person by a provision of a will.

**bequest:** a gift of personal property by a will.

**bocland:** (also *boc land* or bookland) A term from Saxon law denoting allodial lands held by deed or other written evidence of title.

**cedunt solo:** in the same way. (Lat.)

**cestuy que trust:** He who has a right to a beneficial interest in and out of a legal estate the title to which is vested in another. The person who possesses the equitable right to property and receives the rents, issues, and profits generated by that property, legal possession of which is vested in the trustee. The beneficiary of a trust. (Law Fr.; variant of *cestui que trust*)

**cestuy que vie:** The person whose life measures the duration of a trust, gift, estate, or insurance contract. The person for whose life any lands, tenements, or hereditaments are held. (Law Fr.)

**chattels personal:** articles of personal property (as opposed to real property [q.v.]). Also known as movables or *mobilia* (q.v.).

**chattels real:** articles or items of real property; an interest in real estate less than a freehold or fee.

**codicil:** supplement or addition to a will.

**conveyance:** a disposition of property by written agreement executed by a living person.

**copyhold:** a type of estate at will, or customary estate, the only visible title to which consisted of the copies of the court rolls; the general or common law tenure of the country.

**copyholder:** a tenant by copyhold tenure.

**coram:** in the presence of. (Lat.)

**coram non judice:** a phrase used to describe a judgment rendered by a court lacking jurisdiction to hear and decide a case, and thus deemed void. (Law Lat.; literally, "in the presence of a person not a judge.")

**cum testamento annex:** with the will attached. (Law Lat.)

**curia cancellaria:** Court of Chancery. (Law Lat.)

**curial proceedings:** civil, as distinguished from ecclesiastical, proceedings.

**currente calamo:** the words of the day, usage at that time. (Lat.; literally, "the pen of the time")

**debet and detinet:** The phrase denoting a writ in the common law in an action of debt brought by an original contracting party who gave credit, against the party who incurred the debt, or his heirs. (Law Lat.; from Lat. *debet et detinet* — "He owes and detains.")

**debita in praesentia, solvenda in futuro:** debts at present, to be paid at a future time. (Law Lat.)

**defalcation:** The act of embezzling; failure to meet an obligation; misappropriation of trust funds or money held in any fiduciary capacity; failure to account properly for such funds.

**dehors:** out of, without, beyond, foreign to, unconnected with. (Law Fr.)

**demurrer:** initial plea of a defendant that, while taking as true the facts alleged by the plaintiff, denies that these facts are sufficient in law as a basis on which plaintiff may proceed or to require the defendant to answer.

**deposition:** a written record of a witness's sworn answers to questions posed to the witness by an attorney.

**detinue:** in common law, an action for the recovery, in specie (that is, hard cash), of the value of personal chattels from one who acquired possession of them lawfully but retains possession without right, together with damages for the wrongful detention.

**devastavit:** the act of an executor or administrator in wasting the goods of the dedecent; mismanagement of the estate by which a loss occurs. (Law Lat.; literally, "he has wasted.")

**devise** (or **divise**): (*verb*) to dispose of real property by will. (*noun*) a grant of real property by provision of a will.

**devisee:** one who receives real property by will.

**devisor:** one who disposes of real property by will.

**dictum:** an observation or remark made by a judge in pronouncing an opinion in a case, concerning some rule, principle, or application of law, or a solution of a question suggested by a case at bar, but not necessarily involved in that case or essential to its determination. Any statement of the law enunciated by the court merely by way of illustration, argument, analogy, or suggestion. (Law Lat.; also *obiter dictum.*)

**disseised:** dispossessed or deprived of a possessory interest in land.

**disseisor:** one who dispossesses or deprives another of a possessory interest in land.

**distreinable:** seizable, usually by a landlord upon default of a tenant; detaining personal property, whether lawful or unlawful, for any purpose. (var. *distrainable.*)

**divise:** see *devise.*

**dower:** at common law, the doctrine by which a widow may secure financial support for herself and the nurture of her children out of the lands and tenements of her deceased husband.

**dubitatur:** doubtful, wavering, uncertain. (Law Lat.)

**econtra:** from the opposite; on the contrary. (Law Lat.; variant of Latin *e contra.*)

**ejudsem generis:** of the same kind, class, or nature. In interpreting wills and other instruments, the *ejusdem generis* rule provides that, where general words follow an enumeration of persons or things, by words of a particular and specific meaning, such general words are not to be construed in their widest extent, but are to be held as applying only to persons or things of the same general kind or class as those specifically mentioned. (Law Lat.)

**emblements:** crops annually produced by the labor of a tenant.

**escheat:** (*noun*) a reversion of property to the state due to the lack of any person eligible to inherit.
(*verb*) For a property to escheat is for it to revert to the state for that reason.

**estate pur autre vie:** a possessory interest in land the duration of which is limited by the life of a person not the holder. (Law Fr.; literally, "an estate for another life.")

**estate tail:** a possessory interest in land subject to a condition defining the class of heirs who may take possession of the property — most often, heirs directly descended by blood from the current owner so long as the owner's posterity endures in a regular order and course of descent.

**estovers:** a tenant's right or privilege to furnish himself with wood from the demesned premises as may be sufficient or necessary for fuel, fences, or agricultural operations.

**evidence parol:** *see* parol evidence.

**ex relatione magistri:** upon relation or information of the authority named. (Law Lat.)

**ex vi terminorum:** from or by the force of the term. (Law Lat.)

**executor:** a person appointed by a testator to carry out directions and requests in the testator's will, including offering the will for probate after the testator's death and disposing of the property in the testator's estate according to the will's provisions. (See also *administrator.*)

**extinguishment:** the destruction or cancellation of a right, power, contract, or estate.

**extrajudicial opinion:** an opinion given by a judge or judges that did not grow out of an actual case or controversy legitimately before the court.

**in fee:** as a possessory interest; applied to real property.

**fee simple:** a possessory interest in land clear of any condition or restriction to a particular period of time or to particular heirs; the broadest interest that one can have in land. (Also "fee simple absolute.")

**feme covert:** a married woman. (Law Fr.)

**feme sole:** a single woman, including those divorced, widowed, and judicially separated. (Law Fr.)

**feoffment:** the act or instrument giving a freehold interest in land accompanied by *livery of seisin* (that is, by an act transferring actual possession of the land). To *infeoff* is to create a feoffment.

**fidei commissary:** one who has the real or beneficial interest in an estate, the title or administration of which is temporarily confided to another.

**fiduciary:** person bound by an obligation, as a trustee.

**frank-almoigne:** free alms; a spiritual tenure whereby religious corporations, aggregate or sole, held lands of the donee to them and their successors forever.

**frank-marriage:** a species of entailed estate.

**freehold (estate):** a possessory estate in land for life or in fee of uncertain (i.e., not limited) duration.

**in futuro:** in future. (Lat.)

**haeres factus:** in civil law, an heir made by a will; a testamentary heir. (Law Lat.)

**haeres natus:** in civil law, an heir born; the next of kin by blood, in cases of intestacy. (Law Lat.)

**hereditaments:** things capable of being inherited.

**hotchpot:** the combining of properties into a common lot to ensure equality of division among heirs.

**immobilia:** immovable things; land or buildings. (Lat.)

**infeoff:** to perform an act or execute an instrument giving a freehold interest in land accompanied by *livery of seisin* (an act symbolically transferring actual possession of the land).

**inrollment:** (var. of *enrollment*) act of recording, enrolling, or registering.

**inter alia:** among other things. (Lat.)

**inter vivos:** between the living, from one living person to another. Often used to describe property transferred by a conveyance, as distinguished from a case of succession or devise. (Lat.)

**ipso facto:** by the fact itself, by the mere fact. (Lat.)

**joint tenants** (also **jointenants**): in common law, a form of owner ship of real property in which two or more persons hold real property. Joint tenants have one and the same interest and a right of survivorship; that is, if either joint tenant dies, the other succeeds to the full interest in the property. Most often applied to husbands and wives, as in the text.

**knight's service:** personal feudal obligation to render military service to one's lord; later taking the form of pecuniary commutation of the obligation to give service.

**legataries:** legatees; those to whom a testator bequeaths personal property.

**legatory:** of or pertaining to a legacy.

**legatory depositum:** a depositum is one of the four real contracts specified by Justinian, under which the depositee is not liable for negligence but only for fraud, yet the depository has only possession of the deposit, legal title to which remains in the depositor. A legatory depositum is a depositum of money created by a will.

**legibus patriae optime instituti:** those best instructed in the laws of their country. (Lat.)

**letters of administration:** a formal instrument of authority and appointment given to an administrator by the proper court empowering the administrator to enter on the discharge of that office.

**letters testamentary:** a formal instrument of authority and appointment given to an executor by the proper court, upon the admission of the will to probate, empowering the executor to enter on the discharge of that office.

**life estate:** a possessory interest in land the duration of which is limited to the life of the party holding it or of some other specified person.

**logomachy:** contention about words.

**Master of the Rolls:** In English law, an assistant judge of the court of chancery, who held a separate court ranking next to that of the Lord Chancellor, and had the keeping of the rolls and grants which passed the Great Seal, and the records of the chancery.

**messuage:** dwelling-house with the adjacent buildings and curtilage (that is, enclosed space of ground).

**mobilia:** movable things; personal property or chattels personal. (Lat.)

**moiety:** the half of everything; joint tenants (q.v.) are said to hold by moieties.

**mortis causâ:** by reason of, or in contemplation of, death. (Lat.)

**nisi argumentative:** except argumentatively. (Law Fr.)

**nolens volens:** whether willing or unwilling, consenting or not. (Lat.)

**non est factum:** in common law, a plea denying execution of an instrument that is the basis of plaintiff's action. (Law Lat.)

**non sequitur:** something that does not follow logically. (Lat.)

**nova provisio apud Merton facta:** new provision made at Merton. (Law Lat.)

**obiter dictum:** *see* dictum. (Law Lat.)

**obiter opinion:** *see* dictum. (Law Lat.)

**ordinary:** at common law, one who had exempt and immediate jurisdiction in ecclesiastical causes.

**outlawry:** process by which a defendant or other person in contempt of criminal or civil process was declared an outlaw.

**oyer:** hearing or examination in court. (Law Fr.)

**pari materia:** of the same matter, on the same subject. (Lat.)

**pari numero:** of the same number or quantity. (Lat.)

**pari ratione:** for the like reason; by the like mode of reasoning. (Lat.)

**parol evidence:** oral (spoken) evidence as opposed to documentary or physical evidence.

**parol testimony:** parol evidence taking the form of testimony by a witness (whether presented orally or by deposition).

**per curiam:** for the court. (Lat.)

**per ignotus:** by the unknown. (Lat.)

**possessio fratris facit sororum es haeredem:** The brother's possession makes the sister to be heir. (Law Lat.)

**postulata:** things laid down as facts or postulates. (Lat.)

**praecipe:** In common-law practice, an original writ drawn up in the alternative, commanding the defendant to do the thing required, or show the reason why he had not done it. (Law Lat.)

**praetermit:** to let pass or to neglect (also *pretermit*).

**praeteritorum memoria eventorum:** the memory of past events. (Lat.)

**prima facie:** at first sight; on the first appearance. (Lat.)

**privity:** mutual or successive relationship to the same rights of property; *privity of blood* indicates that the relationship is one of family or blood.

**pro placito:** for her plea. (Law Lat.)

**pro tanto:** for so much, for as much as may be, as far as it goes. (Lat.)

**prohibition:** at common law, a writ by which a superior court directs the judge and parties of a suit in an inferior court to cease proceedings, on the suggestion that the suit itself or an issue arising therein lies outside the inferior court's jurisdiction.

**proprietate probanda:** the proving of property — the legal methods by which a person would establish a claim to property. (Law Lat.)

**protestando:** emphatic word formerly used in pleading by way of protestation.

**protestation:** the indirect affirmation or denial of the truth of some matter which cannot with propriety or safety be positively affirmed, denied, or entirely passed over; the exclusion of a conclusion.

**prove a will:** to offer a will for confirmation by the authorities according to law.

**publici juris:** public right; when a thing is common property so that anyone can make use of it. (Lat.)

**pur autre vie:** for the life of another. (Law Fr.)

**quaere:** wherefore, for what reason, on what account. (Lat.)

**quaestio diu vexata:** a vexed question or mooted point; a question often agitated or discussed but not determined; a question or point which has been differently decided, and so left doubtful. (Law Lat.)

**quantum:** something, a finite quantity. (Lat.)

**quare clausum fregit ac maeremium suum cepit:** wherefore he broke the close and took the timber; in common law, a species of the action of trespass. (Law Lat.)

**qui sendit onus sentire debet et commodum quod:** He who sustains the burden shall derive the benefit. (Law Lat.)

**quia emptores terrarum:** "Because purchasers of land..." (Law Lat.) The phrase generally used as the title for 18 Edw. I, c. 1 (1290), from the statute's preamble.

**quicquid plantatur solo, solo cedit:** Whatever is affixed to the soil, belongs to the soil. (Law Lat.)

**quitrent:** rent paid by tenant of freehold by which he is discharged from any other rent.

**quoad hoc:** as to this; with respect to this. (Lat.)

**quod nota: per totam curiam:** which note: by the whole court. (Law Lat.) This note is usually inserted by the reporter in older case reports.

**quod sentit onus sentire debit et commodum:** That which sustains the burden shall derive the benefit. (Law Lat.)

**ratio decidendi:** ground or reason of decision; the point in a case that determines the judgment. (Lat.)

**remainder:** that possessory interest in an estate in land left over after those interests specifically limited by time or identity have expired — for example, O gives a life estate to A, remainder to B.

**replication:** in common-law pleading, plaintiff's reply to defendant's plea; in chancery, plaintiff's reply to defendant's answer.

**residuary devise:** the clause of a will by which the testator grants the residuary estate or residuum (q.v.).

**residuary estate:** the part of a testator's estate not otherwise specifically bequeathed by the testator's will. Also known as *residuum.*

**residuum:** (or *residuam*) residuary estate (q.v.). (Lat.)

**reversion:** the residue possessory interest in an estate — belonging to the grantor or his heirs (or the heirs of a testator) — which takes effect by operation of law at the termination of a particular possessory interest granted or devised. For example, when O gives Blackacre to A for life, O and his heirs retain a reversion by which Blackacre returns to their hands on A's death. (A *reversion for years* gives Blackacre to O and his heirs, but only for a specified time period.)

**in rotulurus:** in the rolls. (Law Lat.)

**Satum cedit solo:** Crops accede to the soil. (Law Lat.)

**seised:** possessed of real property under claim of freehold estate.

**solus deus facit haeredem, non homo:** God alone makes the heir, not man. (Law Lat.)

**special occupancy:** entry into lands held for the life of another under the original grant, or as heir of the tenant.

**specialty debt:** a debt due by deed or instrument under seal.

**spiritual court:** one of the English local courts devoted principally to ecclesiastical cases.

**sub modo:** under a qualification; subject to a restriction or condition. (Law Lat.)

**sui generis:** of its own kind or class, unique. (Lat.)

**sur cui in vita:** a writ available to the heir of a woman whose husband had alienated her land in fee, but who had omitted to bring the writ sur cui in vita for recovery of that land; the heir might have the writ against the tenant after her decease. (Law Lat.)

**synonyma:** a word or phrase having the same sense as another, a synonym. (Lat.)

**in tail:** limited to a certain order of succession or to certain heirs.

**tantum:** such a quantity, so much. (Lat.)

**tenant at will:** one who holds possession of premises by permis sion of a landlord or owner, but without a fixed term.

**tenant for life:** one who holds possession of premises by permission of a landlord or owner for the duration of his (that is, the tenant's) life.

**tenant for years:** one who holds possession of premises by permission of a landlord or owner for a specified period of time.

**tenants in common:** in common law, a form of ownership of real property in which two or more persons hold real property. Each tenant in common has an undivided interest in the property; if a tenant dies, his or her interest does not pass to the surviving tenant or tenants, but instead goes to the deceased tenant's heir.

**tenement:** everything that may be held or possessed, provided it be of a permanent nature, whether it be of a substantial and sensible, or of an insubstantial, ideal kind. At common law, "tenements" includes lands, other inheritances, capable of being held in freehold, and rents. *Tenemental land* is land distributed by a lord among his tenants, as opposed to the demsnes which he and his servants occupied.

**testator:** one who devises or transfers real and personal property by a will.

**tortiously:** wrongfully.

**totidem verbis:** in so many words. (Lat.)

**trespass:** at common law, unlawful interference with one's person, property, or rights; in the civil as opposed to the criminal branch of common law, a form of action to recover damages for any injury to one's person, property, or relationship with another.

**trover:** in common law, an action to recover damages against a person who found another's goods and wrongfully converted them to his own use.

**trust estate:** a trust, all or part of the income from which is to be accumulated during the surviving spouse's life and added to the corpus of the trust, all such funds (corpus and accumulated income) to be paid to the estate of the surviving spouse at that person's death.

**ubi supra:** where above mentioned. (Lat.)

**usufructuaries:** in civil law, those who have the *usufruct* or right of enjoying anything in which they have no property interest.

**utile per inutile non vitiatur:** Surplusage shall not vitiate the essentials. (Law Lat.)

**vi termini:** the force of the term, the meaning of the expression used. (Law Lat.)

**villein:** in feudal law, a person attached to the manor; a subject of property of the lord of the manor.

**vox et praetera nihil:** empty words and sound. (Lat.)

**waste:** an abuse or destructive use of property by one in rightful possession.

**Westminster Hall:** The building in London where the English law and chancery courts met.

**writ of error:** a writ issued by a court of appellate jurisdiction, directed to the judge or judges of a lower court of record, requiring them to remit to the appellate court the records of an action before them in which a final judgment has been entered, to permit the appellate court to examine errors alleged to have been committed in adjudicating the action and, if necessary, reverse, correct, or affirm the lower court's judgment.

**writ of formedon:** a writ for the recovery of an estate brought by a person claiming as issue in tail, or by the remainderman or reversioner after the termination of the entail.

# Index

prepared by Barbara Wilcie Kern and R. B. Bernstein

NOTE: This Index has two parts. Part I, the General Index, deals with persons, things, concepts, and events. Footnotes providing identifying information are marked by an asterisk and appear italicized in parentheses following the page number — 147(*n27**). Part II, the Index of Authorities, indexes references to statutes, cases, legal treatises and commentaries, form books, and law dictionaries cited in the *Bolling v. Bolling* manuscript.

## I. General Index

# II. Index of Authorities

Where the authority is discussed in text and cited in an accompanying note, the entry gives the page number (or numbers) followed by the note number (or numbers) italicized and in parentheses: 155(*nn*68–69). Where the authority is mentioned in text without a citation, the entry gives the page number alone: 208. Where the authority is mentioned only in a note, the entry gives the page number followed by the note number: 325n583. Listings of statutes give the citation, the year, and a bracketed identification. Listings of cases give the case name, the court, and the year. Listings of treatises, commentaries, and alw dictionaries give the author and the book's short title. The full citation of each authority appears in the first note cited. For full citations to the editions of statutes and cases used in this edition of *Bolling v. Bolling*, see the Statement of Editorial Method.

## Statutes: England and Great Britain

## Statutes: Virginia

## Cases: England and Great Britain

### 1. Year Books



### 2. Cases

### 3. Untitled Cases



## Cases: Virginia



## Treatises, Commentaries, and Law Dictionaries

*Thomas Jefferson and*
*Bolling v. Bolling: Law and*
*the Legal Profession in*
*Pre-Revolutionary America*

Designed by Edward Hughes

Formatted in Adobe Garamond
in QuarkXpress on a MacIntosh
Power PC

Printed by BookCrafters, Chelsea,
Michigan, on Booktext Natural
and bound in Roxite B linen